My Bag of Book Tricks

MY BAG OF BOOK TRICKS

Sharron L. McElmeel
Drawings by Deborah L. McElmeel

1989
TEACHER IDEAS PRESS
A Division of
Libraries Unlimited, Inc.
Englewood, Colorado

TEACHER IDEAS PRESS
A Division of Libraries Unlimited, Inc.
P.O. Box 3988
Englewood, Colorado 80155-3988

Library of Congress Cataloging-in-Publication Data

McElmeel, Sharron L.
    My bag of book tricks / Sharron L. McElmeel ; drawings by Deborah
L. McElmeel.
    xiii, 276p. 22x28 cm.
    ISBN 0-87287-722-1
    1. Literature--Study and teaching (Elementary)--United States.
2. Children--Books and reading.   I. Title.
LB1575.5.U5M38   1989
372.6'4--dc20   89-36236
                                                             CIP

For Suzanne
Matthew
Steven
Thomas
Deborah
Michael
and Jack
with thanks and love

Contents

**Section I
Celebrations**

Section II
Connections

Acknowledgments

Grateful acknowledgment goes to those who read *An Author a Month (for Pennies)* and encouraged this book. Thanks to Cheryl Kolar for sharing Thursday morning thoughts and allowing me to share mine, and to Geri Hasley who does the same over the dining room table. A special thanks to Marj McCarty for her years of teaching hundreds of children (including all six of mine) to love learning and life. She is an inspiration. I am especially grateful for the continued professional support from the staff of the Cedar Rapids Community Schools (Iowa), in particular those special people—administrators, teachers, and support staff—at Wright Elementary School. They are important because they help the seeds of reading and writing to propagate, grow, and spread throughout the school. They make the sharing of ideas a rewarding experience and every day a new one. And special thanks once again to Joan Goldsberry who listens to my musings each day of the school year.

Introduction

From the Bookshelves to the Hands of Readers

John Newbery (1731-1767) is sometimes said to have originated books for children in the 1740s with his publication *The Little Pretty Pocket Book*. Scholars of the history of children's books call into question the notion that Newbery did indeed originate the idea of books for children, though few will question the part Newbery played in popularizing books for children. He regularly published books for children and did much to influence those who were to follow him by making a success of publishing books intended for young people. We must look to John Newbery as the first person who thought it worth the time and effort to appeal to children and to give them something of pleasure. Many children's books are published each year by those who carry on the trend of publishing established by John Newbery.

As trends evolved over the years the emphasis went from pure didacticism to amusement. Gradually we have come to reflect our society rather than to preach morals and behavior. The art within books has evolved from the sweat shops where very young children dabbed the color in each book individually to the present museum-quality art found between the pages of books for children. The writing has focused on the interests of young people. Books are promoted to those who can't recognize the words, to those who only want to look at the illustrative material, to those who are emerging readers, to those who wish to escape to another world and another time, to those wishing information, to those who read fluently, and to those who wish simply to enjoy. Few of the books listed in this book will have grades or age levels designated. I have had first graders read what others would term "sixth-grade material," and I have had older children delight in reading picture books. I think each reader will seek what is appropriate to him or her depending on the purpose and the time. Of course, that presupposes that there are no artificial restrictions imposed on the reader. The current professional research is full of suggestions for using picture books with older students and emphasizes the value of exposing early readers to the world of nonfiction and other books meant for older readers. The current trend is to allow children a wide range of choice, to offer encouragement at every crossroad. The number of pages or pictures in a book should not be the controlling factor in deciding the usefulness of a book for a particular child. The usefulness should be determined by interest and content. The choice must be with the reader. Choice is the key element, the key motivator. The meaning of the story is more important for ease of reading than is limited vocabulary.

In a conversation with Jack Prelutsky (April 8, 1988, Des Moines, Iowa), he commented that even though he had written some poems with specific aged youngsters in mind, he found children (and adults) of all ages reading his poems. He had seen children of preschool age—children who probably did not understand the concept of homework—reading or listening to (and enjoying) his poem about homework, "Homework! Oh, Homework!" in *The New Kid on the Block* (Greenwillow, 1984), while intermediate students are often seen reading *Ride a Purple Pelican* (Greenwillow, 1986), a book of modern nursery rhymes he intended for much younger readers. Good books of literature are like onions. Different layers of understanding may be peeled away. Some readers will only get to the first membrane while other readers will be able to peel down to the inner core of meaning. In that way readers of all ages are able to enjoy the literature without regard to the arbitrary grade designations; readers will peel away as many layers as they can handle. One of my favorites is a story called "The Green Ribbon" in Alvin Schwartz's *In a Dark Dark Room and Other Scary Stories* (Harper & Row, 1984). That book is an I Can Read book intended for primary-age readers. They enjoy it very much both as a story to read and as a read aloud story. But I have read aloud that particular story to parents, graduate students, teachers, librarians, intermediate grade students, and high school students. Each time I have enjoyed the ending as much as I did the very first time I read the story. And each time the response from the listeners has been to fill the room with laughter. The book immediately becomes a hot item with the adults as well as with the children who hear the story. The older readers will quickly read the other stories and then go on to discover other books by Schwartz, but the younger students will first focus on reading and rereading the other stories in the first book. Different groups accept the story and the book at their own level. The use of literature in the classroom has as a primary goal that of immersing children in fine literature—to demonstrate the value of reading. We must model not only how to read but teach and model the love of reading as well. And as we do that we will also be modeling the joy of writing, sharing, and communicating.

Surround children with literature. Demonstrate and model responses to literature and the enjoyment of reading. Expect every child to be a reader and provide positive encouragement. Accept their approximation of the written word as parents have traditionally accepted approximation of the spoken word. Finally, encourage children to employ their skills to glean meaning from the written word. The learning of language is through the use of language. Literature experiences help to give children the total experiences through which they begin to build the parts to make their own whole experience. Children will take from each experience the parts they need to complete the puzzle forming their whole.

This book will attempt to focus on bringing together natural experiences and literature, providing much stimulus and motivation for writing, talking, and expression through the visual arts. For the teacher who already provides a literature-rich classroom these suggestions will quickly be seen as providing reinforcement and seeds from which more ideas will grow. Those who are searching for book titles and ways to incorporate more literature into their classrooms might take these suggestions and use them as presented. These suggestions will provide a beginning to many. The ideas will be adapted and altered to provide meaningful experiences for a variety of readers. It is important that as specific titles are located other good literature will become apparent so that many books will be found to share. Immersion and demonstration are most important as a beginning. Immerse the children in good literature. Demonstrate the benefits of reading and writing. Allow children to explore and enjoy. They should be encouraged to develop responsibility for their own choices and to maximize their enjoyment of literature with a personal response to the literature. That response can be in the form of a smile, a picture, a written entry in a journal, something shared with another person, a play, a book advertisement, or a feeling of satisfaction when the book is completed. Sometimes the response may be inspired by a teacher suggestion. Judy Blume's *Freckle Juice* (Dell, 1971) might bring about a class project to create freckle juice. Arnold Lobel's *The Book of Pigericks* (Harper & Row, 1983) might inspire children to read some of Edward Lear's limericks, to read other pig stories, to locate on a map some of the towns that Lobel's pigs inhabit, or to write their own limericks. Whatever the response it must be accompanied by a positive-feeling tone. The climate surrounding the reading experience must be one of support and positive reinforcement, and it must include the joy of discovery. Involve parents by regularly sending home reading bulletins that note the titles and authors of books children are reading in your classroom or library. Add some suggestions for other good books to read. Send notes suggesting book titles for gift giving. Keep reading as an important component in the child's life.

Ideally the suggestions given in this book would not be used as individual mandated writing or speaking assignments. A writing and reading workshop successfully integrates free choice and response within the classroom. Adults need to pattern responses and to model thinking, reading, and writing skills. The suggestions in this book are intended to be a resource for the teacher, a resource that will assist the modeling of creative responses. The use of big books, transparencies of the text, and group activities will all help focus on that objective. At each junction the element of choice must be kept in mind. The reader of this book will know that the suggestions included here can be utilized in many ways—the limit is only in the creativity and ability of the teacher. You must supply the implementation plan. Take the activity suggestions in this book, adapt them, mold them, but use them. Share and enjoy and read!

Section I:

Chapter

1

Book Tricks—From Alphabet to Do-Nothing

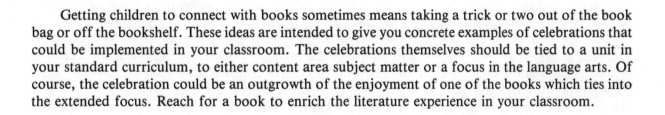

Getting children to connect with books sometimes means taking a trick or two out of the book bag or off the bookshelf. These ideas are intended to give you concrete examples of celebrations that could be implemented in your classroom. The celebrations themselves should be tied to a unit in your standard curriculum, to either content area subject matter or a focus in the language arts. Of course, the celebration could be an outgrowth of the enjoyment of one of the books which ties into the extended focus. Reach for a book to enrich the literature experience in your classroom.

ALPHABET BOOKS—AN ONGOING CELEBRATION

Until the present century the "calling of the letters" was considered a necessary first step toward learning to read. Often children were required to recite the entire alphabet before being allowed to begin to learn to read. Now the emphasis is more on the reading of whole words in context, in order that meaning can be constructed. However, we still feel it is necessary for children to know the names of the letters of the alphabet as they begin to read and write. Teachers, parents, and the children themselves relate to "knowing the alphabet."

The ABCs are often used as an organizational device to present a variety of information to others. One of the first alphabet books to be published was Kate Greenaway's *A Apple Pie* (Warne, 1886); since then many others have been published. Several have been named Caldecott Medal Honor Books. In 1942, Maud and Miska Petersham's *An American ABC* (Macmillan, 1941) was the first to make the Caldecott Honor list. Later four others were included as honor books. *Ape in a Cape: An Alphabet of Odd Animals* by Fritz Eichenberg (Harcourt, Brace & World, 1952) was a humor-filled book with rhyming captions like "Goat in a Boat" and "Fox in a Box." *Hosie's Alphabet* (Viking, 1972) was a sophisticated alphabet book created by Leonard Baskin for his son. While the illustrations are brilliant the very youngest reader will have difficulty comprehending "quintessential quail" or "quasi kiwi." *Jambo Means Hello: A Swahili Alphabet Book* by Muriel Feelings (Dial, 1974) features rich and detailed illustrations by Tom Feelings. The book introduces readers to the Swahili alphabet while it extends their understanding of one aspect of the African culture. An alphabet book by Arnold Lobel, *On Market Street* (Greenwillow, 1981), illustrated by Anita Lobel, shows merchants selling various types of goods. The merchants are outfitted in the goods they sell. The quilt merchant is draped in quilts, the zipper merchant is shown dressed in zippers that make him look long and lanky, the orange merchant is round and plump and orange. In 1977, an alphabet book by Margaret Musgrove, illustrated by Leo Dillon and Diane Dillon, was awarded the prestigious Caldecott Medal for distinguished illustrations in a children's book. That book, *Ashanti to Zulu: African Traditions* (Dial, 1976), focuses on twenty-six African tribes. While the text highlights one notable fact about each particular tribe, the Dillons's illustrations attempt to cover many aspects of each tribe's way of life: terrain, clothing, homes, family structure, animals or birds native to the area, and a typical cooking utensil, tool, or other artifact significant to the tribe's existence. The illustrations add much information to the brief text.

During a study of a specific geographical location an alphabet book might be created depicting the important information about the locale. An excellent model is *Alaska ABC* by Charlene Kreeger and Shannon Cartwright (Alaska ABC Book, 1978).

Within the genre of alphabet books are various types of books utilizing the alphabet. Some follow the traditional "A is for _____" format, others use each letter to build alliterative sentences and rhyming phrases, and still others group words and phrases that go from A to Z. By reading many different alphabet books children will develop ideas for creating their own alphabet books. Encourage rhymes, alliteration, and alphabet antics to tickle the imagination. Create an ABC of the world's countries, or of the Midwest's farm animals, or create an ABC of toys. Experiment with unusual ways to use the letters of the alphabet. For example, in *Ed Emberley's ABCs* (Little, Brown, 1978) the author uses the "i" as the medial vowel sound (pig, wig) and the "x" as the final consonant sound as in fox. Locate ABC books by using the subject category ALPHABET BOOKS in your school or public library's card catalog. My favorite titles include Chris Van Allsburg's *The Z Was Zapped* (Houghton Mifflin, 1987), Mary Elting and Michael Folsom's *Q Is for Duck* (Clarion, 1980) and Graeme Base's *Animalia* (Viking Kestrel, 1986). In *Q Is for Duck* the authors give a pictorial clue as well as the letter clue to the second part of the phrase. On the right-hand page is the text and accompanying picture for "Q is for duck. Why?" and when the page is turned the left-hand page of the next double-page spread shows the duck with an open beak, quacking. This picture is accompanied by the text, "Because a duck quacks." The entire alphabet is treated in a similar manner. Most of the phrases are within the scope of a child's experience. Van Allsburg's *The Z Was Zapped* uses exquisite black and white drawings to show large three-dimensional letters on stage with something happening or being done to them. For example, the "M" is shown as a letter carved from a large block of ice. The letter is melting. Base's *Animalia* is a very unusual alphabet book. The illustrator has created an incredible fantasy world. In this world are familiar animals in unfamiliar situations. Each double-page spread highlights the letter and objects that begin with that letter. The variety of lettering styles, the composition, and color schemes, the presence of dragons, and Graeme Base as a boy hiding in each double-page spread all combine to make this title a visual delight.

Although over twenty-five years old, one of my all-time favorite alphabet books is Jan Garten's *The Alphabet Tale* (Random House, 1964). The illustrations are not particularly exotic but they do enhance the story. I am intrigued by the interplay of the word meaning for "tale" and "tail" and the riddles themselves. Garten has managed to incorporate riddles into the book. On the first page for a letter we see the letter, the tail of the animal, and the text giving riddle clues to the animal's name. The animals range from alligator to zebra and include commonplace animals like the cat and a horse as well as exotic ones like the unicorn and the xenurus.

Other books show life in the big city, as in Michael Deasy's *City ABC's* (Walker, 1974), and life in the country, as in Mary Azarian's *A Farmer's Alphabet* (David R. Godine, 1981). Eric Carle's *All about Arthur (an absolutely absurd ape)* (Watts, 1974) takes us on a fanciful trip to various cities in the United States. The concept of an alphabet book is one that can be utilized in every area of study and knows no age boundaries. Children might be encouraged to write ABC books for their own state and for other countries. They might write an ABC book of pioneer days, an ABC of favorite books, an ABC of inventors, an ABC of heroes in our country's history, or an ABC of our own families. Much research would have to be completed. Children might choose to research their family tree and use the alphabet to name their ancestors or the countries or cities of their ancestors' origins. Other children might focus on traditions or objects in their family homes. This will be a very personal piece of writing which might be a treasured gift for parents or grandparents. Children might use their initials and examine many alphabet books to see what kind of words, phrases, and ideas their initials inspired. A list of those words and phrases could be used to help them compose a book about one of those letters.

Below is a sampling of alphabet books that may prove useful as literary models as well as provide good reading. You may locate other titles by using the subject heading ALPHABET BOOKS in your school or public library.

Booklist—Alphabet Books

Ackerman, Karen. *Flannery Row: An Alphabet Rhyme*. Atlantic Monthly, 1986.

Alda, Arlene. *Arlene Alda's ABC Book*. Celestial Arts, 1981.

Anno, Mitsumas. *Anno's Alphabet: An Adventure in Imagination*. Crowell, 1975.

Azarian, Mary. *A Farmer's Alphabet*. David R. Godine, 1981.

Baldwin, Ruth M. *100 Nineteenth-Century Rhyming Alphabets in English*. Southern Illinois University Press, 1972.

Balian, Lorna. *Humbug Potion: An ABC Cipher*. Abingdon, 1984.

Base, Graeme. *Animalia*. Viking Kestrel, 1986.

Baskin, Leonard. *Hosie's Alphabet*. Viking, 1972.

Bayer, Jane. *A My Name Is Alice*. Illustrated by Steven Kellogg. Dutton, 1984.

Boynton, Sandra. *A Is for Angry: An Animal and Adjective Alphabet*. Workman, 1983.

Brown, Marcia. *All Butterflies: An ABC*. Scribner, 1974.

Burningham, John. *John Burningham's ABC*. Bobbs-Merrill, 1967.

Cameron, Elizabeth. *A Wildflower Alphabet*. Morrow, 1984.

Carle, Eric. *All about Arthur (an absolutely absurd ape)*. Watts, 1974.

Carson, Patti and Janet Dellosa. *A-Z Alphabet Kids*. Carson-Dellosa, 1984.

Chess, Victoria. *Alfred's Alphabet Walk*. Greenwillow, 1969.

Chwast, Seymour and Martin Stephen Moskof. *Still Another Alphabet Book*. McGraw-Hill, 1969.

Crane, Walter. *Baby's Own Alphabet*. Dodd Mead, n.d.

Crowther, Robert. *The Most Amazing Hide and Seek Alphabet Book*. Viking, 1977.

Deasy, Michael. *City ABC's*. Walker, 1974.

Duke, Kate. *The Guinea Pig ABC*. Dutton, 1983.

Duvoisin, Roger. *A for the Ark*. Lothrop, Lee & Shepard, 1952.

Eichenberg, Fritz. *Ape in a Cape: An Alphabet of Odd Animals*. Harcourt, Brace & World, 1952.

Elting, Mary, and Michael Folsom. *Q Is for Duck*. Illustrated by Jack Kent. Clarion, 1980.

Emberley, Ed. *Ed Emberley's ABCs*. Little, Brown, 1978.

Farber, Norma. *As I Was Crossing Boston Common*. Illustrated by Arnold Lobel. Dutton, 1975.

_____. *I Found Them in the Yellow Pages*. Illustrated by Marc Brown. Little, Brown, 1973.

_____. *This Is the Ambulance Leaving the Zoo*. Illustrated by Tomie dePaola. Dutton, 1975.

Feelings, Muriel. *Jambo Means Hello: A Swahili Alphabet Book*. Dial, 1974.

Ferguson, Charles W. *Abecedarian Book*. Little, Brown, 1964.

Fisher, Leonard. *Alphabet Art: Thirteen ABCs from around the World*. Scholastic, 1978.

Folsom, Marcia, and Michael Folsom. *Easy As Pie: A Guessing Game of Sayings*. Illustrated by Jack Kent. Clarion, 1985.

Fujikawa, Gyo. *A to Z Picture Book*. Grosset & Dunlap, 1974.

Gag, Wanda. *The ABC Bunny*. Coward McCann, 1933.

Gardner, Beau. *Have You Ever Seen?* Dodd, Mead, 1986.

Gardner, John. *A Child's Bestiary*. Knopf, 1977.

Garten, Jan. *The Alphabet Tale*. Random House, 1964.

Grafton, Carol Belanger, editor. *Bizarre and Ornamental Alphabets*. Dover, 1981.

_____. *Historic Alphabets and Initials: Woodcut and Ornamental*. Dover, 1977.

Greenaway, Kate. *A Apple Pie*. Warne, 1886.

Grossbart, Francine. *A Big City*. Harper, 1966.

Hague, Kathleen. *Alphabears*. Holt, Rinehart & Winston, 1984.

Harrison, Ted. *A Northern Alphabet*. Tundra, 1982.

Hoban, Tana. *A, B, See!* Greenwillow, 1982.

Hoguet, Susan Ramsay. *I Unpacked My Grandmother's Trunk*. Dutton, 1983.

Johnson, Crockett. *Harold's ABC*. Harper & Row, 1963.

Kennedy, X. J. *Did Adam Name the Vinegarroon?* David R. Godine, 1982.

Kitamura, Satoshi. *What's Inside? The Alphabet Book*. Farrar, Straus & Giroux, 1985.

Korab, Balthazar. *Archabet: An Architectural Alphabet*. Preservation, 1985.

Kreeger, Charlene and Shannon Cartwright. *Alaska ABC*. Alaska ABC Book, 1978.

Larcher, Jean. *Fantastic Alphabets: 24 Original Alphabets*. Dover, 1976.

Lear, Edward. *ABC*. McGraw-Hill, 1965.

_____. *An Edward Lear Alphabet*. Lothrop, Lee & Shepard, 1983.

_____. *Edward Lear's ABC: Alphabet Rhymes for Children*. Salem House, 1986.

Lillie, Patricia. *One Very, Very Quiet Afternoon*. Greenwillow, 1986.

Lobel, Arnold. *On Market Street*. Illustrated by Anita Lobel. Greenwillow, 1981.

MacDonald, Suse. *Alphabatics*. Bradbury, 1986.

Maddex, Diane, editor. *Built in the U.S.A.: American Buildings from Airports to Zoos*. Preservation, 1985.

Maddex, Diane. *Architects Make Zigzags: Looking at Architecture from A to Z*. Preservation, 1986.

Matthiesen, Thomas. *ABC: An Alphabet Book*. Platt Munk, 1966.

Mazzarella, Mimi. *Alphabatty Animals and Funny Foods*. Liberty, 1984.

McGinley, Phyliss. *All around the Town*. Lippincott, 1948.

Mendoza, George. *Alphabet Sheep*. Grosset & Dunlap, 1982.

Miles, Miska. *Apricot ABC*. Atlantic-Little, Brown, 1969.

Munari, Bruno. *Bruno Munari's ABC*. World, 1960.

Musgrove, Margaret. *Ashanti to Zulu: African Traditions*. Illustrated by Leo Dillon and Diane Dillon. Dial, 1976.

Neumeier, Marty and Byron Glaser. *Action Alphabet*. Greenwillow, 1984.

Nicholason, William. *An Alphabet*. Heineman/Alan Wofsy, 1975.

Niland, Deborah. *ABC of Monsters*. McGraw-Hill, 1976.

Obligado, Lilian. *Faint Frogs Feeling Feverish: And Other Terrifically Tantalizing Tongue Twisters*. Viking, 1983.

Oxenbury, Helen. *Helen Oxenbury's ABC of Things*. Watts, 1972.

Pearson, Tracey C. *A Apple Pie*. Dial, 1986.

Petersham, Maud, and Miska Petersham. *An American ABC*. Macmillan, 1941.

Piatti, Celestino. *Celestino Piatti's Animal ABC*. Atheneum, 1966.

Poulin, Stéphane. *Ah! Belle Cité! A Beautiful City ABC*. Tundra, 1985.

Rice, James. *Cajun Alphabet*. Pelican, 1976.

Rojankovsky, Feodor. *Animals in the Zoo*. Knopf, 1962.

Rosenblum, Richard. *The Airplane ABC*. Atheneum, 1986.

Sarasas, Claude. *The ABC's of Origami: Paper Folding for Children*. Tuttle, 1964.

Schmiderer, Dorothy. *The Alphabeast Book: An Abecedarium*. Holt, Rinehart & Winston, 1971.

Sendak, Maurice. *Alligators All Around*. Harper & Row, 1962.

Sloane, Eric. *The ABC Book of Early Americana*. Doubleday, 1963.

Steig, William. *CDB*. Simon & Schuster, 1968.

Stockham, Peter, editor. *The Mother's Picture Alphabet*. Dover, 1974.

Tudor, Tasha. *A Is for Annabelle*. Walck, 1954.

Van Allsburg, Chris. *The Z Was Zapped*. Houghton Mifflin, 1987.

Walters, Marguerite. *The City-Country ABC*. Doubleday, 1966.

Weil, Lisl. *Owl and Other Scrambles*. Dutton, 1980.

Wildsmith, Brian. *Brian Wildsmith's ABC*. Watts, 1962.

Williams, Garth. *Big Golden Animal ABC*. Golden Press, 1954.

Wilson, Ron. *100 Dinosaurs from A to Z*. Grosset & Dunlap, 1986.

Utilize the alphabet to help students synthesize and condense their research findings. For example, ask each student to visit the library for three to four class periods and to read and take notes (copying is okay) on a specific topic. After the note-taking periods have been accomplished, assign students a letter of the alphabet and ask them to write an alliterative report on the topic on which they have taken notes. The report will probably not be any longer than a paragraph or two but should contain the most significant information about the topic. The students will need to make considerable use of a thesaurus to help them locate words starting with their letter. Encourage students to get help from one another. This is an excellent vocabulary builder.

BIRTHDAYS—CELEBRATIONS ALL THROUGH THE YEAR

Bring children and books together with a celebration of authors' birthdays or birthdays honoring specific book characters.

In one year alone (1988) three favorite characters enjoyed memorable birthdays. Clifford the Big Red Dog, the lovable giant dog featured in books by Norman Bridwell, had been in existence for twenty-five years as had Peggy Parrish's Amelia Bedelia. Amelia Bedelia is a wacky housekeeper who interprets every instruction literally rather than figuratively. During the same year the Cat in the Hat was enjoying thirty years of existence. For those special anniversaries, the publishers offered promotional posters and other materials that could be used to facilitate a celebration. But you really don't have to wait for a special birthday to occur. Simply decide on a favorite character and celebrate. One year at the elementary school where I was teaching, the first-grade children were really enjoying Bill Peet's books and all the characters in those books, probably because their teachers were enjoying them. The children and teachers obtained as many books by Bill Peet as they could and then they read and reread them. They laughed at Eli and chuckled at Joel and Jethro. They enjoyed and savoured each book. Houghton Mifflin had produced a videotape *A Visit with Bill Peet* which was obtained. On that video Peet described his early career in illustration and how he came to write books for children. He concludes by demonstrating the procedure that created the Whingdingdilly, a character featured in a book by Peet. The animal begins as Scamp the dog and ends up with the appendages and characteristics of six other animals. Since Bill Peet was already a favorite, the Whingdingdilly soon became the favorite book character. Each time one of the students rediscovers Whingdingdilly a new group of students becomes acquainted with the character—and the excitement starts once again.

Other days might need to be more organized and planned. Declare a week at your school or library as "Clifford Days." Circulate a basket with as many Clifford titles as can be located. Place a routing slip on the basket. When the basket arrives the children and teacher in each class should stop whatever they are doing and read for ten to fifteen minutes (D.E.A.R.: Drop Everything and Read). Offer a ticket to a library read-and-feed event for the student bringing the largest red thing for display, the smallest red thing, the most unusual, the bookiest, and the funniest red thing. Read books with red in the title, books with red covers, and books with red objects in the story. Read the poem "Red Is" from Mary O'Neil's *Hailstones and Halibut Bones, Adventures in Color* (Doubleday, 1961). Go on a search for red in the library. Make a list of books with red in the title. Be sure to include Barbara Park's *The Kid in the Red Jacket* (Knopf, 1987; Bullseye pb, 1988); *The Red Balloon* by Albert Lamorisse (Doubleday, 1956); *The Red Bantam* by Louise Fatio (McGraw-Hill, 1962); "The Red Swan," a story told by Henry Rowe Schoolcraft in *The Fire Plume: Legends of the American Indians*, edited by John Bierhorst (Dial, 1969); all the stories in *The Red Fairy Book* by Andrew Lang (Random House, 1960 [1890]), and *Three Days on a River in a Red Canoe* by Vera B. Williams (Greenwillow, 1981). Don't miss the many versions of "Red Riding Hood," or "The Voyage of a Wee Red Cap" a tale told wonderfully by Ruth Sawyer on a Weston Woods cassette tape, *Ruth Sawyer, Storyteller*.

Celebrate Amelia Bedelia's birthday by focusing on literal interpretations of everyday sayings. First read and reread Peggy Parrish's stories of Amelia. As a group or class list the statements that Amelia took literally rather than figuratively. Add others if you can. Spend one day reacting to everything that is said in a literal manner. As a teacher or librarian be sure to use an abundance of phrases that could be taken literally or figuratively. Declare the day "Amelia Bedelia Day." Encourage students and teachers to dress in costumes depicting Amelia Bedelia. Other book characters could be included in a storybook parade. If full costumes are difficult to handle consider having children make sandwich board style advertisements for their favorite books. On Amelia Bedelia Day, Amelia Bedelia could lead the parade. A storybook parade could become a regular tradition during book week.

Amelia Bedelia's mixed-up interpretation could be extended to intermediate students as they read Bill Brittain's *The Wish Giver* (Harper & Row, 1983). Three youngsters buy a wish from Thaddeus Blinn for only 50 cents. The trouble is that all three are given exactly what they wish. A wish that a traveling salesman plant himself and take root in Coven Tree is granted to a young lady. Another girl wishes to be noticed when she talks, and a young man wishes for water all over his parents' farm. Each of their wishes is granted with disastrous results. Several folk stories present the same wish theme.

A celebration of the *Cat in the Hat* and the other books by Dr. Seuss is a popular activity any year. In 1988 the Cat in the Hat celebrated his thirtieth year. Dr. Seuss marked his eighty-fifth birthday on March 2, 1989. His many books will provide much reading material for any Seuss-related celebration. You may want to include a stuffed Cat in the Hat to guard the reading basket that will circulate to classrooms. Combine literature and the expressive arts: design new tall hats for the Cat in the Hat†—in floral patterns, geometric shapes, and of many varied colors—and fill the halls with them. Publish a cookbook with students' recipes for "Scrambled Eggs Super" or "Green Eggs and Ham." Create other dishes sure to please the Cat in the Hat, Horton the Elephant, and Thing One and Thing Two. Publish those recipes in the cookbook. One creative first-grade teacher†† used Dr. Seuss's *The Foot Book* (Random House, 1968) to inspire a foot poster featuring

---

†Idea credit: Sal Miller, art teacher, Cedar Rapids Community Schools (Iowa).

††Joyce Geater, Cedar Rapids Community Schools (Iowa).

footprints of each of the students in the class and the teacher's footprints too. Red, blue, yellow, or green tempera paint was painted on the soles of each child's feet. The children wrote their own verses to accompany the footprints on the banner, and then hung the banner in a much-used stairwell for all to see and enjoy. The celebration of Dr. Seuss and his books culminated with a day filled with a morning breakfast of green eggs and ham, birthday cake served at lunchtime, and a full day of read alouds. Parents, community leaders, older students, and school administrators took turns throughout the day reading their favorite Dr. Seuss book to groups of children.

Maurice Sendak's *Where the Wild Things Are* was twenty-five years old in 1988. In 1989, Eric Carle's *The Very Hungry Caterpillar* (Philomel, 1969) had been in print for twenty years, and *Madeline* (Viking, 1939) by Ludwig Bemelmans for fifty years. Frances of Russell Hoban's *Bedtime for Frances* (Harper & Row, 1960) and several other books featuring a lovable mischievous badger will be thirty in 1990. In 1991, *Make Way for Ducklings* by Robert McCloskey (Viking, 1941) will be fifty years old.

Choose any character you and the readers enjoy and investigate the year of the character's first appearance in a book. Pick a date of the year and declare a celebration, a day of special activities. As children in your class or school celebrate a birthday make it special by reading and sharing their favorite books or book characters. Celebrate an author or illustrator's birthday by reading his or her books throughout the day or week. Turn any birthday or any book into a book celebration.

Celebrating an Author/Illustrator's Birthday

There are several options for creating a birthday celebration. In your reading corner display a birthday calendar and arrange a space where books by selected authors and illustrators could be displayed for reading and sharing. Weekly or monthly calendars could be created using the extensive lists of birthdays in this section. Standard 8½x11-inch calendars can be made by utilizing *Print Shop Companion*. This computer program is available from Broderbund and is designed to work with the *Print Shop* program. Libraries Unlimited has available a disk, *Print Shop™ Graphics for Libraries—Volume 2: Perpetual Calendars*, which includes a total of forty-eight calendars, twelve of them prepared with the birthdays of favorite authors/illustrators of books in the children's literature category and another twelve in the young adult literature category. During the birthday party students could share a book from the center, give a book talk about one of the books, and in general enjoy the books. A monthly party might include birthday treats and more elaborate preparations, while a very simple routine might be developed to provide a daily focus. Those wishing to have a daily activity might share early in the day the list of the authors/illustrators who are celebrating their birthdays. During the day students could investigate those authors/illustrators and their books in the library. Their findings might be shared during a routine birthday segment at the end of the day.

A weekly party might honor all the authors/illustrators (and students) who celebrated their birthdays during that week. Each day a read aloud could be selected so that the class members could share some common literature experiences. Picture books could be read completely while chapters or other appropriate segments could be read from novels or nonfiction books.

The following list can provide some suggestions for names you may wish to include on your classroom or library author/illustrator calendar. The names are listed by last name; a second list arranges the authors and illustrators by date.

Birthday List for Authors/Illustrators by Last Name

An author/illustrator's year of birth is given in parentheses where that information was available. In appropriate cases we have noted the death of an author or illustrator with a "d" or with the date if available.

Aardema, Verna — June 6 (1911)

Adler, David — April 10

Adoff, Arnold — July 16 (1935)

Ahlberg, Allan — June 5 (1938)

Ahlberg, Janet — October 21 (1944)

Aiken, Joan — September 4 (1924)

Alexander, Lloyd — January 30 (1924)

Alexander, Martha — May 25 (1920)

Alexander, Sue — August 20 (1933)

Alger, Leclaire Gowans (see Nic Leodhas, Sorche)

Aliki (Brandenberg) — September 3 (1929)

Allard, Harry — January 27 (1928)

Amoss, Berthe — September 26 (1925)

Andersen, Hans Christian — April 2 (1805-1875)

Anglund, Joan Walsh — January 3 (1926)

Anno, Mitsumasa — March 20 (1926)

Armstrong, William H. — September 14 (1914)

Arquette, Lois Steinmetz (see Duncan, Lois)

Aruego, Ariane (see Dewey, Ariane)

Aruego, José — August 9 (1932)

Asbjørnson, Peter — January 15 (1816-1885)

Asch, Frank — August 6 (1946)

Asher, Sandy — October 16 (1942)

Asimov, Isaac — January 2 (1920)

Aylesworth, Jim — February 21 (1943)

Baird, Thomas — April 22 (1923)

Balian, Lorna — December 14 (1929)

Bang, Betsy Garrett — July 9 (1912)

Bang, Molly Garrett — December 29 (1943)

Baum, L. Frank—May 15 (1856-1919)

Bellairs, John—January 17 (1938)

Berenstain, Jan—July 26 (1923)

Berenstain, Stan—September 29 (1923)

Beskow, Elsa—February 11 (1874-d.)

Bianco, Margery Williams (see Williams, Margery)

Bierhorst, John—September 2 (1936)

Blake, Quentin—December 16 (1932)

Blos, Joan W.—December 8 (1928)

Blough, Glenn O.—September 5 (1907)

Blume, Judy—February 12 (1938)

Bond, Michael—January 13 (1926)

Bond, Thomas Michael (see Bond, Michael)

Bonsall, Crosby—January 2 (1921)

Bottner, Barbara—May 25 (1943)

Brandenberg, Aliki (see Aliki)

Brandenberg, Franz—February 10 (1932)

Bridwell, Norman—February 15 (1928)

Briggs, Raymond—January 18 (1934)

Brittain, William (Bill)—December 16 (1930)

Brodsky, Beverly—August 16 (1941)

Brown, Marc—November 25 (1946)

Brown, Marcia—July 13 (1918)

Brown, Margaret Wise—May 23 (1910-1952)

Bryan, Ashley—July 13 (1923)

Bulla, Clyde Robert—January 9 (1914)

Bunting, Anne Evelyn (see Bunting, Eve)

Bunting, Eve—December 19 (1928); pseud. of Anne Evelyn Bunting

Burch, Robert—June 26 (1925)

Butterworth, W. E.—November 10 (1929); pseud. of William Edmund Butterworth III

Byars, Betsy—August 7 (1928)

Caldecott, Randolph—March 22 (1846-1886)

Calhoun, Mary—August 3 (1926)

Cameron, Eleanor—March 23 (1912)

Carle, Eric—June 25 (1929)

Carlson, Natalie—October 3 (1906)

Carrick, Carol—May 20 (1935)

Carrick, Donald—April 7 (1929)

Carris, Joan—August 18 (1938)

Carroll, Lewis—January 27 (1832-1898); pseud. of Charles Dodson

Caudill, Rebecca—February 2 (1899-d.)

Charlip, Remy—January 10 (1929)

Chase, Richard—February 15 (1904)

Chorao, Kay—January 7 (1937)

Christopher, Matt—August 16 (1917)

Ciardi, John—June 24 (1916-1986)

Cleary, Beverly—April 12 (1916)

Cleaver, Bill—March 24 (1920)

Cleaver, Vera—January 6 (1919)

Clemens, Samuel (see Twain, Mark)

Clifford, Eth—December 25 (1915); pseud. of Ethel Clifford Rosenberg

Clifton, Lucille—June 27 (1936)

Cohen, Barbara—March 15 (1932)

Cole, Joanna—August 11 (1944)

Cole, William—November 20 (1919)

Collier, Christopher—January 29 (1930)

Collier, James Lincoln—June 27 (1928)

Cone, Molly—October 3 (1918)

Conford, Ellen—March 20 (1942)

Conly, Robert Leslie (see O'Brien, Robert C.)

Coombs, Patricia—July 23 (1926)

Cooper, Susan—May 23 (1935)

Corbett, Scott—July 27 (1913)

Corcoran, Barbara—April 12 (1911)

Cormier, Robert—January 17 (1925)

Courlander, Harold—September 18 (1908)

Coville, Bruce—May 16 (1950)

Dahl, Roald—September 13 (1916)

Dalgliesh, Alice—October 7 (1893-d.)

Danziger, Paula—August 18 (1944)

d'Aulaire, Edgar—September 30 (1898-d.)

d'Aulaire, Ingri—December 27 (1904)

Davies, Andrew—September 20 (1936)

DeAngeli, Marguerite—March 14 (1889-d.)

DeClements, Barthe—October 8 (1920)

DeJong, Meindert—March 4 (1906)

Delton, Judy—May 6 (1931)

dePaola, Tomie—September 15 (1934)

Devlin, Harry—March 22 (1918)

Devlin, Wende—April 27 (1918)

Dewey, Ariane—August 17 (1937)

Dillon, Barbara—September 2 (1927)

Dillon, Diane—March 13 (1933)

Dillon, Leo—March 2 (1933)

Dodson, Charles (see Carroll, Lewis)

Dodson, Susan—January 19 (1941)

Doty, Roy—September 10 (1922)

Duncan, Lois—April 28 (1934); pseud. of Lois Steinmetz Arquette

Dygard, Thomas J.—August 10 (1931)

Elkin, Benjamin—August 10 (1911)

Emberley, Barbara—December 12 (1932)

Emberley, Ed—October 19 (1931)

Ets, Marie Hall—December 16 (1893)

Eyerly, Jeannette—June 7 (1908)

Farber, Norma—August 6 (1909)

Farjeon, Eleanor—February 13 (1882-1965)

Feelings, Muriel L.—July 31 (1938)

Feelings, Tom—May 19 (1933)

Field, Rachel—September 19 (1884-1942)

Fischtrom, Harvey (see Zemach, Harve)

Fischtrom, Margot Zemach (see Zemach, Margot)

Fitzhardinge, Joan Margaret (see Phipson, Joan)

Fitzhugh, Louise — October 5 (1928)

Flack, Marjorie — October 23 (1857-1958)

Fleischman, Paul — September 5 (1952)

Fleischman, Sid — March 16 (1920)

Flora, James — January 25 (1914)

Fox, Paula — April 22 (1923)

Frederiksen, Betty Ren Wright (see Wright, Betty Ren)

Fritz, Jean — November 16 (1915)

Fyleman, Rose — March 6 (1877-1957)

Gackenback, Dick — February 9 (1927)

Galdone, Paul — June 2 (1914-1986)

Gauch, Patricia Lee — January 3 (1934)

Geisel, Theodor Seuss (see Seuss, Dr.)

Giff, Patricia Reilly — April 26 (1935)

Gilson, Jamie — July 4

Gipson, Fred — February 7 (1908)

Goble, Paul — September 27 (1933)

Goode, Diane — September 14 (1949)

Gorman, Carol — February 16 (1952)

Gormley, Beatrice — October 15 (1942)

Gould, Marilyn — February 12 (1928)

Grahame, Kenneth — March 3 (1859-1932)

Gray, Elizabeth — October 6 (1902)

Greenaway, Kate — March 17 (1846-1901)

Greenberg, Jan — December 29 (1942)

Greene, Bette — June 28 (1934)

Greene, Constance C. — October 27 (1924)

Greenfield, Eloise — May 17 (1929)

Griffith, Helen V. — October 31 (1934)

Grimm, Jacob — January 4 (1785-1863)

Grimm, Wilhelm—February 24 (1786-1859)

Hader, Elmer—September 6 (1884-1973)

Hadley, Lee—October 10 (1934); with Ann Irwin joint pseud. Hadley Irwin

Haley, Gail E.—November 4 (1939)

Hall, Donald—September 20 (1928)

Hall, Lynn—November 9 (1937)

Hamilton, Virginia—March 12 (1933)

Hanson, June Andrea—June 2 (1941)

Harris, Joel Chandler—December 9 (1848-1908)

Haviland, Virginia—May 21 (1911-d.)

Haywood, Carolyn—January 3 (1898-d.)

Heide, Florence Parry—February 27 (1919)

Henry, Marguerite—April 13 (1902)

Hermes, Patricia—February 21 (1936)

Hoban, Lillian—May 18 (1925)

Hoban, Russell—February 4 (1925)

Hoff, Syd—September 4 (1912)

Hogrogian, Nonny—May 7 (1932)

Holl, Kristi—December 8 (1951)

Holland, Isabelle—June 16 (1929)

Hopkins, Lee Bennett—April 13 (1939)

Hunter, Molly—June 30 (1922)

Hurd, Clement—January 12 (1908)

Hurwitz, Johanna—October 9 (1937)

Hutchins, Pat (Patricia)—June 18 (1942)

Hyman, Trina Schart—April 8 (1939)

Irwin, Ann—October 8 (1915); with Lee Hadley joint pseud. Hadley Irwin

Irwin, Hadley (see Hadley, Lee and Irwin, Ann)

Jeschke, Susan—October 18 (1942)

Johnson, Crockett—October 20 (1906-1975); pseud. of David Johnson Leisk

Joslin, Sesyle (Hine)—August 30 (1929)

Keats, Ezra Jack—March 11 (1916-1983)

Kelley, Eric—March 16 (1884-1960)

Kellogg, Steven — October 6 (1941)

Kent, Jack — March 10 (1920-1986)

Kerr, M. E. — May 27 (1927); pseud. of Marijane Meaker

Kheridan, David — December 17 (1931)

Kheridan, Nonny Hogrogian (see Hogrogian, Nonny)

Kipling, Rudyard — December 30 (1865-1936)

Klein, Norma — May 13 (1938-1989)

Knight, Kathryn Lasky — June 24 (1944)

Konigsburg, E. (Elaine) L. (Lobl) — February 10 (1930)

Kraus, Robert — June 21 (1925)

Kroll, Steven — August 11 (1941)

Langstaff, John — December 24 (1920)

Lasky, Kathryn (see Knight, Kathryn Lasky)

Latham, Jean Lee — April 19 (1902)

Lauber, Patricia — February 5

Lawson, Robert — October 5 (1892-1957)

Leaf, Munro — December 4 (1905-1976)

Lear, Edward — May 12 (1812-1888)

Leisk, David Johnson (see Johnson, Crockett)

L'Engle, Madeleine — November 29 (1918)

Lent, Blair — January 22 (1930)

Lester, Julius — January 27 (1939)

Lexau, Joan — March 9

Lionni, Leo — May 5 (1910)

Livingston, Myra Cohn — August 17 (1926)

Lobel, Anita — June 2 (1934)

Lobel, Arnold — May 22 (1933-1987)

Lofting, Hugh — January 14 (1886-1947)

Lopshire, Robert — April 14 (1927)

Lowry, Lois — March 20 (1937)

Macaulay, David — December 2 (1946)

MacKellar, William — February 20 (1914)

Mahoney, Elizabeth Winthrop (see Winthrop, Elizabeth)

Mahy, Margaret — March 21 (1936)

Marshall, Edward (see Marshall, James)

Marshall, James—October 10 (1942)

Martin, Jacqueline Briggs—April 15 (1945)

Martin, Patricia Miles (see Miles, Miska)

Mathias, Sharon Bell—February 26 (1937)

Mauser, Patricia Rhoads—January 14 (1943)

Mayer, Marianna—November 8 (1945)

Mayer, Mercer—December 30 (1943)

Mazer, Harry—May 31 (1925)

Mazer, Norma Fox—May 15 (1931)

McCloskey, Robert—September 15 (1914)

McCord, David—November 15 (1898-d.)

McCully, Emily Arnold—July 1 (1939)

McDermott, Beverly Brodsky (see Brodsky, Beverly)

McDermott, Gerald—January 31 (1941)

McGinley, Phyllis—March 21 (1905)

McGinnis, Lila Sprague—May 29 (1924)

McInerney, Judith Whitelock—June 1 (1945)

McKinley, Robin—November 16 (1952)

McPhail, David—June 30 (1940)

Meaker, Marijane (see Kerr, M. E.)

Meigs, Cornelia—December 6 (1884-1973)

Miles, Betty—May 16 (1928)

Miles, Miska—November 14 (1899); pseud. of Patricia Miles Martin

Milne, A. A.—January 18 (1882-1956)

Minarik, Else—September 13 (1920)

Moeri, Louise—November 30 (1924)

Mohr, Nicholasa—November 1 (1935)

Mosel, Arlene—August 27 (1921)

Myers, Walter Dean—August 12 (1937)

Naylor, Phyllis Reynolds—January 4 (1933)

Ness, Evaline—April 24 (1911-d.)

Newton, Suzanne—October 8 (1936)

Nic Leodhas, Sorche—May 20 (1898-1969); pseud. of Leclaire Gowans Alger

Nixon, Joan Lowery—February 3 (1927)

Norton, Mary—December 10 (1903)

Oakley, Graham—August 27 (1919)

O'Brien, Robert C.—January 11 (1918-1973); pseud. of Robert Leslie Conly

O'Neill, Mary—February 16 (1908)

Oxenbury, Helen—June 2 (1938)

Park, Barbara—April 21 (1947)

Parrish, Peggy—July 14 (1927-1988)

Paterson, Katherine—October 31 (1932)

Peck, Richard—April 5 (1934)

Peck, Robert Newton—February 17 (1928)

Peet, Bill—January 29 (1915)

Perrault, Charles—January 12 (1628-1703)

Petersen, P. J.—October 23 (1941)

Pfeffer, Susan Beth—February 17 (1948)

Phipson, Joan—November 16 (1912); pseud. of Joan Margaret Fitzhardinge

Pinkwater, Daniel Manus—November 15 (1941)

Potter, Beatrix—July 28 (1866-1943)

Prelutsky, Jack—September 8 (1940)

Provensen, Alice—August 14 (1918)

Provensen, Martin—July 10 (1916-1987)

Quackenbush, Robert—July 23 (1929)

Raskin, Ellen—March 13 (1928-1984)

Rey, H. A.—September 16 (1898-1972)

Roberts, Willo Davis—May 29 (1928)

Rockwell, Anne—February 8 (1934)

Rockwell, Thomas—March 13 (1933)

Roos, Stephen—February 9 (1945)

Rosenberg, Ethel Clifford (see Clifford, Eth)

Rossetti, Christina—January 5 (1830-1894)

Rounds, Glen—April 4 (1906)

Ruffins, Reynold—August 5 (1930)

Sachs, Marilyn—December 18 (1927)

Sarnoff, Jane—June 25 (1937)

Scarry, Richard—June 5 (1919)

Schwartz, Alvin—April 25 (1927)

Scoppettone, Sandra—June 1 (1936)

Selden, George—May 14 (1929); pseud. of George Selden Thompson

Selsam, Millicent E.—May 30 (1912)

Sendak, Maurice—June 10 (1928)

Seuss, Dr.—March 2 (1904); pseud. of Theodor Seuss Geisel

Shannon, George—February 14 (1952)

Sharmat, Marjorie Weinman—November 12 (1928)

Shepard, Ernest H.—December 10 (1879)

Shulevitz, Uri—February 27 (1935)

Shura, Mary Francis—February 27 (1923)

Siegal, Aranka—June 10 (1930)

Silverstein, Alvin—December 30 (1933)

Silverstein, Virginia B.—April 3 (1937)

Simon, Seymour—August 9 (1931)

Singer, Isaac Bashevis—July 14 (1904)

Skurzynski, Gloria—July 9 (1930)

Sleator, William—February 13 (1945)

Slobodkin, Louis—February 19 (1903)

Slote, Doris Buchanan—June 1 (1934)

Smith, Robert Kimmel—July 31 (1930)

Sobol, Donald J.—October 4 (1924)

Speare, Elizabeth George—November 21 (1908)

Spinelli, Jerry—February 1 (1941)

Steig, William—November 14 (1907)

Stevens, Carla—March 26 (1928)

Stevenson, Robert Lewis—November 13 (1850-1894)

Stewart, Mary—September 17 (1916)

Tafuri, Nancy—November 14 (1946)

Taylor, Theodore—June 23 (1921)

Terris, Susan—May 6 (1937)

Thompson, George Selden (see Selden, George)

Thurber, James—December 8 (1894-1961)

Tresselt, Alvin—September 30 (1916)

Twain, Mark—November 30 (1835-1900); pseud. of Samuel Clemens

Udry, Janice—June 14 (1928)

Ungerer, Tomi—November 28 (1931)

Van Allsburg, Chris—June 18 (1949)

Van Leeuwen, Jean—December 26 (1937)

Viorst, Judith—February 2

Voigt, Cynthia—February 25 (1942)

Vugteveen, Verna Aardema (see Aardema, Verna)

Waber, Bernard—September 27 (1924)

Wahl, Jan—April 1 (1933)

Wallner, John C.—February 3 (1945)

White, E. B.—July 11 (1899-d.)

Whitney, Phyllis A.—September 9 (1903)

Wilder, Laura Ingalls—February 7 (1867-1957)

Wildsmith, Brian—January 22 (1930)

Willard, Nancy—June 26 (1936)

Williams, Margery—July 22 (1881-1944); pseud. of Margery Williams Bianco

Williams, Vera B.—January 28 (1927)

Winthrop, Elizabeth—September 14 (1948)

Wojciechowska, Maia—August 7 (1927)

Wolkstein, Diane—November 11 (1942)

Wright, Betty Ren—June 15 (1927)

Yep, Laurence—June 14 (1948)

Yolen, Jane—February 11 (1939)

Zemach, Harve—December 5 (1933-1974); pseud. of Harvey Fischtrom

Zemach, Margot (Fischtrom)—November 30 (1931)

Zindel, Paul—May 15 (1936)

Birthday List for Authors/Illustrators by Date

The year of birth is given in parentheses for those authors or illustrators for whom that information was available. In appropriate cases we have noted the death of an author or illustrator with a "d" or with the date if available.

JANUARY

January 2 (1920)—Isaac Asimov

January 2 (1921)—Crosby Bonsall; Crosby Barbara Newell Bonsall

January 3 (1898-d.)—Carolyn Haywood

January 3 (1926)—Joan Walsh Anglund

January 3 (1934)—Patricia Lee Gauch

January 4 (1785-1863)—Jacob Grimm

January 4 (1933)—Phyllis Reynolds Naylor

January 5 (1830-1894)—Christina Rossetti

January 6 (1919)—Vera Cleaver

January 7 (1937)—Kay Chorao

January 9 (1914)—Clyde Robert Bulla

January 10 (1929)—Remy Charlip

January 11 (1918-1973)—Robert C. O'Brien; pseud. of Robert Leslie Conly

January 12 (1628-1703)—Charles Perrault

January 12 (1908)—Clement Hurd

January 13 (1926)—Michael Bond; pseud. of Thomas Michael Bond

January 14 (1886-1947)—Hugh Lofting

January 14 (1943)—Patricia Rhoads Mauser

January 15 (1816-1885)—Peter J. Asbjørnson

January 17 (1925)—Robert Cormier

January 17 (1938)—John Bellairs

January 18 (1882-1956)—A. A. Milne

January 18 (1934)—Raymond Briggs

January 19 (1941)—Susan Dodson

January 22 (1930)—Blair Lent

January 22 (1930)—Brian Wildsmith

January 25 (1914)—James Flora

January 27 (1832-1898) — Lewis Carroll; pseud. of Charles Dodson

January 27 (1928) — Harry Allard

January 27 (1939) — Julius Lester

January 28 (1927) — Vera B. Williams

January 29 (1915) — Bill Peet

January 29 (1930) — Christopher Collier

January 30 (1924) — Lloyd Alexander

January 31 (1941) — Gerald McDermott

FEBRUARY

February 1 (1941) — Jerry Spinelli

February 2 (1899-d.) — Rebecca Caudill

February 2 — Judith Viorst

February 3 (1927) — Joan Lowery Nixon

February 3 (1945) — John C. Wallner

February 4 (1925) — Russell Hoban

February 5 — Patricia Lauber

February 7 (1867-1957) — Laura Ingalls Wilder

February 7 (1908) — Fred Gipson

February 8 (1934) — Anne Rockwell

February 9 (1927) — Dick Gackenback

February 9 (1945) — Stephen Roos

February 10 (1930) — E. L. Konigsburg; pseud. of Elaine Lobl Konigsburg

February 10 (1932) — Franz Brandenberg

February 11 (1874-d.) — Elsa Beskow

February 11 (1939) — Jane Yolen

February 12 (1928) — Marilyn Gould

February 12 (1938) — Judy Blume

February 13 (1882-1965) — Eleanor Farjeon

February 13 (1945) — William Sleator

February 14 (1952) — George Shannon

February 15 (1904) — Richard Chase

February 15 (1928) — Norman Bridwell

February 16 (1908) — Mary O'Neill

February 16 (1952) — Carol Gorman

February 17 (1928) — Robert Newton Peck

February 17 (1948) — Susan Beth Pfeffer

February 19 (1903) — Louis Slobodkin

February 20 (1914) — William MacKellar

February 21 (1936) — Patricia Hermes

February 21 (1943) — Jim Aylesworth

February 24 (1786-1859) — Wilhelm Grimm

February 25 (1942) — Cynthia Voigt

February 26 (1937) — Sharon Bell Mathias

February 27 (1919) — Florence Parry Heide

February 27 (1923) — Mary Francis Shura

February 27 (1935) — Uri Shulevitz

MARCH

March 2 (1904) — Dr. Seuss; pseud. of Theodor Seuss Geisel

March 2 (1933) — Leo Dillon

March 3 (1859-1932) — Kenneth Grahame

March 4 (1906) — Meindert DeJong

March 6 (1877-1957) — Rose Fyleman

March 9 — Joan Lexau

March 10 (1920-1986) — Jack Kent

March 11 (1916-1983) — Ezra Jack Keats

March 12 (1933) — Virginia Hamilton

March 13 (1928-1984) — Ellen Raskin

March 13 (1933) — Diane Dillon

March 13 (1933) — Thomas Rockwell

March 14 (1889-d.) — Marguerite DeAngeli

March 15 (1932) — Barbara Cohen

March 16 (1884-1960) — Eric Kelley

March 16 (1920) — Sid Fleischman

March 17 (1846-1901) — Kate Greenaway

March 20 (1926) — Mitsumasa Anno

March 20 (1937) — Lois Lowry

March 20 (1942) — Ellen Conford

March 21 (1905) — Phyllis McGinley

March 21 (1936) — Margaret Mahy

March 22 (1846-1886) — Randolph Caldecott

March 22 (1918) — Harry Devlin

March 23 (1912) — Eleanor Cameron

March 24 (1920) — Bill Cleaver

March 26 (1928) — Carla Stevens

APRIL

April 1 (1933) — Jan Wahl

April 2 (1805-1875) — Hans Christian Andersen

April 3 (1937) — Virginia B. Silverstein

April 4 (1906) — Glen Rounds

April 5 (1934) — Richard Peck

April 7 (1929) — Donald Carrick

April 8 (1939) — Trina Schart Hyman

April 10 — David Adler

April 12 (1911) — Barbara Corcoran

April 12 (1916) — Beverly Cleary

April 13 (1902) — Marguerite Henry

April 13 (1939) — Lee Bennett Hopkins

April 14 (1927) — Robert Lopshire

April 15 (1945) — Jacqueline Briggs Martin

April 19 (1902) — Jean Lee Latham

April 21 (1947) — Barbara Park

April 22 (1923) — Paula Fox

April 22 (1923) — Thomas Baird

April 24 (1911-d.) — Evaline Ness

April 25 (1927) — Alvin Schwartz

April 26 (1935) — Patricia Reilly Giff

April 27 (1918)—Wende Devlin

April 28 (1934)—Lois Duncan; pseud. of Lois Steinmetz Arquette

MAY

May 5 (1910)—Leo Lionni

May 6 (1931)—Judy Delton

May 6 (1937)—Susan Terris

May 7 (1932)—Nonny Hogrogian (Kheridan)

May 12 (1812-1888)—Edward Lear

May 13 (1938-1989)—Norma Klein

May 14 (1929)—George Selden; pseud. of George Selden Thompson

May 15 (1856-1919)—L. Frank Baum

May 15 (1931)—Norma Fox Mazer

May 15 (1936)—Paul Zindel

May 16 (1928)—Betty Miles

May 16 (1950)—Bruce Coville

May 17 (1929)—Eloise Greenfield

May 18 (1925)—Lillian Hoban

May 19 (1933)—Tom Feelings

May 20 (1898-1969)—Sorche Nic Leodhas; pseud. of Leclaire Gowans Alger

May 20 (1935)—Carol Carrick

May 21 (1911-d.)—Virginia Haviland

May 22 (1933-1987)—Arnold Lobel

May 23 (1935)—Susan Cooper

May 23 (1910-1952)—Margaret Wise Brown

May 25 (1920)—Martha Alexander

May 25 (1943)—Barbara Bottner

May 27 (1927)—M. E. Kerr; pseud. of Marijane Meaker

May 29 (1924)—Lila Sprague McGinnis

May 29 (1928)—Willo Davis Roberts

May 30 (1912)—Millicent E. Selsam

May 31 (1925)—Harry Mazer

JUNE

June 1 (1934) — Doris Buchanan Slote

June 1 (1936) — Sandra Scoppettone

June 1 (1945) — Judith Whitelock McInerney

June 2 (1914-1987) — Paul Galdone

June 2 (1934) — Anita Lobel

June 2 (1938) — Helen Oxenbury

June 2 (1941) — June Andrea Hanson

June 5 (1919) — Richard Scarry

June 5 (1938) — Allan Ahlberg

June 6 (1911) — Verna Aardema (Vugteveen)

June 7 (1908) — Jeannette Eyerly

June 10 (1928) — Maurice Sendak

June 10 (1930) — Aranka Siegal

June 14 (1928) — Janice Udry

June 14 (1948) — Laurence Yep

June 15 (1927) — Betty Ren Wright (Frederiksen)

June 16 (1929) — Isabelle Holland

June 18 (1942) — Pat (Patricia) Hutchins

June 18 (1949) — Chris Van Allsburg

June 21 (1925) — Robert Kraus

June 23 (1921) — Theodore Taylor

June 24 (1916-1986) — John Ciardi

June 24 (1944) — Kathryn Lasky Knight

June 25 (1929) — Eric Carle

June 25 (1937) — Jane Sarnoff

June 26 (1925) — Robert Burch

June 26 (1936) — Nancy Willard

June 27 (1928) — James Lincoln Collier

June 27 (1936) — Lucille Clifton

June 28 (1934) — Bette Greene

June 30 (1922) — Molly Hunter

June 30 (1940) — David McPhail

JULY

July 1 (1939)—Emily Arnold McCully

July 4—Jamie Gilson

July 9 (1912)—Betsy Garrett Bang

July 9 (1930)—Gloria Skurzynski

July 10 (1916-1987)—Martin Provensen

July 11 (1899-d.)—E. B. White

July 13 (1918)—Marcia Brown

July 13 (1923)—Ashley Bryan

July 14 (1904)—Isaac Bashevis Singer

July 14 (1927-1988)—Peggy Parrish

July 16 (1935)—Arnold Adoff

July 22 (1881-1944)—Margery Williams (Bianco)

July 23 (1926)—Patricia Coombs

July 23 (1929)—Robert Quackenbush

July 26 (1923)—Jan Berenstain

July 27 (1913)—Scott Corbett

July 28 (1866-1943)—Beatrix Potter

July 31 (1930)—Robert Kimmel Smith

July 31 (1938)—Muriel L. Feelings

AUGUST

August 3 (1926)—Mary Calhoun

August 5 (1930)—Reynold Ruffins

August 6 (1909)—Norma Farber

August 6 (1946)—Frank Asch

August 7 (1927)—Maia Wojciechowska

August 7 (1928)—Betsy Byars

August 9 (1931)—Seymour Simon

August 9 (1932)—José Aruego

August 10 (1911)—Benjamin Elkin

August 10 (1931)—Thomas J. Dygard

August 11 (1941)—Steven Kroll

August 11 (1944) – Joanna Cole

August 12 (1937) – Walter Dean Myers

August 14 (1918) – Alice Provensen

August 16 (1917) – Matt Christopher

August 16 (1941) – Beverly Brodsky; earlier work under name of Beverly Brodsky McDermott

August 17 (1926) – Myra Cohn Livingston

August 17 (1937) – Ariane Dewey; earlier work under name of Ariane Aruego

August 18 (1938) – Joan Carris

August 18 (1944) – Paula Danziger

August 20 (1933) – Sue Alexander

August 27 (1919) – Graham Oakley

August 27 (1921) – Arlene Mosel

August 30 (1929) – Sesyle (Hine) Joslin

SEPTEMBER

September 2 (1927) – Barbara Dillon

September 2 (1936) – John Bierhorst

September 3 (1929) – Aliki (Brandenberg)

September 4 (1912) – Syd Hoff

September 4 (1924) – Joan Aiken

September 5 (1907) – Glenn O. Blough

September 5 (1952) – Paul Fleischman

September 6 (1884-1973) – Elmer Hader

September 8 (1940) – Jack Prelutsky

September 9 (1903) – Phyllis A. Whitney

September 10 (1922) – Roy Doty

September 13 (1916) – Roald Dahl

September 13 (1920) – Else Minarik

September 14 (1914) – William H. Armstrong

September 14 (1948) – Elizabeth Winthrop (Mahoney)

September 14 (1949) – Diane Goode

September 15 (1914) – Robert McCloskey

September 15 (1934) – Tomie dePaola

September 16 (1898-1972)—H. A. Rey

September 17 (1916)—Mary Stewart

September 18 (1908)—Harold Courlander

September 19 (1884-1942)—Rachel Field

September 20 (1928)—Donald Hall

September 20 (1936)—Andrew Davies

September 26 (1925)—Berthe Amoss

September 27 (1924)—Bernard Waber

September 27 (1933)—Paul Goble

September 29 (1923)—Stan Berenstain

September 30 (1898-d.)—Edgar d'Aulaire

September 30 (1916)—Alvin Tresselt

OCTOBER

October 3 (1906)—Natalie Carlson

October 3 (1918)—Molly Cone

October 4 (1924)—Donald J. Sobol

October 5 (1892-1957)—Robert Lawson

October 5 (1928)—Louise Fitzhugh

October 6 (1902)—Elizabeth Gray

October 6 (1941)—Steven Kellogg

October 7 (1893-d.)—Alice Dalgliesh

October 8 (1915)—Ann Irwin; with Lee Hadley joint pseud. Hadley Irwin

October 8 (1920)—Barthe DeClements

October 8 (1936)—Suzanne Newton

October 9 (1937)—Johanna Hurwitz

October 10 (1934)—Lee Hadley; with Ann Irwin joint pseud. Hadley Irwin

October 10 (1942)—James Marshall

October 15 (1942)—Beatrice Gormley

October 16 (1942)—Sandy Asher

October 18 (1942)—Susan Jeschke

October 19 (1931)—Ed Emberley

October 20 (1906-1975)—Crockett Johnson; pseud. of David Johnson Leisk

October 21 (1944) — Janet Ahlberg

October 23 (1857-1958) — Marjorie Flack

October 23 (1941) — P. J. Petersen

October 27 (1924) — Constance Greene

October 31 (1932) — Katherine Paterson

October 31 (1934) — Helen V. Griffith

NOVEMBER

November 1 (1935) — Nicholasa Mohr

November 4 (1939) — Gail E. Haley

November 8 (1945) — Marianna Mayer

November 9 (1937) — Lynn Hall

November 10 (1929) — W. E. Butterworth; pseud. of William Edmund Butterworth III

November 11 (1942) — Diane Wolkstein

November 12 (1928) — Marjorie Weinman Sharmat

November 13 (1850-1894) — Robert Lewis Stevenson

November 14 (1899) — Miska Miles; pseud. of Patricia Miles Martin

November 14 (1907) — William Steig

November 14 (1946) — Nancy Tafuri

November 15 (1898-d.) — David McCord

November 15 (1941) — Daniel Manus Pinkwater

November 16 (1912) — Joan Phipson; pseud. of Joan Margaret Fitzhardinge

November 16 (1915) — Jean Fritz

November 16 (1952) — Robin McKinley

November 20 (1919) — William Cole

November 21 (1908) — Elizabeth George Speare

November 25 (1946) — Marc Brown

November 28 (1931) — Tomi Ungerer

November 29 (1918) — Madeleine L'Engle

November 30 (1835-1900) — Mark Twain; pseud. of Samuel Clemens

November 30 (1924) — Louise Moeri

November 30 (1931) — Margot Zemach (Fischtrom)

DECEMBER

December 2 (1946) — David Macaulay

December 4 (1905-1976) — Munro Leaf

December 5 (1933-1974) — Harve Zemach; pseud. of Harvey Fischtrom

December 6 (1884-1973) — Cornelia Meigs

December 8 (1928) — Joan W. Blos

December 8 (1951) — Kristi Holl

December 8 (1894-1961) — James Thurber

December 9 (1848-1908) — Joel Chandler Harris

December 10 (1879) — Ernest H. Shepard

December 10 (1903) — Mary Norton

December 12 (1932) — Barbara Emberley

December 14 (1929) — Lorna Balian

December 16 (1893) — Marie Hall Ets

December 16 (1930) — William (Bill) Brittain

December 16 (1932) — Quentin Blake

December 17 (1931) — David Kheridan

December 18 (1927) — Marilyn Sachs

December 19 (1928) — Eve Bunting; pseud. of Anne Evelyn Bunting

December 24 (1920) — John Langstaff

December 25 (1915) — Eth Clifford; pseud. of Ethel Clifford Rosenberg

December 26 (1937) — Jean Van Leeuwen

December 27 (1904) — Ingri d'Aulaire

December 29 (1942) — Jan Greenberg

December 29 (1943) — Molly Garrett Bang

December 30 (1865-1936) — Rudyard Kipling

December 30 (1933) — Alvin Silverstein

December 30 (1943) — Mercer Mayer

Booklist — Stories and Poems to Read about Birthdays

Asch, Frank. *Happy Birthday, Moon*. Prentice-Hall, 1982. A six-minute filmstrip of this book is available from Weston Woods.

Barrett, Judith. *Benjamin's 365 Birthdays*. Atheneum, 1974.

Blume, Judy. "Birthday Bash," in *Tales of a Fourth Grade Nothing*. Illustrated by Roy Doty. Dutton, 1972.

Bornstein, Ruth. *Little Gorilla*. Seabury, 1976.

Brandenberg, Franz. *A Secret for Grandmother's Birthday*. Illustrated by Aliki. Greenwillow, 1983.

_____. *Aunt Nina and Her Nephews and Nieces*. Greenwillow, 1983.

Carle, Eric. *The Secret Birthday Message*. Crowell, 1972.

Carrick, Carol. *Paul's Christmas Birthday*. Illustrated by Donald Carrick. Greenwillow, 1978.

Da Rif, Andrea. *The Blueberry Cake That Little Fox Baked*. Atheneum, 1984.

de Brunhoff, Laurent. *Babar's Birthday Surprise*. Random House, 1970.

deRegniers, Beatrice Schenk. "First Day of Spring." In *A Bunch of Poems and Verses*. Clarion, 1977.

Emberley, Ed. *A Birthday Wish*. Little, Brown, 1977. (wordless)

Flack, Marjorie. *Ask Mr. Bear*. Macmillan, 1932.

Heilbroner, Joan. *The Happy Birthday Present*. Illustrated by Mary Chalmers. Harper & Row, 1962.

Hoban, Russell. *A Birthday for Frances*. Harper & Row, 1968.

Hopkins, Lee Bennett and Misha Arenstein. *Do You Know What Day Tomorrow Is? A Teacher's Almanac*. Scholastic/Citation, 1975.

Hughes, Shirley. *Alfie Gives a Hand*. Lothrop, Lee & Shepard, 1983.

Hurwitz, Johanna. "The Birthday Party." In *Aldo Applesauce*. Illustrated by John Wallner. Morrow, 1979.

Hutchins, Pat. *Happy Birthday, Sam*. Greenwillow, 1978.

_____. *The Surprise Party*. Macmillan, 1969.

Ichikawa, Satomi. *Happy Birthday! A Book of Birthday Celebrations*. Philomel, 1988.

Keats, Ezra Jack. *A Letter to Amy*. Harper & Row, 1968. A six-minute filmstrip of this book is available from Weston Woods.

Kellogg, Steven. *The Mysterious Tadpole*. Dial, 1977.

_____. *Won't Somebody Play With Me?* Dial, 1972.

Livingston, Myra Cohn. *Callooh! Callay!: Holiday Poems for Young Readers*. Atheneum, 1978.

_____. *Happy Birthday*. Illustrated by Eric Blegvad. Harcourt Brace Jovanovich, 1964. (poems)

_____. *O Frabjous Day: Poetry for Holidays and Special Occasions*. Atheneum, 1977.

Milne, A. A. "In Which Eeyore Has a Birthday and Gets Two Presents." In *Winnie-the-Pooh*. Illustrated by Ernest H. Shepard, colored by Hilda Scott. Dutton, 1974.

Minarick, Else Holmelund. *Little Bear*. Harper & Row, 1957.

Moore, Lilian. "Monster's Birthday." In *Spooky Rhymes and Riddles*. Scholastic, 1972.

Munari, Bruno. *The Birthday Present*. World, 1959.

Newman, Dana. *The Teacher's Almanack: A Complete Guide to Every Day of the School Year*. Center for Applied Research, 1973.

Nordqvist, Sven. *Pancake Pie*. Morrow, 1984.

Parker, Nancy Winslow. *Love from Uncle Clyde*. Dodd Mead, 1977.

Perl, Lila. *Candles, Cakes, and Donkey Tails: Birthday Symbols and Celebrations*. Illustrated by Victoria deLarrea. Clarion, 1984.

Pomerantz, Charlotte. *The Half-Birthday Party*. Illustrated by DiSalvo-Ryan. Houghton Mifflin, 1984.

Rice, Eve. *Benny Bakes a Cake*. Greenwillow, 1981.

Sendak, Maurice. *Chicken Soup with Rice*. Harper & Row, 1962.

Seuss, Dr. *Happy Birthday to You!* Random House, 1959.

Stevenson, James. *Barbara's Birthday: A Pop-up Book*. Greenwillow, 1983.

Waber, Bernard. *Lyle and the Birthday Party*. Houghton Mifflin, 1966.

Wahl, Jan. *Margaret's Birthday*. Illustrated by Mercer Mayer. Four Winds, 1971.

Watson, Nancy Dingman. *The Birthday Goat*. Crowell, 1974.

Zion, Gene. *No Roses for Harry*. Illustrated by Margaret Bloy Graham. Harper & Row, 1958.

Zolotow, Charlotte. *Mr. Rabbit and the Lovely Present*. Harper & Row, 1962.

Characters such as Ramona (books by Beverly Cleary), Eddie (books by Carolyn Haywood), Anatasia (books by Lois Lowry), and Curious George (books by H. A. Rey), who have been included in a continuing series of books, sometimes find themselves celebrating their birthday within the pages of one of the books written about them. Students might set out to locate birthday chapters in these books. The chapters might describe the character's birthday activities in enough detail that a similar birthday celebration could be recreated in the classroom. Interesting insights into the traditions in specific countries and during specific periods in history may be obtained by comparing the family celebrations.

Generic Activities for Any Birthday Celebration

The following are some activities that would be appropriate for any birthday celebration.

- Read and share books written by the birthday person(s).

- Read a book or story about the celebration of a birthday.

- Read a poem about birthdays.

- Make a birthday card to send to the author/illustrator.

For those authors and illustrators who have summer birthdays consider sending "half-birthday" cards. If you don't have the author's address send the card in care of his or her publisher. Enclose the card in an envelope addressed with only the author's or illustrator's name and the class's return address. Attach a note asking that the address on the envelope (with the card) be completed and that the envelope be forwarded. Put the request note and the envelope with the card into another envelope to send to the publisher.

The End of the Birthday Celebration

Culminate any birthday celebration by singing the traditional "Happy Birthday to You." Two sisters, Mildred J. Hill and Patty S. Hill, wrote this song in 1934. Although the song was written in the United States of America, the song is now sung in many different languages all over the world. Perhaps your students could arrange to learn the song in a different language or two. Happy Birthday to You! Don't forget to celebrate your own birthday by reading a chapter or two from your favorite book.

PIG WEEK

Make your own celebration by declaring a non-traditional holiday on any day you wish. Some days, like National Pig Day on March 1st, seem to lend themselves to a special celebration. But Pig Week activities could also come as the result of reading any book that features a pig as a main character. Everybody knows that most holidays result in a lot of "pigging out." So start the celebration by researching the origin of sayings about pigs. In reality one does not need any special impetus—just decide to focus on pigs, announce the dates for Pig Week and prepare to send out a daily newsletter, *Pig Week News*. If this is to be a schoolwide activity, send two to five copies of the news to each classroom. If only one or two classrooms are participating, individual copies of the news might be distributed to the students. The newsletter can suggest reading and writing activities for student participation, and collaborative assignments, all focusing on pigs. Pig riddles and jokes can be shared, and pig stories read and compared. In classrooms with older students let a planning committee do some of the preliminary preparation. They could write the *Pig Week News* and have it ready for production. Let them search out the pig poems and riddles to share. Make sure they have some of the resources mentioned below and let them pick and choose the appropriate material to share with their classmates or the rest of the school.

Begin your Pig Week celebration planning by arranging to have pigs everywhere. Have copies of a daily news sheet, *Pig Week News*, for leisure reading. In the *Pig Week News* share pig riddles, a pig poem or two, pig jokes, and other news about pigs. Announce group sessions where discussion groups will compare different versions of "The Three Little Pigs" or group viewings of the Reading Rainbow®* program featuring Perfect, the title character of *Perfect the Pig* by Susan Jeschke (Holt, Rinehart & Winston, 1981). Include student written reviews of pig-filled books in the *Pig Week News*, introduce authors of other pig books, and use pigs to motivate writing. Share the list of pig books for students to read.

Research the origin of piggy banks and the term itself. Piggy banks were not always in the shape of pigs. In fact, piggy banks were really "pyggy banks." That spelling is a clue to the real origin of the term "piggy bank." Clay was once known as *pyg*. Early potters made pots and jars of pyg. These clay pots and jars were often used as collection jars for coins. They were referred to as "pyggy banks." Later when people asked potters to make a pyggy bank some potters did not know what they were being asked to make. So they made a bank in the shape of a pig. The shape caught on—and so did the piggy bank.

Hans Christian Andersen wrote a story called "The Swineherd." Introduce Andersen as the writer of fairy tales. Use the card catalog in your library to locate collections of tales by Andersen, then use the index or the table of contents to find this story. Read it aloud to your students and encourage further reading by booktalking and displaying other stories by Andersen. Among his famous tales is "The Ugly Duckling."

---

*Reading Rainbow is a public television children's series funded by the Corporation for Public Broadcasting, Public Broadcasting Stations, and the National Science Foundation.

Share this information: According to the *Oxford English Dictionary*, the word "pig" has the following meanings:

Pig, pigge, pygge, pygg, pigg, pyg

- young swine
- young of a badger
- a swine of any age; a hog
- food
- applied to various other animals, sea pig (porpoise)
- contemptuously applied to a person or another animal
- Slang—a sixpence (an obsolete term—1622); a police officer (an obsolete term—1812, 1821); a pressman in a printing office
- oblong mass of metal; an ingot
- weight—rock salt is cut into square pigs weighing about 60 pounds
- a type of clay

Investigate the multiple meanings of other usual words. Read pig poems and share others in the daily newsletter. Invite students to illustrate the poems and to write some poems of their own.

Booklist—Pig Poems

Brooks, Walter R. "Flying Pigs." In *The Collected Poems of Freddy the Pig*. Knopf, 1952.

Demong, Phyllis. *It's a Pig World Out There*. Avon, 1981. (A collection of poems)

Fyleman, Rose. "Mary Middling." In *Read-Aloud Rhymes for the Very Young*, selected by Jack Prelutsky. Knopf, 1986.

Lobel, Arnold. *The Book of Pigericks*. Harper & Row, 1983. (A collection of original limericks by the author)

_____. "There Was a Small Pig Who Wept Tears." In *Read-Aloud Rhymes for the Very Young*, selected by Jack Prelutsky. Knopf, 1986.

Nash, Ogden. "The Pig." In *Verses from 1929 On*. Little, Brown, 1933.

Poulsson, Emilie. "The Pigs." In *Read-Aloud Rhymes for the Very Young*, selected by Jack Prelutsky. Knopf, 1986.

Smith, William Jay. "Pig." In *Laughing Time*. Delacorte Press/Seymour Lawrence, 1980.

Worth, Valerie. "Pig." In *Small Poems*. Farrar, Straus & Giroux, 1972.

Begin a unit on fables by introducing Arnold Lobel's *Fables* (Harper & Row, 1980). Read "The Pig at the Candy Store" from Lobel's *Fables*. Follow with a discussion of the characteristics of fables. Fables are short tales in which animals appear as characters, talking and acting like human beings, though usually keeping their animal traits; fables have as their purpose the pointing of a moral. Fables consequently have two parts: the narrative, which exemplifies the moral, and the statement of the moral, often appended in the form of a proverb. A fable is one of the earliest forms of a folktale.* Introduce other fables, including those of Aesop (Greece), La Fontaine (France), Lessing (Germany), Bidpai, or sometimes known as fables from the "Panchatantra" (India). As students become widely read in the area of fables initiate and participate in a discussion of the morals and the characterizations generally given to specific animals, for example, the fox as sly, the wolf as greedy, and the lion as courageous and dignified. Discuss the characteristics of pigs as portrayed in fables, other folk tales, and literary tales. Encourage students to try their hand at writing their own fables.

Compare and contrast versions of the classic "Three Little Pigs" story. Look for the characterization of the pigs, the language used to gain sympathy for certain characters, descriptions of the action, and the variant endings found in different retellings. Make story maps for each of the stories. Compare the story grammar. Examine illustrations and discuss the message conveyed through the pictorial representations. Use versions of the "Three Little Pigs" in a critical reading exercise.

Booklist—"Three Little Pigs"

Blegvad, Erik. *The Three Little Pigs*. Illustrated by Erik Blegvad. Atheneum, 1980.

Bucknall, Caroline. *The Three Little Pigs*. Illustrated by Caroline Bucknall. Dutton, 1986.

---

*Marie Leach, editor. *Funk & Wagnalls Standard Dictionary of Folklore Mythology and Legend*. Funk & Wagnalls, 1949. p. 361.

du Bois, William Pene. *The Three Little Pigs*. Illustrated by William Pene du Bois. Viking, 1962.

Galdone, Paul. *The Three Little Pigs*. Illustrated by Paul Galdone. Seabury, 1970.

Jacobs, Joseph. "The Three Little Pigs." In *Tomie dePaola's Favorite Nursery Tales*. Illustrated by Tomie dePaola. Putnam, 1986.

Mayer, Marianna, reteller. "The Three Little Pigs." In *My First Book of Nursery Tales: Five Favorite Bedtime Tales*. Illustrated by William Joyce. Random House, 1983.

Rockwell, Anne. "The Three Little Pigs." In *The Three Bears & 15 Other Stories*. Illustrated by Anne Rockwell. Crowell, 1975.

Develop vocabulary by searching out the meanings of pig-related words and phrases: pigment, in a pig's eye, pork barrel, hog-wild, hogwash, pig Latin, pig tail, piggy bank, and swineherd. Give a specific number of points for an appropriate use of any one of these pig terms throughout the day. The team that receives the most points at the end of the day is feted with a special privilege.

Ask children to write a "biHOGraphy" of a pig personality such as Miss Piggy (of Muppet fame), Arnold the Pig (of TV's Green Acres), Porky Pig (cartoon character), Wilbur (from E. B. White's *Charlotte's Web*), and Orville (from Jim Davis's comic strip *U.S. Acres*). Or they might create their own pig personality and write about that pig's life.

Expressive art activities might include designing "valenswines" for next year's Valentine's Day, creating stylish "Calvin Swines" jeans, or sketching beautiful gowns to be worn in the "Miss HAMerica" contest.

Make a wacky-word dictionary. Think of pig-related words and give them wacky definitions. For example a "pigsty" might be defined as a sty on a pig's eye. Some of the words might be variations of real words, as in "oinkment." Individual dictionaries might be created or collaborative efforts may result in combined products.

Introduce children to the books of Bill Peet, including *Chester, the Worldly Pig*. Visit Bill Peet in his studio via a videotape, *A Visit with Bill Peet*, available from Houghton Mifflin. Display Peet's books and enjoy the many interesting characters he has created. Write other adventures for Chester, Kermit the Hermit, Homer, and the Whingdingdilly. Write Bill Peet a letter.

Go on a pig hunt with Mr. and Mrs. Simkin (from *Mrs. Simkin's Bed*) and share other pigs-in-hiding books.

Booklist — Pigs-in-Hiding

Allen, Linda. *Mrs. Simkin's Bed*. Illustrated by Loretta Lustig. Morrow, 1980.

Dubanevich, Arlene. *Pigs in Hiding*. Four Winds, 1983.

Lobel, Arnold. *A Treeful of Pigs*. Illustrated by Anita Lobel. Greenwillow, 1979.

Introduce other pig books to your students by using them for read alouds and booktalks to interest the children in the books. In the following list (P) indicates that the book is a picture book.

Booklist—Other Pig Books

Bawden, Nina. *The Peppermint Pig*. Lippincott, 1975.
A runt pig is saved and helps a family through a difficult time.

Blegvad, Lenore, editor. *This Little Pig-a-Wig*. Illustrated by Erik Blegvad. Margaret K. McElderry, 1978. (P)
Nursery rhymes featuring pigs.

Bowman, Sarah and Lucinda Vardey. *Pigs*. Macmillan, 1981.
A collection of literary stories and paintings featuring pigs.

Browne, Anthony. *Piggybook*. Knopf, 1986. (P)
The Piggot family males gain a new understanding of family life when Mrs. Piggot leaves them on their own. Mrs. Piggot returns to a more understanding and appreciative family.

Christelow, Eileen. *Mr. Murphy's Marvelous Invention*. Clarion, 1983. (P)
A birthday surprise causes more problems than pleasure.

DeJong, Meindert. *The House of Sixty Fathers*. Illustrated by Maurice Sendak. Harper & Row, 1946.
A classic World War II tale of Tien Pao and his pig who are separated from Tien Pao's family.

Edmonds, Walter D. "Perfection of Orchard View." In *The Night Raider and Other Stories*. Little, Brown, 1980.
A gentleman farmer and his hired hand have decisively differing views on the proper way to raise pigs.

Galdone, Paul. *The Amazing Pig*. Clarion, 1981. (P)
In order to win the king's daughter a suitor tells imaginative stories about his pig.

Geisert, Arthur. *Pa's Balloon and Other Pig Tales*. Houghton Mifflin, 1984.
Three ballooning adventures of a family of pigs.

Getz, Arthur. *Humphrey, the Dancing Pig*. Dial, 1980. (P)
When he loses weight, Humphrey is given a job chasing mice.

Greenberg, Jan. *The Pig-Out Blues*. Farrar, Straus & Giroux, 1982.
Jodie, a fifteen year old, tries to eat her way into oblivion by "pigging-out." She has to come to realize that others have problems, too, before she can handle her own.

Hoban, Lillian. *Mr. Pig and Family*. Harper & Row, 1980. (P)
An *I Can Read* book.

Hopf, Alice L. *Pigs Wild and Tame*. Holiday House, 1979.
Information about real pigs.

Jeschke, Susan. *Perfect the Pig*. Holt, Rinehart & Winston, 1981; Scholastic pb, 1985. (P)
    An unscrupulous street performer kidnaps Perfect. Her happiness comes because of her own endeavors.

Lavine, Sigmund A. and Vincent Scuro. *Wonders of Pigs*. Dodd Mead, 1981.
    Descriptions of and information about ten different breeds of pigs. Explanation of how various parts of the pig are used commercially.

Lobel, Arnold. *Small Pig*. Harper & Row, 1969. (P)
    A nice cool mud hole turns out to be wet cement.

MacLachlan, Patricia. *Arthur, for the Very First Time*. Illustrated by Lloyd Bloom. Harper & Row, 1980.
    Bernadette chooses to have her piglets in the rain even though Arthur has built a pen for her.

Milne, A. A. "In Which Piglet Meets a Heffalump." In *Winnie-the-Pooh*. Illustrated by Ernest H. Shepard. Dutton, 1926.
    Piglet and Pooh set a trap for a Heffalump.

Milne, A. A. "Piglet Nearly Meets the Heffalump Again." In *The House at Pooh Corner*. Illustrated by Ernest H. Shepard. Dutton, 1926.
    Piglet and Pooh look for Small, the beetle. Much dialogue that could be used for readers' theater.

Oxenbury, Helen. *Pig Tale*. Morrow, 1973. (P)
    Riches bring two pigs a loss of freedom.

Peet, Bill. *Chester, the Worldly Pig*. Houghton Mifflin, 1965. (P)
    When Chester runs away to a circus he must perform with five tigers.

Potter, Beatrix. *The Tale of Pigling Bland*. Warne, 1913. (P)
    One of Potter's classic little books.

Rayner, Mary. *Garth Pig and the Ice Cream Lady*. Atheneum, 1977. (P)
    The Big Bad Wolf dresses up as the Ice Cream Lady but still cannot outsmart the piglets.

Rayner, Mary. *Mr. and Mrs. Pig's Evening Out*. Atheneum, 1976. (P)
    A wolf babysitter is outwitted by ten piglets.

Rayner, Mary. *Mrs. Pig's Bulk Buy*. Atheneum, 1981. (P)
    Mrs. Pig's children want ketchup on everything she prepares for them to eat. When she gets an opportunity to purchase many bottles of ketchup in a cost-saving "bulk buy" so she does and gives her piglets only ketchup foods to eat.

Ruby, Lois. *Pig-Out Inn*. Houghton Mifflin, 1987.
    Dovi and her mother move to a small town on the Kansas prairie where they begin to operate a truck stop. An abandoned nine year old and an ensuing custody battle helps Dovi assess her own situation more realistically. The name of the truck stop is the only connection to pigs.

Steig, William. *The Amazing Bone*. Farrar, Straus & Giroux, 1976. (P)
   A talking bone befriends Pearl the Pig.

Stine, Jovial Bob. *The Pigs' Book of World Records*. Illustrated by Peter Lippman. Random House, 1980.
   Jokes, riddles, and a collection of other miscellaneous information about pigs.

Weston, Martha. *If I Only Had a Rainbow*. Lothrop, Lee & Shepard, 1981. (P)
   Peony Pig attempts to discover what it is like to catch a rainbow.

White, E. B. *Charlotte's Web*. Harper & Row, 1952.
   Charlotte, a spider, and Wilbur, a pig, live on the Zuckerman farm and become best of friends.

Yolen, Jane. *Piggins*. Illustrated by Jane Dyer. Harcourt Brace Jovanovich, 1987. (P)
   Piggins, the perfectly proper butler, solves the mystery of the cursed and missing lavaliere.

Read some limericks by Edward Lear. Discuss the poetic form usually found in limericks. (Lines 1, 2, and 5 are three measures long, and rhyme. Lines 3 and 4 are two measures long and rhyme with one another.) After becoming familiar with the limerick form (see index; Booklists—Limericks), read *The Book of Pigericks* by Arnold Lobel (Harper & Row, 1983). Try writing some "pigericks" of your own. Collaborative writing may be a successful technique to use here. Encourage pigerick writers to illustrate their poems. They may wish to draw the illustration first; drawing first often helps the creative writing process.

Invite students and parents alike to display their pig memorabilia in the classroom or library. Give out a generous number of Perfect Pig Awards for Outstanding Behavior. A Perfect Pig Award stamp is available from Kid-stamps, Inc.

By the end of your scheduled celebration your room will be filled with pig-related writing, pictures, books, and memorabilia. Culminate with a pig-out feast—a read and feed.

BEARS — ANOTHER CELEBRATION FOR A DAY,
A WEEK, OR HERE AND THERE ANY DAY OF THE YEAR

Almost every school, library, or classroom has used the bear theme—it is not a new idea. But to omit bears from any list of tricks to get children together with books would be remiss. Teddy bears have become the undisputed darlings of both children and adults. In the United States during the 1970s, over $40 million a year was spent on teddy bears. In 1983 that figure had risen to $125 million and each Christmas the bear market grows larger. In 1985, Workman Publishing printed and sold over 300,000 copies of its Teddy Bear Calendar. B.Y.O.B. (Bring Your Own Bear) conventions are being held nationally and entire stores devoted to bears are being opened. Bear stores feature "bearaphernalia"—teddy tote bags, ties, towels, sleeping bags, trivets, and even hot-water bottles. E. P. Dutton even published a bear spoof on the multitude of exercise books on the market. Their book, *Pooh's Workout Book* (Dutton, 1984), featured original drawings by E. H. Shepard. There are nurse bears, doctor bears, Paddington bears and bears similar to those featured in paintings by Norman Rockwell. Bears seem to be everywhere. In 1985, Greta Bear made her appearance complete with backpack and a book about Yellowstone Park, and Barbara Isenberg brought out a line of Very Important Bears—including Humphrey Beargate and Kareem Abdul Jabear. Collecting bears is the fourth largest collecting hobby, after coins, stamps, and dolls.

Bears and books make for a natural connection. Even the origins of the teddy bear can take us into books. The name (and the stuffed toy) came about as a result of a hunting trip taken by Theodore Roosevelt in 1902. Much media attention was given to Roosevelt's refusal to shoot a black bear under unsportsmanlike conditions. That incident resulted in the development of the first "teddy bear" when a Russian immigrant, Morris Michtom, sought to recognize the president's humanity. Michtom owned a candy store and asked his wife to stitch up a bear to sit in the store window in commemoration of the hunting event. The bear caught the attention of the townspeople and Michtom wrote the president for permission to name the bear "Teddy." Roosevelt responded with permission and the teddy bear launched a new endeavor for Michtom and led eventually to the founding of the Ideal Toy Company. The story of the teddy bear's origins as told in a nonfiction book by Helen Kay, *The First Teddy Bear* (Stemmer House, 1985), will attract early and middle grade readers with its easy-to-understand text and abundance of pictures. Older students will find the book a concise informative account of one incident in President Theodore Roosevelt's life.

Many bear activities can be incorporated into a celebration of bears and books. It's a "Beary Good Time to Read" signs may be displayed throughout the school or library. Each sign can announce "bear and book" events or advertise "beary good books to read." Displays may include favorite bears with their favorite books, bears dressed as storybook characters, and a multitude of bear books. Use the opportunity to develop critical reading skills by comparing and contrasting the many versions of "Goldilocks and the Three Bears." The various versions of the story will have the obvious similarities in basic story grammar and setting. But note the differences and similarities in the conclusion, the illustrations, the time period, and the manner in which each of the characters is portrayed. How do the author and illustrator convey their message about each of the characters' personality?

Another favorite activity of mine includes reading many versions of "The Three Bears," followed by a shared book experience with *Deep in the Forest* by Brinton Turkle (Dutton, 1976). *Deep in the Forest* is a wordless story of a family of three: father, mother, and little girl. The family lives in a log cabin deep in the forest. One day while the family is out taking a walk, a bear cub enters their home and tastes their cereal, sits in their chairs, and sleeps in their beds. The consequences are predictable. The resulting discussion will bring out the similarity of the characters and their reversed roles, the similarity in story grammar, and the similar story setting. While providing a clear opportunity for critical analysis of two stories, the Turkle title, because it is wordless, provides an invitation for children to write the text that will tell the story of *Deep in the Forest*.

Other bear programs could include an invitation for children to attend a reading of *Ira Sleeps Over* by Bernard Waber (Houghton Mifflin, 1972; 1975). A seventeen-minute 16mm film version of *Ira Sleeps Over* is also available from Coronet/Bfa (1977).

Promote the Bears and Books theme by putting bear books in a reading basket accompanied by a teddy bear. Dress the bear in seasonally appropriate clothing and attach a tag (similar to the tag Paddington Bear has attached around his neck) giving information about routing the reading basket to participating classrooms. When the basket arrives in each room the students and teacher should drop everything and read.

Booklist—Bears

Asch, Frank. *Bear Shadow*. Prentice-Hall, 1985.

_____. *In the Eye of the Teddy*. Harper & Row, 1973.

_____. *Mooncake*. Prentice-Hall, 1984.

_____. *Sand Cake*. Parents, 1979.

Banks, Kate. *Alphabet Soup*. Knopf, 1988.

Blathwayt, Benedict. *Bear's Adventure*. Knopf, 1988.

Bond, Michael. *A Bear Called Paddington*. Houghton Mifflin, 1960. (series)

Browne, Anthony. *Bear Hunt*. Atheneum, 1979.

Bunting, Eve. *The Valentine Bears*. Clarion, 1983.

Carlstrom, Nancy White. *Jesse Bear, What Will You Wear?* Macmillan, 1987.

Dabcovich, Lydia. *Sleepy Bear*. Dutton/Unicorn, 1982.

Dahl, Roald. "Goldilocks and the Three Bears." In *Roald Dahl's Revolting Rhymes*. Knopf, 1982; Bantam Skylark, 1982.

Delton, Judy. *A Birthday Bike for Brimhall*. Carolrhoda, 1985.

Eastman, P. D. *The Alphabet Book*. Random House, 1974.

Freeman, Don. *A Pocket for Corduroy*. Viking, 1978.

———. *Beady Bear*. Viking, 1954.

———. *Corduroy*. Viking, 1968.

Fujikawa, Gyo. *Gyo Fujikawa's A to Z Picturebook*. Random House, 1987.

Gage, Wilson. *Cully Cully and the Bear*. Greenwillow, 1984.

Galdone, Joanna. *The Little Girl and the Big Bear*. Clarion, 1980.

Galdone, Paul. *The Three Bears*. Clarion, 1972.

Ginsburg, Mirra. *Two Greedy Bears*. Macmillan, 1976.

Graham, Thomas. *Mr. Bear's Chair*. Dutton, 1987.

Hale, Irwin. *Brown Bear in a Brown Chair*. Atheneum, 1984.

Hayes, Sarah. *This Is the Bear*. Lippincott, 1986.

Hissey, Jane. *Little Bear's Trousers (An Old Bear Story)*. Philomel, 1987.

———. *Old Bear*. Philomel, 1986.

Hofmann, Ginnie. *The Runaway Teddy Bear*. Random House, 1986.

———. *Who Wants an Old Teddy Bear?* Random House, 1978.

Isenberg, Barbara, and Marjorie Jaffe. *Albert the Running Bear Gets the Jitters*. Clarion, 1987.

———. *Albert the Running Bear's Exercise Book*. Clarion, 1984.

Isenberg, Barbara, and Susan Wolfe. *The Adventures of Albert the Running Bear*. Clarion, 1982.

Jeschke, Susan. *Angela and Bear*. Holt, Rinehart & Winston, 1979.

Johnston, Ginny, and Judy Cutchins. *Andy Bear*. Morrow, 1985.

Kay, Helen. *The First Teddy Bear*. Stemmer House, 1985.

Kennedy, Jimmy. *The Teddy Bears' Picnic*. Green Tiger Press, 1983.

Lapp, Eleanor. *The Blueberry Bears*. Weekly Reader Books, 1983.

Mack, Stan. *Ten Bears in My Bed: A Goodnight Countdown*. Pantheon, 1974.

Martin, Bill Jr. *Brown Bear, Brown Bear, What Do You See?* Holt, Rinehart & Winston, 1984.

McCloskey, Robert. *Blueberries for Sal*. Viking, 1948.

Milne, A. A. *Pooh's Bedtime Book*. Dutton, 1980.

Minarik, Else Holmelund. *Little Bear*. Harper & Row, 1957. (series)

Muntean, Michaela. *Bicycle Bear*. Parents, 1984.

Murphy, Jill. *Peace at Last*. Dial, 1980.

Myers, Bernice. *Not This Bear!* Four Winds, 1967.

Parker, Nancy Winslow. *The Ordeal of Byron B. Blackbear*. Dodd Mead, 1979.

Patent, Dorothy Hinshaw. *The Way of the Grizzly*. Clarion, 1987.

Pinkwater, Daniel. *Bear's Picture*. Dutton, 1985.

Seuss, Dr. *Dr. Seuss's ABC*. Random House, 1963.

Sharp, Gene. *The Three Bears*. Golden Press, 1965.

Singer, Arthur. *Wild Animals from Alligator to Zebra*. Random House, 1973.

Steiner, Jörg. *The Bear Who Wanted to Be a Bear*. Atheneum, 1976.

Stevenson, James. *The Bear Who Had No Place to Go*. Harper & Row, 1972.

Turkle, Brinton. *Deep in the Forest*. Dutton, 1976.

Waber, Bernard. *Ira Sleeps Over*. Houghton Mifflin, 1972; 1975.

Watanabe, Shigeo. *How Do I Put It On?* Collins, 1979.

Wildsmith, Brian. *Bear's Adventure*. Pantheon, 1981.

Winter, Paula. *Bear and Fly*. Crown, 1976.

Yektai, Niki. *Bears in Pairs*. Bradbury, 1987.

Yolen, Jane. *The Three Bears Rhyme Book*. Harcourt Brace Jovanovich, 1988.

Begin the Beary Important Reading focus by reading Kay's book *The First Teddy Bear* and discuss the origin of the teddy bear. Older children might enjoy learning about the popularity of the teddy bear in the United States. Encourage them to compile information about the popularity of teddy bears in their own community. Both primary and middle-grade students might research an investigative report concerning the number of teddy bears sold during a month or a year in toy stores, department stores, and other specialty stores. Surveys may be taken as to the number of children who own teddy bears. This information can be charted and shown pictorially. The types of bears owned might be classified and categorized on the chart. Intermediate students might take their favorite bears to primary classrooms to read a bear book or a favorite bear bedtime story. This focus on books and bears might lead to reading books about other favorite things—favorite blankets (quilts) or other special things. Kidstamps has available several appropriate stamps featuring bears. Robert Blake has designed a "Book Bear." Don Freeman's "Corduroy" is available on another stamp. Several of the Ray Cruz's designs feature bears, and Sandra Boynton has a "Teddy" design. All are available from Kidstamps. Mark reading logs with a bear logo stamp, design bookmarks, and mark special notebooks or papers with theme stamps.

Encourage students to investigate information about the different types of bears found in the world. Are panda bears really bears? Are koala bears really bears? Are black bears always black? Are polar bears found only in the polar regions? What is the largest a bear will get? What is the smallest bear? Chart the information. Display a world map showing where each type of bear lives. Use pictorial representations to depict, on the map, the bear population in each region of the world. Have a Beary good time.

HERITAGE DAY

A Heritage Day celebration might be held at the end of a research unit. Begin this celebration by reading *Gooseberries to Oranges*, written by Barbara Cohen and illustrated by Beverly Brodsky (Lothrop, Lee & Shepard, 1982), or *They Were Strong and Good* by Robert Lawson (Viking, 1941). These books are picture books focusing on people who came to America. With older students read these books and discuss where the children think their ancestors came from. Or were they already here when the white settlers came? Were their ancestors brought as slaves? Were they recent refugees? Proceed to investigate some of the backgrounds of the various groups that came to America. Search out the feelings inherent in the struggles of the Native American Indians by reading several of the books on the Native Americans booklist (see index), particularly the realistic titles. For recent refugees read aloud Jamie Gilson's *Hello, My Name Is Scrambled Eggs* (Lothrop, Lee & Shepard, 1985). Harvey has a new mission in this book. This time it is to mold his Vietnamese friend and newcomer Tuan Nguyen into an American. The results are hilarious. Gilson did extensive research before writing this book. Many of the incidents really did happen. The struggles of the blacks who were brought on the slave ships are portrayed in *The Slave Dancer* by Paula Fox (Bradbury, 1973) and in *Amos Fortune, Free Man* by Elizabeth Yates (Dutton, 1950). The plight of the slaves during slavery is told by Julius Lester in *To Be a Slave* (Dial, 1968) and *This Strange New Feeling* (Dial, 1982).

Research the founders of your city or state. Locate the names of some of the earliest founders of the area where you live. What happened to those founders after their initial contributions? Visit the local history section of your local library or your state or local historical society to gather information about the founding. Interview older residents and solicit their memories about the early days in the area. To stimulate the gathering and recording of these stories share some of the following books.

Booklist—Family Memories

Angell, Judie. *One-Way to Ansonia*. Bradbury, 1985.

Cohen, Barbara. *Gooseberries to Oranges*. Illustrated by Beverly Brodsky. Lothrop, Lee & Shepard, 1982.

Coolidge, Olivia. *Come by Here*. Illustrated by Milton Johnson. Houghton Mifflin, 1970.

Fair, Sylvia. *The Bedspread*. Morrow, 1982.

Gould, Deborah. *Grandpa's Slide Show*. Illustrated by Cheryl Harners. Lothrop, Lee & Shepard, 1987.

Hartley, Deborah. *Up North in Winter*. Illustrated by Lydia Dabcovich. Dutton, 1986.

Harvey, Brett. *Cassie's Journey: Going West in the 1860's*. Illustrated by Deborah Kogan Ray. Holiday House, 1988.

Hest, Amy. *The Purple Coat*. Illustrated by Amy Schwartz. Macmillan, 1986.

Hiser, Berniece T. *The Adventures of Charlie and His Wheat Straw Hat*. Illustrated by Mary Szilagyi. Dodd Mead, 1986.

Johnston, Tony. *The Quilt Story*. Illustrated by Tomie dePaola. Putnam, 1985.

Jukes, Mavis. *Blackberries in the Dark*. Illustrated by Thomas B. Allen. Knopf, 1985.

Levinson, Riki. *I Go with My Family to Grandma's*. Illustrated by Diane Goode. Dutton, 1986.

_____. *Watch the Stars Come Out*. Illustrated by Diane Goode. Dutton, 1985.

Mathis, Sharon Bell. *The Hundred Penny Box*. Illustrated by Leo Dillon and Diane Dillon. Viking, 1975.

Pellowski, Anne. *First Farm in the Valley: Anna's Story*. Illustrated by Wendy Watson. Philomel, 1982.

Rylant, Cynthia. *The Relatives Came*. Illustrated by Stephen Gammell. Bradbury, 1985.

_____. *When I Was Young in the Mountains*. Illustrated by Diane Goode. Dutton, 1982.

Sandin, Joan. *The Long Way to a New Land*. Harper & Row, 1981.

Tresselt, Alvin. *What Did You Leave Behind?* Illustrated by Roger Duvoisin. Lothrop, Lee & Shepard, 1978.

Turner, Ann. *Dakota Dugout*. Illustrated by Ronald Himler. Macmillan, 1985.

Yolen, Jane. *Owl Moon*. Illustrated by John Schoenherr. Putnam/Philomel, 1987.

In addition to recording family stories and memories invite some members of your community who have historical stories to tell to come to your school. Arrange for students to interview them, record their stories, and take photographs if possible. Students can use the interviews to write stories about their guests' memories of earlier days. They should illustrate the stories and include biographical notes (and pictures) about the storytellers. Make copies of the stories so that several copies can be bound into a Heritage Book. Invite some or all of the storytellers to a Heritage Day party. Plan to serve punch and cookies to thank them for their participation. Sing songs from early America and read cuttings from the Heritage Book. If practical, present each storyteller with a copy of the Heritage Book.

Heritage Day may be celebrated in conjunction with a celebration of the 100th day of school. Other books may be brought into the celebration by focusing on the number 100. What books might tell us about life 100 years ago? Be sure to read Doreen Rappaport's *Trouble at the Mines* (Crowell, 1987). Rappaport tells the true story of Mary Harris Jones who worked long and tiring hours helping miners unite to get better working conditions for themselves and better wages so that they could support their families. Mary Harris Jones was jailed, chastised, and ridiculed for her active role in helping the miners. She was a lady of courage who lived what she believed. The stories of Laura Ingalls Wilder tell about other aspects of life in the 1800s. Gwenda Blair's simple biography of Wilder, *Laura Ingalls Wilder* (Putnam, 1981), helps children make the connection between Wilder's stories and the real Laura Ingalls Wilder.

Other books focus on the number 100 in other ways. Keiko Kasza has written a delightful book, *The Wolf's Chicken Stew* (Putnam, 1987), about a wolf who envisions a chicken becoming a fat plump chicken for his chicken stew. While the wolf's mouth waters in anticipation he decides to bake scrumptious goodies for the chicken so that she will indeed become fat and plump. He bakes 100 doughnuts, 100 pancakes, and a 100-pound cake. Each of these he leaves on the chicken's doorstep. Finally the wolf goes to the door of the chicken's house to gather his nice fat plump chicken for his stew and he is greeted by the hen who promptly invites him in to meet her 100 chicks, and together they thank a surprised "Uncle Wolf" for his generosity with 100 kisses. Wolf leaves without the chicken for his stew but he does get a good chicken-cooked meal and he resolves that maybe tomorrow he'll bake "those little critters 100 cookies."

Another title that focuses on 100 is *Horton Hatches the Egg* by Dr. Seuss (Random House, 1940). In this story Horton sits on a bird's egg. He stays through rainstorms, relocations, winds, and other difficult situations because an elephant is faithful 100 percent. An "elephant-bird" eventually hatches from the egg.

Bring in some antiques from 100 years ago. Display 100 objects in your room. This could be as simple as 100 books, 100 jelly beans in a jar, books with exactly 100 pages, 100 pennies, and so forth.

Read Sharon Bell Mathis's *The Hundred Penny Box* (Viking, 1975). Encourage the children to make their own box and to put a penny in the box for each year they are old. For each penny they should write a memory from their life.

The following are some other activities for the hundredth day of school.

1. Bounce a ball 100 times.

2. Eat 100 crackers during the day. (This would be a class count.)

3. Enjoy a treat after the first 100 minutes of school that day.

4. Sing songs from 100 years ago.

5. Send up 100 balloons.

6. Count to 100 by fives and by tens.

7. Write a 100-word story.

8.   Use newspaper advertisements to help decide how to spend exactly $100.

9.   List all the possible combinations of coins that would make exactly $1.00.

10.   Send 100 greetings to a nursing home.

11.   Measure 100 feet down the school hall.

12.   Measure 100 inches across the room.

13.   Make a list of your favorite 100 words.

14.   Read 100 books on this day (class activity).

15.   Read 100 pages of a favorite book.

16.   Compute with 100. Create math problems using the number 100.

17.   Tell what you would do if you had 100 _____ .

18.   List the names and ages of other people in your classroom whose ages, when added to yours, would equal 100 years.

19.   Figure out whose birthday is 100 days from today.

20.   Make a timeline for the last 100 years.

21.   Locate places that are 100 miles from your home city.

22.   Write 100 in roman numerals.

23.   Make a list of 100 favorite books.

24.   Make a list of 100 sports figures, actors, authors, illustrators, or other well-known people.

25.   Make a list of 100 things you would like to do on a rainy or snowy day.

26.   Make a three-dimensional "100."

27.   Make a painting or drawing 100 inches long.

28.   Find out events that occurred on this day 100 years ago or facts about that day. Who was president of the United States? How many states were in the Union? What kind of clothing did the men and women wear? What did children wear to school? Were there schools?

Culminate the day by burying a time capsule for children who will be here 100 years from today. Hold a 100-minute read and feed. Eat trail mix made from 100 peanuts, 100 raisins, and other good things in 100s. Enjoy.

POPCORN DAY

A Popcorn Day is a celebration for any time, any day — just because. A cool day in the fall makes a perfect day to celebrate the origins of popcorn but any day will do. When the harvest season begins or on the first day of fall celebrate the day by reading popcorn stories, making popcorn, stringing popcorn on chains, and making popcorn sculptures. For the sculptures use a recipe for popcorn balls and form into other shapes. The origins of popcorn are aptly told by Tomie dePaola in *The Popcorn Book* (Holiday House, 1978). Introduce the day's activities by sharing dePaola's book or one of the other popcorn books or stories. Write information about popcorn on popcorn-shaped pieces of paper. Make a list of books with popcorn in them. Tell about the taste, feel, and appearance of popcorn. Staple the popcorn-shaped papers together with a cover and at the end of the day send home small bags of unpopped popcorn with the booklet.

Booklist — Popcorn

Asch, Frank. *Popcorn*. Parents, 1979.

Carrick, Carol. *The Dragon of Santa Lalia*. Illustrated by Benjamin Levy. Bobbs-Merrill, 1971.

dePaola, Tomie. *The Popcorn Book*. Holiday House, 1978.

Green, Ellie. "Princess Rosetta and the Popcorn Man." In *The Pot of Gold* by Mary E. Wilkins. Illustrated by Trina Schart Hyman. Lothrop, Lee & Shepard, 1971.

Kusche, Larry. *Popcorn Cookery*. H. P. Books, 1977.

Sandburg, Carl. "The Huckabuck Family and How They Raised Popcorn in Nebraska." In *The Sandburg Treasury: Prose and Poetry for Young People*. Illustrated by Paul Bacon. Harcourt Brace Jovanovich, 1970.

Selsam, Millicent. *Popcorn*. Illustrated by Jerome Wexler. Morrow, 1976.

Williams, Barbara. *Cornzapoppin! Recipes and Party Ideas for All Occasions*. Illustrated by Royce L. Blair. Holt, Rinehart & Winston, 1976.

Woodside, Dave. *What Makes Popcorn Pop!* Illustrated by Kay Woon. Atheneum, 1980.

DO-NOTHING DAY

My favorite book day is a Do-Nothing Day. One book is an absolute must. Read *Shenandoah Noah* by Jim Aylesworth, illustrated by Glen Rounds (Holt, Rinehart & Winston, 1985). The story is set in the Appalachian region where all of Shenandoah Noah's kin are farmers, but Shenandoah Noah lives up in the hills where he spends most of his time sitting in the shade doing nothing. Shenandoah Noah does not like to work much. After reading the story and laughing out loud, declare the next hour, or any other time span as a do-nothing period. Brainstorm a list of activities that Shenandoah Noah might do when he is doing nothing. The list might include rocking in a rocking chair, whistling, fishing, or reading. Discuss the literal and figurative meaning of "doing nothing." Can a person really do nothing for even a minute? Or when we say someone is doing nothing do we really mean that that person is not doing something others consider productive.

Enjoy doing nothing—if you can.

Create Your Own Celebration—From A to Z

CELEBRATE BOOKS

Celebrations of books can be brought into every corner of the school day. Celebrate books every day. Create your own special days. Celebrate the rain and rainbows by reading a "rainbow." Celebrate summer on a cold winter day. Celebrate winter on a hot summer day. Bring the celebrations to your classroom as naturally as possible. Use any excuse to bring in books. When children read one book, suggest another. When an activity calendar gives one fact, explore books to discover more information. Allow children to share with other children and with you. Teachers need to share their own favorite books, poems, and writing. Modeling is the key. Teachers should share books that make them laugh; books that make them smile. Those books will make children laugh and smile and learn to read and write, to speak and listen, and to think.

The discovery of a snake may bring a unit focusing on snakes and books about snakes. Apples and Johnny Appleseed will provide a focus for September 26, as that is the birthday of John Chapman. However, the creative teacher or librarian will recognize that the material might just as well be used during October (National Apple Month), on March 11 (Johnny Appleseed Day), or during a companion unit on tall-tale or folklore heroes. The observation of our own shadows can provide a focus on books about shadows and might culminate in a good old-fashioned game of shadow tag. A rainy day can bring poems and stories about rain and the rainbow.

Byrd Baylor's *I'm in Charge of Celebrations* (Macmillan, 1986) begins, "Last year I gave myself one hundred and eight celebrations—besides the ones they close school for." Give yourself one hundred and eight celebrations. Use some of the suggestions in other chapters and look over the booklists that follow. Put books from the bookshelves into the hands of children. Every celebration needs a thread that brings the content and literature together. The thread can be tightly strung or loosely held. Some refer to these ties as webbing. Book webs show the connections that are being spun. The threads of the web can connect a specific title to other books by the author or illustrator and to other books by theme, or the thread can connect literature to specific areas of curriculum.

Suggestions for appropriate books can be given but it is the process of motivating responses that is important. It is the teacher or librarian who must give the suggestions their spark.

Begin to develop some suggestions for celebrations that will fit into your classroom or library by using Lee Bennett Hopkins and Misha Arenstein's *Do You Know What Day Tomorrow Is? A Teacher's Almanac* (Scholastic/Citation, 1975) or Dana Newman's *The Teacher's Almanack: A Complete Guide to Every Day of the School Year* (Center for Applied Research, 1973). You will be able to discover some days of interest and connect them with the booklist topics or with individual books listed. Curriculum will and should dictate some of the focuses on books. While choice must remain with the reader, I have yet to see a quality book that is recommended by the teacher or fellow students go unclaimed. Children respond to the recommendations of their peers and teachers who love books. Their choices need to be informed choices. Artificial restrictions should not be put upon the reader, for example, that the book read must be at least 100 pages and may not be a picture book. The goal is to get children to read and to enjoy reading. Let the choice be theirs. Give them time to read. Two important components in encouraging students to read are choice and time.

You will have to be creative and know the materials that are available to you. For example, in the critical reading list Marcia Brown's *Stone Soup* (Scribner, 1947) is listed along with other comparison titles. In some calendars of notable dates and observations January is listed as National Soup Month. Given this information several literature-related activities might be generated. Celebrate National Soup Month by reading Marcia Brown's *Stone Soup*, or you might find a book such as the story about duck soup in Charles Downing's *Tales of the Hodja* (Walck, 1965) or *Chicken Soup with Rice* by Maurice Sendak (Harper & Row, 1962). Your celebration might include enjoying a lunch of stone soup or chicken soup with rice and an introduction to fairy tale indexes to learn how to find more soup stories. Discuss the story grammar in the comparison tales. An awareness of plot line, setting sequence, and attributes of the characters will emerge. Researchers might locate information about the development of the Campbell Soup Company and other companies that produce soups for commercial sale. Family soup recipes and soup stories might be collected into a class book. Bulletin boards might refer to "souper work." The word *souper* might be depicted rebus style with a can of soup + er. Innovations on a soup story, for example, *Stone Soup*, might be written on paper shaped like a soup can or a soup cauldron.

The booklist for poultry and eggs (see index) might be used in conjunction with a focus on National Egg Month, another designation for January. Make charts of egg-laying animals, research eggs and eggs-related topics, make egg-shaped booklets, have scrambled eggs for breakfast.

February is American Music Month, so celebrate by bringing out the books with folk songs in them. Learn a few of the songs and then invite parents and community residents to a cookie and punch celebration of music. Several books with songs are listed in the booklist—Songs in Books (see index).

February is also Black History Month. Use the card catalog to locate information about Langston Hughes, Charles Drew, Sojourner Truth, Harriet Tubman, Booker T. Washington, George Washington Carver, Mary McLeod Bethune, Frederick Douglass, Carter Goodwin Woodson, Marian Anderson, Ralph Bunche, Shirley Chisholm, Martin Luther King, Jr., Bill Cosby, Hank Aaron, Sidney Poitier, and Garrett Morgan. Read Elizabeth Yates's *Amos Fortune, Free Man* (Dutton, 1950); Julius Lester's *This Strange New Feeling* (Dial, 1982), or Jacob Lawrence's *Harriet and the Promised Land* (Windmill, 1968). Write a poetic biography of one of these people. Use Maxine Kumin's poetic biography of Anton Leeuwenhoek, *The Microscope* (Harper & Row, 1986), as an example.

On February 8, National Inventor's Day, is a perfect time to research and read about some of our modern conveniences. For suggestions refer to the Inventors and Inventions booklist (see index). One might read a story set in the early days of our United States to ascertain which conveniences the pioneers did not have yet.

And don't always think in terms of the traditional or the usual. February 14 is traditionally celebrated as Valentine's Day, but turn the tables and bring out the dragons by introducing Shirley Rousseau Murphy's *Valentine for a Dragon* (Atheneum, 1984). When the little demon attempts to give flowers to the fire-breathing dragon, the dragon's fire turns the flowers to straw, valentines are burnt, and chocolates are melted. Fervicent, the dragon, is really longing to be loved and accepted. She finally holds her breath so flames "won't spurt out on people." Follow this introduction by reading other dragon books.

A date, curriculum goal, or other observation does not always need to bring together an extended focus; the date might inspire just one short book experience. For example, on February 24, 1839 the first steam shovel was patented—read Virginia Lee Burton's *Mike Mulligan and His Steam Shovel* (Houghton Mifflin, 1939).

Almost any calendar-related fact can bring a connection to books. The flower of the month might bring to mind a specific book. In March the flower of the month is a jonquil or daffodil. That may be a good time to read *Golden Daffodils* by Marilyn Gould (Addison-Wesley, 1982; Harper & Row, 1982).

March is National Peanut Month. Read a biography of Booker T. Washington and research the products produced from peanuts or peanut by-products. Jimmy Carter, former president of the United States, was a peanut farmer. Connect with information about him through research about presidents. The month also includes National Pig Day on March 1. Celebrate the day or parlay the rather unusual observance into a week-long celebration. You will want to adapt the suggestions we give but they will provide a good start.

The Hopkins and Arenstein almanac and the one compiled by Newman list special days for each month of the year. Professional periodicals, such as *Instructor*, and *Teaching K-8*, often include monthly calendars that note special days or events. And of course the school's curriculum should give an infinite number of opportunities to incorporate literature into the classroom. When the study of a specific state or region of the United States is the focus in social studies, begin to introduce books set in that area. If another country is being studied consider introducing folklore from that country. By looking for common elements in a country's folklore one can glean much information about the country itself. Each country's folklore has its own characteristics. Welsh tales usually include talking animals, hills and vales, and people who are transformed into enchanted objects (and back again). French tales are usually less gruesome tales; they include fairies, magic, and godmothers who bring good things. English tales include large and small, giants and little people in stories such as "Tom Thumb" and "Jack and the Beanstalk." The folklore of Japan often includes fish, rice, the oni, and the sea. In the Japanese people's everyday life rice, fish, and the sea are very important components. Folktales reflect the cultures of the people about whom they are written. Comparison tales are interesting to use to highlight this. For example, it is not a coincidence that Lynnette Dyer Vuong's oriental version of "Cinderella," *The Brocaded Slipper* (Addison-Wesley, 1982), has a silk slipper rather than the glass slipper of Perrault's version or the golden slipper of other cultures.

On the date a specific state was admitted into the Union, booktalk a book set in that locale. For example, on the day Utah was admitted to the United States (January 4, 1869), bring out Gloria Skurzynski's *Lost in Devil's Desert* (Lothrop, Lee & Shepard, 1982). Mention the significance of the day. Say a few words about the book and make sure the book is available for reading. This is known as a "minute commercial." You could choose to begin reading the book aloud to your class. The minute commercials are important to your ongoing goal of motivating everyday readers. On the day New Mexico was admitted into the Union (January 6, 1912) Gerald McDermott's *Arrow to the Sun* (Viking, 1974), a Pueblo Indian tale, might make a short read aloud to the class. Vibrant illustrations, predominantly in oranges, yellows, and browns, show the pueblo homes, the earthy existence, and a little of the culture of that region (corn raising, pottery making, traditional dances). A major element in *Arrow to the Sun* is transformation. Gerald McDermott's birthday is January 31 (1941), so that connection might also be used to extend the five- to ten-minute class experience into additional individual reading. A display of McDermott's books might be appropriate in conjunction with the focus on *Arrow to the Sun*. His other books are stories from other cultures.

Book celebrations can be any length. They may be minute commercials or last a month. The celebration may focus on a group of books by theme or author or on a specific thinking skill appropriate to a group of books or to an individual title. The celebration may stimulate innovative texts, expression through the expressive arts, or more reading.

Read books by authors who use language in a natural manner to help establish the model for reading and writing and provide stimulus and motivation for all of the communication skills. Responses to literature must be based on the integrity of the literature. Situations can be used throughout the year to bring a focus on reading and enjoying more books. As the literature provides models, children will begin to respond by using the rhythm and pattern for their own writings, and they will use characters they like in writings of their own. Innovations on an author's text can result naturally from a total experience. One class discovered *Ten Bears in My Bed: A Goodnight Countdown*, by Stan Mack (Pantheon, 1974). The book is a delightful verse that starts out with: "There were 10 in the bed and the little one said, 'Roll over! Roll over!' So they all rolled over and one flew out." The illustration shows one bear flying out the window. Subsequent verses have the bears, one at a time, galloping out, skating out, roaring out, chugging out, jumping out, bouncing out, pedaling out, tootling out, and finally rumbling out until there are none in the little boy's bed and he can turn off the lights and say goodnight.

One of the first graders in this class experimented with her own parody called *Ten in the Hall*. Her story starts with: "There were ten in the hall and Heather R. said 'Go to lunch. Go to lunch.' So they all stepped back and Allan walked out." Subsequent verses in this story have Emily skipping out, Liza flying out, Garan marching out, the teacher waddling out, Aubrey hopping out, Tom bouncing out, Adam running out, Matt tiptoeing out, and finally "there was one in the hall and Heather R. said, 'Go to lunch. Go to lunch.' So she did." The student's book came not as a result of an assignment but as the result of a particular class's enjoyment of a special book. After using the book as a read aloud the teacher put it where children could go back to it (along with many other books) again and again. The thrill of the *Ten in the Hall* was complete when the author read the story aloud for her classmates. Her lilting sing-song rendition of "Go to lunch. Go to lunch" with each verse was a real delight. Eventually the children discovered another book with a similar theme. *Roll Over!* by Mordicai Gerstein (Crown, 1984) is small in size and utilizes foldout pages. The first illustration shows a wide bed filled with a little boy and nine animals. The inhabitants of the bed have only the top tufts of their hair showing from under the covers. The second page shows the youngster half sitting up saying "roll over." "So they all rolled over and ... Papa Pig fell out." Papa Pig is revealed when the page's foldout portion is opened. As each page is turned one more animal is revealed falling out of the bed. In quick succession Mama Mouse, Brother Beaver, Sister Seal, Aunt Alligator, Uncle Unicorn, Grandpa Goat, Grandma Goose, and Cousin Camel fall out of bed until finally "there was 1 in the bed and that little one said, 'Good night.' " But when the page is turned we see not one bed but one plus nine other lumps indicating that the animals have crawled into bed on the other side. The enjoyment of these stories continued as other children played with the theme and passed their own books back and forth to one another.

It is important that books of many different types and levels are included in any program or focus. Picture books are needed in first grade for those not yet reading. Picture books are also needed in the intermediate and middle school to stimulate thinking, provide whole classroom modeling, and to provide critical reading material. A picture book shared with older students can become the stimulus for the reading of novels that extend a similar theme. Younger children may compare two picture book versions of "Beauty and the Beast" while older students might use Robin McKinley's novel *Beauty* (Harper & Row, 1978) as a comparison book with any picture book version of "Beauty and the Beast." The comparison exercise can be used equally well with a novel and a picture book as with two picture books or two novels. Another dimension is added when students are able to extend their interpretation of the story to the mood created by the illustrations in the picture book. Different illustrations will evoke different moods and feelings about what is going on in the text of the story. Young children need to see and hear longer books that give them the sense of text and inspire them to aspire for higher levels. They will not be frustrated if allowed the element of choice. They will choose their appropriate level.

A IS FOR THE AMERICAN REVOLUTION AND APPLES

American Revolution

Content area topics are naturals for bringing in historical fiction and biographies and other informational books. Fiction books help the young learner experience the real feel for the time period and to gain some understanding of the human elements behind every period of history. *Johnny Tremain* by Esther Forbes (Houghton Mifflin, 1943) has long been a favorite title set in the Revolutionary period, but there are other titles that provide an insight into the times. The following titles include fiction and nonfiction featuring men, women, boys, and girls as heroes. In conjunction with the basic curricular material on the American Revolution ask that students select and read a historical fiction book set in that same period. In their reading journals the readers should note the facts and impressions about the era that they find in the fiction book. During small group discussions the children should share the facts and impressions that they are gaining from the reading. The facts should be assessed as to their accuracy. The discussions and the journals will help facilitate the readers' understanding of the historical period.

Booklist — American Revolution

Avi. *The Fighting Ground*. Lippincott, 1984.

Bourne, Miriam Anne. *The Children of Mount Vernon: A Guide to George Washington's Home*. Doubleday, 1981.

Brandt, Keith. *Paul Revere, Son of Liberty*. Troll Associates, 1982.

Clyne, Patricia Edwards. *Patriots in Petticoats*. Dodd Mead, 1976.

Colby, Jean Poindexter. *Lexington and Concord, 1775*. Hastings House, 1975.

Collier, James Lincoln, and Christopher Collier. *Jump Ship to Freedom*. Delacorte, 1981.

_____. *My Brother Sam Is Dead*. Scholastic, 1974.

_____. *Who Is Carrie?* Delacorte, 1984.

Costiner, Merle. *The Rebel Courier and the Redcoats*. Meredith Press, 1968.

Fritz, Jean. *And Then What Happened, Paul Revere?* Coward, McCann & Geoghegan, 1973.

_____. *Early Thunder*. Coward McCann, 1967.

_____. *Traitor: The Case of Benedict Arnold*. Putnam, 1981.

_____. *What's the Big Idea, Ben Franklin?* Coward, McCann & Geoghegan, 1976.

_____. *Why Don't You Get a Horse, Sam Adams?* Coward, McCann & Geoghegan, 1974.

_____. *Will You Sign Here, John Hancock?* Coward, McCann & Geoghegan, 1976.

Monjo, F. N. *King George's Head Was Made of Lead*. Coward, McCann & Geoghegan, 1974.

O'Dell, Scott. *Sarah Bishop*. Houghton Mifflin, 1980.

Perl, Lila. *Slumps, Grunts, and Snickerdoodles: What Colonial America Ate and Why*. Seabury Press, 1975.

Phelan, Mary Kay. *Four Days in Philadelphia 1776*. Crowell, 1967.

Stein, R. Conrad. *The Story of Lexington and Concord*. Children's, 1983.

Other eras of history may be enhanced with collaborative readings in the fiction category. Try Irene Hunt's *Across Five Aprils* (Follett, 1964) for a look into one family's emotional trials during the United States's Civil War. Newer historical fiction titles set during the Civil War include Patricia Beatty's *Turn Homeward, Hannalee* (Morrow, 1984). Johanna Reiss's *The Upstairs Room* (Crowell, 1972) is an important reading for the World War II era as is *A Pocketful of Seeds* by Marilyn Sachs (Doubleday, 1973). A newer title in the World War II setting is Sigrid Heuck's *The Hideout* (Dutton, 1988). Use your library's card catalog subject index to locate other books set in specific historical periods. These books might be used as collaborative readings, a common novel for a structured reading activity, or a read aloud for the entire group. Use journaling techniques and discussion groups similar to those used for the American Revolution unit to help develop an understanding of any historical period.

Apples

Apples can fit into the school year in many ways. Set a zany tone for your classroom by reading "Mrs. Gorf" from Sachar's *Sideways Stories from Wayside School* (Avon, 1978). Be sure to have a big juicy red apple on your desk while you read. Polish it once or twice on your shirt or blouse while you read and just before you reach the part where Louis is about to bite into the lone apple on Mrs. Gorf's desk, take a bite of your apple, and then finish reading the story. The timing is all important here but the result will be well worth the effort.

Apples might become the focus in September (the 26th is Johnny Appleseed's birthday), October (National Apple Month), or March (the 11th has been designated Johnny Appleseed Day), and in the fall during the harvest season. During a celebration of apples read many stories focusing on apples. Discuss the traits apples represent in fairytales. How do they fare in picture books? Are apples a symbol of love, hate, evil, or good? Research and compare the varieties of apples grown (7,500 varieties in the world; more than 2,500 in the United States). Choose those varieties most frequently found in your area. Compare the size, shape, color, texture, etc. Graph the results. Have a tasting session. Rate the apple varieties on taste, appearance and other criteria specified by the members of the class. Chart the results.

Use apples to provide the data for mathematical computation. Ask each student to bring an apple to be cut open.

Count the number of seeds.

Figure the average number of seeds per apple.

Compute the total number of seeds.

Estimate how many apple trees would grow from the seeds if it took five seeds to produce each tree.

Create additional computations based on the number of seeds, the slices per apple, the weight of the apples, etc.

Determine from research (may include interviews with parents or other adults) the best variety of apple for eating, baking, cooking, pies, etc.

Other activities might include: reading recipes and making applesauce, apple cider, apple crisp, and other apple treats; planting an apple tree in the school yard; visiting an apple orchard; charting the growth of an apple tree; reading about Johnny Appleseed; or writing an apple shaped book about an apple topic.

While focusing on apples and apple related topics be sure to read plenty of apple books. The following list cites some of my favorites.

Booklist—Apples

Aliki. *The Story of Johnny Appleseed*. Prentice-Hall, 1963.

Barrett, Judi. *An Apple a Day*. Illustrated by Tim Lewis. Atheneum, 1973.

Blair, Walter. "Johnny Appleseed." In *North American Legends*, edited by Virginia Haviland, illustrated by Ann Strugnell. Collins, 1979.

Gibbons, Gail. *The Seasons of Arnold's Apple Tree*. Harcourt Brace Jovanovich, 1984.

Hogrogian, Nonny. *Apples*. Macmillan, 1972. (wordless)

Johnson, Hannah Lyons. *From Apple Seed to Applesauce*. Lothrop, Lee & Shepard, 1977.

Kellogg, Steven. *Johnny Appleseed*. Morrow, 1988.

Kohn, Bernice. *Apples: A Bushel of Fun and Facts*. Illustrated by Roland Rodegast. Parents, 1976.

McMillan, Bruce. *Apples: How They Grow*. Houghton Mifflin, 1979.

Noble, Trinka Hakes. *Apple Tree Christmas*. Dial, 1981.

Orbach, Ruth. *Apple Pigs*. Collins World, 1977.

Rothman, Joel. *A Moment in Time*. Illustrated by Don Leake. Scroll Press, 1973.

Sachar, Louis. "Mrs. Gorf." In *Sideways Stories from Wayside School*. Avon, 1978.

B IS FOR BALLET, BALLOONS, AND BUBBLE GUM

Ballet

Art and artists portrayed in art are sometimes overlooked. But in this focus ballet takes center stage. The following books are most appropriate to the middle-grade reader (grades 2-4) but with some adaptation can be utilized by younger and older readers. Be sure to display posters or photographs of actual ballet performances.

Booklist—Ballet

Baylor, Byrd. *Sometimes I Dance Mountains*. Scribner, 1973.

Bullard, Brian. *I Can Dance*. Putnam, 1979.

Draper, Nancy. *Ballet for Beginners*. Knopf, 1951.

Elliott, Donald. *Frogs and the Ballet*. Gambit, 1979.

Gordon, Suzanne. *Off Balance*. Pantheon, 1983.

Goulden, Shirley. *Royal Book of Ballet*. Follett, 1962.

Gross, Ruth. *If You Were a Ballet Dancer*. Dial, 1979.

Haney, Lynn. *I Am a Dancer*. Putnam, 1981.

Hautzig, Deborah. *The Story of the Nutcracker Ballet*. Illustrated by Diane Goode. Random House, 1986.

Isadora, Rachel. *Max*. Macmillan, 1976.

Jessel, Camilla. *Life at the Royal Ballet School*. Methuen, 1979.

Krementz, Jill. *A Very Young Dancer*. Knopf, 1976.

Maiorano, Robert. *Backstage*. Greenwillow, 1978.

Mara, Thalia. *First Steps in the Ballet*. Doubleday, 1955.

Sorine, Stephanie. *At Every Turn! It's Ballet*. Knopf, 1981.

_____. *Our Ballet Class*. Knopf, 1981.

Streatfield, Noel. *A Young Person's Guide to Ballet*. Warne, 1975.

Walker, Katherine. *Ballet for Boys and Girls*. Prentice-Hall, 1979.

This may be a good time to build an understanding of specialized vocabulary for specific activities or career fields. In this case such terms as *barre* and *tutu* might be discussed. Keep a class chart of new words relating to ballet that children uncover through their reading. Utilize the context in which the word is used to help children discuss the meaning of the new word. As the word is noticed in other books readers may suggest further refinements of the meaning. The end result will be a ballet word list, which might be placed in individual dictionaries or word bank lists. These word bank lists or personal dictionaries are great assists for children searching for just the right word to use in their writing.

Other books might lead to other connections. Try moving into tap dancing through Tomie dePaola's *Oliver Button Is a Sissy* (Harcourt, 1979) or into the area of biographical information and biographies by introducing information about artists who portrayed the ballet in their art.

Artists who portrayed ballet in their art include Edgar Degas, Henri de Toulouse-Lautrec, Auguste Rodine, and Edouard Manet. The art of Toulouse-Lautrec is discussed in *Henri de Toulouse-Lautrec* by Ernest Raboff (Harper & Row, 1988; Harper Trophy, 1988). For information about the other artists consult art encyclopedias and art biographical sources in library reference areas and art history books. If possible attend a ballet performance or invite some advanced dance students to visit your class or school to demonstrate the standard positions and to share information about ballet.

Balloons

Hot-air balloons are the basis for much fascination. Small wicker baskets with helium-filled balloons held to the basket with silver streamers will give the effect of a hot-air balloon as this topic is introduced. Since Brian Wildsmith's *The Bear's Adventure* (Pantheon, 1981) features both a bear and a hot-air balloon it might be the natural link between the Bears and Book week and a focus on books featuring hot-air ballooning. The Reading Rainbow Public Television series features Mary Calhoun's *Hot-Air Henry* (Morrow, 1981) in one of its segments. *Hot-Air Henry* is the story of a sassy Siamese cat who stows away on a hot-air balloon and ends up on a fur-raising flight across the mountains. Feature hot-air balloons on a bulletin board and fill the basket section of the balloon with jackets from many books. Fill a hot-air balloon (or a reading basket) with some of the following titles—both fiction and nonfiction.

Booklist—Balloons

Adams, Adrienne. *The Great Valentine's Day Balloon Race*. Scribner, 1980.

Adler, Irene. *Ballooning: High and Wild*. Troll, 1976.

Becker, Beril. *Dreams and Realities of the Conquest of the Skies*. Atheneum, 1967.

Brown, Dick. *Hot Air Ballooning*. Tab Books, 1979.

Burchard, Peter. *Balloons from Paper Bags to Skyhooks*. Macmillan, 1960.

Calhoun, Mary. *Hot-Air Henry*. Morrow, 1981.

Coerr, Eleanor. *The Big Balloon Race*. Harper & Row, 1981.

Dean, Anabel. *Up, Up, and Away!* Westminster, 1980.

Douglass, Barbara. *The Great Town and Country Bicycle Balloon Chase*. Lothrop, Lee & Shepard, 1984.

Douty, Esther M. *The Brave Balloonists: America's First Airmen*. Garrard, 1974.

Dwiggins, Don. *Riders of the Winds: The Story of Ballooning*. Hawthorn Books, 1973.

Kellogg, Steven. *Tallyho, Pinkerton!* Dial, 1982.

Mohn, Peter B. *Hot Air Ballooning*. Crestwood House, 1975.

Park, Ruth. *The Gigantic Balloon*. Parents, 1976.

Piccard, Joan Russell. *Adventure on the Wind*. Nash Publishing, 1971.

Radlauer, Ed, and Ruth Radlauer. *Hot Air Balloons*. Bowmar, 1974.

Scarry, Huck. *Balloon Trip—A Sketchbook*. Prentice-Hall, 1982.

Stehling, Kurt and William Beller. *Skyhooks*. Doubleday, 1962.

Timmermans, Gommaar. *The Great Balloon Race*. Addison-Wesley, 1976.

Wegen, Ron. *Balloon Trip*. Clarion, 1981.

Wildsmith, Brian. *The Bear's Adventure*. Pantheon, 1981.

If you want to include other balloon stories add these.

Bright, Robert. *Georgie and the Runaway Balloon*. Doubleday, 1983.

Carrick, Carol. *The Highest Balloon on the Common*. Greenwillow, 1977.

Henkes, Kevin. *Margaret & Taylor*. Greenwillow, 1983.

Willard, Nancy. *The Well-Mannered Balloon*. Harcourt Brace Jovanovich, 1976.

Use permanent magic markers to decorate balloons advertising a favorite book. Inflate the balloons, hang them from the ceiling, attach them to chair backs or to tables and desks, or otherwise display them for all to see. Many cities have hot-air balloon enthusiasts; perhaps one would agree to visit your school to discuss the art of hot-air ballooning.

Before any visit by a guest speaker or before any research projects are undertaken ask students to generate a list of what they know about hot-air ballooning. Mark those "facts" that all the class members agree are actual facts. Discuss those comments where there is disagreement. Indicate whether each comment is considered a fact, probably a fact, or not sure. Divide the group into teams to substantiate the validity of each comment as fact or not. Topics that the discussion facilitator may want to submit for comments include uses of balloons—scientific, in war time, and for pleasure; history of ballooning—including the first balloon and the development of balloons over time; important balloon records or trips; and balloon events and races. Basic research should uncover the several kinds of balloons: radiosondes (used in weather forecasting), passenger balloons, and captive or observation balloons (those that remain attached to the ground by means of cables or ropes). Balloons may be either round or shaped like sausages. Sausage-shaped balloons are called barrage balloons. They are the type that were flown over England in World War II, trailing cables to trap enemy aircraft. Basically three types of gases are used in balloons: hydrogen, helium, and coal gas. Each gas has different characteristics that must be considered when the decision is made regarding the type of gas to be used. Include encyclopedia articles as one of the resources to be checked. Famous balloonists that might be investigated include François Blanchard, André J. Garnerin, Joseph Louis Gay-Lussac, Thaddeus S. C. Lowe, the Montgolfier brothers, the Piccard brothers, and Ferdinand von Zeppelin.

Bubble Gum

During National Bubble Gum Week (last week in March), or any time bubble gum becomes a fad in your community, read Myra Cohn Livingston's poem "Bubble Gum." One source for this poem is Livingston's *4-Way Stop* (Margaret K. McElderry/Atheneum, 1976). Then sponsor a contest asking student readers to identify as many books as possible that include gum-chewing incidents in the plot.

Booklist—Bubble Gum in Books

Blume, Judy. *Tales of a Fourth Grade Nothing*. Dutton, 1972.

Paterson, Katherine. *The Great Gilly Hopkins*. Crowell, 1978.

Rogers, Mary. *Freaky Friday*. Harper & Row, 1972.

Thompson, Kay. *Eloise*. Simon & Schuster, 1955.

The card catalog will not be directly helpful in locating books for this list. Students will need much reading time to locate the books. Books that include chewing gum episodes will more often be books of humorous fiction or fiction about school. The card catalog will be helpful in locating those categories of books. A display of bubble gum cards could be set up and a bubble gum blowing contest held.

C IS FOR CLOUDS, CHRISTMAS, COUNTING, AND CRAFTS

Clouds

On a nice clear day, when the sky is filled with clouds, take a group of children outside to observe the interesting cloud shapes. Discuss the shapes. A few days later, give each child a 5 x 7-inch piece of white construction paper. Ask that the paper be torn into a shape. The shape should be put aside while the group shares *It Looked Like Spilt Milk* by Charles G. Shaw (Harper & Row, 1947; Harper Trophy, 1988). Ask each child to decide what his or her shape resembles. Glue the shape onto a piece of sky blue paper and caption the paper with "It looked like (insert the resembled object's name here), but it wasn't (insert object's name here)." Compile the pages as a bulletin board story or fasten them together to make a class book. A title page will need to be added along with a final page stating "It was just a cloud in the sky." *It Looked Like Spilt Milk* and the class book should be available for rereading. A more in-depth discussion of clouds might begin with the use of the section on clouds in Franklyn M. Branley's *It's Raining Cats and Dogs: All Kinds of Weather, and Why We Have It* (Houghton Mifflin, 1987) or by sharing some of the information in Tomie dePaola's *The Cloud Book* (Holiday House, 1975). Available books about clouds might be advertised on cloud-shaped papers and displayed on a bulletin board. Place cloud books close to the bulletin board so they will be available for reading, and declare the day a "cloudy day."

Booklist—Clouds

Bendick, Jeanne. *How to Make a Cloud*. Parents, 1971.

Branley, Franklyn M. *Flash, Crash, Rumble, and Roll*. Crowell, 1985.

Branley, Franklyn M. and Leonard Kessler. *Owlie Skywarn's Lightning Book*. U.S. Government Printing Office, 1978.*

Broekel, Ray. *Storms: A New True Book*. Children's, 1982.

Cummings, Pat. *C.L.O.U.D.S.* Lothrop, Lee & Shepard, 1986.

Davis, Hubert. *A January Fog Will Freeze a Hog and Other Weather Folklore*. Crown, 1977.

Fisher, Aileen. *I Like Weather*. Crowell, 1963.

Fisher, Leonard Everett. *Storm at the Jetty*. Viking, 1981.

Lambert, David. *Weather*. Watts, 1983.

McFall, Gardner. *Jonathan's Cloud*. Harper & Row, 1986.

---

*Order from the U.S. Government Printing Office, Washington, D.C., 20402. Include stock number (003-018-00086-5) and a check or money order made out to the Superintendent of Documents in the amount of $1.75.

Moncure, Jane Bells. *What Causes It?* Child's World, 1977.

Rayner, Mary. *The Rain Cloud*. Atheneum, 1980.

Renberg, Dalia Hardof. *Hello, Clouds!* Illustrated by Alona Frankel. Harper & Row, 1985.

Rubin, Louis D., Sr., and Jim Duncan. *The Weather Wizard's Cloud Book*. Algonquin Books of Chapel Hill, 1984.

Spier, Peter. *Dreams*. Doubleday, 1986.

Szilagyi, Mary. *Thunderstorm*. Bradbury Press, 1985.

Wolff, Barbara. *Evening Gray, Morning Red*. Macmillan, 1976.

Zim, Herbert S. *Lightning and Thunder*. Morrow, 1952.

Encourage students to observe and classify clouds and to record that information in a personal cloud observation notebook or keep a class notebook. Each student would view the clouds in the sky sometime during the day. The cloud shapes could be sketched, the date and the time noted, and the entry signed by the observing student. Be sure to keep a book showing the various types of clouds next to the window with the observation notebook. Initially the three basic types of clouds should be considered: cirrus, cumulus, and stratus. Various intermediate types of clouds are based on these basic classifications. Allow the observers to refine the cloud classifications if they wish.

Christmas

Books about Christmas are abundant and readily available. Locate those that are available in your library by using the subject cards of the library's card catalog. Sources for Christmas stories that will not be indexed in the card catalog are those Christmas chapters that are found within chapter books. The following chapters within favorite books will provide many short Christmas stories to read aloud or to share during the holiday season. The reading of a particular chapter can serve as an appropriate way to introduce a book and a series of books about a particular character. Most of these authors have additional books that feature some of the same characters.

Booklist — Christmas Chapters in Books

Bond, Michael. *More About Paddington*. Houghton Mifflin, 1962. Chapters 6 and 7.

_____. *Paddington at Large*. Houghton Mifflin, 1963. Chapter 7.

Carris, Joan. *Hedgehogs in the Closet*. Lippincott, 1988. Chapters 16 and 17.

Cleary, Beverly. *Henry Huggins*. Morrow, 1950. Chapter 4.

_____. *Ramona and Her Father*. Morrow, 1977. Chapters 6 and 7.

Cone, Molly. *A Promise Is a Promise*. Houghton Mifflin, 1964. Chapter 10.

Delton, Judy. *Angel's Mother's Boyfriend*. Houghton Mifflin, 1986. Chapter 10.

Estes, Eleanor. *The Middle Moffat*. Harcourt Brace Jovanovich, 1942. Chapter 6.

Fitzgerald, John D. *The Great Brain Does It Again*. Dial, 1975. Chapter 5.

George, Jean Craighead. *My Side of the Mountain*. Dutton, 1975. Chapter 18.

Grahame, Kenneth. *The Wind in the Willow*. Scribner, 1933. Chapter 5.

Haywood, Carolyn. *Back to School with Betsy*. Harcourt Brace Jovanovich, 1943. Chapter 8.

_____. *Eddie and the Fire Engine*. Morrow, 1949. Chapters 6 and 7.

Lawson, Robert. *The Tough Winter*. Viking, 1954. Chapter 8.

Lindgren, Astrid. *Pippi in the South Seas*. Viking, 1959. Chapter 12.

Uchida, Yoshiko. *Journey to Topaz*. Scribner, 1971. Chapter 3.

Wilder, Laura Ingalls. *Little House in the Big Woods*. Harper & Row, 1953. Chapter 4.

_____. *Little House on the Prairie*. Harper & Row, 1953. Chapter 19.

The reading of these chapters can well serve to introduce companion titles (books featuring some of the same characters) or a series of books to children. For example, Carris's *Hedgehogs in the Closet* is just one of several books featuring the Howard family. While the story line is not continued from one book to another, the characters are familiar and will encourage children to move from one book onto another. Sequels, such as the Wilder titles, follow the story line sequentially from one book to another. Children who wish to continue the story will be highly motivated to read the next book.

While all the Wilder titles were not listed in the previous booklist, they all contain a Christmas chapter. Sharing the Christmas chapters from all of Wilder's books might allow for the class to duplicate a pioneer Christmas celebration complete with the striped hard candies and button necklaces. A celebration could be shared with residents of a nearby nursing home, or older residents of the school or library neighborhood might be invited in to share the festivities.

Some favorite book characters are featured in novels that focus on the Christmas season throughout the book. Laura Ingalls Wilder's *The Long Winter* (Harper & Row, 1953), describes the long hard winter of the Dakota Territory in 1880-1881. The Christmas celebration that year is simple and unique. Robert Burch features Ida Early in *Christmas with Ida Early* (Viking, 1983) and Carolyn Haywood collected five previously published and very funny holiday stories about Eddie, added four new stories featuring Eddie, and brought out the nine stories in a collection titled *Merry Christmas from Eddie* (Morrow, 1986).

There are many picture books available to help celebrate the Christmas season. Some of my favorites are included in the list that follows, along with resource books and others that focus on the Christmas holiday. Picture books are noted with a (P) designation. One of my favorites on this list is Chris Van Allsburg's Caldecott Award-winning *The Polar Express*. Locate a large, silver, single sleigh bell. Attach a ribbon to the bell. Before reading the story aloud ring the bell and discuss the tone and tinkling sound of the ring. Encourage each child to acknowledge his or her ability to hear the bell ringing. Then proceed to read the story. As the conclusion is read the children will realize the significance of the discussion about hearing the bell. Extend the idea by discussing the idea of something being so because a person's belief is so strong. I am more comfortable reading *The Polar Express* to an audience of children who are past the age of believing in Santa Claus. The story works well for middle school and junior high students.

Perhaps rivaling any of the previous titles mentioned as my favorites is Tomie dePaola's *Merry Christmas, Strega Nona*. Strega Nona (Grandmother Witch) is my favorite dePaola character, partially because I am intrigued by Strega Nona's relationship with Big Anthony. In previous stories Big Anthony manages to get himself in big trouble. This time Big Anthony shows that he is capable of pulling off a big surprise. It is a delightful story with an important message. DePaola's other Christmas books have much utility in providing the springboard to other response activities. His book *The Legend of Old Befana: An Italian Christmas Story* could be used to begin a research study of holiday gift bearers, and his illustrated version of Clement Moore's *The Night before Christmas* could provide the initial focus for a look at the many published versions of the classic poem. DePaola's illustrations include borders that feature authentic quilt patterns represented in his own collection of antique quilts. When the illustrations for this poem are surveyed it may be interesting to focus on the way in which each of the illustrators depicted a particular character or a scene. Discuss the different moods conveyed through each of the different illustrations.

Booklist – Christmas Books

Adams, Adrienne. *The Christmas Party*. Scribner, 1978. (P)

Amoss, Berthe. *What Did You Lose, Santa?* Harper & Row, 1987. (P)

Andersen, Hans Christian. *The Fir Tree*. Illustrated by Nancy Ekholm Burkert. Harper & Row, 1970; Harper Trophy, 1986. (P)

_____. *The Fir Tree*. Illustrated by Diane Goode. Random House, 1988. (P)

Anglund, Joan Walsh. *A Christmas Book*. Random House, 1983. (P)

Arico, Diane, editor and compiler. *A Season of Joy: Favorite Stories and Poems for Christmas*. Illustrated by Daniel San Souci. Doubleday, 1987.

Bahr, Howard. *Home for Christmas: A Story of the South*. Illustrated by Kathleen Hardin. St. Luke's Press, 1987.

Bonsall, Crosby. *Twelve Bells for Santa*. Harper & Row, 1977. (P)

Bricusse, Leslie. *Christmas 1993 or Santa's Last Ride: An Absolutely Amazing Christmas Story*. Illustrated by Errol Le Cain. Faber & Faber, 1987.

Brown, Margaret Wise. *Christmas in the Barn*. Illustrated by Barbara Cooney. Crowell, 1952; Harper Trophy, 1985. (P)

_____. *The Little Fir Tree*. Illustrated by Barbara Cooney. Crowell, 1954; Harper Trophy, 1985. (P)

Chalmers, Mary. *A Christmas Story*. Harper & Row, 1956; reissued 1986. (P)

Cohen, Barbara. *The Christmas Revolution*. Illustrated by Diane deGroat. Lothrop, 1987.

Cozet, Denys. *Christmas Moon*. Bradbury Press, 1984. (P)

Cummings, E. E. *Little Tree*. Illustrated by Deborah Kogan Ray. Crown, 1987.

dePaola, Tomie. *An Early American Christmas*. Holiday House, 1987.

_____. *The Legend of Old Befana: An Italian Christmas Story*. Harcourt Brace Jovanovich, 1980. (P)

_____. *Merry Christmas, Strega Nona*. Harcourt Brace Jovanovich, 1986. (P)

_____. *Tomie dePaola's Book of Christmas Carols*. Putnam, 1987.

Gantos, Jack. *Rotten Ralph's Rotten Christmas*. Houghton Mifflin, 1984. (P)

Goode, Diane. *The Nutcracker*. Random House, 1988. (P)

Harrison, Susan J. *Christmas with the Bears*. Dutton, 1987. (P)

Hautzig, Deborah. *The Christmas Story*. Random House, 1981. (P)

Helldorfer, M. C. *Daniel's Gift*. Illustrated by Julie Downing. Bradbury, 1987.

Heller, Nicholas. *The Monster in the Cave*. Greenwillow, 1987. (P)

Henrik, Drescher. *Looking for Santa Claus*. Lothrop, Lee & Shepard, 1984. (P)

Hoff, Syd. *Santa's Moose*. Harper & Row, 1979; Harper Trophy, 1986. (P)

Hoffman, E. T. A. *The Nutcracker*. Retold by Anthea Bell, illustrated by Lisbeth Zwerger. Picture Book Studio, 1987. (P)

Hollyn's Lynn. *Lynn Hollyn's Christmas Toyland*. Knopf, 1985. (P)

Hurd, Edith Thatcher. *Christmas Eve*. Harper & Row, 1962. (P)

King, B. A. *The Christmas Junk Box.* Illustrated by Michael McCurdy. Godine, 1987.

Langstaff, John. *What a Morning! The Christmas Story in Black Spirituals.* Illustrated by Ashley Bryan. Margaret K. McElderry, 1987.

L'Engle, Madeline. *The Twenty-four Days before Christmas.* Harold Shaw, 1984. (P)

McCully, Emily Arnold. *The Christmas Gift.* Harper & Row, 1988. (P)

Mikolaycak, Charles. *Babushka.* Holiday House, 1984. (P)

Minarik, Else Holmelund. *What If?* Illustrated by Margaret Bloy Graham. Greenwillow, 1987. (P)

Moore, Clement C. *The Night before Christmas.* Illustrated by Douglas Corsline. Random House, 1975. (P)

_____. *The Night before Christmas.* Illustrated by Robin Spowart. Dodd Mead, 1986. (P)

_____. *The Night before Christmas.* Illustrated by Diane Goode. Random House, 1988. (P)

_____. *The Night before Christmas.* Illustrated by Anita Lobel. Knopf, 1984. (P)

_____. *The Night before Christmas.* Illustrated by Tomie dePaola. Holiday House, 1980. (P)

Naylor, Phyllis Reynolds. *Old Sadie and the Christmas Bear.* Atheneum, 1984. (P)

Olson, Arielle North. *Hurry Home Grandma.* Dutton, 1984. (P)

Overton, Jenny. *The Thirteen Days of Christmas.* Illustrated by Joseph A. Smith. Greenwillow, 1987. (P)

Parker, Nancy Winslow. *The Christmas Camel.* Dodd Mead, 1983. (P)

Pepper, Dennis. *An Oxford Book of Christmas Stories.* Illustrated by Judy Brown and others. Oxford University Press, 1987.

Peterson, Cheryl. *The Animals' Christmas.* Random House, 1983. (P)

Pienkowski, Jan, illustrator. *Christmas.* Text from the St. James Bible. Knopf, 1984. (P)

Quackenbush, Robert. *The Boy Who Waited for Santa Claus.* Watts, 1981. (P)

Rydberg, Victor. *The Christmas Tomten.* Coward, McCann & Geoghegan, 1981. (P)

Rylant, Cynthia. *Children of Christmas: Stories for the Season.* Illustrated by S. D. Schindler. Orchard Books/Watts, 1987.

Schweninger, Ann. *Christmas Secrets.* Viking Kestrel, 1984. (P)

Seuss, Dr. *How the Grinch Stole Christmas.* Random House, 1957. (P)

Speare, Jean. *A Candle for Christmas*. Illustrated by Ann Blades. Margaret K. McElderry, 1987.

Spier, Peter. *Christmas*. Doubleday, 1983. (P)

Van Allsburg, Chris. *The Polar Express*. Houghton Mifflin, 1985. (P)

Vincent, Gabrielle. *Merry Christmas, Ernest and Celestine*. Greenwillow, 1983. (P)

Weil, Lisl. *Santa Claus Around the World*. Holiday House, 1987.

Williams, Marcia. *The First Christmas*. Random House, 1988.

Winstanley, Rita. *The Oxford Merry Christmas Book*. Oxford University Press, 1987.

Zimelman, Nathan. *The Star of Melvin*. Illustrated by Oliver Dunrea. Macmillan, 1987.

Poems, Songs, and Crafts for the Christmas Season

Cummings, E. E. "Little Tree." In *Scott, Foresman Anthology of Children's Literature*, edited by May Hill Arbuthnot. Scott, Foresman, 1984.

Fisher, Aileen. "Merry Christmas." In *Random House Book of Poetry*, edited by Jack Prelutsky. Random House, 1983.

Fleming, Denise, illustrator. *The Merry Christmas Book: A First Book of Holiday Stories and Poems*. Random House, 1986.

Goode, Diane, illustrator. *Christmas Carols*. Random House, 1988.

Harrison, Michael and Christopher Stuart Clark, editors. *Oxford Book of Christmas Poems*. Oxford University Press, 1984.

Hopkins, Lee Bennett. *Sing Hey for Christmas Day!* Harcourt Brace Jovanovich, 1975.

Olliver, Jane. *The Doubleday Christmas Treasury: A Collection of Stories, Poems, Carols and Traditions*. Doubleday, 1986.

Purdy, Susan. *Christmas Decorations for You to Make*. Lippincott, 1965.

Tennyson, Noel, illustrator. *Christmas Carols*. Random House, 1981.

Wenk, Diana, editor. *A Holiday Treasury*. Doubleday, 1983.

Very Special Information Books about Christmas

Barth, Edna. *Balder and the Mistletoe: A Story for the Winter Holidays.* Illustrated by Richard Cuffari. Clarion, 1979.

_____. *Holly, Reindeer, and Colored Lights: The Story of the Christmas Symbols.* Illustrated by Ursula Arndt. Clarion, 1971.

Borland, Hal. *Plants of Christmas.* Crowell, 1987.

Giblin, James Cross. *The Truth about Santa Claus.* Crowell, 1985.

Sandak, Cass. *Christmas.* Watts, 1980.

Any planned emphasis on the Christmas holiday should be very sensitive to library patrons or school population who may not share the Christian holiday of Christmas. Alternative focuses could incorporate winter holidays around the world. This focus could include the New Year's Day celebration in many countries and the holidays celebrated by other religious or secular groups during the winter season. Investigate the makeup of the population in your community and invite speakers into your classroom, school, or library to share some of their traditions during the winter holidays. A classic title that describes an old-fashioned celebration of Hanukkah is Sydney Taylor's *More All-of-a-Kind Family* (Follett, 1954).

Counting 1-2-3

One, two, three climb the tree/Four, five, six flowers for us to pick. Counting books and rhymes help develop number concepts. The following are fairly simple counting books.

Booklist—Counting

Allen, Robert. *Numbers: A First Counting Book.* Illustrated by Mottke Weissman. Platt & Munk, 1968.

Anno, Mitsumas. *Anno's Counting Book.* Day, 1977.

Aylesworth, Jim. *One Crow: A Counting Rhyme.* Illustrated by Ruth Young. Lippincott, 1988.

Bang, Molly. *Ten, Nine, Eight.* Greenwillow, 1983.

Brown, Marc. *One Two Three: An Animal Counting Book.* Little, Brown, 1976.

Carle, Eric. *1, 2, 3 to the Zoo.* Collins, 1968.

_____. *My Very First Book of Numbers.* Crowell, 1974.

_____. *The Very Hungry Caterpillar.* Collins, 1969.

Chwast, Seymour and Martin Moskof. *Still Another Number Book*. McGraw-Hill, 1971.

Crews, Donald. *Ten Black Dots*. Scribner, 1968.

Dalgliesch, Alice. *The Little Wooden Farmer*. Macmillan, 1968.

Dee, Ruby. *Two Ways to Count to Ten: A Liberian Folk Tale*. Illustrated by Susan Maddaugh. Henry Holt, 1988.

Ehrlich, Amy. *The Everyday Train*. Dial, 1977.

Eichenberg, Fritz. *Dancing in the Moon: Counting Rhymes*. Harcourt, Brace & World, 1955.

Elkin, Benjamin. *Six Foolish Fishermen*. Illustrated by Katherine Evans. Children's, 1957.

Ets, Marie Hall. *In the Forest*. Viking, 1945.

Feelings, Muriel. *Moja Means One: Swahili Counting Book*. Illustrated by Tom Feelings. Dial, 1971.

Gretz, S. *Teddy Bears 1 to 10*. Follett, 1969.

Hoban, Russell. *Ten What? A Mystery Counting Book*. Illustrated by Sylvie Selig. Scribner, 1975.

Hoban, Tana. *Count and See*. Macmillan, 1972.

Hutchins, Pat. *The Doorbell Rang*. Greenwillow, 1986.

Ipcar, Dahlov. *Brown Cow Farm*. Doubleday, 1959.

———. *Ten Big Farms*. Knopf, 1958.

Keats, Ezra Jack. *Over in the Meadow*. Four Winds, 1971.

Kirn, Ann. *Nine in a Line*. Norton, 1966.

Langstaff, John. *Over in the Meadow*. Illustrated by Feodor Rojankovsky. Harcourt, Brace & World, 1957.

Leydenfrost, Robert. *Ten Little Elephants*. Doubleday, 1975.

Livermore, Elaine. *One to Ten. Count Again*. Houghton Mifflin, 1973.

Mack, Stan. *Ten Bears in My Bed: A Goodnight Countdown*. Pantheon, 1974.

Maestro, Giulio. *One More One Less*. Crown, 1974.

Mendoza, George. *The Marcel Marceau Counting Book*. Doubleday, 1971.

Merriam, Eve. *Project 1-2-3*. Illustrated by Harriet Sherman. McGraw-Hill, 1971.

Moncure, J. *Magic Monsters Count to Ten*. Child's World, 1979.

Oxenbury, Helen. *Number of Things*. Watts, 1968.

Peek, Merle. *The Balancing Act: A Counting Book*. Clarion, 1987.

_____. *Roll Over! A Counting Song*. Clarion, 1981.

Petie, Harris. *Billions of Bugs*. Prentice-Hall, 1975.

Rosenberg, Amye. *1 to 100 Busy Counting Book*. Golden Book/Western Pub., 1988.

Sendak, Maurice. *One Was Johnny: A Counting Book*. (The Nutshell Library) Harper & Row, 1962.

Tudor, Tasha. *1 Is One*. Walck, 1956.

Wahl, Jan. *I Can Count the Petals of a Flower*. National Council of the Teachers of Mathematics, 1976.

Wildsmith, Brian. *Brian Wildsmith's 1, 2, 3's*. Watts, 1965.

Kidstamps has available stamps designed by Giulio Maestro for numerals one through ten and four mathematical symbols. Students might use these to create their own counting books. Each of the stamps features a whimsical animal riding in a car or truck with the numeral on the vehicle's side. An eleventh stamp has an alligator in a blank car to allow for using other numerals. A caravan of numbers could carry children to a renewed understanding of number concepts.

Crafts

Traditional folk crafts from different cultures will provide hands-on experiences in the classroom. The use of the crafts could be part of an overall exploration of various cultural heritages or could be used one at a time to integrate with specific social studies units, holidays, or special months. Examine the crafts and compare them with those from other cultures. For example, compare the Jewish art of paper cutting with the time-honored Japanese art of origami (paper folding). Most importantly give students a chance to test their reading comprehension by organizing the materials that will enable them to read the directions for some of the projects and to actually create the crafts according to those directions. Paper-cut scenes could be backed with contrasting paper, matted, and framed for a very special gift to someone. Small origami objects could be attached to folded greeting cards to make three-dimensional cards. A study of various pop-up books might give some children ideas on how to use some of these crafts, particularly the origami, in the making of a "toy" book, most often referred to today as a pop-up book.

Booklist — Crafts

African — D'Amato, Janet and Alex D'Amato. *African Crafts for You to Make*. Messner, 1969.

Japanese — Montroll, John. *Origami for the Enthusiast: Step-by-Step Instructions in Over 700 Diagrams*. Dover, 1979.

Jewish — Strassfeld, Sharon and Michael Strassfeld, editors. *The Second Jewish Catalog*. Jewish Publication Society, 1976.

Native American — Blood, Charles L. *American Indian Games and Crafts*. Watts, 1981.

D IS FOR DENTISTS, DINOSAURS, DRAGONS, DRAWING, AND THE DEMOCRATIC PROCESS

Dentists and Dental Health

In addition to providing a focus during Dental Health Month books might be used to spur discussion on the loss of a tooth or to mark the point where all children have lost at least one baby tooth or when a molar is lost. Make several paper toothbrushes and note the title of an available book on each. Discuss good dental hygiene, the tooth fairy (and other traditions), the structure of teeth and the jaw, the need for braces and special care, and the careers related to dentistry (such as dental hygienist, oral surgeon, laboratory worker who makes dentures). Answer questions about how many teeth will be lost and other such matters. Culminate the celebration by holding a tasting party of good, healthful food for the teeth, especially foods that clean the teeth.

Booklist — Dentists and Dental Health

Gaskin, John. *Your Body — Teeth*. Watts, 1984.

Barnett, Naomi. *I Know a Dentist*. Putnam, 1977.

Barr, George. *Young Scientist and the Dentist*. McGraw-Hill, 1970.

Betancourt, Jeanne. *Smile! How to Cope with Braces*. Knopf, 1982.

Kessel, Joyce K. *Careers in Dental Care*. Lerner, 1984.

LeSeig, Theo. *The Tooth Book*. Beginner Books/Random House, 1981.

Silverstein, Dr. Alvin and Virginia Silverstein. *So You're Getting Braces*. Lippincott, 1978.

Steig, William. *Doctor DeSoto*. Farrar, Straus & Giroux, 1982.

Wolf, Bernard. *Michael and the Dentist*. Four Winds, 1980.

For a humorous and fun culmination to this focus read Tom Birdseye's *Airmail to the Moon*, illustrated by Stephen Gammell (Holiday, 1988). In this story Ora Mae Cotton of Crabapple Orchard loses her tooth. Then the tooth comes up missing. She attempts to figure out who might have taken the tooth and when she finds them she is going to spray them with a can of "Gotch ya" and send them airmail to the moon. The conclusion is predictable. She finds it in her own pants pocket. This book contains many metaphors.

Dinosaurs

Dinosaurs are popular themes with many ages of children. There is something fascinating about these large extinct animals that lived thousands of years ago. People were not living during the period when dinosaurs roamed the earth. Today, however, some descendants of the dinosaur are thought to live. Some of the books on the following list suggest that the information will be factual, others provide fictional settings for these real animals. Other books provide riddles and jokes focusing on dinosaurs. Display as many books as possible in your dinosaur center.

Booklist—Dinosaurs

Aliki. *Digging up Dinosaurs*. Crowell, 1981.

_____. *Dinosaur Bones*. Crowell, 1988.

_____. *Dinosaurs Are Different*. Crowell, 1985.

_____. *My Visit to the Dinosaurs*. Harper & Row, 1985.

Berman, Sam. *Dinosaur Joke Book*. Grosset & Dunlap, 1970.

British Museum. *Dinosaurs and Their Living Relatives*. British Museum, 1979.

Brown, Marc, and Stephen Krensky. *Dinosaurs, Beware!* Little, Brown, 1982.

Carrick, Carol. *Patrick's Dinosaurs*. Illustrated by Donald Carrick. Clarion, 1983.

_____. *What Happened to Patrick's Dinosaurs?* Illustrated by Donald Carrick. Clarion/Ticknor & Fields, 1986.

Cauley, Lorinda Bryan. *The Trouble with Tyrannosaurus Rex*. Harcourt Brace Jovanovich, 1988.

Cole, William. *Dinosaurs and Beasts of Yore*. Illustrated by Susanna Natti. William Collins Publishers, 1979. (poems)

Davidson, Rosalie. *Dinosaurs from A to Z*. Illustrated by John Forsberg. Children's, 1983.

Dixon, Dougal. *Prehistoric Reptiles*. Gloucester, 1984.

Elting, Mary, and Ann Goodman. *Dinosaur Mysteries*. Illustrated by Susan Swan. Platt & Munk, 1980.

Emberley, Michael. *Dinosaurs! A Drawing Book*. Little, Brown, 1980.

_____. *More Dinosaurs!* Little, Brown, 1983. (a drawing book)

Foreman, Michael. *Dinosaurs and All That Rubbish*. Crowell, 1972.

Freedman, Russell. *Dinosaurs and Their Young*. Illustrated by Leslie Morrill. Holiday House, 1983.

Granger, Judith. *Amazing World of Dinosaurs*. Illustrated by Pamela Baldwin Ford. Troll Associates, 1982.

Hobhouse, Sarah and David Mackay. *Wesley and the Dinosaurs*. Illustrated by Tony Ross. Wright Group, 1987. Other titles in this graded text set are *Brachiosaurus in the River, Dinosaurs on the Motorway, A Diplodocus in the Garden, Pterodactyl at the Airport, Triceratops on the Farm, Tyrannosaurus the Terrible*.

Horenstein, Sidney. *Big Strawberry Book of Dinosaurs and Other Prehistoric Animals*. McGraw-Hill, 1978.

Knight, David. *Battle of the Dinosaurs*. Prentice-Hall, 1982.

Kredenser, Gail. "Brontosaurus." In *The Random House Book of Poetry*, selected by Jack Prelutsky. Illustrated by Arnold Lobel. Random House, 1983.

Malam, Charles. "Steam Shovel." In *The Random House Book of Poetry*, selected by Jack Prelutsky. Illustrated by Arnold Lobel. Random House, 1983.

Milton, Joyce. *Dinosaur Days*. Illustrated by Richard Roe. Random House, 1985.

Moseley, Keith. *Dinosaurs a Lost World*. Illustrated by Robert Cremins. Putnam, 1984.

Most, Bernard. *Dinosaur Cousins?* Harcourt Brace Jovanovich, 1987.

_____. *If the Dinosaurs Came Back*. Harcourt Brace Jovanovich, 1978.

_____. *Whatever Happened to the Dinosaurs?* Harcourt Brace Jovanovich, 1984.

Packard, Mary. *Dinosaurs*. Illustrated by Christopher Santoro. Simon & Schuster, 1981.

Parish, Peggy. *Dinosaur Time*. Harper & Row, 1974.

Petty, Kate. *Dinosaurs*. Illustrated by Alan Baker. Watts, 1984.

Polhmus, Jean Burt. *Dinosaur Funny Bones*. Illustrated by Mamoru Funai. Prentice-Hall, 1974. (poems)

Prelutsky, Jack. "I'd Never Dine on Dinosaurs." In *The New Kid on the Block*. Illustrated by James Stevenson. Greenwillow, 1984.

Pringle, Laurence, *Dinosaurs and People: Fossils, Facts, and Fantasies*. Harcourt Brace Jovanovich, 1978.

Rosenbloom, Joseph. *Dictionary of Dinosaurs*. Messner, 1980.

Sattler, Helen Roney. *Baby Dinosaurs*. Illustrated by Jean Day Zallinger. Lothrop, Lee & Shepard, 1984.

Selsam, Millicent E. and Joyce Hunt. *A First Look at Dinosaurs*. Scholastic, 1972.

Silverstein, Shel. "Prehistoric." In *A Light in the Attic*. Illustrated by Shel Silverstein. Harper & Row, 1974.

Simon, Seymour. *The Largest Dinosaurs*. Macmillan, 1986.

Sterne, Noelle. *Tyrannosaurus Wrecks*. Illustrated by Victoria Chess. Crowell, 1979. (riddles)

Many children have an intense interest in and curiosity about dinosaurs. Most of the books published about dinosaurs deal with the factual aspects of a dinosaur's existence. Carrick's books begin to make the transition to establishing the dinosaur's role as a fanciful, imaginative character who is part of a story, as animals often are in fairy tales and fables. Lorinda Bryan Cauley completes the transition when she presents *The Trouble with Tyrannosaurus Rex*. In her story Tyrannosaurus Rex is determined to gobble up all the other dinosaurs in the neighborhood. The littlest dinosaur will hardly come out of hiding even for a drink of water. Duckbill and Ankylosaurus remember the peaceful life they enjoyed before the trouble with Tyrannosaurus. The two of them come up with a plan. As in traditional fables cleverness triumphs over brute strength. While this is a purely imaginative story the dinosaurs are accurately rendered and their characteristics are in keeping with the facts about dinosaurs as we know them.

Use the factual books to help build charts, graphs, and timelines showing information about the various types of dinosaurs and how they lived. Make books, bookmarks, posters, and three-dimensional displays showing favorite dinosaurs and information about them.

Dragons

An excellent book with which to start focusing on dragons is Tomie dePaola's *The Knight and the Dragon* (Putnam, 1980). In this wordless book a knight who has never fought a dragon is set to spar with an equally inexperienced dragon. The story line is humorous and has a unique ending which is sure to bring laughter and a rush toward more books about dragons. Another title that will provide an interesting beginning is James Seidelman and Grace Mintonye's *The 14th Dragon* (Harlin Quist, 1968). Rhymes describe thirteen dragons being captured by thirteen hunters. Each dragon shows a unique mood and personality through body gestures and facial expression. The fourteenth dragon is left for the reader to imagine and create.

Booklist—Dragons

Alexander, Sue. *World Famous Muriel and the Scary Dragon*. Little, Brown, 1985.

Aylesworth, Thomas G. *The Story of Dragons and Other Monsters*. McGraw-Hill, 1980.

Craig, Helen. *The Knight, the Princess, and the Dragon*. Knopf, 1985.

dePaola, Tomie. *The Knight and the Dragon*. Putnam, 1980.

Drescher, Henrik. *Simon's Book*. Scholastic, 1983.

Estes, Rose. *Children of the Dragon*. Random House, 1985.

Gannett, Ruth Stiles. *My Father's Dragon*. Random House, 1948.

Godden, Rumer. *The Dragon of Og*. Viking, 1981.

Gonzalez, Merce Company. *Killian and the Dragons*. Silver Burdett, 1986.

Hodges, Margaret. *Saint George and the Dragon: A Golden Legend*. Little, Brown, 1984.

Hope, Christopher. *The Dragon Wore Pink*. Macmillan, 1985.

Kellogg, Steven. *Ralph's Secret Weapon*. Dutton, 1983.

Konigsburg, E. L. *The Dragon in the Ghetto Caper*. Dell, 1984.

Korschunow, Irina. *Adam Draws Himself a Dragon*. Harper & Row, 1986.

Leaf, Margaret and Ed Young. *Eyes of the Dragon*. Lothrop, Lee & Shepard, 1987.

McGowan, Tom. *Encyclopedia of Legendary Creatures*. Rand McNally, 1981.

Nesbit, Edith. *The Book of Dragons*. Dell, 1986.

_____. *The Deliverers of Their Country*. Picture Book Studio USA, 1985.

Schaeffer, Susan Fromberg. *The Dragons of North Chittendon*. Simon & Schuster, 1986.

Seidelman, James and Grace Mintonye. *The 14th Dragon*. Harlin Quist, 1968.

Wallace, Ian. *Chin Chiang and the Dragon's Dance*. Atheneum, 1984.

Yep, Lawrence. *Dragon Steel*. Harper & Row, 1985.

Yolen, Jane, et al. *Dragons and Dreams*. Harper & Row, 1986.

Dragon language often includes similes and metaphors. Any reading of dragon books is sure to uncover some very poetic phrases. Keep a list of picturesque phrases to use in your own writing. Draw ferocious dragons, timid dragons, city dragons, and country dragons. Examine the art work in each of these books. Which art medium gives the dragon a look of strength? Which makes the dragon seem more vulnerable? Which colors make the dragon seem more ferocious?

Drawing and Writing

Authors and illustrators Lee J. Ames and Ed Emberley have provided several basic books demonstrating the how-to of drawing. Typically the books by both Ames and Emberley are light on text while presenting a step-by-step approach to drawing an object or scene. Those books will continue to be library staples. Other books are available that will balance the step-by-step approach presented in the popular titles by Ames and Emberley. Some titles describe ways to ease into writing by encouraging children to illustrate their own work. For some children the drawing must come before the writing. Try the following titles to stimulate more drawing and more writing.

Booklist—Drawing and Writing

Ames, Lee J. *Draw Draw Draw*. Doubleday, 1962.

_____. *Draw 50 Animals*. Doubleday, 1984.

_____. *Draw 50 Athletes*. Doubleday, 1985.

_____. *Make 25 Crayon Drawings of the Circus*. Doubleday, 1980.

Arnosky, Jim. *Drawing from Nature*. Lothrop, Lee & Shepard, 1982.

Benjamin, Carol Lea. *Cartooning for Kids*. Crowell, 1982.

_____. *Writing for Kids*. Crowell, 1985; Harper Trophy, 1985.

Bernstein, Joanne E. *Fiddle with a Riddle: Write Your Own Riddles*. Dutton, 1979.

Bolognese, Don and Robert Thornton. *Drawing and Painting with the Computer*. Watts, 1983.

Browne, Anthony. *Bear Hunt*. Atheneum, 1979.

Demi. *Liang and the Magic Paint Brush*. Holt, Rinehart & Winston, 1980.

Emberley, Ed. *Ed Emberley's Drawing Book: Make a World*. Little, Brown, 1975. (There are several other books in Ed Emberley's drawing book series.)

_____. *Ed Emberley's Great Thumbprint Drawing Book*. Little, Brown, 1977.

_____. *Ed Emberley's Picture Pie, A Circle Drawing Book*. Little, Brown, 1984.

Emberley, Michael. *Dinosaurs! A Drawing Book*. Little, Brown, 1980.

Frame, Paul. *Drawing the Big Cats*. Watts, 1981.

Hawkinson, John. *Pastels Are Great*. Albert Whitman, 1968.

Hoff, Syd. *How to Draw Cartoons*. Scholastic, 1975.

Ivenbaum, Elliott. *Drawing People*. Watts, 1980.

Jackson, Jacqueline. *Turn Not Pale, Beloved Snail: A Book About Writing and Other Things*. Little, Brown, 1974.

Judy, Susan and Stephen Judy. *Gifts of Writing, Creative Projects with Words and Art*. Scribner, 1980.

Kilroy, Sally. *Copycat Drawing Book*. Dial, 1981.

McPhail, David M. *The Magical Drawings of Moony B. Finch*. Doubleday, 1978.

Nicklaus, Carol. *Drawing Your Family and Friends*. Watts, 1980.

Purdy, Susan. *Books for You to Make*. Lippincott, 1973.

Weiss, Harvey. *Pencil, Pen and Brush: Drawing for Beginners*. Scholastic, 1974.

Zaidenberg, Arthur. *How to Draw and Compose Pictures*. Harper & Row, 1971.

_____. *How to Draw People: A Book for Beginners*. Harper & Row, 1952. (There are several other How-to titles by Zaidenberg.)

Establish an ongoing practice of showcasing the drawings and writings of children. Provide a forum where children may share their creations with others. Sponsor a weekly or monthly authors' lunch where writers and creative artists are encouraged to read their written papers or display their art work for other participants to hear and see. Establish a writers' workshop forum in your classroom or school. Provide an opportunity for children to respond to literary selections and their own writing through the expressive arts. An area in the classroom might be set aside for expressive arts activities. Each week a different medium might be made available. The ready availability of water paints and brushes, paper, and water containers at the art center will encourage responses using that medium. At other times colored chalk, crayons, drawing pencils, tempera paint, or a supply of tissue paper and glue will evoke quite a different type of artistic response. An equally important center is a writing center. Here children are encouraged to focus their energy on the writing process. Plenty of paper and pencils should be readily available along with standard writing tools, such as dictionaries and thesauri, appropriate to the age and needs of the writer.

Democratic Process

While nonfiction books on the democratic process will present the basic elements of a democratic society, fiction books will breathe life into the concepts of nominations, committee work, campaigns, and elections. The fiction books included in the following booklist cleverly weave the mechanics and terminology of the democratic process into the fictional tales. The humor and adventure contained within each of the books will serve to bring the world of politics into the realm of the student reader and help to make the concepts inherent in politics a viable part of the reader's world. Use the democratic process to establish classroom rules or practices. Establish a procedure for determining favorite authors and book titles in the school or classroom. Follow the entire process: nominations, campaigns, campaign speeches, media advertising, and finally the voting.

Booklist—Democracy

Bailard, Virginia and Harry C. McKown. *So You Were Elected!* McGraw-Hill, 1966.

Clymer, Eleanor. *My Mother Is the Smartest Woman in the World.* Atheneum, 1982.

Cohen, Dan. *The Mystery of the Hidden Camera.* Carolrhoda, 1979.

Conford, Ellen. *Dreams of Victory.* Little, Brown, 1973.

Fife, Dale. *Who'll Vote for Lincoln?* Illustrated by Paul Galdone. Coward, McCann & Geoghegan, 1977.

Giff, Patricia Reilly. *Fourth Grade Celebrity.* Dell, 1979.

Hicks, Clifford B. *Alvin Fernald, Mayor for a Day.* Holt, Rinehart & Winston, 1970.

Kibbe, Pat. *My Mother the Mayor, Maybe.* Scholastic, 1981.

Morton, Jane. *I Am Rubber, You Are Glue.* Beaufort Books, 1981.

E IS FOR ENEMIES

Enemies—"Let's Be Enemies"

Introduce the theme of Let's Be Enemies Day by reading *Let's Be Enemies* by Janice May Udry and illustrated by Maurice Sendak (Harper & Row, 1961). Discuss the difference between friends and enemies. How does one think a person becomes an enemy? Generate incidents that might make someone consider themselves an enemy of another. Be sure to include the idea of nature's natural enemies, for example, the cat as an enemy of the mouse. Then introduce books that feature enemy relationships. Read and discuss and add situations to the Let's Be Enemies list. Eventually discuss how enemies could be changed into friends. You will want to include some of the following books in your Let's Be Enemies celebration. Some of these enemies got away and some did not.

Booklist—Enemies

Aruego, José and Ariane Aruego. *A Crocodile's Tale*. Scribner, 1972.

Asbjørnsen, P. C. and J. E. Moe. *The Three Billy Goats Gruff*. Illustrated by Marcia Brown. Harcourt, Brace & World, 1957.

Christelow, Eileen. *Henry and the Red Stripes*. Clarion, 1982.

Freschet, Bernice. *Porcupine Baby*. Putnam, 1978.

_____. *Skunk Baby*. Crowell, 1973.

Galdone, Paul. *The Gingerbread Boy*. Seabury, 1975.

_____. *The Monkey and the Crocodile*. Seabury, 1969.

Grimm, Jacob and Wilhelm Grimm. *Hansel and Gretel*. Illustrated by Arnold Lobel. Delacorte, 1971.

Hyman, Trina Schart. *Little Red Riding Hood*. Holiday House, 1983.

Kalan, Robert. *Jump, Frog, Jump!* Greenwillow, 1981.

Lobel, Anita. *The Pancake*. Greenwillow, 1978.

Massie, Diane Redfield. *Briar Rose and The Golden Eggs*. Parents, 1973.

Udry, Janice May. *Let's Be Enemies*. Illustrated by Maurice Sendak. Harper & Row, 1961.

F IS FOR FAMILIES, FARMS, FEARS, FLIGHT, FOSTER CARE, FRIENDS, FRONTIER LIFE, FOXES, AND FROGS

Families (and Siblings)

Mothers and fathers, brothers and sisters often find their relationships changing. The following books will confirm for children that they are not alone in their feelings of jealousy, hurt, and anger and that the line between love and hate is very fine. (P indicates a must book for primary children; I indicates a particularly special book for intermediate-age children; and M indicates middle school priority.)

Booklist—Families (and Siblings)

Adler, C. S. *Get Lost, Little Brother*. Clarion, 1983 (I, M)

_____. *The Shell Lady's Daughter*. Coward McCann, 1983. (M)

Asher, Sandy. *Missing Pieces*. Delacorte, 1984. (M)

Baker, Betty. *My Sister Says*. Illustrated by Tricia Taggart. Macmillan, 1984. (P, I)

Baron, Nancy. *Tuesday's Child*. Atheneum, 1984. (I, M)

Bloss, Janet Adele. *My Brother the Creep*. Willowisp, 1983. (I)

Blume, Judy. *The One in the Middle Is the Green Kangaroo*. Dell, 1981. (P, I)

_____. *Superfudge*. Dutton, 1980. (I, M)

Buckley, Helen E. *Someday with My Father*. Harper & Row, 1985. (P, I)

Byars, Betsy. *The Night Swimmers*. Delacorte, 1980. (I, M)

Cassedy, Sylvia. *M. E. and Morton*. Crowell, 1987. (I)

Cazet, Denys. *Big Shoe, Little Shoe*. Bradbury, 1984. (P, I)

Ciardi, John. "Mummy Slept Late and Daddy Fixed Breakfast." In *The Random House Book of Poetry*, edited by Jack Prelutsky. Random House, 1983. (P, I, M)

Cleary, Beverly. *Ramona and Her Mother*. Morrow, 1979. (I)

Cole, Babette. *The Trouble with Mom*. Coward McCann, 1983. (P)

Dahl, Roald. "Aunt Sponge and Aunt Spiker." In *The Random House Book of Poetry*, edited by Jack Prelutsky. Random House, 1983. (P, I, M)

deRegniers, Beatrice Schenk. *Waiting for Mama*. Illustrated by Victoria deLarrea. Clarion, 1984. (P, I)

Dragonwagon, Crescent. *I Hate My Brother Harry*. Harper & Row, 1983. (P)

Fisher, Aileen. "On Mother's Day." In *The Random House Book of Poetry*, edited by Jack Prelutsky. Random House, 1983. (P, I, M)

Flournoy, Valerie. *The Patchwork Quilt*. Dial, 1985. (P, I)

Gomi, Taro. *Coco Can't Wait*. Morrow, 1984. (P, I)

Grant, Eva. *Will I Ever Be Older?* Raintree, 1981. (P, I)

Greenberg, Jan. *The Pig-Out Blues*. McGraw-Hill, 1982. (I, M)

Hall, Lynn. *The Leaving*. Scribner, 1980. (M)

Harris, Robie H. *Rosie's Double Dare*. Knopf, 1980. (I)

Hazen, Barbara Shook. *Tight Times*. Viking, 1979. (P)

Henderson, Rose. "Growing Old." In *The Random House Book of Poetry*, edited by Jack Prelutsky. Random House, 1983. (P, I, M)

Hermes, Patricia. *You Shouldn't Have to Say Good-bye*. Harcourt Brace Jovanovich, 1982. (I, M)

Hest, Amy. *The Crack-of-Dawn Walkers*. Illustrated by Amy Schwartz. Macmillan, 1984. (P, I)

Hirsch, Karen. *My Sister*. Carolrhoda, 1977. (P, I)

Hogan, Paula Z. *Will Dad Ever Move Back Home?* Raintree, 1980. (P, I)

Holz, Loretta. *Foster Child*. Messner, 1984. (P, I)

Hughes, Ted. "My Brother Bert." In *The Random House Book of Poetry*, edited by Jack Prelutsky. Random House, 1983. (P, I, M)

Hurwitz, Johanna. *DeDe Takes Charge*. Morrow, 1984. (I, M)

Hutchins, Pat. *You'll Soon Grow into Them, Titch*. Greenwillow, 1983. (P)

Jonas, Ann. *The Quilt*. Greenwillow, 1984. (P)

Katz, Bobbi. "The Runaway." In *The Random House Book of Poetry*, edited by Jack Prelutsky. Random House, 1983. (P, I, M)

Keats, Ezra Jack. *Apt. 3*. Macmillan, 1971. (P)

———. *Peter's Chair*. Harper & Row, 1967. (P)

Leigh, Henry S. "The Twins." In *The Random House Book of Poetry*, edited by Jack Prelutsky. Random House, 1983. (P, I, M)

Locker, Thomas. *Where the River Begins*. Dial, 1984. (P, I)

Lowry, Lois. *Anastasia on Her Own*. Houghton Mifflin, 1985. (I, M)

McCully, Emily Arnold. *Picnic*. Harper & Row, 1984. (P, I)

McPhail, David. *Fix-it*. Dutton, 1984. (P)

Nixon, Joan Lowry. *Maggie, Too*. Harcourt Brace Jovanovich, 1982. (I, M)

Paterson, Katherine. *Jacob, Have I Loved*. Crowell, 1980. (I, M)

Pellowski, Anne. *Betsy's Up and Down Year*. Philomel, 1983. (I, M)

———. *Stairstep Farm*. Philomel, 1981. (I, M)

Pevsner, Stella. *And You Give Me a Pain, Elaine*. Seabury, 1978. (I)

Quigley, Susan. *Do I Have To?* Raintree, 1980. (P, I)

Ridlon, Marci. "My Brother." In *The Random House Book of Poetry*, edited by Jack Prelutsky. Random House, 1983. (P, I, M)

Robinson, Nancy K. *Mom, You're Fired*. Scholastic, 1981. (I)

Roos, Stephen. *My Horrible Secret*. Delacorte, 1983. (I, M)

Silverstein, Shel. "Little Abigail and the Beautiful Pony." In *A Light in the Attic*. Harper & Row, 1981. (P, I, M)

———. "Surprise." In *A Light in the Attic*. Harper & Row, 1981. (P, I, M)

Simon, Norma. *I Wish I Had My Father*. Illustrated by Arieh Zeldich. Albert Whitman, 1983. (P, I)

Stecher, Miriam B. and Alice S. Kandell. *Daddy and Ben Together*. Lothrop, Lee & Shepard, 1981. (P, I)

Titherington, Jeanne. *A Place for Ben*. Greenwillow, 1987. (P)

Vigna, Judith. *Daddy's New Baby*. Albert Whitman, 1982. (P)

Viorst, Judith. "Some Things Don't Make Any Sense At All." In *The Random House Book of Poetry*, edited by Jack Prelutsky. Random House, 1983. (P, I, M)

Zindel, Paul. *The Effects of Gamma Rays on Man-in-the-Moon-Marigolds*. Bantam, 1970. (M)

These books could be used quite successfully to discuss relationships in our culture and to compare and contrast them with relationships, as we perceive them, in other countries. The journaling approach and discussion groups will facilitate the use of these books to focus on our own family relationships and to focus on the influence society's pressures have on those relationships.

Farms

Traditional farm animals are often the focus of farm units. But the real essence of the country or a farm is the feeling of calm and tranquility that goes with living there. After reading several of the titles on the booklist below compare and contrast one's own life with the life presented in these books. Is there more hustle and bustle in our life or in the country life? How would life change if we moved to the country? Or, for those living in the country, how realistic is this presentation of life in the country? After reading these books about farm or country life create original books about farm life. Counting books, alphabet books, and imaginative stories can be built on a farm theme.

Booklist—Farms and Country Living

Brown, Ruth. *The Big Sneeze*. Lothrop, Lee & Shepard, 1985.

Dragonwagon, Crescent. *Jemima Remembers*. Illustrated by Troy Howell. Macmillan, 1984.

Gibbons, Gail. *Farming*. Holiday House, 1988.

Locker, Thomas. *The Mare on the Hill*. Dial, 1985.

_____. *Where the River Begins*. Dial, 1984.

McPhail, David. *Farm Morning*. Harcourt Brace Jovanovich, 1985.

Parnall, Peter. *Winter Barn*. Macmillan, 1986.

Rylant, Cynthia. *Night in the Country*. Illustrated by Mary Szilagyi. Bradbury, 1986.

Tejima, Keizaburo. *Fox's Dream*. Illustrated by Tejima. Philomel, 1987.

_____. *Owl Lake*. Illustrated by Tejima. Philomel, 1987.

Yolen, Jane. *Owl Moon*. Illustrated by John Schoenherr. Philomel, 1987.

Fears (and Scary Things)

All children will be fearful of something at some time or another. Introduce this focus by reading Beatrice Schenk deRegniers's poem "When I Tell You I'm Scared," in her book *The Way I Feel Sometimes*, illustrated by Susan Meddaugh (Clarion, 1988). Discuss scary or fearful things. Follow the discussion by reading one of my all-time favorite scary stories, "The Green Ribbon," in

Alvin Schwartz's *In a Dark, Dark Room and Other Scary Stories* (Harper & Row, 1984). The book is designated as an *I Can Read* book but this story has been read aloud to children and adults alike. The response is always one which includes generous chuckles at the end of the story. The illustrations by Dirk Zimmer add to the fun of the story which is as humorous as it is scary. After this two-fold introduction set up a scary center. Be sure to include some of the following books.

Booklist—Fears and Scary Things

Andersen, Karen. *What's the Matter, Sylvie, Can't You Ride?* Dial, 1982.

Blaine, Marge. *The Terrible Thing That Happened at Our House.* Parents, 1975.

Blegvad, Lenore. *Anna Banana and Me.* Margaret K. McElderry, 1985.

Blume, Judy. *The One in the Middle Is the Green Kangaroo.* Dell, 1981.

Bottner, Barbara. *Horrible Hannah.* Crown, 1980.

Brown, Marc. *Spooky Riddles.* Random House, 1983.

Bunting, Eve. *Scary, Scary Halloween.* Illustrated by Jan Brett. Clarion, 1986.

Calhoun, Mary. *The Night the Monster Came.* Illustrated by Leslie Morrill. Morrow, 1982.

Carlson, Nancy. *Harriet the Roller Coaster.* Carolrhoda, 1982.

_____. *Loudmouth George and the Sixth Grade Bully.* Carolrhoda, 1983.

Carrick, Carol. *The Climb.* Clarion, 1980.

Christelow, Eileen. *Henry and the Dragon.* Clarion, 1984.

Cohen, Miriam. *Jim Meets the Thing.* Greenwillow, 1981.

_____. *Will I Have a Friend?* Collier, 1967.

Conford, Ellen. *Eugene the Brave.* Little, Brown, 1978.

Corbett, Scott. *Jokes to Read in the Dark.* Dutton, 1980.

Crowe, Robert L. *Clyde Monster.* Dutton, 1976.

deRegniers, Beatrice Schenk. *The Way I Feel Sometimes.* Illustrated by Susan Meddaugh. Clarion, 1988.

Fujikawa, Gyo. *Fraidy Cat.* Grosset & Dunlap, 1982.

Hamilton, Morse. *Who's Afraid of the Dark?* Avon, 1983.

Harris, Robie H. *Don't Forget to Come Back*. Knopf, 1978.

Hefter, Richard. *Very Worried Walrus*. Holt, Rinehart & Winston, 1977.

Heide, Florence Parry and Roxanne Heide. *A Monster Is Coming! A Monster Is Coming!* Illustrated by Rachi Farrow. Watts, 1980.

Hill, Susan. *Go Away Bad Dreams!* Random House, 1985.

Howe, James. *There's a Monster under My Bed*. Illustrated by David Ross. Atheneum, 1986.

Johnston, Tony. *Four Scary Stories*. Putnam, 1978.

_____. *Night Noises and Other Mole and Troll Stories*. Putnam, 1977.

Jones, Rebecca C. *The Biggest, Meanest, Ugliest Dog in the Whole Wide World*. Macmillan, 1982.

Keller, Victor. *The Scary Woods*. Illustrated by Cheryl Pelavin. Four Winds, 1971.

Krasilovsky, Phyllis. *The Shy Little Girl*. Houghton Mifflin, 1970.

MacDonald, Golden and Leonard Weisgard. *Little Frightened Tiger*. Doubleday, 1953.

Martin, Ann M. *Stage Fright*. Holiday House, 1984.

Martin, Bill, Jr. and John Archambault. *The Ghost-Eye Tree*. Illustrated by Ted Rand. Holt, Rinehart & Winston, 1985.

Martin, Jacqueline Briggs. *Bizzy Bones and Uncle Ezra*. Lothrop, Lee & Shepard, 1984.

Mayer, Mercer. *There's an Alligator under My Bed*. Dial, 1987.

_____. *There's a Nightmare in My Closet*. Dial, 1968.

_____. *There's Something in My Attic*. Dial, 1988.

McMillan, Sally Hudson. *I Used to Be Afraid*. Willowisp, 1985.

Memling, Carl. *What's in the Dark?* Illustrated by John E. Johnson. Parents, 1971.

Pinkwater, Daniel. *I Was a Second Grade Werewolf*. Dutton, 1983.

Prelutsky, Jack. *Nightmares*. Illustrated by Arnold Lobel. Greenwillow, 1976.

Rockwell, Ann and Harlow Rockwell. *The Night We Slept Outside*. Macmillan, 1983.

Ross, Tony. *I'm Coming to Get You!* Dial, 1984.

Roy, Ron. *Awful Thursday*. Pantheon, 1979.

Schwartz, Alvin. *In a Dark, Dark Room and Other Scary Stories*. Illustrated by Dirk Zimmer. Harper & Row, 1984.

Sharmat, Marjorie Weinman. *Frizzy the Fearful*. Holiday House, 1983.

_____. *Gila Monsters Meet You at the Airport*. Macmillan, 1980.

_____. *Lucretia the Unbearable*. Holiday House, 1981.

_____. *Sometimes Mama and Papa Fight*. Harper & Row, 1980.

Simon, Norma. *Why Am I Different?* Albert Whitman, 1976.

Stevenson, James. *That Dreadful Day*. Greenwillow, 1985.

_____. *What's under My Bed?* Willowisp, 1988.

Waber, Bernard. *Ira Says Good-bye*. Houghton Mifflin, 1988.

_____. *Ira Sleeps Over*. Houghton Mifflin, 1972.

Walker, Barbara. *Teeny-Tiny and the Witch Woman*. Illustrated by Michael Foreman. Pantheon, 1975.

Warren, William E. *The Graveyard and Other Not-So-Scary Stories*. Illustrated by Edward Frascino. Prentice-Hall, 1984.

Weil, Lisl. *The Riddle Monster*. Scholastic, 1981.

Willoughby, Elaine Macmann. *Boris and the Monsters*. Houghton Mifflin, 1980.

Wolf, Bernard. *Michael and the Dentist*. Four Winds, 1980.

Zelonky, Joy. *I Can't Always Hear You*. Raintree, 1980.

_____. *My Best Friend Moved Away*. Raintree, 1980.

Ziefert, Harriet and Jon Ziefert. *The Small Potatoes and the Sleep-Over*. Dell, 1985.

Flight

Flight, things that fly, airplanes and helicopters, hot-air balloons, space shuttles, and space ships. "Fly high with reading." These books could become part of a celebration of Charles A. Lindbergh's first solo flight across the Atlantic Ocean. The flight was made in a single-engine airplane, *Spirit of St. Louis*. Lindbergh took off from Roosevelt Field, Garden City, New York (near New York City), at 7:52 A.M. on May 20, 1927. He landed at Le Bourget Field near Paris on May 21 at 10:21 P.M. Paris time (5:21 P.M. New York time). He had flown more than 3,600 miles in 33½ hours. The Wright Brothers could also be the subject of a celebration. Wilbur and Orville

Wright invented and built the first successful airplane. On December 17, 1903 they made the world's first flight in a power-driven, heavier-than-air machine at Kitty Hawk, North Carolina. Prepare for the day by building and displaying model airplanes hung from the ceiling with fishing line or by encouraging experimentation with paper airplanes. Then pull out the books and read, read, and read. Use the following booklist and some additional titles from the Balloons booklist (see index).

Booklist—Flight

Branley, Franklyn M. *Is There Life in Outer Space?* Illustrated by Don Madden. Crowell, 1984.

Calhoun, Mary. *Hot-Air Henry*. Illustrated by Erick Ingraham. Morrow, 1981.

Cameron, John. *If Mice Could Fly*. Atheneum, 1979.

Coerr, Eleanor. *The Big Balloon Race*. Illustrated by Carolyn Croll. Harper & Row, 1981.

Douglass, Barbara. *The Great Town and Country Bicycle Balloon Chase*. Illustrated by Carol Newsom. Lothrop, Lee & Shepard, 1984.

Dwiggins, Don. *Flying the Space Shuttles*. Dodd Mead, 1985.

Kelly, James E. and William R. Park. *The Airport Builders*. Illustrated by Joel Snyder. Addison-Wesley, 1973.

Fradin, Dennis B. *Spacelab*. Children's, 1982.

Friskey, Margaret. *Space Shuttles*. Children's, 1982.

Hazen, Barbara Shook. *Amelia's Flying Machine*. Doubleday, 1977.

Moochli, Dinah L. *The Astronauts*. Random House, 1978.

Packard, Edward. *Hyperspace*. Bantam, 1983.

Percefull, Aaron W. *Balloons, Zeppelins & Dirigibles*. Watts, 1983.

Petty, Kate. *On a Plane*. Watts, 1984.

Provensen, Alice and Martin Provensen. *The Glorious Flight Across the Channel with Louis Bleriot*. Viking, 1983.

Ransome, Arthur. *The Fool of the World and the Flying Machine*. Farrar, Straus & Giroux, 1968.

Scarry, Huck. *Balloon Trip*. Prentice-Hall, 1982. (a sketchbook)

Stein, R. Conrad. *The Spirit of St. Louis*. Illustrated by Len Meents. Children's, 1984.

_____. *The Story of the Flight at Kitty Hawk*. Illustrated by Len Meents. Children's, 1984.

Young, Miriam. *If I Flew a Plane*. Illustrated by Robert Quackenbush. Lothrop, Lee & Shepard, 1970.

Foster Care (and Other Family Arrangements)

While some children do not live with both natural parents, other children do not live with either natural parent. Some live with grandparents or foster families, and others live with aunts and uncles or other relatives. The children for whom that is true must find themselves in books. They must see that their situation is one that can bring them to a full and productive life. And others will gain an awareness of the problems their classmates face just to survive in a daily routine. Consider using one or more of the following books as a read aloud for your class. Use these books in conjunction with those focusing on stepfamilies and other family members.

Booklist—Foster Families

Byars, Betsy. *The Pinballs*. Harper & Row, 1977; Scholastic, 1979.
> Three foster children find themselves in the same home and prove to each other and the world that they are not "pinballs" to be knocked around from one place to the next. While dealing with a very serious topic, Byars has created a hopeful, loving, and witty book.

Eige, Lillian. *Cady*. Illustrated by Janet Wentworth. Harper & Row, 1987.
> When Cady's grandmother dies Cady runs away to the home of a family friend. The friend eventually must send him away, this time to the home of a woman whom he hardly knows. There is something strange about her. Somewhere there is a connection but Cady cannot find it. Through the encouragement of this strange woman Cady builds a relationship with a hermit-like man who lives on the edge of her land. That man turns out to be Cady's father and the woman Cady's aunt.

Gibbons, Faye. *Mighty Close to Heaven*. Morrow, 1985.
> Since his mother's death three years ago, Dave has lived unhappily with his grandparents. Now he is running away to find his father. He eventually does find a place he can call home.

Hall, Lynn. *Mrs. Portree's Pony*. Scribner, 1986.
> Mrs. Portree is a proud woman who has alienated and lost her own daughter. She is the owner of a pony which is the source of comfort to a foster child who otherwise feels unloved and unneeded. The pony brings the two of them together and fosters an enriching relationship between the two people.

MacLachlan, Patricia. *Mama One, Mama Two*. Illustrated by Ruth Lercher Bornstein. Harper & Row, 1982.
> When a young girl's mother becomes "sad" and cannot cope with the world she is hospitalized. The girl is put into a foster home. She needs to be comforted during the night and at other times. As she is comforted, given love, and assimilated into the family's activities the girl realizes that Mama Two is there to take care of her until Mama One is better. Maybe she'll come home in the spring or maybe she won't but Mama Two will be there until she does.

Means, Florence Crannell. *Us Maltbys*. Houghton Mifflin, 1966.
> The two Maltby girls are shocked when they find out that their parents are going to open their home to five teenage girls with problems. All seven of the girls have problems adjusting to their new situation. The Maltby family eventually extends their home to a charming black boy who challenges the town's rule forbidding blacks from staying overnight in the town.

Neufeld, John. *Edgar Allan*. S. G. Phillips, 1968; NAL, 1969.
When a white family adopts a black child the pressure from the community forces them to give him up. A classic tale.

Paterson, Katherine. *The Great Gilly Hopkins*. Crowell, 1978.
Gilly is a spunky preteen, suffering the same growing pains as many other preteens. The difference; Gilly is a foster child. She must reach through the natural alienation preteenagers often feel for their parents to uncover a sense of her own worth and to find a permanent family.

Voigt, Cynthia. *Dicey's Song*. Atheneum, 1982.
After their mother abandons them and enters an asylum, Dicey and her two brothers and one sister make their way to their grandmother's home. Dicey finds that survival in the new surroundings requires love, trust, humor, and courage.

Wosmek, Frances. *A Brown Bird Singing*. Lothrop, Lee & Shepard, 1986.
A Chippewa Indian leaves his daughter, in a small Minnesota town, to be raised by his white friends. As time goes on she comes to love her new family and lives in fear that her father will return and take her away from the only family she has known.

Friends

Most children wish to have a special friend that they can call when they want someone to talk to, sleep over, or someone to go with them to a movie. The books on the following list could be combined with the Enemies booklist to provide books for a Friends and Enemies Day. Or friendship could be celebrated during the month of February to promote the feeling of friendship among all races and ages. With any group discussions about friends and friendships be careful about promoting questions and remarks that will single out any of the students as not having a friend. Keep the experience positive for everyone including the less popular members of the class. The majority of the books listed here are picture books. Many of the books of fiction for children and young adults include a friendship relationship. Allow those who wish to read a novel to select any of their choice and then discuss it with the focus on the friendship relationship.

Booklist—Friends

Aliki. *The Two of Them*. Greenwillow, 1979.

_____. *We Are Best Friends*. Greenwillow, 1982.

Bond, Felicia. *Poinsettia and Her Family*. Crowell, 1981.

Brown, Marc. *The True Francine*. Little, Brown, 1981.

Cohen, Miriam. *Will I Have a Friend?* Collier, 1967.

Cosgrove, Stephen. *Morgan and Yew*. Rourke, 1984.

Delton, Judy. *Lee Henry's Best Friend*. Albert Whitman, 1980.

Ehrlich, Amy. *Leo, Zack and Emmie*. Dial, 1981.

Gackenbach, Dick. *Hattie Rabbit*. Harper & Row, 1976.

_____. *Hound and Bear*. Seabury, 1976.

Gretz, Susana. *Teddy Bears Cure a Cold*. Four Winds, 1984.

Hermes, Patricia. *Friends Are Like That*. Harcourt Brace Jovanovich, 1984.

Hoban, Lillian. *Best Friends for Francis*. Harper & Row, 1969.

Kellogg, Steven. *Best Friends*. Dial, 1986.

_____. *Can I Keep Him?* Dial, 1971.

Kent, Jack. *Joey*. Prentice-Hall, 1984.

Kroll, Stephen. *The Biggest Pumpkin Ever*. Scholastic, 1984.

Litchfield, Ada B. *Making Room for Uncle Joe*. Illustrated by Gail Owens. Albert Whitman, 1984.

Lobel, Arnold. *Frog and Toad Are Friends*. Harper & Row, 1970.

Marshall, James. *George and Martha, Tons of Fun*. Houghton Mifflin, 1980.

Peet, Bill. *Zella, Zach, and Zodiac*. Houghton Mifflin, 1986.

Ruckman, Ivy. *Night of the Twister*. Crowell, 1984.

Schulman, Janet. *The Great Big Dummy*. Greenwillow, 1978.

Stevenson, James. *Emma*. Greenwillow, 1985.

_____. *The Worst Person in the World*. Greenwillow, 1978.

Stock, Catherine. *Emma's Dragon*. Lothrop, Lee & Shepard, 1984.

Weiss, Nicki. *Maude and Sally*. Greenwillow, 1983.

Wells, Rosemary. *Timothy Goes to School*. Dial, 1981.

Yorinks, Arthur. *Hey, Al*. Illustrated by Richard Egielski. Farrar, Straus & Giroux, 1986.

To introduce this focus view the Reading Rainbow segment that features Kellogg's *Best Friends*. This program segment not only reads the Kellogg book aloud but includes book talks for several other books that have friends and friendships as a common theme.

Frontier and Early Life in America

The chronicles of Laura Ingalls Wilder's growing-up years in America's frontier country have been unparalleled to this date. That series, beginning with *Little House in the Big Woods* (Harper & Row, 1932), was first published during the Depression in the 1930s. The first editions of her titles were illustrated by Helen Sewall. Later, in the 1950s, Garth Williams agreed to provide new illustrations for the books. The project took him ten years and many miles on the same roads and trails travelled years before by the Ingalls family.

After sharing one or more of her books, build on the interest in these books by researching the late 1800s and the early 1900s. Who was president? What states were already admitted as states of the United States? To continue the interest in the frontier and the history surrounding the era use some of the following books as read alouds, or as collaborative or common readings.

Booklist—Frontier Life

Calvert, Patricia. *The Snowbird*. Scribner, 1980.
A brother and sister travel to the Dakota territory in the 1880s to begin a new life with their aunt and uncle. Willanna Bannerman shows a strength of character that brings her to discover the real meaning of frontier living.

Conrad, Pam. *Prairie Songs*. Harper & Row, 1985.
Women coping with the rigors of frontier living.

DeClue, Denise. *Women Shaping History*. Raintree, 1979.
A history of women's liberation from colonial days to the present time.

Flournoy, Valerie. *The Patchwork Quilt*. Illustrated by Jerry Pinkney. Dial, 1985.
A grandmother shows her granddaughter, a young black girl, the significance of a quilt and the proper way to make one.

Hoare, Robert. *Turn of the Century*. Holiday House, 1975.
New inventions, fashions, and social changes at the turn of the century.

MacLachlan, Patricia. *Sarah Plain and Tall*. Harper & Row, 1985.
Two young girls are faced with the acceptance of their father's mail-order bride. And the bride is faced with two young girls and their memories of their mother.

Terris, Susan. *Nell's Quilt*. Collings, 1987.
At the turn of the century, an eighteen year old looks toward her future as a college student. That future becomes clouded with pressure from her family to marry a cousin who farms. Faced with a marriage she does not want Nell withdraws into a solitary world of her own and makes her quilt, a quilt that helps her focus on her real future.

Foxes

In Eric Carle's *The Mixed-Up Chameleon* (Crowell, 1975; revised, 1984), the chameleon wishes for the attributes of various animals. One of the animals the chameleon meets is a fox. The fox is described as being "smart," and the physical attribute the chameleon receives is the fox's fluffy red tail. Read the story and during a subsequent rereading use it to focus on the attributes and depiction of the fox in folklore and in fiction and nonfiction literature. Introduce the folktale component by reading *One Fine Day* by Nonny Hogrogian (Macmillan, 1971). Hogrogian presents matchless simplicity in her drawings as she tells the story of an old woman who caught a fox licking up her pail of milk and she cut off his tail. She agreed to sew it back on only when he replaced the milk. The tale is based on Armenian folk stories and while the focus of the story is on the cumulative effect of the tail, the story can also serve as an introduction to foxes as they are depicted in folklore. The fox as presented in traditional literature is quite different from the story of a real-life fox. Compare and contrast the image of a fox as presented in each type of story. Compare legends and stories to the real life of a fox. Compare the European and American Indian view of the fox. Compile information about foxes. As children research and read books and encyclopedias they should record facts and impressions they receive about foxes on 3x5 cards. Each fact and impression should be designated as fact or impression and the source should be noted. Working in small groups the children should combine their fact and impression cards to build some generalizations and opinions which they can support from their reading.

Booklist—Foxes in Books

Ahlstrom, Mark. *The Foxes*. Crestwood House, 1984.

Burton, Jane. *Fancy the Fox*. Random House, 1988. (series: How Animals Grow)

Carle, Eric. *The Mixed-Up Chameleon*. Crowell, 1975; rev. 1984.

Fox, Mem. *Hattie and the Fox*. Illustrated by Patricia Mullins. Bradbury, 1987. (traditional literature)

George, Jean. *The Moon of the Fox Pups*. Crowell, 1968.

Ginsburg, Mirra. *One Trick Too Many: Fox Stories from Russia*. Illustrated by Helen Siegl. Dial, 1972. (traditional literature—Russia)

_____. *The Fox and the Hare*. Illustrated by Victor Nolden. Crown, 1969. (traditional literature—Russia)

Hess, Lilo. *Foxes in the Woodshed*. Scribner, 1966.

Hogrogian, Nonny. *One Fine Day*. Macmillan, 1971. (traditional literature—Armenia)

Lane, Margaret. *Fox*. Dial, 1982.

McDearmon, Kay. *Foxes*. Dodd Mead, 1981.

McKissack, Pat. *Flossie and the Fox*. Dial, 1987.

Ripper, Charles. *Foxes and Wolves*. Morrow, 1961.

Roach, Marilynne. *Dune Fox*. Little, Brown, 1977.

Sarett, Lew. "Four Little Foxes." In *Favorite Poems Old and New* by Helen Ferris, compiler. Illustrated by Leonard Weisgaard. Doubleday, 1957. (poem)

Spier, Peter. *The Fox Went Out on a Chilly Night*. Doubleday, 1961. (traditional literature)

Tejima, Keizaburo. *Fox's Dream*. Illustrated by Tejima. Philomel, 1987.

Thomas, Jane Resh. *Fox in a Trap*. Illustrated by Troy Howell. Clarion, 1987.

Frogs

Frogs, frogs, everywhere. A frog found in the meadow or the realization that frogs are green and toads are brown can bring an excuse for celebrating frogs. Create a celebration by asking children to wear, on Frog Day, as much green as possible. Research information about frogs, what they eat, and where they live. Write frog poems (including "frogericks"—limericks about frogs) and frog stories. Celebrate by reading with stories and poems about frogs and stories with frogs as main characters. Begin by sharing the *Frog and Toad* books by Arnold Lobel, folktales like Wang's "The Frog Prince," and the following books by Mercer Mayer featuring frogs (and himself as a boy with his dog).

Booklist—Frogs (wordless)

Mayer, Mercer. *A Boy, a Dog, and a Frog*. Dial, 1978.
The story of a little boy and his dog who try to catch an enterprising frog. (Filmstrip available from Random House.)

Mayer, Mercer and Marianna Mayer. *A Boy, a Dog, a Frog, and a Friend*. Dial, 1971.
A boy, his dog, and his frog go fishing and end up catching a turtle.

Mayer, Mercer. *Frog Goes to Dinner*. Dial, 1974.
Frog stows away in the boy's pocket when the family goes out to dinner. (Filmstrip available from Random House.)

Mayer, Mercer. *Frog on His Own*. Dial, 1973.
Frog decides to part company with his friends so that he might have an afternoon of adventure on his own. (Filmstrip available from Random House.)

Mayer, Mercer. *Frog, Where Are You?* Dial, 1969.
     A boy and his dog have a number of adventures searching for their missing pet, Frog. (Film-strip available from Random House.)

Mercer Mayer has illustrated several wordless books. One might use Mayer's wordless books above and those on the Wordless bibliography (see index) to stimulate verbal language expression. This verbal expression should first be shared in a group. The group could compose some dialogue about the action in each book. (The use of one of the available filmstrips of Mayer's books will facilitate the showing of the illustrations to a large group.) Later smaller groups could discuss a book and its plot development. Finally individuals could compose a summary or text to accompany the story line developed with the pictures in the wordless book. The text could either be tape recorded by the students or written with the help of a "secretary." For the student who is just beginning to write, it is best to have a parent volunteer or an adult or student teacher associate write the story and later type it so that each student may have a copy of the text that the group develops. Able individuals might do their own writing in story form.
     Then take a look at how frogs are represented in books, both imaginative stories and traditional folk stories.

Booklist—Other Frog Books

Blake, Quentin. *Story of the Dancing Frog.* Knopf, 1984.

Isele, Elizabeth. *The Frog Princess.* Crowell, 1984.

Langstaff, John. *Frog Went a-Courtin'.* Illustrated by Feodor Rojankovsky. Harcourt, Brace & World, 1955.

Lionni, Leo. *Fish Is Fish.* Knopf, 1970.

Lobel, Arnold. *Days with Frog and Toad.* Harper & Row, 1979.

_____. *Frog and Toad All Year.* Harper & Row, 1976.

_____. *Frog and Toad Are Friends.* Harper & Row, 1970.

_____. *Frog and Toad Together.* Harper & Row, 1972.

Thaler, Mike. *In the Middle of the Puddle.* Illustrated by Bruce Degen. Harper & Row, 1988.

Wang, Mary Lewis. *The Frog Prince.* Illustrated by Gwen Connelly. Children's, 1986. (series: Start-Off Stories)

Send the readers on a search in your school or public library to locate other books featuring frogs. As the books are read ask the readers to keep notes in their journals concerning how frogs are depicted in stories. Research true facts about frogs and then discuss the depiction of frogs in relation to those facts.

G IS FOR GAMES, GHOSTS, AND GRANDPARENTS

Games

Chris Van Allsburg's book *Jumanji* (Houghton Mifflin, 1981) tells the story of Judy and her brother Peter who begin to play the board game of Jumanji. The game's directions warn them that once the game is begun it must be finished. Judy and Peter do not heed the directions and proceed only to find themselves in the midst of a mysterious and mystical jungle adventure that provides them with more excitement than the two of them ever anticipated.

Plan a day when children bring their favorite board game and introduce it to some of their classmates. Children should be given the opportunity to play several different types of games. Follow the board game activity with a reading of *Jumanji*. Discuss the implications for the development of a board game titled *Jumanji* or other board games with a "come to life" theme. The following books will assist children in developing the games and with drawing the animals.

Booklist—Making Games

Ames, Lee J. *Draw 50 Animals*. Doubleday, 1974.
  Step-by-step instructions for drawing fifty different animals.

Arnosky, Jim. *Drawing from Nature*. Lothrop, Lee & Shepard, 1982.
  Instructional steps for drawing water, land, plants, and animals.

Caney, Steven. *Steven Caney's Playbook*. Workman, 1975.
  Projects, constructions, games, and puzzles for children to make and do.

Simons, Robin. *Recyclopedia*. Houghton Mifflin, 1976.
  Suggestions for making games and crafts from recycled materials.

Ghosts

Ghosts are not just for Halloween, they are for those who love suspense and adventure any time of the year. Young children hear monsters in their room at night; older children fantasize about ghosts. Use these books to tie into the booklist featuring books on fears and scary things. To begin the ghost unit make a paper-tissue ghost for each child or better yet give the children the instructions and let them make their own ghosts. Make the paper-tissue ghosts by using one tissue. Drape the tissue over a tightly wadded-up paper ball. The paper ball should be about the size of a walnut. Use a piece of string to tie the tissue under the ball making the tissue appear to have a head and a loosely flowing garment over a nonexistent body. Use a black marker to make two dots on the ball, to represent eyes. Follow through with a booktalk featuring some of the following ghostly tales for readers of all ages.

Booklist—Ghostly Tales

Adler, C. S. *Footsteps on the Stairs*. Delacorte, 1982.

Adler, David. *Jeffrey's Ghost and the Fifth Grade Dragon*. Holt, Rinehart & Winston, 1985.

Alcock, Vivian. *The Haunting of Cassie Palmer*. Delacorte, 1980.

Alexander, Sue. *Witch, Goblin and Ghost in the Haunted Woods*. Pantheon, 1981.

Barth, Edna. *Witches, Pumpkins, and Grinning Ghosts*. Clarion, 1972.

Bellairs, John. *The Curse of the Blue Figurine*. Dial, 1983.

———. *The Mummy, the Will, and the Crypt*. Dutton, 1983.

———. *The Revenge of the Wizard's Ghost*. Dial, 1985.

Boston, Lucy M. *The Children of Green Knowe*. Harcourt, Brace & World, 1955.

———. *An Enemy at Green Knowe*. Harcourt, Brace & World, 1958.

———. *The Stones of Green Knowe*. Atheneum, 1976.

———. *Treasures of Green Knowe*. Harcourt, Brace & World, 1958.

Brittain, Bill. *Who Knew There'd Be Ghosts?* Harper & Row, 1985.

Bunting, Eve. *The Ghost of Summer*. Warne, 1977.

Cameron, Eleanor. *The Court of the Stone Children*. Dutton, 1973.

Carlson, Natalie Savage. *Spooky Night*. Lothrop, Lee & Shepard, 1982.

Christopher, Matt. *Favor for a Ghost*. Westminster, 1983.

———. *Return of the Headless Horseman*. Westminster, 1982.

Clapp, Patricia. *Jane-Emily*. Lothrop, 1969.

Corbett, Scott. *The Discontented Ghost*. Dutton, 1978.

Curry, Jane. *Poor Tom's Ghost*. Atheneum, 1977.

Duncan, Lois. *Summer of Fear*. Little, Brown, 1976.

Dunlop, Eileen. *The Maze Stone*. Coward McCann, 1983.

Fleischman, Sid. *McBroom's Ghost*. Atlantic Monthly Press, 1981.

Flora, James. *Grandpa's Ghost Stories*. Atheneum, 1978.

Gage, Wilson. *Mrs. Gaddy and the Ghost*. Greenwillow, 1979.

Galdone, Joanne. *The Tailypo: A Ghost Story*. Clarion, 1977.

Garfield, Leon. *The Ghost Downstairs*. Pantheon, 1972.

Hahn, Mary Downing. *Time of the Witch*. Clarion, 1982.

_____. *Wait till Helen Comes*. Clarion, 1986.

Hancock, Sibyl. *Esteban and the Ghost*. Dial, 1983.

Hildick, E. W. *Ghost Squad Breaks Through*. Dutton, 1984.

Hunter, Mollie. *The Haunted Mountain*. Harper & Row, 1972.

Irving, Washington. *Legend of Sleepy Hollow*. Illustrated by Dan Sans Souci. Doubleday, 1986.

Kay, Mary. *A House Full of Echoes*. Crown, 1980.

Klaveness, Jan O'Donell. *The Griffin Legacy*. Macmillan, 1983.

Kroll, Steven. *Amanda and the Giggling Ghost*. Holiday House, 1980.

Lane, Carolyn. *Echoes in an Empty Room and Other Supernatural Tales*. Holt, Rinehart & Winston, 1981.

Levin, Betty. *The Keeping Room*. Greenwillow, 1981.

Lively, Penelope. *The Ghost of Thomas Kempe*. Dutton, 1973.

MacDonald, Roby Edmond. *The Ghosts of Austwick Manor*. Atheneum, 1982.

MacKellar, William. *A Ghost around the House*. David McKay, 1970.

Mahy, Margaret. *The Haunting*. Atheneum, 1982.

Martin, Bill and John Archambault. *The Ghost-Eye Tree*. Holt, Rinehart & Winston, 1985.

Mayne, William. *It*. Greenwillow, 1978.

McGinnis, Lila Sprague. *The Ghost Alarm*. Hastings, 1989.

_____. *The Ghost Upstairs*. Hastings, 1982.

McKillip, Patricia. *The House on Parchment Street*. Atheneum, 1974.

Pearce, Philippa. *Tom's Midnight Garden*. Dell, 1979.

Peck, Richard. *Blossom Culp and the Sleep of Death*. Delacorte, 1986.

_____. *The Dreadful Future of Blossom Culp*. Delacorte, 1983.

_____. *The Ghost Belonged to Me*. Viking, 1975.

_____. *Ghosts I Have Been*. Viking, 1977.

Prelutsky, Jack. *The Headless Horseman Rides Tonight*. Greenwillow, 1980.

Snyder, Zilpha. *The Headless Cupid*. Atheneum, 1971.

_____. *The Truth about Stone Hollow*. Atheneum, 1975.

Stahl, Ben. *Blackbeard's Ghost*. Houghton Mifflin, 1965.

Wallin, Luke. *The Slavery Ghosts*. Bradbury, 1983.

Westall, Robert. *The Scarecrows*. Greenwillow, 1981.

Wibberley, Leonard. *The Crime of Martin Coverly*. Farrar, Straus & Giroux, 1980.

Wright, Betty Ren. *Christina's Ghost*. Holiday House, 1985.

_____. *The Dollhouse Murders*. Holiday House, 1983.

Grandparents

Grandparents are very special people in extended families. Some children live near enough to their grandparents and are able to have a meaningful relationship. Others live too far away to see their grandparents often and still others may not have living grandparents. For this celebration of grandparents begin by identifying the situation of the children and their grandparents. Set up a grandparents corner. On the bulletin board feature pictures of each child's grandparents. Use a map to locate the cities and towns where their grandparents live or lived during their lives. Encourage children to write letters to their grandparents, to interview their parents about their parents (the child's grandparents), and to write brief biographical profiles of their grandparents. The collected writings could be made into personal or class books featuring "Our Grandparents." During all of these activities be sure to include time to read and share the many books that deal with the child-grandparent, such as those on the following list. Design a special day to honor grandparents or older friends (stand-in grandparents). Invite grandparents to come to school to eat lunch with their grandchildren. Hold an afternoon read-in where the grandparents read to the children and the children recite poems and choral readings for the assembled grandparents. Have children interview grandparents and gather information about their lives in order that they might write a story about their grandparents. They can then make the story into a book, add photographs, bind, and give the book as a gift.

Booklist — Grandparents

Abercrombie, Barbara. *Cat-Man's Daughter*. Harper & Row, 1981.

Bartoli, Jennifer. *Nonna*. Harvey House, 1975.

Beattie, Ann. *Spectacles*. Workman, 1985.

Blue, Rose. *Grandma Didn't Wave Back*. Illustrated by Ted Lewin. Watts, 1972.

Burningham, John. *Granpa*. Crown, 1984.

Clifford, Eth. *The Remembering Box*. Houghton Mifflin, 1985.

_____. *The Rocking Chair Rebellion*. Houghton Mifflin, 1978.

Clymer, Eleanor. *The Get-Away Car*. Dutton, 1978.

Coutant, Helen. *First Snow*. Knopf, 1974.

dePaola, Tomie. *Nana Upstairs and Nana Downstairs*. Putnam, 1973.

_____. *Now One Foot, Now the Other*. Putnam, 1981.

_____. *Watch Out for the Chicken Feet in Your Soup*. Prentice-Hall, 1974.

Farber, Norma. *How Does It Feel to Be Old?* Dutton, 1979.

Flournoy, Valerie. *The Patchwork Quilt*. Dutton, 1985.

Gauch, Patricia Lee. *Grandpa and Me*. Coward, McCann & Geoghegan, 1972.

Greenfield, Eloise. *Grandmama's Joy*. Illustrated by Carole Byard. Philomel, 1980.

Griffith, Helen V. *Georgia's Music*. Illustrated by James Stevenson. Greenwillow, 1986.

_____. *Granddaddy's Place*. Illustrated by James Stevenson. Greenwillow, 1987.

Guernsey, JoAnn Bren. *Journey to Almost There*. Clarion, 1985.

Hall, Donald. *The Man Who Lived Alone*. Illustrated by Mary Azarian. David R. Godine, 1984.

Haller, Danita Ross. *Not Just Any Ring*. Knopf, 1982.

Hanson, June Andrea. *Winter of the Owl*. Macmillan, 1980.

Hicks, Clifford B. *Pop and Peter Potts*. Holt, Rinehart & Winston, 1984.

Holl, Kristi. *Just Like a Real Family*. Atheneum, 1983.

_____. *The Rose beyond the Wall*. Atheneum, 1985.

Irwin, Hadley. *The Lilith Summer*. Feminist Press, 1979.

_____. *What about Grandma?* Atheneum, 1983.

Jackson, Louise A. *Grandpa Had a Windmill, Grandma Had a Churn*. Parents, 1977.

Jukes, Mavis. *Blackberries in the Dark*. Illustrated by Thomas B. Allen. Knopf, 1985.

Kirk, Barbara. *Grandpa, Me and Our House in the Tree*. Macmillan, 1978.

Lapp, Eleanor J. *In the Morning Mist*. Albert Whitman, 1978.

Lasky, Kathryn. *I Have Four Names for My Grandfather*. Little, Brown, 1976.

Lowry, Lois. *Anastasia Again*. Houghton Mifflin, 1981.

Lundgren, Max. *Matt's Grandfather*. Illustrated by Fibber Hald. Putnam, 1972.

MacLachlan, Patricia. *Through Grandpa's Eyes*. Harper & Row, 1980.

Miles, Miska. *Annie and the Old One*. Little, Brown, 1971.

Nixon, Joan Lowery. *The Gift*. Macmillan, 1983.

Numeroff, Laura Joffe. *Does Grandma Have an Elmo Elephant Kit?* Greenwillow, 1980.

Raynor, Dorka. *Grandparents around the World*. Albert Whitman, 1977.

Root, Phyllis and Carol A. Marron. *Gretchen's Grandma*. Raintree, 1983.

Rylant, Cynthia. *When I Was Young in the Mountains*. Illustrated by Diane Goode. Dutton, 1982.

Seuss, Dr. *You're Only Old Once*. Random House, 1986.

Smith, Robert Kimmel. *The War with Grandpa*. Delacorte, 1984.

Stevens, Carla. *Anna, Grandpa, and the Big Storm*. Illustrated by Margot Tomes. Clarion, 1982.

Stevenson, James. *Grandpa's Great City Tour*. Greenwillow, 1983.

Streich, Corrine. *Grandparents' Houses: Poems about Grandparents*. Greenwillow, 1984.

Tolan, Stephanie S. *Grandpa and Me*. Scribner, 1978.

Vigna, Judith. *Grandma without Me*. Albert Whitman, 1984.

Voigt, Cynthia. *Dicey's Song*. Atheneum, 1983.

Williams, Barbara. *Kevin's Grandma*. Illustrated by Kay Chorao. Dutton, 1975.

Williams, Vera B. *A Chair for My Mother*. Greenwillow, 1982.

Worth, Richard. *You'll Be Old Someday, Too*. Watts, 1986.

Zolotow, Charlotte. *My Grandson Lew*. Illustrated by William Pene du Bois. Harper & Row, 1974.

H IS FOR HALLOWEEN, HANDICAPPED, HATS, AND HOSPITALS

Halloween and Scary Things

Halloween is an exciting and fun holiday. The following books will help play on the basic theme. Use books from the Fears and Scary Things booklist (see index) to provide additional reading material for this holiday. Provide a varied focus for the traditional Halloween costume parade. Start weeks early and encourage children to create their own costumes based on favorite book characters.

Booklist—Halloween, Witches, and Things

Adams, Adrienne. *A Woggle of Witches*. Atheneum, 1971.

Bang, Betsy. *The Old Woman and the Red Pumpkin: A Bengali Folk Tale*. Macmillan, 1975.

Bang, Molly. *The Goblins Giggle and Other Stories*. Scribner, 1973.

Barth, Edna. *Jack O'Lantern*. Illustrated by Paul Galdone. Clarion, 1974.

Bond, Felicia. *The Halloween Performance*. Harper & Row, 1983.

Bright, Robert. *Georgie's Halloween*. Doubleday, 1958.

Brown, Marc. *Arthur's Halloween*. Little, Brown, 1982.

_____. *Spooky Riddles*. Random House, 1983.

Bunting, Eve. *Ghost's Hour, Spook's Hour*. Clarion, 1987.

_____. *Scary, Scary Halloween*. Clarion, 1986.

Calhoun, Mary. *The Night the Monster Came*. Morrow, 1982.

Collins, Trish. *Grinkles: A Keen Halloween Story*. Watts, 1981.

Credle, Ellis. "The Preambulatin' Pumpkin." In *Clever Cook: A Concoction of Stories, Charms, Recipes and Riddles*, edited by Ellin Greene. Lothrop, Lee & Shepard, 1973.

Dillon, Barbara. *What Happened to Harry?* Morrow, 1982.

Finger, Charles G. "The Hungry Old Witch." In *Witches, Witches, Witches*, compiled by Helen Hoke. Watts, 1958.

Gantos, Jack. *Rotten Ralph's Trick or Treat!* Houghton Mifflin, 1986.

Gorey, Edward, editor. *The Haunted Looking Glass*. Random, 1959.

Hardendorff, Jeanne B. *The Bed Just So*. Four Winds, 1975.

_____. *Witches, Wit and a Werewolf*. Lippincott, 1971.

Hoban, Lillian. *Arthur's Halloween Costume*. Harper & Row, 1984.

Hoke, Helen, editor. *Spooks, Spooks, Spooks*. Watts, 1966.

Hopkins, Lee Bennett. *Hey-How for Halloween*. Harcourt Brace Jovanovich, 1974.

Howe, Deborah and James Howe. *Bunnicula*. Atheneum, 1980.

Howe, James. *Howliday Inn*. Atheneum, 1982.

Jack, Adrienne. *Witches and Witchcraft*. Watts, 1980.

Kahn, Joan, editor. *Some Things Strange and Sinister*. Harper & Row, 1973.

Levy, Elizabeth. *Dracula Is a Pain in the Neck*. Harper & Row, 1983.

Martin, Bill, Jr. and John Archambault. *The Ghost-Eye Tree*. Holt, Rinehart & Winston, 1985.

Merriam, Eve. *Halloween ABC*. Macmillan, 1987.

Nevins, Dan. *Creepy Creatures*. Watermill Press, 1982.

Prelutsky, Jack. *Nightmares*. Greenwillow, 1976.

Ross, Tony. *I'm Coming to Get You!* Dial, 1984.

Schwartz, Alvin. *In a Dark, Dark Room and Other Scary Stories*. Harper & Row, 1984.

Stevenson, James. *That Terrible Halloween Night!* Greenwillow, 1980.

Titherington, Jeanne. *Pumpkin Pumpkin*. Greenwillow, 1986.

Wilkins, Mary E. *The Pumpkin Giant*. Retold by Ellin Greene. Lothrop, Lee & Shepard, 1970.

Williams, Linda. *The Little Old Lady Who Was Not Afraid of Anything*. Crowell, 1986.

Handicapped—Stories with Hope

Share some of the following information about successful handicapped people. Discuss types of handicaps and how those handicaps might affect a person's life and success. If possible, contact local agencies to see if there are people in your community who are handicapped and can share with your class or group information about their efforts and successes. Then read and discuss some of the titles in the booklist. Intermediate or middle school students will be able to read the titles independently. Other children may enjoy the titles as a read aloud.

Information about Handicapped People

World-renowned poet, author, and television producer Maya Angelou was so emotionally disturbed as a youngster (as a result of a rape and subsequent killing of her rapist) that she did not talk for several years. She went on to become a noted Broadway star, writer, television producer, poet, and public speaker. Her autobiographical works, the first being *I Know Why the Caged Bird Sings*, have been widely acclaimed for their literary quality.

Edward Lear overcame a physical handicap to begin a career in painting birds and animals. He became known for his nonsense verses and landscape paintings. He is known for popularizing the limerick verse form.

Franklin D. Roosevelt is the only man to be elected president of the United States four times. He served while in a wheel chair. His legs had been paralyzed by polio. Senator John East is also paralyzed because of polio.

Gilbert Ramirez, a New York Supreme Court justice is blind, as is a successful computer programmer Robert LaGrone, who works for IBM. Ray Charles, a famous musician and vocalist, also achieved success even though he was blinded by a childhood case of glaucoma. Homer, a famous poet of ancient Greece, was also blind.

Al Capp, the creator of the Lil' Abner cartoon, had just one leg. Jay J. Armes became a top private eye despite having no hands.

Other handicaps have not kept success from coming for other determined individuals. Kitty O'Neil is a stunt person who has broken many land and water speed records. She is deaf. Mel Tillis overcame a severe stuttering problem to become a popular country and western singer. Anne Glenn, the wife of astronaut and senator John Glenn, has overcome a similar speech problem to allow her to speak in public.

Albert Einstein did not speak until he was four years old. His teachers felt he was too slow to ever accomplish anything of value. Thomas Edison was sent home from school because of deficient mental capabilities. The school staff felt that he had reached his potential. They thought he was "too slow."

Theodore Roosevelt had poor vision and suffered from a severe case of asthma. Napoleon Bonaparte, one of the greatest military strategists in the history of the world, is believed to have suffered from epilepsy.

Douglas Bader was a pilot when he lost both legs in a flying accident. He continued in the air service and went on to become a top ace in the Battle of Britain during World War II. Later he golfed with a handicap of seven.

If these people can make it so can others. The following books are fictional stories about people dealing with their handicap. Extend the theme of success and determination by researching the lives of the people mentioned in the previous information and then relate those struggles to those depicted in the fictional accounts of a handicapped person's life. Discuss how realistic the stories are and how all of this relates to the real world in which we live.

Booklist—Handicapped in Fiction

Brancato, Robin. *Winning*. Knopf, 1977.
  A football game accident results in spinal injuries for Gary Madden. Gary must deal first with the shock of the injury, later with the anger and depression; and finally he must learn to accept and get on with his rehabilitation.

Carrick, Carol. *Stay Away from Simon*. Houghton Mifflin, 1985.
  Simon is retarded and in the early nineteenth century people thought retarded people were somehow dangerous. When Simon manages to save two children from getting lost in the storm, the children realize how wrong their ideas had been.

Coleman, Hila Crayder. *Accident*. Morrow, 1980.
  Adam has enormous guilt to face when Jenny, a passenger on the motorcycle he was driving, is paralyzed. Jenny must work through her own anger and hopelessness to bring her life together once again.

Cook, Marjorie. *To Walk on Two Feet*. Westminster, 1978.
  Fifteen-year-old Carrie Karns struggles to accept herself as a girl with legs amputated below the knees. She refuses a wheelchair or prostheses. She does cope and comes to accept her situation and make the best of it.

Corcoran, Barbara. *Child of the Morning*. Atheneum, 1982.
  Susan is diagnosed as having epilepsy. At first she must deal with the "little spells" her family doctors dismissed as not indicative of anything. And after the diagnosis, Susan must deal with the reality of her situation.

Gerson, Corinne. *Passing Through*. Dial, 1978.
  Fifteen-year-old Liz comes to grips with her brother's suicide when she helps Sam Benedict, a young man with cerebral palsy. Both learn to adjust to their situation.

Gilson, Jamie. *Do Bananas Chew Gum?* Lothrop, Lee & Shepard, 1980.
  Finally in sixth grade Sam is tested and found to have a learning disability. He must try to put behind him all the years of feeling dumb and different.

Gould, Marilyn. *Golden Daffodils*. Addison-Wesley, 1982; Harper & Row, 1982.
  Daffodils were a symbol of hope and beauty to Janis. This fall Janis needed hope more than ever. She had cerebral palsy and she was starting a new school and she wanted to be "just another student" at that school. She does meet good friends, including Barney Fuchs, and her cousin Rhoda is close at hand. But Cheryl and Garth set out deliberately to be nasty and unkind to Janis. Janis and her friends triumph but not before some moving episodes.

Gould, Marilyn. *The Twelfth of June*. Lippincott, 1986.
In this sequel to *Golden Daffodils* the friendship of Janis and Barney Fuchs continues to develop.

Groshkopf, Bernice. *Shadow in the Sun*. Atheneum, 1975.
Thirteen-year-old Fran becomes a summer companion to Wilma, a partially paralyzed girl confined to a wheelchair. Wilma is a bitter child who finds herself faced with danger and the realization that she must learn to live the life she now has.

Hall, Lynn. *Half the Battle*. Scribner, 1982.
Loren is resentful of the attention his blind brother, Blair, is getting as they both prepare for a 100-mile endurance race with their horses. Loren feels he is doing much of the preparation and in many ways carrying Blair along. Loren must deal with his relationship with Blair, and Blair must come to grips with his dependency on Loren's help.

Hautzig, Deborah. *Second Star to the Right*. Greenwillow, 1981.
Leslie's feelings about herself and her mother bring confusion. She finally concludes that she will only be happy when she is thin. Anorexia nervosa is the result.

Jones, Rebecca Castaldi. *Angie and Me*. Macmillan, 1981.
Juvenile rheumatoid arthritis plagues Jenna. But with the help of a terminally ill friend, Jenna does come to terms with her affliction. She is determined not to be known as "the crippled kid."

Kerr, M. E. *Little, Little*. Harper & Row, 1981.
Born a dwarf complicates and frustrates Little, Little. But she is determined that her dwarf condition will not be defeating. Two dwarfs vie for the heart of Little, Little who is an heiress tired of being treated like a doll.

Kingman, Lee. *Head over Wheels*. Houghton Mifflin, 1978.
An automobile accident forever changes the lives of identical twins. One emerges as a quadriplegic and the other suffers guilt for being the uninjured person. Both must adjust and establish a new life.

Levison, Nancy Smiler. *World of Her Own*. Harvey House, 1981.
Leaving her safe secure world with other deaf children, Anne becomes frightened and angry when she is told that she will be mainstreamed into a regular public school. With frustration and pain, Anne makes friends and soon is at home in her expanded world.

Peck, Robert Newton. *Clunie*. Knopf, 1979.
One teenage boy assaults and taunts Clunie, but the second boy does care for her feelings. Clunie is retarded but feels the hurt of being shunned for something she cannot change.

Peterson, Jeanne Whitehouse. *I Have a Sister—My Sister Is Deaf*. Harper & Row, 1977.
Sisters define their relationship as one child sees what the other cannot hear.

Riskind, Mary. *Apple Is My Sign*. Houghton Mifflin, 1981.
Set in the early 1900s this is the story of ten-year-old Harry Berger who is deaf, as is the rest of his family. His family sends him to a school for the deaf in Philadelphia. The first of the family to go away to school, Harry finds a whole new world opened to him.

Sachs, Elizabeth Ann. *Just Like Always*. Atheneum, 1981.
Sclerosis causes Janie to be hospitalized for treatment. She and her hospital roommate refuse to harness their mischief making, even when both are put into full body casts.

Terris, Susan. *Wings and Roots*. Farrar, Straus & Giroux, 1982.
A four-year friendship results when Jeannie West volunteers to help in a post-polio ward and meets polio victim Kit Hayden. Both learn to deal with challenge and risks.

Wartski, Maureen Crane. *My Brother Is Special*. Westminster, 1979.
Noni's brother is retarded. She cannot understand why some people consider retarded people as "creatures from another planet." Noni helps her brother toward a fulfilling life.

Hats Everywhere

Begin the Hats Everywhere unit by brainstorming with the children to make a list of all the types of hats they may know about, for example, baseball caps, cowboy hats, hard hats, uniform hats, top hats. After a list is generated and recorded ask children to choose one of the hats, draw a picture of the hat, and, finally, write a description of the hat. Encourage children to bring in examples of the hats on the list. If they bring in types of hats that are not on the list, add the type to the list. Then read one of the hat books from the following booklist. I prefer to begin with Ron Roy's *Whose Hat Is That?* or Margaret Miller's *Whose Hat?* They are excellent models depicting various hats and the people who wear them. Follow by reading a book that incorporates a hat as an integral part of the story. Once the topic of hats has been extended to the concept of hats in stories, make hat books available for immersion reading.

Booklist—Hats

Blos, Joan. *Martin's Hats*. Morrow pb, 1987.

Chambers, Aidan. "The Irishman's Hat." In *Funny Folk: A Book of Comic Tales*, illustrated by Trevor Stubley. Collins, 1976.

Corney, Estelle. *Pa's Top Hat*. Deutsch, 1980.

Couldridge, Alan. *The Hat Book*. Prentice-Hall, 1980.

Courlander, Harold. "The Hatshaking Dance." In *The Hatshaking Dance, and Other Tales from the Gold Coast*. Harcourt, Brace & World, 1957.

Drawson, Blair. *I Like Hats!* Scholastic-TAB, 1977.

Frances, Marian. *The Christmas Santa Almost Missed*. Troll Associates, 1970.

Gelman, Rita Golden. *Hello Cat You Need a Hat*. Scholastic, 1979.

Geringer, Laura. *A Three Hat Day*. Pictures by Arnold Lobel. Harper & Row, 1985.

Goodall, John S. *Paddy's New Hat*. Atheneum, 1980.

Hart, Johan. "The Magic Cap." In *Laughing Matter*, edited by Helen R. Smith. Scribner, 1949.

Keats, Ezra Jack. *Jennie's Hat*. Harper & Row, 1966.

Leach, Maria. "Holding Down the Hat." In *Noodles, Nitwits, and Numskulls*. Collins/Philomel, 1961.

Lear, Edward. *The Pelican Chorus and The Quangle Wangle's Hat*. Viking, 1981.

Lee, Tanya. "Hats to Disappear With." In *Floating Clouds, Floating Dreams: Favorite Asian Folktales*, compiled by I. K. Junne. Doubleday, 1974.

Levoy, Myron. *The Magic Hat of Mortimer Wintergreen*. Harper & Row, 1988. (a novel)

Lobel, Arnold. "The Hats." In *Days with Frog and Toad*. Harper & Row, 1979.

Miller, Margaret. *Whose Hat?* Greenwillow, 1988.

Munari, Bruno. *Jimmy Has Lost His Cap, Where Can It Be?* World, 1959.

Nodset, Joan L. *Who Took the Farmer's Hat?* Harper & Row, 1963.

Rey, H. A. *Curious George Rides a Bike*. Scholastic, 1952.

Rice, Inez. *The March Wind*. Lothrop, Lee & Shepard, 1957.

Robison, Deborah. *Anthony's Hat*. Scholastic, 1976.

Roy, Ron. *Whose Hat Is That?* Illustrated by Rosmarie Hausherr. Clarion, 1987.

Seuss, Dr. *The 500 Hats of Bartholomew Cubbins*. Vanguard, 1938; Random House, 1989.

Silverstein, Shel. "Hat." In *Where the Sidewalk Ends*. Harper & Row, 1974.

Slobodkina, Esphyr. *Caps for Sale*. W. R. Scott, 1947.

Stepian, Jan. *The Cat Who Wore a Pot on Her Head*. Scholastic, 1967.

Uchida, Yoshiko. "The Magic Listening Cap." In *The Magic Listening Cap: More Folktales from Japan*. Harcourt, Brace & World, 1955.

_____. "New Year's Hats for the Statues." In *The Sea of Gold, and Other Tales from Japan*. Scribner, 1965.

Ungerer, Tomi. *The Hat*. Parents, 1970.

Wood, Joyce. *Grandmother Lucy and Her Hats*. Atheneum, 1969.

Culminate the unit by creating special hats to wear. Hold a Hat Day where everyone in the school or library wears his or her favorite hat. Write about the hat: Where was the hat obtained? On what occasions is the hat worn? Why is the hat so special? Use plain straw hats to create a fancy hat. Make a hat mural, using pictures of hats cut from magazines and newspapers. Focus on the types of hats worn by people in different occupations. What type of hat does a nurse wear? a construction worker? a police officer? a letter carrier? a football player? This could make an appropriate focus during a study of community workers.

A similar career activity could focus on different types of shoes worn by people in various occupations. Start the unit off with Elizabeth Winthrop's *Shoes* (Harper & Row, 1986) or Ron Roy's *Whose Shoes Are These?* (Clarion, 1988).

Hospitals and Children

After a hospital class visit these books will be especially meaningful. The Colliers title and the Sobol title will be helpful if children are scheduled for a visit to the hospital.

Booklist — Hospitals and Children

Beame, Rona. *Emergency!* Messner, 1977.

Colliers, James. *Danny Goes to the Hospital.* Grossett, 1970.

Howe, James. *The Hospital Book.* Crown, 1981.

Marino, Barbara. *Eric Needs Stitches.* Addison-Wesley, 1979.

Rey, Margaret. *Curious George Goes to the Hospital.* Houghton Mifflin, 1966.

Rowland, Florence. *Let's Go to the Hospital.* Putnam, 1968.

Sharmat, Marjorie. *I Want Mama.* Harper & Row, 1974.

Sobol, Harriet. *Jeff's Hospital Book.* Walck, 1975.

Weber, Alfons. *Elizabeth Gets Well.* Crowell, 1970.

I IS FOR INVENTORS AND ICE CREAM

Inventors and Inventions

Choose a month to honor the many inventors who have contributed to our quality of life. Most information will be gathered by researching individual inventors in the biographical section of your public or school library or in the encyclopedias. A good resource about inventions is *Steven Caney's Invention Book* (Workman, 1985). Another source is Norman Richards's *Dreamers and Doers: Inventors Who Changed Our World* (Atheneum, 1984). Among those inventors which might be researched are

- Alexander Graham Bell, inventor of the telephone (1876)

- Clarence Birdseye, inventor of frozen food (1925)

- Ladislao and George Biro, inventors of the modern ballpoint pen (1938)

- Chester Carlson, inventor of the xerographic copier (1938)

- George Washington Carver, inventor of over 100 items made from peanuts (late 1800s and early 1900s)

- Samuel Colt, inventor of the revolver gun (1836)

- Thomas Edison, inventor of the electric light (1879)

- Benjamin Franklin, inventor of bifocals (1780)

- Robert Goddard, inventor of liquid-propellant rocket (1926)

- Chester Greenwood, inventor of earmuffs (1873)

- Johannes Gutenberg, inventor of printing from movable type, which made books more accessible (1447)

- Margaret Knight, inventor of the bag-folding machine (1870)

- Kirkpatrick Macmillan, inventor of a pedal-powered bicycle (1839)

- Jan Ernst Matzeliger, inventor of a shoemaking machine (1883)

- Elijah McCoy, inventor of the lubricator cup for lubricating machines (1872)

- Garrett Morgan, inventor of the traffic signal (1923)

- Eli Whitney, inventor of the cotton gin (1793)

- Orville and Wilbur Wright, inventors of the engine-powered airplane (1903)

After researching information about inventions and inventors plan an Inventor's Day. Create your own inventions, movable school lockers, self-sharpening pencils, and other new ideas to make your life easier. Make a prototype if you can and display it on Inventor's Day.

Booklist — Inventors and Inventions

Asimov, Isaac. *Break Through in Science*. Houghton Mifflin, 1959.

Bachman, Frank P. *Great Inventors and Their Inventions*. American Book Company, 1941.

Blow, Michael and Robert P. Multhauf. *Men of Science and Invention*. American Heritage, 1960.

Buehr, Walter. *The Story of the Wheel*. Putnam, 1960.

Caney, Steven. *Steven Caney's Invention Book*. Workman, 1985.

Cooke, David. *Inventions That Made History*. Putnam, 1986.

Cooper, Chris. *How Everyday Things Work*. Facts on File, 1984.

Evans, I. O. *Inventors of the World*. Warne, 1962.

Garrison, Webb. *Why Didn't I Think of That?* Prentice-Hall, 1977.

Keller, Charles. *The Best of Rube Goldberg*. Prentice-Hall, 1970.

Montgomery, Elizabeth. *The Story behind Great Inventions*. Dodd Mead, 1944.

Murphy, Jim. *Guess Again: More Weird and Wacky Inventions*. Bradbury, 1986.

_____. *Weird and Wacky Inventions*. Crown, 1978.

Richards, Norman. *Dreamers and Doers: Inventors Who Changed Our World*. Atheneum, 1984.

Taylor, Barbara. *Weekly Reader Presents Be an Inventor*. Harcourt Brace Jovanovich, 1987.

Waller, Leslie. *American Inventions*. Holt, Rinehart & Winston, 1963.

Chris Winn and Jeremy Beadle have created a humorous book *Rodney Rootle's Grown-Up Grappler and Other Treasures from the Museum of Outlawed Inventions* (Little, Brown, 1982). The book details collections of inventions which have been "designed by kids but banned by adults."

Ice Cream

Make ice cream in the classroom. Concoct your own flavors and hold an ice cream tasting party. Enjoy a warm day with a cool treat or make ice cream as part of a Summer in March celebration. And while the treat is being enjoyed, enjoy these stories and poems that feature ice cream.

Booklist—Ice Cream

Cobb, Vicki. *The Scoop on Ice Cream*. Little, Brown, 1985.

deRegniers, Beatrice Schenk. *How Joe the Bear and Sam the Mouse Got Together*. Illustrated by Brinton Turkle. Parents, 1965; Scholastic, 1987.

Krensky, Stephan. *Scoop after Scoop*. Illustrated by Richard Rosenblum. Atheneum, 1986.

Merriam, Eve. "A Vote for Vanilla." In *It Doesn't Always Have to Rhyme*. Illustrated by Malcolm Spooner. Atheneum, 1964. (poem)

Prelutsky, Jack. "Bleezer's Ice Cream." In *The New Kid on the Block*. Illustrated by James Stevenson. Greenwillow, 1984. (poem)

Silverstein, Shel. "Eighteen Flavors." In *Where the Sidewalk Ends*. Harper & Row, 1974. (poem)

Make a graph of children's favorite ice cream flavors. The graph could be a bar or line graph or a picture graph. Cut out a large paper cone for each flavor of ice cream to be included in the survey. For each vote a specific flavor receives, top the cone with a cut out scoop of ice cream. The relative size of the ice cream cones will indicate the popularity of the various flavors. Later use the same cone and scoop patterns to make a reading chart. For each book read add a scoop of ice cream with the title and author of the book noted on the scoop shape. This could be a class ice cream cone representing the books read aloud in the classroom or the ice cream chart could represent books read by individuals or small groups.

Research information about the origin and popularity of this concoction (see the Cobb and Krensky titles). Ice cream is said to be one of the most popular and nourishing of all foods. In the United States alone hundreds of millions of gallons of ice cream are produced each year. The first ice cream is thought to have been made in Italy in 1550. It was first eaten in the United States in the early 1700s. Thomas Jefferson is thought to have made his own ice cream and to have served it in a warm pastry shell. It was still a rare treat when Dolly Madison (wife of President James Madison) first served the delicacy in the White House in 1809. For years the recipe was a closely guarded secret of expert chefs. However, in 1851, Jacob Fussell set up the first ice cream factory in Baltimore. But it was not until the 1900s that ice cream became a national favorite. The cone is popularly believed to have first appeared in St. Louis at the Louisiana Purchase Exposition in 1904.

J IS FOR JEALOUSY AND JEWISH TRADITIONS

Jealousy

One of the most human emotions between siblings, friends, and acquaintances is jealousy. Sometimes the jealousy is the result of competition, sometimes envy, sometimes both. The theme of family relationships might include a discussion of jealousy among family members especially among brothers and sisters. Discuss the origin and meaning of phrases such as "green with envy" and "catty remarks." Locate reference sources for the origin of these phrases by using the subjects WORD ORIGIN and ETYMOLOGY in the card catalog of your school or public library.

Booklist—Jealousy

Bottner, Barbara. *Big Boss! Little Boss!* Pantheon, 1978.

Brandenberg, Franz. *I Wish I Was Sick, Too!* Greenwillow, 1976.

Brown, Marc. *Arthur's Baby*. Little, Brown, 1987.

Cleary, Beverly. *Ramona and Her Mother*. Dell, 1979.

Dragonwagon, Crescent. *I Hate My Brother Harry*. Harper & Row, 1983.

Hall, Lynn. *Half the Battle*. Scribner, 1982.

Hanson, Joan. *I Don't Like Timmy*. Carolrhoda, 1983.

Jones, Penelope. *I Didn't Want to Be Nice*. Bradbury, 1977.

Kingman, Lee. *The Year of the Raccoon*. Houghton Mifflin, 1966.

Kroll, Steven. *Loose Tooth*. Holiday House, 1984.

Paterson, Katherine. *Jacob Have I Loved*. Crowell, 1980.

Wells, Rosemary. *Don't Spill It Again, James*. Dial, 1977.

Zemach, Margot. *To Hilda for Helping*. Farrar, Straus & Giroux, 1977.

Zolotow, Charlotte. *It's Not Fair*. Harper & Row, 1978.

Jewish Traditions

Jewish traditional items such as menorahs, seder plates, and mezuzahs can be displayed with explanations of their tradition and use. An interest in Jewish history and tradition could be sparked by using picture books as part of the introductory segment of this focus.

Booklist—Jewish History (a beginning) Picture Books

Cohen, Barbara. *Gooseberries to Oranges*. Lothrop, Lee & Shepard, 1982.

Hirsh, Marilyn. *Rabbi and the Twenty-Nine Witches*. Holiday, 1976.

Singer, Isaac Bashevis. *Why Noah Chose the Dove*. Farrar, Straus & Giroux, 1974.

Zemach, Margot. *It Could Always Be Worse*. Farrar, Straus & Giroux, 1976.

Themes in Jewish folk literature reflect the common themes and emotions (jealousy, greed, courage, and joy) found in folklore all over the world. The popular Cinderella story has a Jewish version. Howard Schwartz has edited a collection of Jewish folk stories, *Elijah's Violin and Other Stories* (Harper/Jewish Publication Society, 1983). One of the stories in the Schwartz collection is a folk story which can be compared with versions of the Cinderella story from other cultures. A list of twenty-six variant Cinderella stories and detailed comparison notes for Cinderella and its variants are included in *An Author a Month (for Pennies)* by Sharron McElmeel (Libraries Unlimited, 1988). That book contains several groups of folktales for critical reading activities. Those groups could be utilized with other stories from Schwartz's collection of Jewish stories. Refer to the index in this book for additional critical reading booklists.

Paper cutting has been a popular Jewish folk craft for the past few hundred years. Paper cuts have been used as holiday decorations, as adornment for marriage contracts, as amulets, and as wall hangings. Jewish paper cutting and other Jewish folk art are contained in a book edited by Sharon Strassfeld and Michael Strassfeld. The book, *The Second Jewish Catalog* (Jewish Publication Society, 1976) will provide ample information to conduct a craft session focusing on this traditional folk craft.

Poetry is a powerful vehicle to help young people see the similarities and differences in the experiences of many different people. Poetry, such as the following, helps to bridge the gap between culturally diverse peoples.

Poetry

Zim, Jacob, editor. *I Never Saw Another Butterfly: Children's Drawings and Poems from Terezin Concentration Camp, 1942-1944*. McGraw-Hill, 1964.

_____. *My Shalom, My Peace: Paintings and Poems by Jewish and Arab Children*. McGraw-Hill, 1975.

Books of fiction and nonfiction featuring Jewish protagonists and information about the Jewish people can be located by using the card catalog in your school or public library. For starters try locating and sharing the books on the following booklist.

Booklist—Jewish People in Fiction and Nonfiction

Adler, David A. *Our Golda: The Story of Golda Meir*. Illustrated by Donna Ruff. Viking, 1984.

Baldwin, Margaret. *The Boys Who Saved the Children*. Messner, 1981.

Bamberger, David, adapter. *My People: Abba Eban's History of the Jews*. 2 volumes. Behrman House, 1978; 1979. Vol. 1: Genesis to 1776. Vol. 2: From 18th Century to Present Day.

Brodie, Deborah, editor. *Stories My Grandfather Should Have Told Me*. Illustrated by Carmela Tal Baron. Hebrew Publishing Co., 1977.

Frank, Anne. *The Diary of a Young Girl*. Modern Library, 1958.

Ish-Kishor, Shulamith. *A Boy of Old Prague*. Illustrated by Ben Shahn. Scholastic, 1980.

Meir, Mira. *Alina: A Russian Girl Comes to Israel*. Translated by Zeva Shapiro. Illustrated with photos by Yael Rozen. Jewish Publication Society, 1982.

Meltzer, Milton, editor. *The Jewish Americans: A History in Their Own Words, 1650-1950.* Crowell, 1982.

Mezey, Robert, editor. *Poems from the Hebrew.* Harper & Row, 1973.

Singer, Isaac Bashevis. *When Shlemiel Went to Warsaw and Other Stories.* Translated by Singer and Elizabeth Shub. Illustrated by Margot Zemach. Farrar, Straus & Giroux, 1968.

Stadtler, Bea. *The Holocaust: A History of Courage and Resistance.* Illustrated by David Stone Martin. Behrman House, 1974.

Steinberg, Fannie. *Birthday in Kishinev.* Illustrated by Luba Hanuschak. Jewish Publication Society, 1978.

Taylor, Sydney. *All-of-a-Kind Family.* Illustrated by Helen John. Dell, 1982.

K IS FOR KITES, KELLOGG, AND KEATS

Kites

Use the kite theme to connect readers with Bill Peet's *Merle the High-Flying Squirrel* (Houghton Mifflin, 1974) or Mildred Pitts Walter's *Brother of the Wind* (Lothrop, Lee & Shepard, 1985). The Walter book is illustrated by Leo and Diane Dillon. Arnold Lobel included a story, "The Kite," in his book *Days with Frog and Toad* (Harper & Row, 1979).

Study the origin of kites and kite making. A kite is a device flown in the air at the end of a string. Many historians think that the Greeks invented the kite between 400 and 300 B.C. but the Chinese claim the invention as having been the idea of one of their generals, Han Sin, who invented the kite for use in warfare in 206 B.C.

Investigate the uses of kites, particularly in relation to the cloud experiments by Alexander Wilson and Thomas Melville in Scotland in 1749 and Benjamin Franklin's discovery of electricity in 1752. Kites were also used during World War II to send up radar reflectors, and in the early 1900s kites played an important role in the United States Weather Bureau's forecasts. Kites have been used to assist in the building of bridges, to send radio signals across the Atlantic, and to take photographs during wartime.

Explore the Chinese tradition of observing Kite Day. On that day, the ninth day of the ninth month, thousands of kites shaped like dragons, fishes, birds, and butterflies float over the cities and the countryside.

As a culmination of your kite activities hold your own Kite Day. Hold a kite tournament. Be sure to have two divisions: one for kites built from commercial kits and one for kites built from an original design.

Kellogg, Steven

Kellogg here refers to Steven Kellogg, an absolutely wonderful author and illustrator. A focus on Kellogg at any age level is almost a requirement. His books are excellent examples of books that can be read on many different levels of meaning. Kellogg is noted for using illustrations to lead the reader into his story before the text actually begins. Introduce Kellogg and his books to your students by showing the Weston Woods filmstrip *How a Picture Book Is Made: The Making of "The Island of the Skog" from Conception to Finished Book*. Set up an author corner and share as many of Kellogg's books as possible. Of special interest are his wonderfully imaginative detailed illustrations. Complete suggestions for a month-long focus on Steven Kellogg and his books can be found in Sharron McElmeel's *An Author a Month (for Pennies)* (Libraries Unlimited, 1988). Among the titles that are important to share are Kellogg's books featuring Pinkerton, his lovable but rowdy Harlequin Great Dane, and *The Island of the Skog* (Dial, 1977). He has also authored several books in his recent series focusing on tall tale heroes: *Johnny Appleseed* (Morrow, 1988); *Pecos Bill* (Morrow, 1986); and *Paul Bunyan* (Morrow, 1984). These titles will provide a springboard to a complete focus on folklore in the United States.

Keats, Ezra Jack

Another author and illustrator who deserves special recognition is Ezra Jack Keats. Born on March 11, 1916, he died of a heart attack on May 6, 1983. He lived his entire life in the New York area, and views of the streets of New York show up in many of his books. The store fronts, the street signs, graffiti, and posters were all part of his immediate surroundings and became part of all of his books. He became an artist when he was four years old. As he grew older children would follow him on the street and beg him to tell them a story. Even the tough kids in his Brooklyn neighborhood expressed subtle admiration for his work. His mother encouraged him to be an artist but his father thought he would starve. But Keats did become an artist. First he was a muralist and a painter and gradually he began to illustrate children's books. He illustrated thirty-three books for children, twenty-two of which he wrote. In 1967, Keats was the guest of honor of the Empress of Iran at the International Film Festival in Teheran. Seven years later Keats was the guest of honor at the opening of a children's roller skating rink in Tokyo, Japan. The rink has a plaque bearing his name. The rink was the result of the enthusiasm for skating generated by his book *Skates!* (Watts, 1973). His books have been translated into sixteen languages. Believing in the universality of characters, he felt that whether a character was black or white did not matter. Peter in his 1963 Caldecott Award-winning book *The Snowy Day* (Viking, 1962) is black, as are several of his other book characters. Long before Keats thought about creating books for children he clipped a series of photographs from a magazine. The photographs were of a small black child. He tacked the pictures on his wall. Twenty-two years later those photographs became the inspiration for the illustrations for *The Snowy Day*. Keats had been illustrating other people's books for ten years and there had never been a black child in those books as a hero. So when he felt confident enough to do his own book he resolved that his book's hero would be black. Peter, the hero of *The Snowy Day*, was the result. Peter later appeared in four other titles: *Whistle for Willie* (Viking, 1964), *Goggles* (Macmillan, 1969), *A Letter to Amy* (Harper & Row, 1968, Harper Trophy pb, 1984), and *Peter's Chair* (Harper & Row, 1967).

Keats is noted for his illustrations, which represent an acute ability to observe, and for his technique of combining paint and collage with a mixture of textures and brilliant colors.

Ezra Jack Keats is featured in a seventeen-minute Weston Woods Signature Collection film. The interview with Keats is followed by a film adaptation of *A Letter to Amy*. During the interview segment Keats describes the process he utilized to make the marbled background paper for his collage illustrations and how he found collage material that suggested new patterns and relationships to him. If you are able to share the Weston Woods film *Ezra Jack Keats*, be prepared to make collage illustrations. Those who view the film will be anxious to try their hand at collage making.

Make the marbleized background paper with oil paint and heavy art paper. Put the oil paint in a large pan of water. Swirl the colors around in the water. Do not try to mix too thoroughly. Put the top side of the paper onto the water's surface. Allow the paper surface to pick up some of the swirling paint. Dry the paper by laying it flat on the table. When the paper is thoroughly dry it may be used as the background paper for original collages.

Another alternative with a slightly different effect is to use chalk marbling. The advantage to this technique is the nonpermanent nature of the media. If oil paint is spilled on clothing the paint is almost impossible to remove; chalk is fairly easy to clean up. The materials needed for chalk marbleizing are: colored chalk, scissors, a pan or bowl, and white drawing paper. Fill the pan half full of cold water. Shave colored chalk dust onto the surface of the water using open scissors. While the chalk is floating on the water, lay a piece of white paper on the surface. Remove the paper and set aside for drying. The marbling should be sprayed with a fixative after drying. The fixative will help prevent the chalk from smearing. Commercial chalk fixatives are available but a very adequate substitute is hair spray. The cheaper varieties tend to do a better job. Use the marbleized paper as background for your own collages.

Many of Keat's books are available in nonprint format from Weston Woods. These filmstrips and films may be used in an author center and for special activities focusing on Ezra Jack Keats and his books. Share as many of his books as possible.

General Activities

1. Set up all available books by Keats.

2. Make large letters "Keen on Keats" for a bulletin board on which information about Keats and his books will be shared.

3. Make an acrostic poem about Amy, Peter, Archie, or the dog Willie.

4. Draw (or, better yet, make a collage) of a favorite book character from one of Keat's books.

Book Activities

Keats, Ezra Jack. *Apt. 3.* (Macmillan, 1971)

*   Invite a harmonica player to visit.

*   Stop reading at the point the boys enter the apartment; predict what is going to happen. Write your ending. Finish reading the story.

Keats, Ezra Jack. *Goggles.* (Macmillan, 1969)

*   Make some pretend goggles.

*   Draw a picture of your special hideout. Then read Beatrice Schenk deRegniers's *Little House of Your Own* (Harcourt, Brace & World, 1954); Dorothy Aldis's poem "Hiding," in *The Arbuthnot Anthology of Children's Literature*, edited by May Hill Arbuthnot et al., 113. 3rd ed. (Scott, Foresman, 1971); Arbuthnot's *Time for Poetry* (Scott, Foresman, 1968); or Myra Cohn Livingston's *I'm Hiding* (Harcourt, Brace & World, 1961).

Keats, Ezra Jack. *Hi Cat.* (Macmillan, 1970)

- Write a sequel; what will happen tomorrow?

- Make a list of ten reasons you would use on your parents to convince them that you need a cat as a pet.

Keats, Ezra Jack. *Jennie's Hat.* (Harper & Row, 1966)

- Have a hat parade.

- Extend the theme by reading other hats books.

Keats, Ezra Jack. *A Letter to Amy.* (Harper & Row, 1968)

- Write a letter to a friend and send it.

- Extend the theme of birthdays and birthday parties by using some of the book titles on the Birthdays booklist in this book.

Keats, Ezra Jack. *Maggie and the Pirate.* (Four Winds, 1969)

- Utilize the origami source on the Crafts booklist to help instruct in the art of paper folding. Paper folding could be used to create a pirate's hat.

- Investigate some of the famous pirates that actually lived. Famous pirates include the notorious Captain Jack Rackham or "Calico Jack"; Bartholomew Roberts or "Black Bart"; Captain Kidd; Edward Teach or "Blackbeard"; Stede Bonnet; Captain Greaves; Anne Bonney; and Mary Read.

- Discuss feelings and impressions about the pirate in this story.

Keats, Ezra Jack. *Pet Show.* (Macmillan, 1972)

- Hold a pet show.

- Read and discuss Steven Kellogg's *Can I Keep Him.* (Dial, 1971) or Kay Smith's *Parakeets and Peach Pies* (Parents, 1970).

Keats, Ezra Jack. *Peter's Chair.* (Harper & Row, 1967)

- Compare and contrast to several of the titles on the Families (and Siblings) or Jealousy booklist (see index).

- Make a class list that includes those things that are difficult for each of the students to share with siblings, for example, a special toy, a specific book.

Keats, Ezra Jack. *Whistle for Willie*. (Viking, 1966)

- Hold a whistling contest. Invite the school principal, the library director, or other adults.

- Read Jack Prelutsky's poem "Whistling" in his collection *Read-Aloud Rhymes for the Very Young* (Knopf, 1986).

L IS FOR LANGUAGE AND LIMERICKS

Language

Those who are comfortable with the basic elements of using our English language will begin to enjoy playing with the language. Books such as Fred Gwynne's *A Chocolate Moose for Dinner* (Windmill, 1976) and *The King Who Rained* (Windmill, 1970) will provide interesting word play. See the bookshelf entry for Gwynne's *A Chocolate Moose for Dinner* for additional activity suggestions. Collective nouns are always great fun; try Patricia Hooper's *A Bundle of Beasts*, illustrated by Mark Steele (Houghton Mifflin, 1987). Brian Wildsmith also illustrated several books focusing on collective nouns: *Brian Wildsmith's Birds* (Watts, 1967), *Brian Wildsmith's Fishes* (Watts, 1968), and *Brian Wildsmith's Wild Animals* (Watts, 1967).

Limericks

Edward Lear is the person generally credited with popularizing the limerick form of poetry. Read examples of limericks. Others, in addition to those listed below, may be located by using the indexes of available poetry anthologies. After many limericks have been read over a period of several days or weeks, discuss the form. Attempt to use the examples to generalize about the standard form for a limerick. (Limerick, a five-line nonsense poem. Lines 1, 2 and 5 are three measures long, and rhyme. Lines 3 and 4 are two measures long, and rhyme.) Then, in pairs, try writing some limericks.

Booklist—Limericks

Anonymous. "A Young Lady of Lynn." In *The Random House Book of Poetry for Children*. Selected by Jack Prelutsky. Illustrated by Arnold Lobel. Random House, 1983.

Bishop, Morris. "Hog-Calling Competition." In *The Random House Book of Poetry for Children*. Selected by Jack Prelutsky. Illustrated by Arnold Lobel. Random House, 1983.

Brewton, John E. and Lorraine A. Blackburn, editors. *They've Discovered a Head in the Box for the Bread and Other Laughable Limericks*. Illustrated by Fernando Krahn. Crowell, 1978.

Brewton, Sara and John E. Brewton, compilers. *Laughable Limericks*. Crowell, 1965.

Ciardi, John. *I Met a Man*. Illustrated by Robert Osborne. Houghton Mifflin, 1967.

deRegniers, Beatrice Schenk. *A Bunch of Poems and Verses*. Illustrated by Mary Jane Dunton. Clarion, 1977. (Several of the beginning poems in this book are examples of limericks.)

Gorey, Edward. "Number Nine, Penwiper Mews." In *The Random House Book of Poetry for Children*. Selected by Jack Prelutsky. Illustrated by Arnold Lobel. Random House, 1983.

Lear, Edward. "An Old Person of Ware." In *In Read-Aloud Rhymes for the Very Young*. Selected by Jack Prelutsky. Illustrated by Marc Brown. Knopf, 1986.

_____. "There Was an Old Man with a Beard." In *The Random House Book of Poetry for Children*. Selected by Jack Prelutsky. Illustrated by Arnold Lobel. Random House, 1983.

Livingston, Myra Cohn. *A Lollygag of Limericks*. Illustrated by Joseph Low. Atheneum, 1978.

_____. "On Reading: Four Limericks." In *4-Way Stop*. Illustrated by James J. Spanfeller. Atheneum, 1976.

Lobel, Arnold. *The Book of Pigericks*. Harper & Row, 1983.

McCord, David. "Limericks." In *Take Sky*. Illustrated by Henry B. Kane. Little, Brown, 1961.

_____. "Three Limericks." In *Every Time I Climb a Tree*. Illustrated by Marc Simont. Little, Brown, 1967.

Reeves, James. "Doctor Emmanuel." In *The Random House Book of Poetry for Children*. Selected by Jack Prelutsky. Illustrated by Arnold Lobel. Random House, 1983.

M IS FOR MICE AND MISHANDLED SPELLS

Mice

I can't believe I'm including a list of mice books in this resource book. I don't like mice but for some reason they seem to fascinate many others. They are small furry creatures that let some readers enter the world of little things. Stories about mice include stories about the real variety (field mice), fables, and stories that treat mice as people. Begin by making mouse bookmarks. Cut an oval shape of gray construction paper, add gray ears and inner ears of pink, add a yarn tail, two black spots for the eyes, and lines for the whiskers. Then bring out the books and read. After the readers are immersed in many mice books discuss the image of mice as presented in folklore, in fiction, and in nonfiction books. Investigate the facts about mice that authors include in their fiction or folklore books. Get a toy rubber mouse (I wouldn't ever suggest a live mouse) and make a mouse house. Be creative when you furnish the house. For example, use sewing thread spools for chairs, popsicle sticks for rocking chairs, postage stamps framed with yarn for pictures, and swatches of corduroy for floor carpeting. Read many poems and stories (suggestions follow) and write some of your own.

Booklist—Mice

Arnosky, Jim. *Mouse Numbers and Letters*. Harcourt Brace Jovanovich, 1982.
A wordless picture book which counts ten groups of objects and then builds the letters of the alphabet from twigs.

Carle, Eric, reteller. "The Lion and the Mouse." In *Twelve Tales from Aesop*. Philomel, 1980.
A classic fable about the mouse that repays the lion for his previous kindness.

Carryl, Guy Wetmore. "The Fearful Finale of the Irascible Mouse." In *Every Child's Book of Verse*. Selected by Sarah Chokla Gross. Watts, 1968.
A poem similar to "Hickory, Dickory, Dock, The Mouse Ran Up the Clock." The finale, however, is much more graphic.

Cauley, Lorinda Bryan. *The Town Mouse and the Country Mouse*. Illustrated by the author. Putnam, 1984.
Lush illustrations show the wholesome countryside and the luxurious world of a Victorian home. A classic tale retold in simple terms.

Cleary, Beverly. *Mouse on a Motorcycle*. Morrow, 1965.
Ralph, a mouse, rides his motorcycle and risks grave dangers in order to obtain an aspirin for his human friend, Keith.

Cleary, Beverly. *Ralph S. Mouse*. Morrow, 1982.
In this adventure Ralph Smart Mouse goes to school with a boy named Ryan.

Coombs, Patricia. *Mouse Cafe*. Lothrop, Lee & Shepard, 1972.
A mouse tale of "Cinderella" featuring Lollymops and a rags to riches adventure.

Freeman, Don. *The Guard Mouse*. Viking, 1967.
The story of Clyde, a guard just outside Buckingham Palace.

Freeman, Don. *Norman the Doorman*. Viking, 1959.
Norman is an art lover and the responsible doorman at a famous museum. He lives in a knight's helmet in the basement of the museum. He gives his mice friends tours of the museum basement area but longs for a tour of the upstairs part for himself. He gets his wish when he wins a sculpture contest after making a wire sculpture using the wire from the mousetraps a guard sets for the basement mice.

Freschet, Bernice. *Bear Mouse*. Illustrated by Donald Carrick. Scribner, 1973.
Early snow makes for difficult times as a mother meadow mouse struggles to find nourishment for her young family.

Godden, Rumer. *Mouse House*. Puffin, 1957.
A tiny mouse gets squeezed out of his family's flower pot home. He sets out in search of a new home. Once he finds a jewelry box, a just-right home, he accidently gets locked inside. After some moments of terror he is set free but the new home is destroyed. When the box is taken to the basement, the mice family discovers that it is large enough for all of them.

Gordon, Margaret. *Supermarket Mice*. Dutton, 1984.
Mice live in great comfort until Bounce, the fat cat, arrives to clean up the store.

Holl, Adelaide. *Moon Mouse*. Random House, 1969.
When Mouse finally becomes old enough to stay up after dark he discovers something big and round and shining.

King-Smith, Dick. *Magnus Powermouse*. Harper & Row, 1982.
Interesting characters interact with Magnus, the giant baby mouse, to create a rollicking adventure.

Kraus, Robert. *The Good Mousekeeper*. Illustrated by Hilary Knight. Dutton, 1977.
One day in the life of a mousekeeper cat as she tells how she keeps her mice from her neighbor, Miss Tabby.

Kraus, Robert. *Whose Mouse Are You?* Macmillan, 1970.
A little mouse feels unloved and unneeded by his family. He imagines that he earns their love during fantasies in which he rescues each member of his family.

Lionni, Leo. *Alexander and the Wind-up Mouse*. Pantheon, 1969.
Alexander is envious of the attention Willy, the wind-up mouse, receives until he discovers that Willy is about to be thrown out with the other old toys. He asks Lizard to turn Willy into a real mouse and the Lizard does.

Lionni, Leo. *Frederick*. Pantheon, 1967.
A family of field mice gathers food for winter—all except Frederick. He gathers the sun's rays, colors, and words which he shares with the others on the cold bleak winter days.

Lobel, Arnold. "The Mouse at the Seashore." In *Fables* by Arnold Lobel. Harper & Row, 1980.
A literary fable in which a young mouse makes a terror-filled journey to the seashore. At his destination he is overwhelmed by the feeling of deep peace and contentment.

Lobel, Arnold. *Mouse Soup*. Harper & Row, 1977.
Mouse is captured by a weasel who wants to make mouse soup. Mouse convinces Weasel that the soup would be much better with other ingredients. When Weasel leaves to get those ingredients Mouse runs safely home to his own supper and his book.

Low, Joseph. *Mice Twice*. Atheneum, 1980.
Cat invites Mouse to dinner thinking he will actually have Mouse for his dinner. Mouse outsmarts Cat by bringing another guest, Dog. Cat counters by bringing Wolf. But Dog then brings Crocodile. Eventually Cat invites Dog for dinner to meet a relative, Lion. But Dog settles it all when he brings Wasp. Lion and Cat run away leaving the dinner for Dog, Mouse, and Wasp.

Martin, Jacqueline Briggs. *Bizzy Bones and Moosemouse*. Illustrated by Stella Ormai. Lippincott, 1986.
Uncle Ezra takes a trip to Paris Hill while Bizzy Bones stays with Moosemouse. Bizzy is not comfortable with Moosemouse's messy and noisy home so he wanders off to Piney Woods where he gets lost.

Martin, Jacqueline Briggs. *Bizzy Bones and the Lost Quilt*. Illustrated by Stella Ormai. Lippincott, 1988.
> Bizzy Bones forgetfully leaves his precious quilt by the stream's edge. When he returns to get it the quilt is nowhere to be found. With the help of some of his friends the quilt is recovered, but it is damaged. Repairs are made and Bizzy finds comfort with his quilt with new stories.

Martin, Jacqueline Briggs. *Bizzy Bones and Uncle Ezra*. Illustrated by Stella Ormai. Lippincott, 1984.
> Bizzy's fear of the wind cannot be dispelled until Uncle Ezra builds him a wind-propelled carousel.

McCully, Emily Arnold. *The Christmas Gift*. Harper & Row, 1988.
> Christmas carols and Christmas presents make the mouse family joyous until a toy airplane is broken. Happiness is restored when an electric train is brought from the attic. Another wordless tale showing family love.

McCully, Emily Arnold. *First Snow*. Harper & Row, 1985.
> A wordless story about an extended family who get out their red pick-up truck to take everyone sleigh riding.

McCully, Emily Arnold. *New Baby*. Harper & Row, 1988.
> All the attention usually heaped onto a new baby is shown in this wordless tale. The other mice children show their jealousy.

McCully, Emily Arnold. *Picnic*. Harper & Row, 1984.
> In this wordless tale, the family is on the way to the country for a picnic. Baby Mouse bounces out of the red pickup and finds that his family doesn't miss him right away.

McCully, Emily Arnold. *School*. Harper & Row, 1987.
> A wordless story. Baby Mouse is left behind when all the other mice children gather their backpacks and go off to school. Mother Mouse settles down to a good book and Baby Mouse finds that the house is too quiet. He goes out the door to find out what school is all about.

McNulty, Faith. *Mouse and Tim*. Harper & Row, 1978.
> Tim finds a newborn deer mouse in the barn and keeps him as a pet until the mouse is old enough to be interested in finding another mouse.

Mendoza, George. *Need a House? Call Ms. Mouse!* Grosset and Dunlap, 1981.
> Ms. Mouse, Henrietta, is a world-famous home decorator specializing in creating the extraordinary. She, however, prefers a simple tent in the woods.

National Geographic. *Creatures Small and Furry*. Books for Young Explorers. National Geographic Society, 1983.
> Text and photographs present habits and habitats of small furry animals including the door mouse. (nonfiction)

Numeroff, Laura Joffe. *If You Give a Mouse a Cookie*. Illustrated by Felicia Bond. Harper & Row, 1985. (Large book edition by Scholastic, 1988.)
> A circular tale that all starts with giving a mouse a cookie.

Stein, Sara Bonnett. *Mouse*. Harcourt Brace Jovanovich, 1985.
Many facts about mice written to interest young scientists. The life cycle of a mouse shows it to be a hardy survivor who smells, eats strange things, gives birth (shown graphically), and makes a home in many places in the human environment.

Steptoe, John. *The Story of Jumping Mouse*. Lothrop, Lee & Shepard, 1984.
A native American legend about a small mouse and his adventure in the wide world. His transformation from mouse to regal eagle comes with the help of a magical frog.

Mishandled Spells

Magic and magical happenings always intrigue those who don't know how the event occurred. Focus on mishandled spells by discussing what ancient people believed about magic and voodoo spells. Discuss spells they might wish to use. Then discuss what happens when spells go wrong. Choose one of the following books to read aloud, and have the others available. When two or three books have been read discuss the effects of mishandled spells or spells that failed.

Booklist—Mishandled Spells

Corbett, Scott. *The Lemonade Trick*. Little, Brown, 1960.

Coville, Bruce. *The Monster's Ring*. Pantheon, 1982.

Dahl, Roald. *George's Marvelous Medicine*. Knopf, 1981/1982.

dePaola, Tomie. *Strega Nona*. Harcourt Brace Jovanovich, 1986.

Galdone, Paul. *The Magic Porridge Pot*. Seabury, 1976.

Gormley, Beatrice. *Fifth Grade Magic*. Dutton, 1982.

Mahy, Margaret. *The Boy Who Was Followed Home*. Illustrated by Steven Kellogg. Dial/Pied Piper, 1983.

Towle, Faith. *The Magic Cooking Pot*. Houghton Mifflin, 1975.

N IS FOR NATIVE AMERICAN INDIANS

Native Americans, Their Culture and Traditions

Long before the white man came to the Americas there were people on the land. All the states of the United States have their historical roots intertwined in the history of the American Indian. Most often the history of the American Indian is given little attention in the national history books. Books recounting the history of the individual states do somewhat better. Celebrate the contributions of the native Americans in your area by researching the history of your state. Search out the contributions of the native American Indian and other minority groups. Prepare a timeline noting the major dates and events in your state's history. There are some books detailing the stories of the American Indian but few that deal with present-day activities. Most often the books deal with the folklore of the American Indian, for example, *Arrow to the Sun* by Gerald McDermott (Viking, 1974). The other books written about the American Indian generally tend to be concerned with a tribe, an Indian leader, or a specific event. And few of those writing about the American Indian are native Americans themselves. Jamake Highwater is one of the noted writers of American Indian stories who can make a legitimate claim of American Indian heritage. He was born in northern Montana in 1942 of Blackfeet/Eastern Band Cherokee parentage. Until he was nine, Highwater spoke only Blackfeet and a little French learned from his mother. When he was nine, his father died in an automobile accident. That is when Highwater moved to southern California to live with his father's best friend, who adopted him. During this time he met Alta Black, a teacher who helped him bridge into the Western culture. From his total experience come his writings which strive to tell the Indians' story. Other writers have adopted or been adopted into American Indian tribes. Two of the best known are Paul Goble, a native Englishman, who several years ago moved to the Black Hills of South Dakota where he lives and works among the Indians. Robert Hofsinde was adopted by the Chippewas and given the name of Gray-Wolf. But the others are white men or women looking from the outside into the culture of the American Indian.

Set aside a day or more to explore the contributions of the many native American cultures to our life today. While a total integration of the American Indian's role in our country's history should be the goal, perhaps a concentrated focus now will at least begin the process.

Booklist—Native Americans

Allen, Terry, editor. *The Whispering Wind*. Doubleday, 1972.
  Poems by young American Indians.

Bleeker, Sonia. *The Sea Hunters: Indians of the Northwest*. Illustrated by Althea Karr. Morrow, 1951.
  One of a series of books on specific and individual Indian cultures.

Bleeker, Sonia. *The Sioux Indians: Hunters and Warriors of the Plains*. Illustrated by Kisa N. Saski. Morrow, 1962.
  One of a series of books on specific and individual Indian cultures.

Brown, Dee. *Wounded Knee*. Holt, Rinehart & Winston, 1974.
  Adapted by Amy Ehrlich from Brown's adult title *Bury My Heart at Wounded Knee*.

Clark, Ann Nolan. *Circle of Seasons*. Illustrated by W. T. Mars. Farrar, Straus & Giroux, 1970.
  An account of the rites and observances of the Pueblo year.

Folsom, Franklin. *Red Power on the Rio Grande: The Native American Revolution of 1680*. Illustrated by J. D. Roybal. Follett, 1973.
  Presents the American Indian point of view on the Pueblo revolution of 1680.

Goble, Paul and Dorothy Goble. *Brave Eagle's Account of the Fetterman Fight: 21 December 1866*. Illustrated by Paul Goble. Pantheon, 1972.
  A description of the Indian resistance to white encroachment as told by an Oglala Sioux chief.

Goble, Paul and Dorothy Goble. *Red Hawk's Account of Custer's Last Battle*. Pantheon, 1969.
A dramatic telling from the viewpoint of a boy. After the battle at Little Big Horn the boy realizes that while the battle's victory belonged to the Indian the victory in the Indian's overall fight against the white invasion would belong to the white man.

Hassler, Jon. *Jemmy*. Atheneum, 1981.
The story of a seventeen-year-old woman and her struggle from poverty to finding her identity as a woman, an Indian, and an artist. (fiction)

Highwater, Jamake. *Eyes of Darkness*. Lothrop, Lee & Shepard, 1985.
Yesa, a Santee Sioux Indian is raised by his grandmother and immersed in the Indian culture. At age sixteen his father takes him to live among the white men where he becomes the first native American medical doctor. He returns to his boyhood home to live as an Indian. The book shows the struggle between the two cultures: Dr. Alexander East and Yesa.

Hirshfelder, Arlene. *Happily May I Walk*. Scribner, 1986.
New information about the ways native Americans (American Indians and Alaska natives) live in the United States today. The book attempts to dispel some commonly held stereotypes.

Hofsinde, Robert. *Indian Sign Language*. Morrow, 1956.
Glossary of over 500 universal signs of North American Indians.

Hofsinde, Robert. *Indian Warriors and Their Weapons*. Morrow, 1965.
Describes martial weapons and costumes of seven tribes.

Hofsinde, Robert. *Indians at Home*. Morrow, 1964.
A discussion of the six major types of Indian homes.

La Farge, Oliver. *The American Indian*. Golden Press, 1960.
Both historical and contemporary material.

McNeer, May. *The American Indian Story*. Illustrated by Lynd Ward. Farrar, Straus & Giroux, 1963.
Although this volume is intended to be a survey, it is really an introduction to the American Indian's history.

Sneve, Virginia Driving Hawk. *When Thunder Strikes*. Illustrated by Oren Lyons. Holiday House, 1974.

Speare, Elizabeth George. *The Sign of the Beaver*. Houghton Mifflin, 1983.
When Matthew is left in the Maine wilderness to wait for his father to return with their family, he does not know that his family will not be able to return for many months. While striving to eke out food for survival Matthew has a near fatal disaster and is befriended by an Indian and his grandson. Matthew must make a difficult choice, that of moving north with the Indians or continuing to wait for his family—hoping that they are indeed going to return.

Tunis, Edwin. *Indians*. World, 1959.
Factual information about a variety of tribes and cultures.

Wallin, Luke. *Ceremony of the Panther*. Bradbury, 1987.
A young Miccosukee Indian, John Raincrow, is torn between the unstressful life in the Florida Everglades and his father's desires for his son to carry on the Shaman traditions.

Booklist—Native American Folklore

Baylor, Byrd. *When Clay Sings*. Scribner, 1972.

Goble, Paul. *Buffalo Woman*. Bradbury, 1984.

_____. *The Gift of the Sacred Dog*. Bradbury, 1980.

_____. *The Great Race*. Bradbury, 1985.

Haseley, Dennis. *The Sacred One*. Warne, 1983.

Highwater, Jamake. *Moonsong Lullaby*. Lothrop, Lee & Shepard, 1981.

Longfellow, Henry Wadsworth. *Hiawatha*. Illustrated by Susan Jeffers. Dutton, 1975.

McDermott, Gerald. *Arrow to the Sun*. Viking, 1974; Puffin, 1977.

Miles, Miska. *Annie and the Old One*. Atlantic-Little, Brown, 1971.

Steptoe, John. *The Story of Jumping Mouse*. Lothrop, Lee & Shepard, 1984.

Research Project

Research native American tribes in the United States. Attempt to locate a tribe for each letter of the alphabet. When a tribe has been identified for each letter, assign a tribe to each member of the class. The student should spend several class periods in the library searching for information about that tribe. Gather as much information as possible. Then, using Margaret Musgrove's *Ashanti to Zulu: African Traditions* (Dial, 1976) as a model, ask students to create a page focusing on the one tribe they have researched. The Musgrove title focuses on twenty-six African tribes. The text highlights one notable fact about each particular tribe while the Dillons's illustrations attempt to show something of the terrain where each tribe lives, their clothing, their homes, their family structure, the animals or birds native to that particular area, and a typical cooking utensil, tool, or other artifact significant to the tribe's existence. The illustrations add much information to the brief text. The students' text and illustrations should attempt to give this same information for the native American tribe that is being featured.

O IS FOR ORNATE LETTERS AND ODD ANIMALS

Ornate Letters

Ornate or illuminated letters were once very prevalent in published books. While these ornate letters are not as prevalent now some illustrators do use illuminated letters in present day books for children. The letters serve to focus on a main element of the book as in the *Devil with the Three Golden Hairs* by Jacob and Wilhelm Grimm and illustrated by Nonny Hogrogian (Knopf, 1983). Hogrogian's illuminated O uses the letter as a cradle of sorts for a baby wrapped in a softly colored blanket. The baby plays a key role in the development of the Grimm Brothers' tale. Often endpapers and the illustrations on the title page will foreshadow characters or story action in much the same way as does the illuminated letters. Search for other books which use illuminated (ornate) letters to foreshadow the characters or action in the story. Use some of the books which follow to get you started.

Booklist—Ornate Letters

Baker, Betty. *Santa Rat*. Illustrated by Tom Huffman. Greenwillow, 1980.

Base, Graeme. *Animalia*. Viking Kestrel, 1986.

Degen, Bruce. *Jamberry*. Harper & Row, 1983.

Moore, Clement C. *A Visit from St. Nicholas*. Illustrated by T. C. Boyd. A facsimile of the 1848 edition. Simon & Schuster, 1971.

Nyce, Vera. *A Jolly Christmas at the Patterprints*. Illustrated by Helene Nyce. Parents, 1971.

Pearce, Philippa. *The Squirrel Wife*. Illustrated by Derek Collard. Crowell, 1971.

Roy, Ron. *Three Ducks Went Wandering*. Illustrated by Paul Galdone. Clarion, 1979.

Odd Animals

Odd or mixed-up animals can provide some interesting drawing and writing assignments. Make your own mixed-up beasts, draw a picture, name the animal, and write about the animal in either poetry or prose. Use some of the books and poems on the following booklist as models of odd and mixed-up animals.

Booklist—Odd Animals in Story and Poem

Carle, Eric. *The Mixed-Up Chameleon*. Crowell, 1975; revised 1984.

Cox, Kenyon. "The Bumblebeaver." In *The Arbuthnot Anthology of Children's Literature*, 3rd ed. Scott, Foresman, 1971. Reprinted from *The Mixed-up Beasts* by Kenyon Cox. Dodd Mead, n.d.

_____. "The Kangarooster." In *The Arbuthnot Anthology of Children's Literature*, 3rd ed. Scott, Foresman, 1971. Reprinted from *The Mixed-up Beasts* by Kenyon Cox. Dodd Mead, n.d.

_____. "The Octopussycat." In *The Arbuthnot Anthology of Children's Literature*, 3rd ed. Scott, Foresman, 1971. Reprinted from *The Mixed-up Beasts* by Kenyon Cox. Dodd Mead, n.d.

Peet, Bill. *The Whingdingdilly*. Houghton Mifflin, 1970.

P IS FOR POULTRY

Poultry (and Eggs)

Studies of animal groups, how they reproduce, how eggs are hatched, and a general study of farm animals all lend themselves to using the following booklist featuring eggs, hens, chicks, ducks, and geese.

Booklist—Poultry (and Eggs)

Andersen, Hans Christian. *The Ugly Duckling*. Illustrated by Lorinda Bryan Cauley. Harcourt Brace Jovanovich, 1979.

_____. *The Woman with the Eggs*. Crown, 1974.

Burnie, David. *Birds*. Eyewitness Series. Knopf, 1988.

Delton, Judy. *The Goose Who Wrote a Book*. Carolrhoda, 1982.

Eastman, P. D. *Flap Your Wings*. Beginner Books/Random House, 1977.

Edmondson, Madeleine. *The Witch's Egg*. Seabury, 1974.

Flora, James. *Little Hatchy Hen*. Harcourt, Brace & World, 1969.

Heine, Helme. *The Most Wonderful Egg in the World*. Atheneum, 1983.

Heller, Ruth. *Chickens Aren't the Only Ones*. Putnam, 1981.

Hooper, Meredith. *Seven Eggs*. Harper & Row, 1985.

Isenbaart, Hans-Heinrich. *A Duckling Is Born*. Putnam, 1981.

Johnson, Sylvia. *Inside an Egg*. Lerner, 1982.

McCloskey, Robert. *Make Way for Ducklings*. Viking, 1966.

Selsam, Millicent E. *Egg to Chick*. Illustrated by Barbara Wolff. Harper & Row, 1980; Harper Trophy, 1987.

Wolff, Ashley. *A Year of Birds*. Dodd Mead, 1984.

An excellent general reference book focusing on birds is *Birds* by David Burnie (Knopf, 1988), one title in the Eyewitness Books series. Another title which will help focus on other animals that lay eggs is Ruth Heller's *Chickens Aren't the Only Ones* (Putnam, 1981). For activity suggestions see the entry for that title in the Bookshelf section of this book.

Q IS FOR QUEENS (AND KINGS) AND QUILTS

Queens and Kings (or Books and Poems with "Queens" and "Kings" in Them)

Queens and kings are fascinating to Americans. While we have never had a king or queen (although some people feared George Washington might proclaim himself king), we continue to read news magazines and newspaper articles about royalty. Especially fascinating are the British royalty. The queens and kings in the following books hold little resemblance to those who are actually ruling today. Do look for "regal" qualities in the book characters you read about. Discuss and identify what one should consider regal. Learn more about King George of England by reading some of the books on the American Revolution booklist (see index). Research information about current ruling kings and queens or kings and queens who have been prominent figures in the history of the world.

Or just make yourself an aluminum foil-covered royal crown and read some of the following stories aloud.

Booklist—Queens (and Kings)

Alexander, Lloyd. *The High King*. Holt, Rinehart & Winston, 1969.

Burch, Robert. *Queenie Peavy*. Illustrated by Jerry Lazare. Viking, 1966.

Cohen, Barbara. *King of the Seventh Grade*. Lothrop, Lee & Shepard, 1975.

Cooper, Susan. *The Grey King*. Atheneum, 1976.

Fritz, Jean. *Can't You Make Them Behave, King George*. Coward McCann, 1977.

Henry, Marguerite. *King of the Wind*. Illustrated by Wesley Dennis. Rand McNally, 1948.

Jacobs, Leland B. "Queenie." In *The Random House Book of Poetry for Children*. Selected by Jack Prelutsky. Illustrated by Arnold Lobel. Random House, 1983.

King-Smith, Dick. *The Queen's Nose*. Illustrated by Jill Bennett. Harper & Row, 1976.

Prelutsky, Jack. *The Queen of Eene*. Illustrated by Victoria Chess. Greenwillow, 1978.

Watanabe, Shigeo. *I'm King of the Castle*. Illustrated by Yasuo Ohtomo. Putnam, 1982.

Weil, Lisl. *The Foolish King*. Macmillan, 1982. (A new version of Hans Christian Andersen's "The Emperor's New Clothes.")

Quilts

Favorite things, quilt patterns, and a study of days gone past might all involve a look at quilts. The following books will bring into focus the memories and stories associated with most quilts. Some of these books would be appropriate additions to the booklist for the Heritage Day celebration.

Booklist—Quilts

Chorao, Kay. *Kate's Quilt*. Dutton, 1982.
Kate really wanted a doll; instead she received a quilt. But when the night became cold and scary Kate was glad she had the quilt.

Coerr, Eleanor. *The Josefina Story Quilt*. Harper & Row, 1986.
A story quilt tells the story of a young girl's family's journey to the west in the 1850s. Two special patches are made for her pet hen, Josefina.

Daly, Niki. *Joseph's Other Red Sock*. Atheneum, 1982.
A lost red sock leads Joseph to encounter a horrible monster. Featured in the illustrations are several different quilts, including a quilt monster.

Ernst, Lisa Campbell. *Sam Johnson and the Blue Ribbon Quilt*. Lothrop, Lee & Shepard, 1983.
Sam Johnson starts a quilting club when the women will not let him belong to their group. A country fair quilt contest brings competition and then, due to a mishap, cooperation between the two groups. Each page is bordered with a quilt pattern. The border reflects the content of the specific page.

Fair, Sylvia. *The Bedspread*. Morrow, 1982.
Two elderly sisters, Maud and Amelia, generally disagree about things. But they do agree to embroider their plain white bedspread with recollections of the house in which they grew up. The finished bedspread is a surprise to both of them. (Not strictly a quilt story but in the same general theme—memories, stories in quilts.)

Flournoy, Valerie. *The Patchwork Quilt*. Illustrated by Jerry Pinkney. Dial, 1985.
Tanya's family spends a year stitching memories into a quilt. A warm gentle story of a young girl and her grandmother.

Geras, Adèle. *Apricots at Midnight*. Atheneum, 1982.
Older children will enjoy this story of Aunt Pinney, a treasured visitor because at night she told stories of her childhood. Each patch of a quilt has its own special story, from eating apricots at midnight with a highwayman to adventures with the pirate Captain Tramplemousse.

Johnston, Tony. *The Quilt Story*. Putnam, 1985.
Simple poetic words tell the story of a quilt that originated with a young pioneer girl and now belongs to a child who treasures it.

Jonas, Ann. *The Quilt*. Greenwillow, 1984.
A new quilt for a little girl brings her memories of the fond happenings associated with each of the squares. With her quilt she is able to look and dream her memories.

Keller, Holly. *Geraldine's Blanket*. Greenwillow, 1984.
A unique use is found for a pink scrap from a treasured blanket.

Martin, Jacqueline Briggs. *Bizzy Bones and the Lost Quilt*. Lippincott, 1988.
Bizzy Bones loses his quilt by the stream. Friends help him find the quilt and repair it with scraps that bring new memories to the quilt.

Moncure, Jane Belk. *My "Q" Sound Box.* Children's, 1979.
  The little girl's sound box is filled with objects that begin with "Q". Several quilts are shown in the illustrations.

Moore, Clement C. *The Night before Christmas.* Illustrated by Tomie dePaola. Holiday House, 1980.
  Quilt patterns form the borders on each page. Many of dePaola's family quilts are shown in the illustrations.

Vincent, Gabrielle. *Ernest and Celestine's Patchwork Quilt.* Greenwillow, 1982.
  Ernest and Celestine work together to make a patchwork quilt. When they realize that each of them needs one, they make another. (wordless)

Willard, Nancy. *The Mountains of Quilt.* Illustrated by Tomie dePaola. Harcourt Brace Jovanovich, 1987.
  A grandmother is busy making quilts while four magicians gather for lunch. A magpie and a runaway carpet make everything turn topsy-turvy.

Use crayons or felt-tip markers to create a pattern on one-inch square graph paper. Put the patterns together to make a paper quilt banner. Discuss the repetitive patterns of 1-2-1-2 and the 1-2-3-1-2-3 patterns. As this exercise is repeated the patterns will become more and more complicated. Make a miniposter for a favorite book, on a 6x6-inch square of paper. Affix the miniposter to one of the patterned graph pages and you have an illustration advertising a book. The technique of using a quilt-patterned border is shown in dePaola's illustrated version of Moore's *The Night before Christmas* and in Lisa Campbell Ernst's *Sam Johnson and the Blue Ribbon Quilt*.

R IS FOR RAIN AND RUSSIAN FOLKLORE

Rain

Caroline Feller Bauer has collected together twenty-eight stories or poems to celebrate the rain in her book *Rainy Day: Stories and Poems* (Lippincott, 1986). She ends the book with some facts about rain, like the fact that it hasn't rained for over 400 years in the Atacama Desert in Chile, but it rains 350 days a year on the island of Maui in Hawaii. The final three pages list twenty-one additional books that celebrate rain and rainy days. Follow with Franklyn M. Branley's *It's Raining Cats and Dogs* (Houghton Mifflin, 1987) and you'll never have a dull rainy day.

Russian Folklore

Any study of a country could include a look at that country's folklore. The folklore of each country brings information about that country. After reading several of the following Russian stories discuss the apparent characteristics of Russia's folktales. What information can be gleaned from the folklore about Russia's country and its people? Compare and contrast to folklore from other cultures.

Booklist—Russian Folklore

Bogdanovic, Toma, illustrator. *The Firebird*. Scroll Press, 1972.

Ginsburg, Mirra. *The Fox and the Hare*. Illustrated by Victor Nolden. Crown, 1969.

_____. *The Master of the Winds and Other Tales from Siberia*. Crown, 1970.

_____. *One Trick Too Many: Fox Stories from Russia*. Illustrated by Helen Siegl. Dial, 1972.

_____. *Three Rolls and One Doughnut: Fables from Russia*. Illustrated by Anita Lobel. Dial, 1970.

Haviland, Virginia. *Favorite Fairy Tales Told in Russia*. Little, Brown, 1961.

Ransome, Arthur. *The Fool of the World and the Flying Ship*. Illustrated by Uri Shulevitz. Farrar, Straus & Giroux, 1968.

Reyher, Becky. *My Mother Is the Most Beautiful Woman in the World*. Illustrated by Ruth Gannett. Lothrop, Lee & Shepard, 1945.

Shulevitz, Uri. *Soldier and the Tsar in the Forest: A Russian Tale*. Translated by Richard Lourie. Farrar, Straus & Giroux, 1972.

Tolstoy, Alexei. *The Great Big Enormous Turnip*. Illustrated by Helen Oxenbury. Watts, 1969.

Whitney, Thomas P., translator. *In a Certain Kingdom*. Illustrated by Dieter Lange. Macmillan, 1972.

_____. *Vasilisa the Beautiful*. Illustrated by Nonny Hogrogian. Scribner, 1968.

Wyndham, Lee. *Tales the People Tell in Russia*. Illustrated by Andrew Antal. Messner, 1970.

Zemach, Harve. *Salt: A Russian Tale*. Illustrated by Margot Zemach. Follett, 1965.

S IS FOR SCHOOL, SEASONS, SHADOWS, SHAPES, SILLY STORIES, STEPFAMILIES, SNOW, AND SONGS IN BOOKS

School

There are several books that feature teachers and some action taking place in schools. One of the most notable school characters created is Miss Nelson, star of three books written by Harry Allard and illustrated by James Marshall: *Miss Nelson Is Missing* (Houghton Mifflin, 1977), *Miss Nelson Is Back* (Houghton Mifflin, 1982), and *Miss Nelson Has a Field Day* (Houghton Mifflin, 1985). These books should be staples in every library and in every elementary and middle school substitute teacher's survival kit.

But perhaps the funniest book is *Sideways Stories from Wayside School* by Louis Sachar (Avon, 1978). The school was supposed to be thirty classrooms on one story. By mistake the school was built sideways with one classroom on each of thirty floors. These stories are about the one class on the top floor of this school. Please note that before you start sharing this book you must get yourself a shiny red apple to put on your desk. Then read the first story to your class and enjoy. Sachar has written a sequel *Wayside School Is Falling Down* (Lothrop, Lee & Shepard, 1989). It is sure to be another popular book.

Seasons

In science during a study of the seasons, you might celebrate the first day of spring, or the warmth of an autumn day. Discover the changes brought by each season.

Booklist—Seasons

Buscaglia, Leo. *The Fall of Freddie the Leaf*. Charles B. Slack, 1982.

Cavagnario, David and Maggie Cavagnario. *The Pumpkin People*. Scribner, 1979.

Clifton, Lucille. *The Boy Who Didn't Believe in Spring*. Dutton, 1973.

Cole, Brock. *The Winter Wren*. Farrar, Straus & Giroux, 1984.

Gibbons, Gail. *Farming*. Holiday, 1988.

_____. *The Seasons of Arnold's Apple Tree*. Harcourt Brace Jovanovich, 1984. (See entry for this title in the Bookshelf section of this book.)

Hall, Donald. *Ox-Cart Man*. Viking, 1979. (See Bookshelf entry for this title.)

Icikawa, Satomi. *Suzette and Nicholas and the Seasons Clock*. Philomel, 1978.

Johnson, Hannah Lyons. *From Apple Seed to Applesauce*. Lothrop, Lee & Shepard, 1977.

Lasky, Kathryn. *Sugaring Time*. Macmillan, 1983.

Livingston, Myra Cohn. *A Circle of Seasons*. Holiday House, 1982.

Roberts, Bethany. *Waiting for Spring Stories*. Harper & Row, 1984.

Rylant, Cynthia. *This Year's Garden*. Bradbury, 1984.

Tafuri, Nancy. *All Year Long*. Greenwillow, 1983.

Wildsmith, Brian. *Seasons*. Oxford University Press, 1980.

Shadows

Correlate the reading of the following books with science activities focusing on the sun and shadows. In the Bookshelf section of this book are activity suggestions to correlate with Frank Asch's *Bear Shadow* (Prentice-Hall, 1985) and additional ideas relating to shadows and deRegniers's *The Shadow Book*.

Booklist — Shadows

Asch, Frank. *Bear Shadow*. Prentice-Hall, 1985.

Cendrars, Blaise. *Shadow*. Translation of *La Féticheuse*. Illustrated by Marcia Brown. Scribner, 1982.
Won the 1983 Caldecott Award, for illustrations. From the storytellers of East Africa comes this image of the sorcerer whose images are brought forth through the brilliant shadows of their surroundings.

deRegniers, Beatrice Schenk. *The Shadow Book*. Photographs by Isabel Gordon. Harcourt, Brace & World, 1960.
Shows the effects of shadow and shadow plays.

deRegniers, Beatrice Schenk. *Who Likes the Sun?* Illustrated with woodcuts by Leona Pierce. Harcourt, Brace & World, 1961.
The first few pages tell about shadows and their relationship to the sun.

Gardner, Robert and David Webster. *Shadow Science*. Doubleday, 1976.
Very few words and shadow pictures with high contrast.

Goor, Nancy and Ron Goor. *Shadows: Here, There, and Everywhere*. Crowell, 1981.
Shadows change shapes as they help us to distinguish between various shapes, for example, an orange and an egg.

Hader, Berta and Elmer Hader. *The Big Snow*. Illustrated by the authors. Macmillan, 1948.
This book won the 1949 Caldecott Award, for illustrations depicting the imagery of the fresh fallen snow. All the animals of the woodland prepare for winter but the blanket of snow makes food scarce. Friends help the animals by setting out food to help them survive the "big snow." Vivid, clear shadows in the snow.

Hoover, Helen. *Great Wolf and the Good Woodsman*. Parents, 1964.
A folktale in the traditional style. Illustrations are filled with reflections and shadows to observe.

Kent, Jack. *The Biggest Shadow in the Zoo*. Parents, 1981.
Kent's charming illustrations depict Goober, an elephant, as he discovers his new friend. When his new friend disappears Goober becomes ill and longs for his friend to return. Only when the sun shines again does his friend, his shadow, return to make him well once again.

Leopold, A. Starker. *The Desert*. Life Nature Library, 1970.
Many scenes of shadows in the desert are part of the illustrations.

Rothman, Joel. *Night Lights*. Albert Whitman, 1972.
The lights of the night help to create shadows.

Tompert, Ann. *Nothing Sticks Like a Shadow*. Houghton Mifflin, 1984.
Getting rid of a shadow is not as easy as burying it in the ground or nailing it down. Only when the sun's location changes does the shadow show any signs of leaving.

Wolcott, Patty. *My Shadow and I*. Addison-Wesley, 1975.
A young boy finds his shadow can make a great playmate. Correlates with the "shadow tag" game illustrated in deRegniers's *The Shadow Book*.

Shapes

Concepts of geometric shapes can be extended by exposing children to many examples of circles, triangles, squares, and other shapes. After reading these books use construction paper to construct interesting shapes. For intermediate or middle school students, culminate the entire focus on shapes by introducing a computer program from Sunburst Communications, *The Factory: Strategies in Problem Solving*. This program can help children develop their thinking skills. Introduce the software in a large group, modeling the thinking required to solve the questions. Teacher interaction with the students will be the key to the effective use of this software.

Booklist—Shapes

Goor, Nancy and Ron Goor. *Shadows, Here, There, and Everywhere*. Crowell, 1981.

Hoban, Tana. *Circles, Triangles, and Squares*. Collier Macmillan, 1974.

_____. *Is It Red, Is It Blue, Is It Yellow?* Greenwillow, 1978.

_____. *Round and Round and Round*. Scholastic, 1983.

_____. *Shapes and Things*. Macmillan, 1970.

Holt, Delores. *Good Friends Come in Many Shapes*. Children's, 1973.

Jonas, Ann. *Round Trip*. Greenwillow, 1983. (Another meaning for round.)

Kuskin, Karla. *Square as a House*. Harper & Row, 1960.

Moncure, Jane Belk. *Word Bird's Shapes*. Child's World, 1983.

Podendorf, Illa. *Shapes: Sides, Curves and Corners*. Children's, 1970.

Reiss, John J. *Shapes*. Bradbury, 1974.

Schlein, Miriam. *Shapes*. E. M. Hall, 1952.

Youldon, Gillian. *Sizes*. Watts, 1979.

Silly Stories

Often children are told to stop being silly. But what does silly really mean? After reading the books that follow you and your students will have a good idea of the definition of silly. Discuss the definition for being silly. Make a list of "silly" actions from the story and from the children's own experiences. Then let yourself do one silly thing.

Booklist—Silly Stories

Bowman, James Cloyd and Margery Bianco. *Who Was Tricked?* Albert Whitman, 1966.

Duvoisin, Roger. *The Miller, the Son and the Donkey*. McGraw-Hill, 1962.

Elkin, Benjamin. *Six Foolish Fishermen*. Children's, 1957.

Galdone, Paul. *The Table, the Donkey, and the Stick*. McGraw-Hill, 1976.

Goins, Ellen H. *Horror at Hankelmeyer House*. Follett, 1971.

Kent, Jack. *Jim, Jimmy, James*. Greenwillow, 1984.

_____. *Silly Goose*. Prentice-Hall, 1983.

King-Smith, Dick. *Farmer Bungle Forgets*. Illustrated by Martin Honeysett. Atheneum, 1987.

Lobel, Arnold. *Ming Lo Moves the Mountain*. Greenwillow, 1982.

Polushkin, Maria. *Bubba and Babba*. Crown, 1976.

Stepfamilies and Other Family Members

Many families now include stepparents, stepbrothers or stepsisters, grandparents, and aunts and uncles or cousins. The relationships sometimes get complicated but the thread that binds is love. There are celebrations to honor mothers (in May), fathers (in June), and grandparents (in September), but celebrations for other family members that we love are not so prevalent. Try the following books to focus on many different family members who provide nurturing and love. Set aside a V.I.R. (Very Important Reader) Day when each child invites a special person from his or her family to school to read with them. Serve punch and cookies which the children have made.

Booklist—Stepfamilies and Other Family Members

Brandenberg, Franz. *Aunt Nina and Her Nephews and Nieces*. Illustrated by Aliki. Greenwillow, 1983. (Aunt Nina)

_____. *Aunt Nina's Visit*. Illustrated by Aliki. Greenwillow, 1983. (Aunt Nina)

Buckley, Helen E. *Someday with My Father*. Illustrated by Ellen Eagle. Harper & Row, 1985. (Father)

Cooney, Barbara. *Miss Rumphius*. Viking, 1982. (Great Aunt Alice)

Francis, Dorothy Benner. *The Flint Hill Foal*. Abingdon, 1976. (Stepbrother, stepsister, stepmother)

Greenfield, Eloise. *Grandma's Joy*. Illustrated by Carole Byard. Philomel, 1980. (Grandma)

Hunter, Evan. *Me and Mr. Stenner*. Lippincott, 1976. (Stepfather)

Jukes, Marvis. *Like Jake and Me*. Knopf, 1984. (Stepfather)

MacLachlan, Patricia. *Sarah, Plain and Tall*. Harper & Row, 1985. (Stepmother)

McHugh, Elizabet. *Karen and Vicki*. Greenwillow, 1984. (Stepsisters)

Numeroff, Laura Joffe. *Does Grandma Have an Elmo Elephant Kit?* Greenwillow, 1980. (Grandparents)

Pearson, Susan. *Karin's Christmas Walk*. Illustrated by Trinka Hakes Noble. Dutton, 1980. (Uncle Jerry)

Pevsner, Stella. *A Smart Kid Like You*. Seabury, 1975. (Stepmother)

Pfeffer, Susan Beth. *Awful Evalina*. Illustrated by Diane Dawson. Albert Whitman, 1979. (Cousin)

Rylant, Cynthia. *When I Was Young in the Mountains*. Illustrated by Diane Goode. Dutton, 1982. (Grandparents)

Schwartz, Amy. *Her Majesty, Aunt Essie*. Puffin, 1984. (Aunt Essie)

Stevens, Carla. *Anna, Grandpa, and the Big Storm*. Illustrated by Margot Tomes. Clarion, 1982. (Grandfather)

Vigna, Judith. *She's Not My Real Mother*. Albert Whitman, 1980. (Stepmother)

Williams, Vera B. *A Chair for My Mother*. Greenwillow, 1982. (Grandmother)

Zolotow, Charlotte. *But Not Billy*. Illustrated by Kay Chorao. Harper & Row, 1975. (Baby Brother)

Snow

Celebrate the first snow, or an unexpected school holiday resulting from a heavy snowfall, by pulling out Caroline Feller Bauer's *Snowy Day: Stories and Poems* (Lippincott, 1986). And if you live in an area where the snow never falls, bring in the snowy world of winter by sharing Bauer's collection of stories and poems to match the mood of snowflakes landing on your nose, frozen toes, warm mittens, and lots of snow. Continue enjoying the snow by reading even more snow stories. You're sure to find a favorite among the following titles. Make snow cones and enjoy. In addition to Bauer's title enjoy these snow books.

Booklist—Snow

Agee, Jon. *If Snow Falls*. Pantheon, 1982.

Andersen, Hans Christian. *The Snow Queen*. Adapted by Naomi Lewis. Viking, 1979.

Brenner, Barbara. *The Snow Parade*. Crown, 1984.

Briggs, Raymond. *The Snowman*. Random House, 1978.

Burningham, John. *The Snow*. Crowell, 1974.

Craft, Ruth and Erik Blegvad. *The Winter Bear*. Atheneum, 1976.

Duncan, Jane. *Brave Janet Reachfar*. Seabury, 1975.

Duvoisin, Roger. *Snowy and Woody*. Knopf, 1979.

Frost, Robert. "Stopping by the Woods on a Snowy Evening." In *You Come Too*. Illustrated by Thomas W. Nason. Holt, Rinehart & Winston, 1959. (Poem is also available in a picture book version published by Dutton, 1978.)

Hader, Berta and Elmer Hader. *The Big Snow*. Macmillan, 1948.

Hasler, Eveline. *Winter Magic*. Morrow, 1984.

Hoff, Syd. *When Will It Snow?* Harper & Row, 1971.

Keats, Ezra Jack. *The Snowy Day*. Viking, 1962.

Kellogg, Steven. *The Mystery of the Missing Red Mitten*. Dial, 1974.

Kimura, Yasuko. *Fergus and the Snow Deer*. McGraw-Hill, 1979.

Lobe, Mira. *The Snowman Who Went for a Walk*. Morrow, 1984.

Mack, Gail. *Yesterday's Snowman*. Pantheon, 1979.

McPhail, David. *Snow Lion*. Parents, 1982.

Morgan, Allen. *Sadie and the Snowman*. Scholastic, 1985.

Prelutsky, Jack. *It's Snowing! It's Snowing!* Greenwillow, 1984.

Sasaki, Isao. *Snow*. Viking, 1980.

Schick, Eleanor. *City in the Winter*. Collier Books, 1970.

Shire, Ellen. *The Snow Kings*. Walker, 1969.

Stevens, Carla. *Anna, Grandpa and the Big Storm*. Clarion, 1982.

Tresselt, Alvin. *White Snow, Bright Snow*. Lothrop, Lee & Shepard, 1947.

Wheeler, Cindy. *Marmalade's Snowy Day*. Random House, 1982.

Songs in Books

Children learn the alphabet by memorizing the alphabet song. Other rhymes help us learn the days of the week and the months of the year. And now researchers are saying that rhythm and song can also help us learn not only the language but the language patterns necessary for language development. Rhythms are being credited for neurological impressioning. This impressioning does not come with just one exposure but takes firm hold only when the rhythm has been repeated over and over. This repetition is most easily accomplished when the rhythm is in the form of a song. Many single songs have been published as illustrated books complete with musical scores (usually appended at the end). Begin to enjoy these books and let the children take the rhythms for their own.

Booklist—Songs in Books

Abisch, Ros. *'Twas in the Moon of Wintertime*. Prentice-Hall, 1969.

Adams, Adrienne. *Bring a Torch, Jeannette, Isabella*. Scribner, 1963.

Alexander, Cecil Frances. *All Things Bright and Beautiful*. Scribner, 1962.

Aliki. *Go Tell Aunt Rhody*. Macmillan, 1974.

———. *Hush, Little Baby*. Prentice-Hall, 1968.

Bangs, Edward. *Yankee Doodle*. Illustrated by Steven Kellogg. Parents, 1976.

Bonne, Rose and Alan Mills. *I Know an Old Lady*. Rand-McNally, 1961.

Broomfield, Robert. *The Twelve Days of Christmas*. Bodley Head, 1965.

Chase, Richard. *Billy Boy*. Golden Gate, 1966.

dePaola, Tomie. *The Friendly Beasts: An Old English Christmas Carol*. Putnam, 1981.

Domanska, Janina. *I Saw a Ship A-Sailing*. Macmillan, 1972.

Emberley, Barbara. *One Wide River to Cross*. Prentice-Hall, 1966.

_____. *Simon's Song*. Prentice-Hall, 1969.

Emberley, Ed. *London Bridge Is Falling Down*. Little, Brown, 1967.

Gerstein, Mordicai. *Roll Over!* Crown, 1984.

Graboff, Abner. *Old MacDonald Had a Farm*. Scholastic, 1970.

Harriett. *Froggie Went A-Courtin'*. Harvey House, 1967.

Harasz, Ilonka. *The Twelve Days of Christmas*. Harper, 1949.

Hart, Jan. *Singing Bee*. Illustrated by Anita Lobel. Lothrop, Lee & Shepard, 1982. (a collection of songs)

Hoffman, Hilde. *Green Grass Grows All Around*. Macmillan, 1968.

Johnson, J. W. and J. R. Johnson. *Lift Every Voice and Sing*. Hawthorne, 1970.

Keats, Ezra Jack. *The Little Drummer Boy*. Macmillan, 1968.

_____. *Over in the Meadow*. Scholastic, 1971.

Kent, Jack. *Jack Kent's Twelve Days of Christmas*. Parents, 1973.

Langstaff, John. *Frog Went A-Courtin'*. Harcourt, Brace & World, 1955.

_____. *Oh, A-Hunting We Will Go*. Illustrated by Nancy Winslow Parker. Atheneum, 1974.

_____. *Ol' Dan Tucker*. Harcourt, Brace & World, 1963.

_____. *On Christmas Day in the Morning*. Harcourt, Brace & World, 1959.

_____. *Over in the Meadow*. Illustrated by Feodor Rojankovsky. Harcourt, Brace & World, 1967.

_____. *The Swapping Boy*. Harcourt, Brace & World, 1960.

Mills, Alan. *The Hungry Goat*. Hale, 1964.

Nic Leodhas, Sorche. *Always Room for One More*. Illustrated by Nonny Hogrogian. Holt, Rinehart & Winston, 1965.

———. *Kellyburn Braes*. Holt, Rinehart & Winston, 1968.

———. *The Laird of Cockpen*. Holt, Rinehart & Winston, 1969.

Oberhansli, Gertrude. *Sleep, Baby, Sleep*. Atheneum, 1967.

Paterson, A. B. *Waltzing Matilda*. Holt, Rinehart & Winston, 1972.

Peek, Merle. *Roll Over! A Counting Song*. Clarion, 1981.

Quackenbush, Robert. *Clementine*. Lippincott, 1974.

———. *Go Tell Aunt Rhody*. Lippincott, 1973.

———. *Man on the Flying Trapeze*. Lippincott, 1972.

———. *Old MacDonald Had a Farm*. Lippincott, 1972.

———. *Pop! Goes the Weasel and Yankee Doodle*. Lippincott, 1976.

———. *She'll Be Comin' round the Mountain*. Lippincott, 1973.

———. *Skip to My Lou*. Lippincott, 1975.

Rounds, Glen. *Casey Jones: The Story of a Brave Engineer*. Golden Gate, 1968.

———. *The Strawberry Roan*. Golden Gate, 1970.

———. *Sweet Betsy from Pike*. Golden Gate, 1973.

Schackburg, Richard. *Yankee Doodle*. Prentice-Hall, 1965.

Seeger, Pete and Charles Seeger. *The Foolish Frog*. Macmillan, 1973.

Spier, Peter. *The Erie Canal*. Doubleday, 1970.

———. *The Fox Went Out on a Chilly Night*. Doubleday, 1961.

———. *London Bridge Is Falling Down!* Doubleday, 1967.

———. *Star-Spangled Banner*. Doubleday, 1973.

———. *To Market! To Market!* Doubleday, 1967.

Stanley, Diane Zuromskis. *Fiddle-I-Fee*. Little, Brown, 1979.

Taylor, Mark. *Old Blue, You Good Dog You*. Golden Gate, 1970.

Troughton, Joanna. *The Little Mohee*. Dutton, 1971.

Yulga. *Bears Are Sleeping*. Scribner, 1967.

Zemach, Harve. *Mommy Buy Me a China Doll*. Illustrated by Margot Zemach. Follett, 1966.

Zemach, Margot. *Hush, Little Baby*. Dutton, 1976.

Zuromskis, Diane. *The Farmer in the Dell*. Little, Brown, 1978.

T IS FOR THANKSGIVING AND TRANSFORMATION

Thanksgiving

Over the years there has been considerable discussion concerning the real origin of Thanksgiving. During an interview, which was published in the November 1982 *Early Years* magazine, Jamake Highwater is quoted as saying (about Thanksgiving), "It's an Indian holiday, a harvest festival. It wasn't the Pilgrims who invited us, but we invited them." Later when he was asked if he would prefer that the interview be published during a month other than November, Highwater replied, "Not at all. Better to think of us once a year than not at all." So here is a list of Thanksgiving books. Don't expect them to settle the question of the origin of Thanksgiving. Kessel's book may attempt to answer the question but the accuracy will have to depend on you and your students' research.

Booklist—Thanksgiving

Brown, Marc. *Arthur's Thanksgiving*. Little, Brown, 1983.

Cohen, Miriam. *Don't Eat Too Much Turkey*. Morrow, 1987.

Kessel, Joyce. *Squanto and the First Thanksgiving*. Illustrated by Lisa Donze. Carolrhoda, 1983.

Kraus, Robert. *How Spider Saved Turkey*. Simon & Schuster, 1981.

Kroll, Steven. *One Tough Turkey*. Illustrated by John Wallner. Holiday House, 1982.

Prelutsky, Jack. *It's Thanksgiving*. Illustrated by Marilyn Hafner. Scholastic, 1982.

Whitehead, Pat. *Best Thanksgiving Book—ABC Adventures*. Illustrated by Susan T. Hall. Troll Associates, 1985.

Transformation

Many cultures use transformation in their legends. Paul Goble's *Buffalo Woman* (Bradbury, 1984) is the story of an Indian man who marries a female buffalo who has assumed the form of an Indian maiden. Both are rejected by the Buffalo nation. The brave must pass various tests before being allowed to join his wife and son as a buffalo.

Frederick Gurima's *Princess of the Full Moon* (Macmillan, 1970) is an African folktale in which a princess seeks a husband as physically perfect as she. She selects the physically attractive Devil Prince of Midnight. A physically unattractive shepherd assumes the appearances of numerous animals while he attempts to rescue her by fighting the monster prince.

Both stories depict that things (or people) are not always what they seem on the outside.

Three illustrators have shown transformation of their story character in masterful illustrations. In Errol LeCain's illustrations for Perrault's *Cinderella* (Bradbury, 1972), LeCain depicts the transformation of Cinderella from grand lady to peasant girl in a fade-out where five images of Cinderella in various stages of transformation are shown on the same page. All the stars have become clock faces with the hands at midnight. Gerald McDermott uses a similar technique to show the transformation of the young brave into an arrow in *Arrow to the Sun: A Pueblo Indian Tale* (Viking, 1974). Another example of transformation in a pictorial form is included in Elizabeth Cleaver's *The Enchanted Caribou* (Atheneum, 1985).

U IS FOR THE UNKNOWN

Whenever there is something that is unknown that something becomes feared and something to be described as scary. For books that focus on Fears and Scary Things refer to the booklist by that title (see index).

V IS FOR VAN ALLSBURG, VAN LEEUWEN, VOIGT, AND VIORST

Van Allsburg, Van Leeuwen, Voigt, and Viorst are four popular authors and illustrators of children's books. Chris Van Allsburg produces visual delights and mystical texts which delight both the picture book and intermediate or middle school set. Jean Van Leeuwen has written some very successful early readers. Oliver Pig and Amanda are two of her popular book characters. Cynthia Voigt writes books for older readers. Her books, which evoke deep feelings and emotions from the reader, contain many layers of meaning. And Judith Viorst's early writing focused on the problems and incidents in the lives of her three sons, Alexander, Anthony, and Nicholas. Her children are grown now bringing her to look further from home for her inspiration.

Children are always interested in hearing tidbits about an author's or illustrator's life. Make it a point to find out some information about favorite authors and illustrators. Make sure the children are aware of who has written and illustrated their favorite books. Help them learn how to locate books by their favorite creators by using the card catalog or by using the alphabetical arrangement in the library or media center.

Author units can always involve a search in the library for the author's or illustrator's books.

W IS FOR WORDLESS

Using Wordless and Minimal-Text Books

Wordless books are particularly valuable in stimulating the language development of children. These books have little or no text, encouraging children to tell their own stories by interpreting the expressive pictures. Choose one of the titles and tell the story you would tell. Model the storytelling procedure for the children. Eventually the children can work in small groups or in pairs to tell the story. Finally many will want to write individual stories to accompany the illustrations. Intermediate or middle school students will enjoy both writing the story and recording it complete with sound effects. Wordless books really have no age level. A particularly interesting book to use with students is Hutchins's *Rosie's Walk*. This book and several others on the following list are available from Weston Woods or Random House/Miller-Brody in filmstrip or film format. Using that medium will allow you to more effectively share the illustrations while the class creates the text to accompany the illustrations. Filmstrips of other books may be used in the same manner to give additional experience with storytelling. The story in book form may have a great deal of text but if the illustrations carry the story independently, just the filmstrip of a sound filmstrip package could be used. This would in effect create a wordless filmstrip.

Booklist—Wordless or Minimal-Text Books

Arnosky, Jim. *Mouse Numbers and Letters*. Harcourt Brace Jovanovich, 1982.
    A mouse counts ten groups of objects and then builds the letters of the alphabet from twigs.

Briggs, Raymond. *The Snowman*. Random House, 1978.
    The adventures of a snowman-come-to-life and the boy who made him.

Carle, Eric. *Do You Want to Be My Friend?* Crowell, 1971.
    A mouse searches for a friend among the many animals he encounters.

Carle, Eric. *I See a Song*. Crowell, 1973.
    A visual and musical delight shows a performing violinist who creates joy in his audience.

Carroll, Ruth. *Rolling Downhill*. Walck, 1973.
    A cat and a dog, playing with a ball of yarn, roll downhill and meet Skunk, Raccoon, and Bear. At the end of the book Cat and Dog, tired from their adventure, set out for another.

dePaola, Tomie. *The Hunter and the Animals*. Holiday House, 1981.
    A bluebird warns the animals that a hunter is coming. The scared animals hide. When the hunter cannot find the animals he falls asleep, exhausted. The animals befriend the hunter and lead him out of the forest to his home.

dePaola, Tomie. *Pancakes for Breakfast*. Harcourt Brace Jovanovich, 1978.
    An old lady wakes up craving pancakes. To make the pancakes she must gather milk from the cow, collect eggs from the hens, and churn butter from the cream. When she returns from the neighbors with the final ingredient, maple syrup, she finds that the dog and cat have spilled all of the other ingredients and have made a mess of the kitchen. She rectifies the situation by following the aroma of freshly grilled pancakes coming from a neighbor's kitchen.

dePaola, Tomie. *Sing, Pierrot, Sing*. Harcourt Brace Jovanovich, 1983.
    A true incident in the life of a famous clown figure.

Fromm, Lilo. *Muffel and Plums*. Macmillan, 1973.
    Nine short stories about the adventures of a lion and a rabbit.

Goodall, John S. *Creepy Castle*. Atheneum, 1975.
A mouse and his lady friend are chased by a mean rat in a medieval castle. They must escape from a dungeon complete with dragons and bats, and so they go aboard a frog-powered lily pad.

Goodall, John S. *An Edwardian Summer*. Atheneum, 1976.
Double-page spreads tell the story of a brother and sister on their way to a school in an English town during the Edwardian period. The reader sees a pub, a school, a market, and other locations common to the Edwardian period.

Goodall, John S. *Naughty Nancy*. Atheneum, 1975.
An elegant mouse wedding is upset by Nancy the flower girl. She rides up the aisle on the bride's dress train and goes along on the honeymoon.

Goodall, John S. *Paddy Pork's Holiday*. Atheneum, 1976.
A wagon of friendly pigs takes Paddy Pork on a camping adventure.

Goodall, John S. *Paddy's Evening Out*. Atheneum, 1973.
A good-natured pig gallantly attempts to rescue his lady friend's fan which has been dropped over the theater balcony.

Heller, Linda. *Lily at the Table*. Macmillan, 1979.
Lily does not want to eat what the adults want her to eat. While she sits at the supper table she plays with her food and fantasizes about skateboarding down a wedge of cheese, going fishing in a bowl of cereal, and swimming in a glass of milk.

Hogrogian, Nonny. *Apples*. Macmillan, 1972.
An apple vendor eats an apple, tosses the core aside, the core starts another tree, the tree blooms, and the cycle continues until the vendor picks an apple from the new tree and eats the apple. The subtle indication brings us to realize that the cycle will continue over and over again.

Hutchins, Pat. *Changes, Changes*. Macmillan, 1971.
Two wooden dolls arrange and rearrange wooden building blocks to create a wood block house. When the house catches fire the resourceful couple dismantle the house.

Hutchins, Pat. *Rosie's Walk*. Macmillan, 1968.
The most self-reliant hen in the barnyard goes for a walk, unmindful of the fact that she is being stalked by a hungry fox. At every turn she manages to foil his plans to capture her.

Kent, Jack. *The Egg Book*. Macmillan, 1975.
A hen wants to be a mother. She hatches a turtle, an alligator, and a frog. After they are hatched they go home to their real mothers. Finally she lays an egg of her own and is delighted when a chick hatches from the egg.

Krahn, Fernando. *April Fools*. Dutton, 1974.
A cat jumps on a fruit vendor's scale and almost gets run over by a car as he is chased by a boy. The cat leads the boy to a dock where the boy is locked on board a steamship and escapes just in time to save the cat from being thrown into the ocean.

Krahn, Fernando. *A Funny Friend from Heaven*. Lippincott, 1977.
An angel meets a hobo when she lands in a tree. They eat together and then the angel turns them both into clowns. Their antics cause havoc with an ice cream man and create chaos at a ballet. The hobo remains on earth, only this time he is in a circus continuing to make people laugh.

Krahn, Fernando. *The Mystery of the Giant Footprints*. Dutton, 1977.
A little boy and girl follow the trail of giant footprints in the snow. Their parents and neighbors follow them and finally locate the two children in a cave playing with two friendly "monsters," monsters with one giant hairy foot, a triangular body, and fox-like faces.

Krahn, Fernando. *Sebastian and the Mushroom*. Delacorte, 1976.
Sebastian finds a fantasy world of other planets and stars when he climbs a giant mushroom that has been painted by a man. When he falls off the moon he lands back in his own room.

Krahn, Fernando. *The Self-Made Snowman*. Lippincott, 1974.
On the way down a mountain a ball of snow gains a body, arms, a head, and clothes while the townspeople and animals show their amazement.

Krahn, Fernando. *Who's Seen the Scissors?* Dutton, 1975.
The tailor's bright red scissors fly out the window and cause all sorts of problems. The dog's leash is cut and a lantern falls on a customer in a restaurant.

Lisker, Sonia O. *Lost*. Harcourt Brace Jovanovich, 1975.
When a boy gets separated from his parents at the zoo he overcomes his fear but only when he tries to comfort another lost boy. The two of them find their parents and both families sit down to a picnic dinner.

McCully, Emily Arnold. *The Christmas Gift*. Harper & Row, 1988.
A broken gift brings more joy when the gift is replaced with a train from the attic.

McCully, Emily Arnold. *First Snow*. Harper & Row, 1985.
A wordless story about an extended family who gets out their red pickup truck to take everyone sleigh riding.

McCully, Emily Arnold. *New Baby*. Harper & Row, 1988.
The attention given to a new baby in the mouse family brings the other children to exhibit signs of jealousy.

McCully, Emily Arnold. *Picnic*. Harper & Row, 1984.
A wordless story featuring an extended mouse family who goes to the woods for a picnic. Baby Mouse bounces out of the red pickup and finds that his family doesn't miss him right away.

McCully, Emily Arnold. *School*. Harper & Row, 1987.
A wordless story. Baby Mouse is left behind when all the other mice children gather their backpacks and go off to school. Mother Mouse settles down to a good book and Baby Mouse finds that the house is too quiet. He goes out the door to find out what school is all about.

Ramage, Corinne. *The Joneses*. Lippincott, 1975.
Mother goes off on a submarine and father stays home to care for thirty-one children. Father's story is told on the left side of the page and mother's story is told on the right side.

Schweninger, Ann. *A Dance for Three*. Dial, 1979.
The first of three stories tells of the effect three musicians have on the moon. The second is a tale of three friends enjoying some music and dance. The third story is about characters who must figure out what to do when they are confronted with an overcrowded boat.

Spier, Peter. *Peter Spier's Christmas*. Doubleday, 1983.
Traces a family's Christmas from the very first start of the holiday to the placing of the last ornament.

Sugita, Yutaka. *My Friend Little John and Me*. McGraw-Hill, 1973.
A good-natured dog and his little boy master take a bath together. The dog waits to say grace before eating and remains quiet as he lets chickens walk over him. He even responds with appropriate attentiveness when his master plays teacher.

Turk, Hanne. *Bon Appetit Max*. Picture Book Studio, 1987.
————. *Butterfly Max*. Picture Book Studio, 1987.
————. *Chocolate Max*. Picture Book Studio, 1987.
————. *Do It Yourself Max*. Picture Book Studio, 1987.
————. *Friendship Max*. Picture Book Studio, 1987.
————. *A Fright for Max*. Picture Book Studio, 1987.
————. *Goodnight Max*. Picture Book Studio, 1987.
————. *Good Sport Max*. Picture Book Studio, 1987.
————. *Happy Birthday Max*. Picture Book Studio, 1987.
————. *A Lesson for Max*. Picture Book Studio, 1987.
————. *Max the Art Lover*. Picture Book Studio, 1987.
————. *Max Packs*. Picture Book Studio, 1987.
————. *Max versus the Cube*. Picture Book Studio, 1987.
————. *Merry Christmas Max*. Picture Book Studio, 1987.
————. *Rainy Day Max*. Picture Book Studio, 1987.
————. *Raking Leaves with Max*. Picture Book Studio, 1987.
————. *Robinson Max*. Picture Book Studio, 1987.
————. *The Rope Skips Max*. Picture Book Studio, 1987.
————. *Snapshot Max*. Picture Book Studio, 1987.
————. *A Surprise for Max*. Picture Book Studio, 1987.
The wordless tales of Max the mouse who has an adventure with a single focus, as indicated by the title itself. *Butterfly Max, Chocolate Max, Friendship Max, Goodnight Max, Christmas Max*, and *Rainy Day Max* are available in a kit from Society for Visual Education. The kit includes a filmstrip and cassette of each title and a teacher's manual. The kit is titled *Max's Reading Readiness Adventure*.

Turkle, Brinton. *Deep in the Forest*. Dutton, 1976.
A little bear visits the cabin of some people. It is a reverse version of "Goldilocks and the Three Bears."

Vincent, Gabrielle. *Ernest and Celestine's Patchwork Quilt*. Greenwillow, 1982.
Two friends make a patchwork quilt. When they realize that each of them needs one, they make another.

Winter, Paula. *The Bear and the Fly*. Crown, 1976.
A buzzing fly is unaware of the commotion that he is causing in bear's house.

X IS FOR BO*X*

BoXes in Books

Put a mystery object into a box and let the children use their senses to ascertain what the mystery object is. The children can use their senses of hearing, sight, touch, and taste (with supervision). Be sure you caution children not to taste unknown foods, pills, or such unless an adult verifies that it is safe to taste. In conjunction with this use of the boxes read some books that include boxes and their interesting contents.

Booklist — BoXes

deRegniers, Beatrice Schenk. *Catch a Little Fox: Variations on a Folk Rhyme*. Illustrated by Brinton Turkle. Seabury, 1970.

Duvoisin, Roger. *Petunia*. Knopf, 1950.

Goodall, John. *Jacko*. Harcourt Brace Jovanovich, 1972.

Gordon, Margaret. *The Supermarket Mice*. Dutton, 1984.

Hutchins, Pat. *The Silver Christmas Tree*. Macmillan, 1974.

Langstaff, John. *Oh, A-Hunting We Will Go*. Illustrated by Nancy Parker. Atheneum, 1974.

Mathis, Sharon Bell. *The Hundred Penny Box*. Illustrated by Leo Dillon and Diane Dillon. Viking, 1975.

Van Allsburg, Chris. *Jumanji*. Houghton Mifflin, 1981.

Y IS FOR YOLEN AND YORINKS

Yolen, Jane

Jane Yolen is the author of the award-winning *Owl Moon* (Philomel, 1987) and many other books. She writes books for the picture book group as well as full-length novels of science fantasy for young adults. Locate books by Yolen in your library by checking the card catalog.

Yorinks, Arthur

Arthur Yorinks is the author of *Company's Coming* (Crown, 1988), *It Happened in Pinsk* (Farrar, Straus & Giroux, 1983), *Louis the Fish* (Farrar, Straus & Giroux, 1980), and the Caldecott Award-winning *Hey, Al* (Farrar, Straus & Giroux, 1986).

Z IS FOR ZOO

There are several books and poems about zoos and zoo animals. These two are among my favorites.

Campbell, Rod. *Dear Zoo*. Four Winds, 1982.
A variety of flaps and doors reveal hidden animals that arrive from the zoo. The search is an attempt to find just the right animal for a pet.

Gibbons, Gail. *Zoo*. Crowell, 1987.
A working day at the zoo is presented, from the beginning when the workers arrive to the time when the night guard locks the gate.

Activity suggestions are given for these titles in the Bookshelf section of this book.

Section II:

Chapter

3

Connections:
Children and Books

RESPONDING TO BOOKS

Much has been written about connecting children and books through the use of activities designed to allow and encourage children to respond to literature. The truth is that no one can read a piece of literature without having some response. Even a "non-response" is in a sense a response. Responses can take many forms and can assist in reaching various levels of comprehension and aid in promoting the value and enjoyment of reading. A daily time allocation for the discussion of books and reading can provide one type of response opportunity for readers. Discussions of books or booktalking allows readers to communicate their thoughts about a particular selection to other readers. Evaluative thinking is stimulated when judgments about the reality or fantasy qualities of a selection are discussed among the readers. Discussions of the author's purpose and biases can also contribute to the building of evaluative skills. Appreciation for a piece of literature is often enhanced when an emotional and active response to the content is solicited. Relating the content to the reader's own life helps the reader to identify with the characters and incidents in the books. Discussions might center on incidents in books that parallel situations in real life. Appreciation for the written work is also stimulated when the author's craft is examined. How did the author make you feel the way you did? What words did he or she use? How did the words help you visualize, smell, taste, hear or feel? What memorable pictures has the author created? By encouraging readers to discuss and talk about books in a meaningful manner the experience of the book will be extended and will serve to assist in building thinking skills.

Discussions differ from the traditional question and answer format sometimes used by teachers to assess "if a child has completely read a selection." In the first place, the goal of a discussion or conference approach to reading is to enhance the reading, not merely check if the child has read the selection thoroughly enough that he or she can recall literal details from the story. Reader-led discussions and conferences help children reorganize and translate the story into their own words and to make inferential judgments. They learn to classify by putting characters and events into categories. They learn to summarize by describing the action of a story in paraphrased statements. They learn to relay information about the implied actions and events that took place. Encouraging discussions throughout the reading process will stimulate readers to think about what might happen next and to discuss the events that are influencing the actions of the characters. To make a point or to clarify specific assertions, some readers may need to re-read portions of the selection to substantiate what has been said during the discussions. Throughout the discussions readers will begin to examine the cause and effect of relationships, build inferences, and predict outcomes. They will begin to make their own connections and to attach meaning to the text.

Other opportunities for responding to books and stories should also be made available to readers. In addition to discussion sessions responses to the literature might include the expressive arts: art, crafts, music, drama, writing, as well as cooking, games, and more reading. Encouraging a visual or active response to literature has several benefits. The activity itself can be enjoyable and thus may help a reader to connect with a piece of literature in a memorable way. The act of reading is often a solitary activity. The interaction provided through the reading discussions and the sharing of other active responses can do much to help children develop interactive skills. Activity opportunities will allow a reader to reflect upon what he or she has read and will allow a transition between one selection and another. Less able readers may be able to gain confidence and grow in their feeling of self-worth if they are able to respond to literature utilizing an attribute in which they already feel more confident. For example, a child who is a superb artist may gain confidence if he or she is encouraged to draw a favorite scene from the selection and to share the drawing with others. A child who speaks well might be encouraged to "sell" the book by telling about it onto a cassette tape. The tape could be put in a listening center for others to listen to and hopefully be encouraged to read the book. Creative writers might be asked to transform their favorite episode from the book into a puppet play or a minidrama that might be performed for the rest of the class or group.

The teacher's or librarian's role is to encourage and guide children to respond in different ways, to make connections that are meaningful to them. There should be alternatives and guidelines for the selection and completion of the activities. It is important to remember that having alternatives is all-important. Alternatives provide an element of choice which allows for the maximization of the experience. Without choice, opportunities for building a child's sense of self-worth will get buried in an activity that becomes just another assignment. Alternatives for response opportunities should be varied and plentiful. And we must not forget that an important alternative will always be the opportunity to read another book. Sometimes a teacher will need to challenge a particular child and will want to specify a specific type of response. But even then care should be taken to give some type of choice within the parameters of creating the challenge. The same may be true if a teacher wishes to help children make a link with another curriculum area or a connection with a previous reading or activity. Even as the activity is defined within a narrower structure the components of good lesson design should be kept well in mind. Motivation is all-important as is modeling and a chance for the children to mold their responses within the confines of the structure set forth by the teacher or librarian. The enjoyment an adult shares with young readers will have a dramatic effect on the attitude of those readers with regard to the activity and response suggestion.

Activity responses should never take priority over reading itself. In all cases the activity suggested should be purposeful. There is an inherent danger in allowing the activities to become time fillers that neither result naturally from the reading nor extend the reader's enjoyment or understanding of the literature.

While there are several types of activities that could be suggested for many books, most books lend themselves to a merging of activities—to natural connections. Some books appear to be obvious choices for a particular type of response. Frank Asch's *Popcorn* (Parents, 1979) or Tomie dePaola's *The Popcorn Book* (Holiday House, 1978) could provide some reading material on a day when an excuse is desired for a popcorn read and feed. DePaola's book could also provide a model for motivating some research into the origins of other common foods. Gingerbread cookies can be made in conjunction with Paul Galdone's *The Gingerbread Boy* (Seabury, 1975), and older students will want to make tofu shakes when they read the recipe in Jamie Gilson's *Can't Catch Me I'm the Gingerbread Man* (Lothrop, Lee & Shepard, 1981). A taste of camomile tea will extend the experience when Beatrix Potter's *The Tale of Peter Rabbit* (Warne, 1901) is shared. These are rather obvious connections between books and foods but the bookshelves of your library are filled with other books that could be parlayed into response activities encompassing cooking, taste testing, family activities, mathematical concepts, cooperative learning, comprehension, decision making, and practical writing applications.

Recipes sent home can foster involvement between the child and other members of the family. When the cooking is classroom-centered, math concepts, cooperative learning, and practical application of reading skills can be integrated into the activity. Many books lend themselves to enjoying these types of activities associated with food. Harry Devlin and Wende Devlin have incorporated a specific food in several of their books. *Old Witch and the Polka Dot Ribbon* (Parents/Four Winds, 1970) featured the Old Black Witch and her special concoction that was to win her a prize at the county fair. The witch's magic nut cake did win but only after some tomfoolery and havoc spreading on the part of the witch. On the back of the book a recipe for magic nut bread is shared with the readers. This story and recipe can be used in a variety of ways. After reading the book aloud to children send home a copy of the magic nut cake recipe with the suggestion that the cake be tried in the family kitchen. A classroom activity could involve the doubling of the recipe to make a recipe that would yield a quantity sufficient for the class to taste. The cake could actually be made in an activity period. This would involve cooperative planning for the bringing of the ingredients and utensils needed for the recipe. Once the cake was made it could be shared during another session where the story or another story is read. However, my favorite way to use this book and recipe is to create the illusion of a visit by the Old Black Witch. Sometime during the weeks before Halloween the children are introduced to the character of the Old Black Witch through a reading of an earlier story in this sequence, *Old Black Witch* (Parents/Four Winds, 1966). Plan to read this story on a day when the school cafeteria has served pancakes for breakfast since *Old Black Witch* uses blueberry pancakes as a story element. Most important is the development of the character, the Old Black Witch. Nicky's mother has just purchased the Jug and Muffin tea room and it appears that the outspoken but friendly witch is part of the package. Old Black Witch uses her magic to make two thieves disappear (actually she changes them into two spotted toads). The thieves were stealing the money Nicky's mother had made selling blueberry pancakes. A few days or weeks later, but shortly before Halloween, share *Old Witch and the Polka Dot Ribbon*. The magic nut cake recipe specifies golden raisins. Read the story and discuss the recipe and even show children the difference between the more common dark raisins and the golden raisins. Discuss why the raisins are a different color and make a point to mention that some people believe that the golden raisins are magic and that is probably why the witch uses them in her recipe. Continue by suggesting that they could identify magic nut cake by the golden raisins. Then concoct your own story about the witch liking to bake so much that often she bakes cakes for friends. Discuss the witch's clothing so she could be recognized if she were ever seen. At the conclusion of the discussion session make sure that each child has a copy of the recipe to take home for a family baking event. In the next day or two, but before Halloween actually comes, arrange to have a batch of the magic nut cake mysteriously appear in the classroom during a time when the children are out of the room. A note might be left behind, but it probably won't be necessary. The children will certainly suspect who put the cake there but they will not be sure, especially when a witch's black pointed hat shows up in the library, office, or some other central location. They will no longer be quite so sure about the real identity of the Old Black Witch. It is of course with younger children that this whole dramatic scene can be played out with delightful success. They will be ecstatic when someone shows up on Halloween day in full witch costume. The children will read and reread the stories of the Old Black Witch and enjoy them throughout the year, always with memories of the magic nut cake and the drama that accompanied their first encounter with the stories. Older children enjoy the stories (and a taste of the magic nut cake) but their response to the stories might be more appropriately channeled toward reading several of the Old Witch stories by the Devlins and then creating another adventure for the witch. They might also do some wide reading of stories with witches in them and then discuss the portrayal of witches in literature.

Other books can be utilized to motivate similar food-related responses. Read *Pancakes, Pancakes!* by Eric Carle (Knopf, 1970) and then serve up a special readers' lunch or breakfast of pancakes and strawberry jam. Try making doughnuts from tube biscuits after reading the "Doughnuts" chapter in *Homer Price* by Robert McCloskey (Viking, 1943). Make a hundred scrumptious cookies after reading Keiko Kasza's *The Wolf's Chicken Stew* (Putnam, 1978). Older students who read Judy Blume's *Freckle Juice* (Four Winds, 1971) will have great fun forming teams and creating their own versions of the famed freckle juice. An official panel of tasters could judge the concoctions. Of course, each team must record its recipe in standard form. The recording of the recipe would involve perusing cookbooks to ascertain the form and structure generally used for the writing of recipes. The various recipes could be collected into a recipe book complete with illustrations of a scene from the book. It is not only stories and books that can be utilized. Poems often have a food theme. In *The New Kid on the Block* by Jack Prelutsky (Greenwillow, 1986) a poem, "Bleezer's Ice Cream Store," lists many unusual flavors of ice cream, as does "Eighteen Flavors" by Shel Silverstein in *Where the Sidewalk Ends* (Harper & Row, 1974). While a cool luscious ice cream cone might hit the spot on a warm autumn day, just as much fun is creating your own wonderful ice cream flavors through the use of descriptive language. Make a giant cone for the wall and then pile on scoops of ice cream colored to represent the delicious flavor created by each student. Follow by creating a class list of "twenty-nine flavors." Or try listing an alphabet of ice cream flavors. Conduct a class survey of favorite ice cream flavors. Graph the results to create a pictorial report. Expand the survey to other classrooms and compare results class versus class, adults versus children, and intermediate students versus primary students.

So while food might provide the connection to a book, the response is not limited to eating and cooking. Every area of the curriculum could be brought into play. Similar types of activities can be brought about through a focus on the art in books.

In many books the illustrations play a major role as the illustrator can also change the mood or tone of a story. For example, "Hansel and Gretel" is a popular folktale known for many generations. The story text might stay essentially the same but the illustrations might change the mood of the traditional tale by depicting the parents as either cold and harsh or as loving but poor. The characterization of the witch is most often that of a menacing hag but in some versions she is especially wicked. This is a tale that can be foreboding for a very young child. The witch is killed in the same manner that she plans to kill the children. The stepmother also dies and the children are reunited with their joyful father. The illustrations by Anthony Browne create a contemporary setting while Paul Zelinsky uses somber but lush oil paintings to create the dense dark forest and the interior of the poor woodcutter's home, suggesting a more traditional setting. Zelinsky's characters are in period dress. Susan Jeffers meticulously presents each detail in the forest scenes; leaves of the trees and individual birds are exquisite. Her illustrations do not differentiate between the experiences in the forest and those with the witch. She is one of the artists to pictorially suggest that the stepmother and the witch are one and the same. In her illustrations, the witch is wrapped in a shawl identical to the stepmother's. Anthony Browne makes this same suggestion by using a mole on each woman's cheek. He includes other pictorial symbols in his illustrations. He fills the illustrations with reflected images, symbols of cages and flight, and the triangular shape representative of the witch's hat. Browne's edition has been criticized for the contemporary setting; adults feel that the image of a contemporary story brings the story too close to the present and in effect makes it more threatening to the young reader. But the variation makes the story all the more interesting for critical reading by the older reader. Lisbeth Zwerger keeps the time element in the distance by portraying her characters and scenes in a brown wash which gives the feeling of long ago.

Story grammar can be compared and contrasted along with a discussion of the change in the story, if any, brought about by the variety of settings depicted. In addition, some of the elements of storytelling can be identified and discussed. Several versions, including the Scribner translation illustrated by Adrienne Adams, and the versions illustrated by Browne and Zwerger, retain the storyteller's coda or verse that traditionally ends the story. The Scribner version ends the story with this coda.

> My story is done,
> See the mouse run.
> If it's caught in a trap,
> You can make a fur cap.

Gather together as many versions of "Hansel and Gretel" as are available to your class. After the children have read several of the versions share with them some of the comparison information given here. During a first experience with comparing and contrasting different editions of a story a lot of modeling will need to be done with the group. Be sure to give them ample time to discover some of the information for themselves. However, suggestions could be inserted in the discussions to stimulate thinking about both the text and the illustrations and the effect each has on the total retelling.

Booklist—Hansel and Gretel

Alderson, Brian, translator. *The Brothers Grimm: Popular Folk Tales*. "Hansel and Gretel." Illustrated by Michael Foreman. Doubleday, 1978.

Ehrlich, Amy, translator. *The Random House Book of Fairy Tales*. "Hansel and Gretel." Illustrated by Diane Goode. Random House, 1985.

Grimm Brothers. *Hansel and Gretel*. Illustrated by Adrienne Adams. Translated by Charles Scribner, Jr. Scribner, 1975.

_____. *Hansel and Gretel*. Illustrated by Antonella Bolliger-Savielli. Adapted from *Grimm's Fairy Tales*. 1962 ed. Oxford University Press, 1981.

_____. *Hansel and Gretel*. Illustrated by Mildred Boyle. Adapted by Robert Laurence for the story of Humperdinck's opera, authorized by the Metropolitan Opera Guild, Inc. Silver Burdette, 1938.

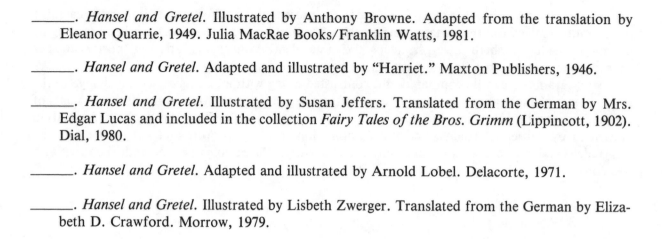

_____. *Hansel and Gretel*. Illustrated by Anthony Browne. Adapted from the translation by Eleanor Quarrie, 1949. Julia MacRae Books/Franklin Watts, 1981.

_____. *Hansel and Gretel*. Adapted and illustrated by "Harriet." Maxton Publishers, 1946.

_____. *Hansel and Gretel*. Illustrated by Susan Jeffers. Translated from the German by Mrs. Edgar Lucas and included in the collection *Fairy Tales of the Bros. Grimm* (Lippincott, 1902). Dial, 1980.

_____. *Hansel and Gretel*. Adapted and illustrated by Arnold Lobel. Delacorte, 1971.

_____. *Hansel and Gretel*. Illustrated by Lisbeth Zwerger. Translated from the German by Elizabeth D. Crawford. Morrow, 1979.

Comparison titles are often more easily identified in the genre of traditional literature. However, there are other titles that could be used, particularly informational books. When only one book is used to obtain information on a particular topic, the information, facts, attitudes, and perspective of the author is more likely to be accepted without question. On the other hand, when two or more books are used the facts are more likely to be compared and evaluated. The purpose of the author will be important as will the author's specificity. Constructing a chart of similarities and differences will be a useful aid to help develop clear thinking. The very simplest of charts would begin with a list of various points covered in the books down the side of a large sheet of paper. Across the top the titles of the comparison books would be listed. Underneath each of the titles a check could be made to indicate whether or not each of the books contained these points. Later more complete charts might supply more details concerning the content, illustrations, or format. A helpful source for using informational books in the classroom is *The Kobrin Letter* edited by Beverly Kobrin. The newsletter is published ten times a year. Each issue reviews new informational books alongside older ones on several topics. Kobrin has also authored a 300-page book focusing on informational books and how to use them. The book, *Eyeopeners! How to Choose and Use Children's Books about Real People, Places, and Things* (Penguin, 1988), focuses on explaining the "total literature connection" and suggests over 500 nonfiction books and over 150 tips for using information books with children.

Illustrated books can also provide sources for critical reading. Many illustrators are noted for their playful additions in their illustrations. Marc Brown usually finds a way to include the names of his three children, Tolon, Tucker, and Eliza, and the name of his wife Laurie in his books. Somewhere in each of his books the names will appear as the signature on a child's painting on the wall, on the ends of baby incubators, on a book, or on other items. In Trina Schart Hyman's *Little Red Riding Hood* (Holiday, 1983) she places a "guardian cat" in the background of the scene where Little Red Riding Hood first encounters the wolf. The cat is present in subsequent pictures. Hyman is the master at hiding interesting material in her illustrations. The dwarfs in *Snow White* (Little, Brown, 1974) resemble her former husband and some of her neighbors. Eric Carle has often included the names of his now-grown children, Kirsten and Rolf, in his picture books, and Tomie dePaola manages to put himself as a child in many of his books. DePaola's illustrations often include one of his Abyssinian cats. Hearts and a stylized bird have become symbolic elements in his pictures. In many of his books he uses the illustrations to include another story element. In *Charlie Needs a Cloak* (Prentice-Hall, 1973) a small mouse tells, wordlessly, a second story at the bottom of the page. Sometimes the pictures have an autobiographical note; Arnold Lobel included himself in his paintings. In *The Book of Pigericks* (Harper & Row, 1983), Lobel appears as a pig with a mustache and glasses on the front of the book jacket and on an opening page. When Stephen Gammell illustrated Cynthia Rylant's *The Relatives Came* (Bradbury, 1985) he included his parents, his wife, and himself. His father is giving a young boy a haircut in one double-page spread while Gammell himself appears on the next double-page illustration as a bearded, bespeckled guitar player in tattered jeans and red sneakers. The next pages show his wife taking a picture with a camera. His mother is at the end of the book waving good-bye to the visiting relatives. Don Wood used his own pillared home as the house model for *The Napping House* (Harcourt Brace Jovanovich, 1984) by Audrey Wood. By integrating information about the author or illustrator when sharing the work by that author or illustrator much enjoyment can be extracted. Explaining the connections between the story and illustrations and actual events and people in the book creator's life provides readers the opportunity to organize their facts and to make inferences from those facts.

The design of a book can provide a collaboration between viewing and reading experiences. Steven Kellogg and Peter Spier are noted for beginning the story visually on the blank sheets and titles pages that precede the beginning of the text and they often make a final statement pictorially at the conclusion of the book. Endpapers and the paper jackets of other books are designed to fulfill a specific purpose, as with the devil's tail that is part of the design for Nonny Hogrogian's version of the Grimm Brothers' *The Devil with the Three Golden Hairs* (Knopf, 1983). The Devil's appearance is successfully foreshadowed by a tail emerging from the marbled paper. Other illustrators utilize foldout pages, as in *Tomie dePaola's Book of Christmas Carols* (Putnam, 1987). Others, such as Brian Wildsmith and John Goodall, use a combination of full and half pages to develop the concept of contrasting roles and to enhance plot development. Eric Carle successfully used pages of graduated size in *The Grouchy Ladybug* (Crowell, 1977) to depict the increasing size of the animals being confronted. As the ladybug's voice became more and more boisterous and as her words increased in size and boldness, so did the typeface.

Traditional symbols or colors and designs to set the mood or setting of a story are often part of a book's design. Persian rugs are depicted on the endpapers of *The Contest* (Greenwillow, 1976), an Armenian tale retold and illustrated by Nonny Hogrogian. African designs are reproduced on the blank leaves of Gerald McDermott's *Anansi the Spider* (Holt, Rinehart & Winston, 1972). Charcoal-colored endpapers focus on the emperor's heartbreak over his daughter's blindness in Jane Yolen's *The Seeing Stick* (Crowell, 1977), illustrated by Remy Charlip and Demetra Marsalis. Mice following one another in a circular fashion surround the text on the title page of Barbara Bartos-Hoppner's version of *The Pied Piper of Hamelin*, illustrated by Annegert Fuchshuber (Lippincott, 1985), foreshadowing the action in the story itself. For Michael Patrick Hearn's *The Porcelain Cat* (Little, Brown, 1987), Leo Dillon and Diane Dillon have created endpapers that use dark silhouettes of cats and rats on a lighter background. These animals foreshadow the cumulative tale within, a tale that centers on obtaining the ingredients for a potion that will bring a porcelain cat to life. The cat then is to rid the sorcerer's house of rats. The conclusion of the tale has the porcelain cat brought to life, pouncing on the rat only to hit the floor too hard and shatter. From the broken pieces of the porcelain cat rises a spirit-like porcelain bird. Only then does the reader realize that in the light spaces between the cats' silhouettes on the endpapers is the lighter figure of a bird.

Dedications also contain interesting pieces of information, sometimes about the content of the book, but more often about the author or illustrator. For example, Steven Kellogg most often dedicates his books to his six children, Pam, Melanie, Laurie, Kim, Kevin, and Colin. Sometimes the dedication mentions his wife, Helen. But in *Prehistoric Pinkerton* (Dial, 1987) a new name showed up. The name was that of his brand-new grandchild. Cynthia Rylant's *The Relatives Came* (Bradbury, 1985) is dedicated to "Aunt Agnes and her brood, Dick Jackson and his, Gerry and ours." This dedication includes Rylant's aunt, who did come from Virginia to Rylant's grandparents' home in West Virginia each summer. The dedication also includes her friend and editor Dick Jackson and his family, and Gerry, and their family, which included her son Nate. Rylant's *When I*

Was Young in the Mountains (Dutton, 1982) is based on Rylant's early years, from the ages of four to eight, when she lived with her grandparents while her mother attended nursing school. The book is dedicated to "my grandparents, Elda and Ferrell Rylant." Chris Van Allsburg used his dedication in *The Mysteries of Harris Burdick* (Houghton Mifflin, 1984) to extend the credibility of the fictitious editor, Peter Wenders, who supposedly supplied Van Allsburg with the mysterious drawings.

Borders and illuminated letters not only decorate the page but communicate motifs, settings, and unifying elements of the text and the illustrations. Critical viewing and reading of all the components of a book will enhance the book experience and will help children develop their critical thinking skills and evaluative techniques.

If children are to become real readers they should be encouraged to read books during a silent reading time, during reading instructional periods, and as they discover history, science, the arts, and all the other content area subjects. The books must provide models of good literature and language. They must read in all genres, including the "literature of fact" — nonfiction or informational books. Informational books, like any other books, should be selected for their good writing, quality illustrations, and high standards in book making. A well-stocked central school or public library and the availability of a selection of books from these libraries in the classroom will support a child's growth in reading and in appreciating good writing and illustrations, and will further their understanding of information presented. On the following pages are some suggestions that might be utilized for a variety of critical reading activities.

TRADITIONAL TALES FOR CRITICAL READING

Beauty and the Beast

Marianna Mayer has retold the favorite fairy tale *Beauty and the Beast* (Four Winds, 1978). The intricate artwork by Mercer Mayer illuminates this tale of romance and adventure. The dominant motif is that of transformation, while the thematic wisdom inherent in the story tells us that one should not trust too much in appearances. Other than the tales of Perrault this is the best-known French tale. It was told in the 1800s by a Madame de Beaumont, a French teacher.

Tales whose theme is that one should not trust appearances too much attempt to show that inner qualities of love and kindness are more important than outer appearances. Goode has retold the "Beauty and the Beast" tale in tightly drawn prose. Her illustrations, especially of the girl, have a romantic element in them. Her lion-maned beast contrasts with the catlike beast of the Mayer version. Mayer uses gnarled and stressed forest backdrops with ornately decorated interiors. LeCain's illustrations (for the Harris edition) attempts to reflect the French origins of the tale with his tapestry borders and elegant French court costumes. The illustrations in the Hutton edition are notable for their light and dark shadows that develop story mood. Apy's writing has been criticized for its lack of economy in words and for its slow-moving dialogue-filled text. Michael Hague's illustrations enhance her text.

Booklist—Beauty and the Beast

Apy, Deborah. *Beauty and the Beast*. Illustrated by Michael Hague. Holt, Rinehart & Winston, 1983.

deBeaumont, Madame Leprince. *Beauty and the Beast*. Translated from the French and illustrated by Diane Goode. Bradbury, 1978. (picture book)

Goode, Diane, translator. *Beauty and the Beast*. Illustrated by Diane Goode. Based on the French tale by Madame Leprince deBeaumont. Bradbury, 1978. (picture book)

Harris, Rosemary. *Beauty and the Beast*. Illustrated by Errol LeCain. Doubleday, 1979. (picture book)

Hutton, Warwick. *Beauty and the Beast*. Atheneum, 1985.

Mayer, Marianna. *Beauty and the Beast*. Illustrated by Mercer Mayer. Four Winds, 1978.

Pearce, Philippa. *Beauty and the Beast*. Illustrated by Alan Barrett. Longman Young Books, 1972. (picture book)

Compare and contrast selected versions from the list above with the novel-length version of "Beauty and the Beast," Robin McKinley's *Beauty* (Harper & Row, 1978).

Examine the transformation theme by reading three other tales with this same theme:

Bierhorst, John, editor. *Ring in the Prairie: A Shawnee Legend*. Illustrated by Leo Dillon and Diane Dillon. Dial, 1970.

d'Aulaire, Ingri and Edgar d'Aulaire. "Widow's Son." In *East of the Sun and West of the Moon*. Viking, 1969 (1938).

Gag, Wanda. "Frog Prince." In *Tales from Grimm*. Translated and illustrated by Wanda Gag. Coward McCann, 1943. (This tale is also available in many other collections of Grimm tales.)

Compare and contrast the story grammar of the preceding titles with the following similar tales, each expanding on the thematic statement of not trusting too much in appearances.

Asbjørnsen, Peter Christian and Jorgen E. Moe. *East O' the Sun and West O' the Moon*. Translated by George Webbe Dasent. Dover, 1970.

Berger, Terry. "The Serpent's Bride." In *Black Fairy Tales*. Illustrated by David Omar White. Atheneum, 1969.

Troughton, Joanna. *Sir Gawain and the Loathly Damsel*. Dutton, 1972.

East of the Sun and West of the Moon

Mercer Mayer's retelling of *East of the Sun and West of the Moon* (Four Winds, 1980) is an intertwining of a plot element from the original fairy tale (in which a frog is changed into a prince by a kiss) with details of his own. Here the heroine and her parents are wealthy farmers until their luck changes and the girl has to toil like a "rough peasant." A frog saves her ailing father's life. She kills the creature when he asks her to marry him although she had promised to grant his wish. The spellbound frog is whisked off to the troll's castle, and the ungrateful lass loses her chance to marry a handsome prince until she creates a happy ending by atoning for her mistakes. Mayer's paintings rival in splendor and vigor the award-winning illustrations created by him for Marianna Mayer's *Beauty and the Beast* (Four Winds, 1978), Jay Williams's *Everyone Knows What a Dragon Looks Like* (Four Winds, 1976), and other beautiful tales.

Compare and contrast the Mayer text to one that more closely reflects the original Asbjørnsen and Moe tale. Compare illustrations to identify the mood each creates for the text. A superb title to use for this comparison is Kathleen Hague and Michael Hague's *East of the Sun and West of the Moon*, illustrated by Michael Hague (Harcourt Brace Jovanovich, 1980). The Hague version of this Scandinavian tale is adapted from the Asbjørnsen and Moe collection and remains true to the original. It begins with the offer of a mysterious white bear. The bear persuades a maiden to be his bride by enriching her destitute family. He takes her to his palatial home, deep in a mountain. By gazing at the beast when he's transformed during sleep into a handsome youth, the girl dooms him to wed a hideous troll. He leaves for the troll's castle where his sad bride cannot follow. Hague's paintings in brilliant colors enhance the classic fantasy throughout the suspenseful events as the plucky girl gets help from the four winds and saves her prince at last.

Stories with the Theme of the Emergence of Power

The motif in these stories is that of power. In each of the mouse stories with this theme mouse parents wish to find a spouse for their lovely and intelligent daughter. Of course an ordinary mouse is not good enough for their daughter. In the mouse tales the mistaken belief that someone else is more powerful does not cause any lasting consequences (see the mouse titles in the following list). However, the same misconception imprisons the lowly stonecutter in the mountain for the rest of his life (see McDermott). Discuss the story grammar and the underlying themes in these tales.

Booklist – Emerging Power

Bulatkin, I. F. "The Match-Making of a Mouse." In *Eurasian Folk and Fairy Tales*. Illustrated by Howard Simon. Criterion, 1965.

Gackenbach, Dick. *The Perfect Mouse*. Macmillan, 1984.

McDermott, Gerald. *The Stonecutter*. Viking, 1975.

Uchida, Yoshiko. "The Wedding of the Mouse." In *The Dancing Kettle and Other Japanese Folk Tales*. Illustrated by Richard C. Jones. Harcourt, Brace & World, 1949.

Three Billy Goats Gruff

Read and compare the version of "The Three Billy Goats Gruff" illustrated by Marcia Brown and the one illustrated by Paul Galdone. Compare and contrast the depiction of the troll and the size of the goats in the two books. Recall the story grammar in each of the stories to ascertain variances in the expressions and statements used by the goats or the troll. Essential elements in this traditional Norse tale are the appearance of the troll as the three goats cross the bridge, the repetition of the "trip, trap, trap," the troll demands, and the goats' responses. Discuss which statements sound the most agitated, mean, cooperative, and so forth. After "The Three Billy Goats Gruff" has become a familiar story to younger students, or after older students have recalled the story line of the goats story, read "Sody Sallyraytus." Examine for comparison and contrast purposes the story grammar in the stories.

The structure of this folktale, as in many others, is based on relating three events with rising action. Readers can anticipate the climax resulting in the overthrow of the troll. This tale reinforces the implications of bad behavior receiving punishment and good behavior being rewarded. It has a happy ending brought about by poetic justice. Brown's illustrative style brings a sense of prancing movement to the goats as they cross the bridge. Her troll is a muddy ugly one. Compare her images of the troll and goats to the images created by Galdone. When comparing either of "The Three Billy Goats Gruff" versions with Chase's "Sody Sallyraytus" concentrate on the story grammar.

Booklist—Three Billy Goats Gruff

Asbjørnsen, P. C. and Jorgen E. Moe. *The Three Billy Goats Gruff.* Illustrated by Marcia Brown. Harcourt, Brace & World, 1957.

Chase, Richard. "Sody Sallyraytus." *Grandfather Tales.* Houghton Mifflin, 1948.

Galdone, Paul. *Three Billy Goats Gruff.* Illustrated by Paul Galdone. Seabury, 1973.

A Native American Legend—Star Husband

The native American Indians are noted for their stories that combine religious beliefs, how-and-why explanations, and references to Indian customs. Mobley has told the story of a young Indian woman who wishes for a star husband. She is granted her wish, marries, and bears a boy child. When she ignores a warning to never dig in the floor of the sky she finds she must leave her star husband and son, the moon. When she dies she is allowed to rejoin them in the sky where she becomes a shining star close by the moon. Goble has used less poetic prose, but his beautiful illustrations authentically represent the Blackfeet artistic traditions. His text differs in that Star Boy is expelled with his mother. He is marked by a facial scar and becomes known as Scarface. In order to marry he must journey to the Sun, who removes the scar. To commemorate this gesture the Blackfeet have a Sun Dance each summer. Star Boy becomes another star and joins his father, Morning Star, and his mother, Evening Star. Goble's illustrated version is based on the original retelling by Grinnell. San Souci's version does not refer to an original source. The illustrations of Daniel San Souci are very striking but the tale has been criticized for its eclectic and embroidered retelling of this Blackfeet tale.

Booklist—Star Husband

Goble, Paul. *Star Boy*. Bradbury, 1983.

Grinnell, George B. *North American Legends*, edited by Virginia Haviland. Illustrated by Ann Strugnell. Collins World, 1979.

Mobley, Jane. *The Star Husband*. Illustrated by Anna Vojtech. Doubleday, 1979.

San Souci, Robert D. *The Legend of Scarface: A Blackfeet Indian Story*. Illustrated by Daniel San Souci. Doubleday, 1978.

Jamake Highwater's *Anpao*, illustrated by Fritz Scholder (Lippincott, 1977), is another version of the Star Boy/Scarface tale. In this novel Anpao meets many traditional Indian characters, such as Coyote, Grandmother Spider, Raven, and the Mouse People, as he journeys to ask the sun for the removal of his scar. For those intermediate and middle school children who are familiar with the outline of the story, portions of this novel would make excellent read aloud material.

Gingerbread Boy

In each of the cumulative stories the title character is attempting to run away from its maker. In each of the stories a series of other animals or people attempt to catch the title character. The character chants a refrain that makes him known as the fastest or cleverest of them all. In most of the tales those animals or people who take up the chase abandon the chase when the next group enters the story. The character finally meets his match when he comes across a crafty fox who tricks him into a position where he is gobbled down. The variations contain some elements of their country of origin; Steel's is a Scottish version while Brown retells a tale from Russia. The Galdone version and the "Johnny Cake" variations are generally thought to be English in origin. In Sawyer's *Journey Cake, Ho!* the ending takes a different twist. Reading the following titles for comparison and contrast purposes will uncover other similarities and differences in the tales.

Booklist—Gingerbread Boy (and Other Tales to Compare)

Brown, Marcia. *The Bun: A Tale from Russia*. Harcourt Brace Jovanovich, 1972.

Galdone, Paul. *The Gingerbread Boy*. Seabury, 1975. Available as a filmstrip/cassette. Listening Library (GFS 700).

Haviland, Virginia. "Johnny Cake." In *Favorite Fairy Tales Told in England*. Little, Brown, 1959.

Jacobs, Joseph. "Johnny Cake." In *Tomie dePaola's Favorite Nursery Tales*, by Tomie dePaola. Putnam, 1986.

Lobel, Anita. *The Pancake*. Morrow, 1978.

"The Pancake." In *The Arbuthnot Anthology of Children's Literature*. 3rd ed. Scott, Foresman, 1971.

Rockwell, Anne. "The Gingerbread Man." In *The Three Bears and 15 Other Stories*. Crowell, 1975; Harper Trophy, 1984.

Sawyer, Ruth. *Journey Cake, Ho!* Illustrated by Robert McCloskey. Viking, 1953. Available as a filmstrip/cassette. Weston Woods (SF80C).

Steel, Flora Annie. "The Wee Bannock." In *English Fairy Tales*. Illustrated by Arthur Rackham. Macmillan, 1962 (1918).

Sedna—An Eskimo Legend

The Eskimo legend of Sedna is told in two versions. Examine the story grammar in each and note the references given for the source of the legend and the illustrations. Discuss which you think is more authentic and why.

McDermott, Beverly Brodsky. *Sedna: An Eskimo Myth*. Viking, 1975.

San Souci, Robert. *Song of Sedna*. Illustrated by Daniel San Souci. Doubleday, 1981.

Rumpelstiltskin

Rumpelstiltskin (German), Tom Tit Tot (English), and Duffy and the Devil (Cornish) all involve a young girl who is depicted as being able to spin either gold or fabric threads to weave beautiful strong cloth. At first, none of the girls can. In each version, when the girl is confronted with a situation where she must spin, an elf-like creature appears and offers to help. In return she offers herself in marriage or her firstborn child to the creature. When the creature appears to claim his reward he relents and offers to give the girl one more chance if she can guess his name. In each case the name is guessed after having been dis-  covered when a friend or servant of the girl overhears the creature chanting a rhyme that divulges his name. The endings in the different versions have variant twists. Watch for the recurrence of the number three in each of the stories.

Booklist—Rumpelstiltskin (and Other Tales to Compare)

Grimm, Jacob and Wilhelm Grimm. *Rumpelstiltskin*. Illustrated by William Stobbs. Walck, 1971. (German)

Grimm, Jacob and Wilhelm Grimm. "Rumpelstiltzkin." In *Arbuthnot Anthology of Children's Literature*. 3rd ed. Scott, Foresman, 1971. (German)

Grimm Brothers. *Rumpelstiltskin*. Illustrated by Diane Diamond. Holiday House, 1983. (German)

Jacobs, Joseph, editor. "Tom Tit Tot." In *English Folk and Fairy Tales*. Putnam, n.d. (English)

Ness, Evaline. *Tom Tit Tot*. Scribner, 1965. (English)

"Tom Tit Tot." In *Arbuthnot Anthology of Children's Literature*. 3rd ed. Scott, Foresman, 1971. (English)

Wilson, Barbara Kerr. "Whippety Stourie." In *Scottish Folk-tales and Legends*. Illustrated by Joan Kiddell-Monroe. Walck, 1954. (Scottish)

Zelinsky, Paul O. *Rumpelstiltskin*. Dutton, 1986. (German)

Zemach, Harve. *Duffy and the Devil*. Illustrated by Margot Zemach. Farrar, Straus & Giroux, 1973. (Cornish)

Soup Stories

In each of these stories a person or persons traveling on foot encounters another person or persons whom they ask for some food. They are refused "because we hardly have enough to eat ourselves." In a show of compassion the traveler produces a stone, nail, or hatchet which is said to have the power to produce the finest soup or gruel, a dish fit for the king. As the water and the object heat up, the traveler comments that while this soup will be delicious it would be even better if just a bit of flour, or carrots, or ground oats, or potatoes could be added. Soon the people produce all the ingredients for a fine soup. All enjoy the feast with bread and butter. The people are grateful to the traveler for having shown them how to always have the ingredients for a fine soup.

Three French soldiers are the travelers in the Brown version. They feed the people of a small French town. Haviland's retelling is very similar to the Zemach retelling and to the story contained in the Greene collection. Rynbach has depicted the story in a post-Revolutionary War setting. A single Revolutionary soldier happens upon a farm family whom he asks for food. His soup stone produces enough soup for him and the entire family. In Ginsburg's Russian version the stone and nail of the other stories is replaced by a hatchet which produces gruel for all to eat.

Booklist—Soup Stories

Brown, Marcia. *Stone Soup*. Scribner, 1947. (French)

Ginsburg, Mirra. "Hatchet Gruel." In *Three Rolls and One Doughnut: Fables from Russia*. Illustrated by Anita Lobel. Dial, 1970. (Russian)

Greene, Ellin. "Old Woman and the Tramp." In *Clever Cooks: A Concoction of Stories, Charms, Recipes and Riddles*. Illustrated by Trina Schart Hyman. Lothrop, Lee & Shepard, 1973.

Haviland, Virginia. "The Old Woman and the Tramp." In *Favorite Fairy Tales Told in Sweden*. Little, Brown, 1966. (Swedish)

Ross, Tony. *Stone Soup*. Dial, 1987.

Rynbach, Iris Van. *The Soup Stone*. Greenwillow, 1988. (Set in post-Revolutionary America)

Zemach, Harve. *Nail Soup*. Adapted from the text by Nils Djurklo. Illustrated by Margot Zemach. Follett, 1964. (Swedish)

In Lloyd Alexander's *The Cat Who Wished to Be a Man* (Dutton, 1973) a wizard transforms his cat Lionel into a young man. The man's catlike ways wear off only gradually. In one of the episodes a good-hearted rogue named Tudbelly uses trickery and a "stone soup recipe" to share a special stew with inhospitable townspeople. Readers of Brown's *Stone Soup* will surely recognize Tudbelly's "delicious Pro Bono Publico" stew as having been made from the same recipe.

Cinderella

There are over 200 variant forms of the "Cinderella" tale. A few of the versions are cited below. Basically the French and the German versions differ in the method by which the cindergirl obtains her finery for the ball. The end in the German version is traditionally much harsher than the all-forgiving ending in the French version. Many other countries have a version as well. Many of those are cited in a booklist, "Cinderella and Variant Tales from around the World," in a book published by Libraries Unlimited in 1988, *An Author a Month (for Pennies)*. That list is followed by "Comparison Notes for Cinderella and Its Variants," which expands on the possibilities for critical reading activities and the "Cinderella" tale. In the shortened list that follows, the Murphy title is a novel that has several of the most common elements from Cinderella woven into it, and the Myers title is a humorous modern-day parody.

Booklist—Cinderella

Ehrlich, Amy. *Cinderella*. Illustrated by Susan Jeffers. Dial, 1985.

Evans, C. S. *Cinderella*. Illustrated by Arthur Rackham. Viking, 1972.

Galdone, Paul. *Cinderella*. McGraw-Hill, 1978.

Grimm Brothers. *Cinderella*. Illustrated by Nonny Hogrogian. Greenwillow, 1981.

_____. *Cinderella*. Illustrated by Otto S. Svend. Larousse, 1978.

Murphy, Shirley Rousseau. *Silver Woven in My Hair*. Illustrated by Alan Tiegreen. Atheneum, 1977. (novel)

Myers, Bernice. *Sidney Rello and the Glass Sneaker*. Macmillan, 1985.

Perrault, Charles. *Cinderella*. Illustrated by Marcia Brown. Scribner, 1954.

Jack and the Beanstalk

The commonality of all of the following "Jack and the Beanstalk" tales is quite evident. Discuss the story grammar and the illustrations in terms of setting, mood established, and story told. The elements relating to the setting in the Appalachian versions are particularly interesting. The Briggs title is actually a modern-day sequel to the original tale.

Booklist – Jack and the Beanstalk

Briggs, Raymond. *Jim and the Beanstalk*. Coward McCann, 1970.

Cauley, Lorinda Bryan. *Jack and the Beanstalk*. Putnam, 1983. (English)

Chase, Jack. "Jack and the Bean Tree." In *The Jack Tales*. Illustrated by Berkeley Williams, Jr. Houghton Mifflin, 1943. (Appalachian – U.S.)

Galdone, Paul. *The History of Mother Twaddle and the Marvelous Achievements of Her Son Jack*. Seabury, 1974. (Published in paperback as *Jack and the Beanstalk*.) (English)

Haley, Gail. *Jack and the Bean Tree*. Crown, 1986. (Appalachian – U.S.)

Ross, Tony. *Jack and the Beanstalk*. Delacorte, 1981. (English)

Still, James. *Jack and the Wonder Beans*. Illustrated by Margot Tomes. Putnam, 1977. (Appalachian – U.S.)

Johnny Appleseed

The following list contains three versions of the "Johnny Appleseed" story. Steven Kellogg is known for his unusual new twists in each of his folktales. The Ormondroyd tale is the modern story of a little boy whose sand castle is washed away, taking "seeds" to other parts of the beach where soon several other castles are being built. Aliki's version is perhaps the most traditional of each of the offerings.

Booklist—Johnny Appleseed

Aliki. *The Story of Johnny Appleseed*. Prentice-Hall, 1963.

Kellogg, Steven. *Johnny Appleseed*. Morrow, 1988.

Ormondroyd, Edward. *Johnny Castleseed*. Illustrated by Diana Thewlis. Parnassus, 1985.

Little Red Hen

Compare the very worldly animals in Margot Zemach's *Little Red Hen* to the comfortable but lazy household depicted in Paul Galdone's version of the same story. The illustrations in the Domanska version have a stained glass effect in bold bright oranges, greens, yellows and blacks. Note how the illustrations change the mood of the tale.

Booklist—Little Red Hen

Domanska, Janina. *Little Red Hen*. Macmillan, 1973.

Galdone, Paul. *Little Red Hen*. Seabury, 1973.

Jacobs, Joseph. "The Little Red Hen." In *Tomie dePaola's Favorite Nursery Tales*, edited by Tomie dePaola. Putnam, 1986.

McQueen, Lucinda. *Little Red Hen*. Scholastic, 1985. (A Big Book of this title is available from Scholastic.)

Zemach, Margot. *The Little Red Hen*. Farrar, Straus & Giroux, 1983.

Rapunzel

Compare and contrast the following two versions of the "Rapunzel" tale. Dark and mysterious drawings highlight the illustrations by Trina Schart Hyman while Hoffman's seem lighter and less crowded. The mood of the tale changes significantly as the illustrations extend the mood of the text. Hyman's dark brown borders seem to separate the reality of the reader's world from the fantasy world within the book. Her lush paintings enhance the setting of the story. Hoffman attempts to include the reader directly in the fantasy by using light colors in large expressive illustrations rendered through the medium of stone lithography.

Booklist—Rapunzel

Grimm, Jacob and Wilhelm Grimm. *Rapunzel.* Retold by Barbara Rogasky. Illustrated by Trina Schart Hyman. Holiday House, 1982.

_____. *Rapunzel.* Illustrated by Felix Hoffman. Harcourt, Brace & World, 1967.

STORIES FOR CRITICAL READING FROM TODAY'S WRITERS AND ILLUSTRATORS

It has been said that any two books can provide material activities involving critical reading. The story grammar, the illustrations, the characterization, the plot development, and other elements from each book can be utilized to bring the author's and illustrator's craft into focus. However, most of us look toward a common theme or other element to help us make the connection between books and critical reading activities. Each time stories are read and their subtle messages uncovered the collaboration between reader and the author and illustrator is strengthened and the literature experience enhanced.

Child and Parents

In his earlier book, *Come Away from the Water, Shirley* (Harper & Row, 1967), John Burningham used a combination of media to compose the visual jokes in his book. He used crayons on one side of the page to depict Shirley's parents as they sit in their beach chairs while giving frequent admonitions to Shirley. Shirley's imaginative pirate adventures are depicted on the opposite side of the pages through the media of rich paints, collages, and crayon. The use of different media and color tones helps to create the humor by producing a contrasting image for the parents' and child's thinking. In his second book, Burningham uses the same technique to depict Shirley's exciting adventures. This time Shirley is taking a bath while her mother weighs herself and cleans up the bathroom. Most of the time she is also admonishing Shirley for being so messy. Meanwhile, Shirley's imagination has taken her down the drain, on the back of her duck, and into a wide river where she is rescued by a knight in armor, meets the King and Queen, and defeats them in a tilting match on the river while all are riding on ducks. The endpapers of these books are notable, combining pipes and sewers with all of Shirley's adventures. As these two books are read, compared and contrasted, discuss the techniques used to juxtapose the parents' thinking with the imaginative escapades of Shirley.

Booklist—Child and Parents

Burningham, John. *Come Away from the Water, Shirley.* Harper & Row, 1967.

_____. *Time to Get Out of the Bath, Shirley.* Harper & Row, 1978.

Hiroshima

Use these two tales about Hiroshima to examine the mood and depiction of a serious and sad episode in our world's history. Discuss how the illustrations impact our understanding of the text and influence our attitude toward the Hiroshima tragedy which took place in August 1945. The format of the books might provide an interesting discussion point. Maruki uses paintings in vibrant oranges, yellows, and reds to enhance the fire image of the tragedy, while Lifton uses actual photographs. One would think that photographs might have a greater impact on the emotional reaction to the book. But many readers have found that in comparing these two books the Maruki book is very powerful and overshadows the more realistically illustrated account. The appropriateness of using the Maruki book with young children might be considered.

Booklist — Hiroshima

Lifton, Betty Jean. *Return to Hiroshima*. Illustrated with photographs by Eikoh Hosoe. Atheneum, 1970.

Maruki, Toshi. *Hiroshima No Pika*. Translated by Komi Shoten Co. Lothrop, Lee & Shepard, 1982.

Memories

In the Miles and Miller stories in the following list a young child is faced with the death of a grandparent. In *Annie and the Old One*, the grandmother says that when her weaving is finished so will her days on earth be finished. In an attempt to prolong the time, Annie sneaks out each night and unweaves some of the weaving. Her grandmother talks to her and helps her understand that her memory will remain even after she is gone. Annie comes to accept the eventuality and lets go. In *My Grandmother's Cookie Jar* a young child is again faced with death. She is left with the very special cookie jar which will evoke memories to fill her heart and keep the sadness out. In both the Gould and Jukes titles a young child must face the death of a grandfather. In one story the ritual of getting out the slides to view is just not the same without Grandpa nor is the ritual of picking blackberries in the dark the same without that grandparent. Each of the grandchildren begins to realize that the memories can go on; while the grandparent will be missed the memories can stay.

Booklist — Memories of Grandparents

Gould, Deborah. *Grandpa's Slide Show*. Illustrated by Cheryl Harness. Lothrop, Lee & Shepard, 1987.

Jukes, Mavis. *Blackberries in the Dark*. Knopf, 1985.

Miles, Miska. *Annie and the Old One*. Illustrated by Peter Parnall. Little, Brown, 1971.

Miller, Montzalee. *My Grandmother's Cookie Jar*. Illustrated by Katherine Potter. Price Stern Sloan, 1987.

Drawing and Imagination

Each of the following stories involves someone drawing an object or objects which then come alive and enter the action of the story. The Alexander and Browne books depict a story where the drawn object is given life for the amusement of the other characters in the story, while the animals and things in the Bang and Demi tales come alive in an effort to save their creator from danger or from grave circumstances. Note especially how the illustrations depict the lifelike quality of the objects that have been drawn or painted.

Booklist—Drawings Come to Life

Alexander, Martha. *Blackboard Bear*. Dial, 1969.

Bang, Molly Garrett. *Tye May and the Magic Brush*. Greenwillow, 1981.

Browne, Anthony. *Bear Hunt*. Atheneum, 1979.

Demi. *Liang and the Magic Paint Brush*. Holt, Rinehart & Winston, 1980.

Gackenbach, Dick. *Mag, the Magnificent*. Clarion, 1985.

Magic and Mishandled Chants

In the dePaola, Towle, and Galdone stories the pot is the property of a person who has the power to stop and start the action to create food. When another person attempts to use the pot and then bungles the chant that will stop the pot, the pot continues to produce the porridge, spaghetti, or other food, and the contents spill out over many homes and such. Examine the story grammar of these three stories carefully. By retelling each of them a pattern will emerge. Note the elements in the retellings. Create your own stories by deciding on the specific elements to be included in your story and write it using the pattern. The Coombs and Mosel tales are variants on the pattern but do contain many of the same elements contained in the other three versions.

Booklist—Magic and Mishandled Chants

Coombs, Patricia. *The Magic Pot*. Lothrop, Lee & Shepard, 1977. (Modern literary)

dePaola, Tomie. *Strega Nona*. Prentice-Hall, 1975. (Italy)

Galdone, Paul. *The Magic Porridge Pot*. Seabury, 1976. (Germany)

Mosel, Arlene. *The Funny Little Woman*. Illustrated by Blair Lent. Dutton, 1972. (Japan)

Towle, Faith M. *The Magic Cooking Pot*. Houghton Mifflin, 1975. (India)

Counting Tales

A counting book depicting ten in a bed has as its roots a folk song. As each of the animals and people rolls out of bed the number in bed is reduced until there is only one left.

Peek's version shows a little boy in bed with ten animals. Each time they roll over one of the animals falls out. And each time children can see that the animal has found a resting place in the room. At last only the boy remains. A lion in a picture in his room appears to be winking and all the other animals are seen in a wall frieze that rings the ceiling. Gerstein's version is a small-sized book featuring a fold-out flap which reveals the fallen animal falling out of the huge bed. Finally the little boy is asleep in his bed, but he is not alone; all of the animals have crawled back in on the other side. The last page shows a darkened room as the moon says "Good Night" to the ten humps in the bed. Another variation of that book is *Ten Bears in My Bed: A Goodnight Countdown*. The variation in this tale is that the animals are all bears but when they are told to roll over each of the bears departs in a different manner. One galloped out, another skated out, and so forth.

Booklist—Counting Tales

Gerstein, Mordicai. *Roll Over!* Crown, 1984.

Mack, Stan. *Ten Bears in My Bed: A Goodnight Countdown*. Pantheon, 1974.

Peek, Merle. *Roll Over! A Counting Song*. Clarion, 1981.

SPECIAL ILLUSTRATORS WITH SPECIAL TOUCHES

In addition to enhancing and expanding on the text the illustrations in a book can foreshadow the action that will take place in the story and can establish mood and clarify themes. Many illustrators also take the opportunity to provide visual games within their books. While creating powerful visual alliterative pictures for each letter of the alphabet in *Animalia* (Viking Kestrel, 1986), Graeme Base's hides himself as a boy in every double-page spread. Other illustrators hide their name or the names of others or hide messages and insert their own family and friends in their illustrations. Maurice Sendak managed to inject much information relating to his own life into his books. After researching information about Sendak's personal life one might read his books to uncover the references to the events that Sendak evidently viewed as significant in his life.

Maurice Sendak—His Books and His Illustrations

Maurice Sendak was born the same year as Mickey Mouse (1928). The house he lives in in the Connecticut woods has an intricate burglar alarm system and a Mickey Mouse night light. A large collection of Mickey Mouse memorabilia sits among his family photographs. A backdrop curtain (a large face of a wild thing) designed for the Brussels opera production of *Where the Wild Things Are* was inspired by Mickey Mouse's huge face. When Sendak was asked to illustrate a cover design for a book about children's literature, *Celebrating Children's Books* by Betsy Hearne and Marilyn Kaye (Lothrop, Lee & Shepard, 1981), he included many of his popular book characters along with Mickey Mouse. As a child Maurice Sendak had many favorite stories, among which was *Mickey Mouse in Pygmyland* (he has long since forgotten the author or publisher).

From this early love of story Sendak has been inspired to use his own gift for storytelling. All of his books are personal statements about people, places, and times. Hidden in most of his books is information about his friends, his pets, and incidents in his life. Before beginning this critical look at the hidden information in Sendak's books arrange to have as many of Sendak's books as possible available for reading. Then share some bits of information about Sendak's life and reread and enjoy the stories while focusing on the interplay between Sendak's storytelling and his real life.

Higglety Pigglety Pop! (Harper & Row, 1967) was written as a tribute to Sendak's Sealyham terrier, Jennie. She is shown throughout that book but Jennie made her way into many of his other books as well. Search for Jennie throughout Sendak's books. Don't forget to take a look at books that Sendak illustrated for other authors. Jennie first appeared in Betty MacDonald's *Mrs. Piggle Wiggle's Farm* (Lippincott, 1954) and appeared regularly in almost every one of Sendak's works in the years following. *Higglety Pigglety Pop!* was published just one month after his beloved Jennie died of cancer in 1967. In one illustration, featuring Jennie with paws on the table, which holds a dish marked "Jennie," there is a picture on the wall. The picture is the famous painting, Mona Lisa. Mona Lisa is the name that Jennie's breeders had given her before Sendak obtained her and changed her name to Jennie. Today he has io, a golden retriever named after the Greek maiden Zeus turned into a heifer, and Runge, a German shepherd named in honor of the eighteenth-century painter Philipp Otto Runge. Like faithful friends they too show up in his books.

Read *A Kiss for Little Bear* by Else Minarik, illustrated by Maurice Sendak (Harper & Row, 1968). This is an I Can Read book that gives a clue to the other books Sendak has illustrated. A close look at this book's illustrations will reveal a wild thing within the picture showing Little Bear unveiling a picture he has drawn for his mother. Children will need to have had some experience with Sendak's *Where the Wild Things Are* (Harper & Row, 1963) before they recognize the illustration as significant.

Look at each of the books illustrated by Sendak. Compare and contrast Sendak's use of the moon and moonlight in his illustrations.

In the Night Kitchen (Harper & Row, 1970) contains many references to Sendak's own life. As the boy, Mickey (in tribute to Mickey Mouse), falls out of bed and into the night, the words "Q. E. Gateshead" may be seen on the building outside the window. That is the hospital where Sendak recovered after he suffered a major heart attack during a trip to Europe in 1967. As a child, Maurice Sendak enjoyed many movies with his older brother, Jack, and his sister, Natalie. Among his favorites where those that featured Laurel and Hardy, who came back into his life as the bakers in this book.

At the bottom of the page where the three bakers are shown mixing "Mickey in batter, chanting," there is a sack of shortening lying on its side. At the bottom of the sack is the name "Killingworth, Connecticut." That town is where his beloved Jennie was born. One of the bakers is holding a sack that has the partial name "Jennie" visible, along with the names of Jennie's breeders. The date 1953 is also on the sack. During the summer of 1953 Sendak was desperate for a dog and arranged to have the runt of the litter. Also, as Mickey flies over the top of the Milky Way in the night kitchen he flies over "Jennie Street." Jennie was Sendak's friend and companion for fourteen years.

In the scenes where Mickey is turning his plane's propellor there is a building in the background. Lettering on the building says, "Patented June 10th 1928." That date is the date of Sendak's birth.

In the four-section illustration where "he kneaded and punched it and pounded and pulled," buildings in the background carry the phrases, "Eugene's," "Philip's Best Tomatoes," and "Sadie's Best." Philip and Sadie were the names of Sendak's father and mother. Eugene was a very close friend who took Jennie to be put out of her misery.

As Mickey falls into the bowl of batter and "into the light of the night kitchen" a background building, in the shape of a bottle, has the name "Kneitel's Fandango." That refers to Kenny Kneitel, a collector and dealer of Mickey Mouse figures and other nostalgia items from the 1930s.

On the following page the salt tube held by another baker is labeled "Woody's Salt." That name is in reference to Wood Gelman, editor of the Nostalgia Press and a very close friend.

Another building has the name "Schickel." This is a reference to Richard Schickel. It was his biography of Walt Disney that prodded Sendak's memory of his childhood love of Mickey Mouse and of Disney himself.

Sendak's *Outside Over There* includes pictorial references to Sendak's admiration of the famed composer Mozart. The setting is that of Mozart's time, and in one illustration Mozart is shown in the background playing his flute.

Many of Sendak's books contain a lion. A Sendak lion appears first in Ruth Krauss's *A Very Special House*. He put lions next in his illustrations for Jack Sendak's *Circus Girl*, then lions appeared in his own *Pierre, Hector Protector* and later in *Higglety Pigglety Pop!* The lions seem to bear some relationship to the many MGM movies Sendak saw from the age of six.

Alligators are also favorite animals showing up in several of the books Sendak illustrated. *Alligators All Around*, however, went through several drafts. The first draft featured a family of apes, but in later drafts the animals became the more favored alligators. Alligators also show up in Else Holmelund Minarik's *No Fighting! No Biting!*

Be sure to arrange for time for children to share and enjoy the bits and pieces of Sendak's life that they find in his books.

The Ahlbergs and Anno—Hidden Images

Other illustrators cleverly bring to mind other books through the inclusion in their literary tales of references to traditional characters and events. Janet and Allan Ahlberg successfully utilize this technique in two titles. In their *Each Peach Pear Plum* (Viking Kestrel, 1978; Scholastic, 1978) they combine the familiar "I spy" rhyme with hidden images of Tom Thumb, Jack and Jill, The Three Bears, Cinderella, and a host of other nursery characters. In the Ahlbergs' *The Jolly Postman and Other People's Letters* (Little, Brown, 1986), a plump postman delivers letters to some of the same characters. The letters, which can be removed from the book and read, vary from handwritten notes of apology from Goldilocks to The Three Bears to an advertising brochure delivered to the ginger-bread house of the witch. One of the masters of this technique is Mitsumasa Anno. He is a Japanese artist who has created books filled with literally hundreds of hidden visual images. In *Anno's Britain* (Philomel, 1982), Anno arrives in Britain by boat, then travels about the countryside and through the cities before sailing away again. As he travels throughout Britain the alert "reader" will be able to find a copper craftsman and a tinker, Prince Charles and Princess Diana, the Tower of London, King Lear, the Merchant of Venice, Peter Pan, Tinkerbell, Alice in Wonderland, Jack and the Giant, Winnie the Pooh, the Loch Ness monster and Toad from *Wind in the Willows*. More famous places, animals, fictional and fairy tale characters, as well as other craftsmen can be located. In *Anno's USA* (Philomel, 1983), Anno uses the same technique. This time the boat takes him to Hawaii and then to the San Francisco Bay area. He travels through the United States on horseback. As he travels he samples many historic events and places of interest and spots John Muir, Betsy Ross, Orville and Wilbur Wright, the Boston Tea Party, King Kong, Dorothy of Oz, Superman, and other fictional characters. Anno has included himself in each of the books. By utilizing Anno's books significant events and people can be identified. Research could uncover why a Japanese artist would consider the specific person or event significant enough to single out for inclusion in his book. A discussion of the merits of Anno's choices might result in a debate of those merits.

PROMOTING BOOKS

Use the suggestions in this chapter to start the focus on promoting active and sharing responses to books. The specific methodology you use to bring the ideas and books to children must be yours and must fit your personality, your group of children, and your goals. The shell is here, the beginning of several opportunities to tie meaningful experiences together for children. *You* must bring the warmth, the expression of enjoyment, and the excitement to the activities as you share these books and ideas with children.

Chapter

4

BookShelf

It is important in literature experiences as in other conceptual activities that children are given an opportunity to manipulate the story elements in some concrete form. When children have an opportunity to discuss and work with a story in ways that are meaningful to them—through the expressive arts, drama, or puppetry, or by creating innovations on the text or recreating the story characters and scenes in their own paintings and models—they will gain a better understanding of the literature. Experiencing a book in a concrete manner will extend the experience and make it a memorable one. Reading aloud to children is the single most effective activity to help children both learn to read and enjoy reading. The literature will also provide children with models of good writing and will present opportunities for the building of writing skills through innovations on the text and extension of the story. This can be done by encouraging the development of episodic chapters or sequels. Cynthia Rylant, author of the Newbery honor book *A Fine White Dust* (Bradbury, 1986), and *The Relatives Came* (Bradbury, 1985), has said that in order to teach children to write she would probably "read to them day after day for ten years."* Reading aloud introduces children to new and interesting words and sounds and helps the children extend their imagination. Good oral reading helps children to develop a taste for the best in literature and to extend their thinking skills. The importance of reading aloud is expressed by Cynthia Rylant when she commented, in reference to her son Nate, "I'd pay his teachers a million dollars if I had it if they'd just read aloud to him."†

Reading aloud will allow a specific title to be shared with a group of children. Children respond to what has been read in many different ways, but by sharing a common reading experience children can join together to dramatize an event from the book, to share their favorite episodes, to explore and discuss characterization and plot development, or to build an innovation on the story grammar. Often the only response to the reading of the book is to read another book. A good read aloud of one author will often promote the reading of other books by the same author or will become the stimulation for reading a group of books tied together with a thematic thread.

---

*Cynthia Rylant. "Questions and Answers Session" (presentation at Workshop: Authors/Illustrators of Children's Literature, University of Northern Iowa, Cedar Falls, Iowa. 5 August 1988).

†Ibid.

In the bookshelf entries that follow we have tried to give a variety of titles that lend themselves to sharing through oral reading. For each we have given brief suggestions for expressive activities which you might wish to suggest to groups of children for the cooperative development of an active response to the literature. In many cases, the activity suggestions might be used to model the type of activity being suggested. After a type of activity is modeled successfully with the young readers and they are given a chance to respond in guided situations, they will be more confident and successful in developing their own responses. It will be that success that promotes more reading.

While there are literally thousands of books that could have been chosen for our bookshelf entries we have simply chosen a random sampling of books from our own bookshelf. Many of the titles included are authored or illustrated by either Mercer Mayer, Gail Gibbons, Nonny Hogrogian, or Maurice Sendak. By including these titles in the entries we have given another option that might be utilized. Pulling the titles by a specific author or illustrator, together with biographical information about that author or illustrator, could create an author or illustrator unit to be shared with children. The utility of such a focus is immeasurable. Focusing on the people who create the books allows us to connect the books while offering the opportunity for wide reading. Choose one or more of the books by a particular author or illustrator, share it as a read aloud, discuss it, motivate and model group responses to that selection, and then share or introduce many of the other books by that same book creator. The remaining books could be read independently, in small groups, and viewed in listening centers (if nonprint formats are available). Activities focusing on the body of work by the specific author or illustrator could be developed and shared over a period of time.

Focusing on a specific book person provides a structure for the organization of activities and a time to read in such a way as to provide for the achievement of curriculum or program goals. Through this type of focus a respect for the body of work of a writer or illustrator is developed and the connections between his or her many works become apparent. All of the library's bookshelves become a potential reading source as children search for more of the author's works and for connecting themes. A sense of achievement is felt as connections are identified between the works of different writers and artists. As connecting threads between two books are sewn the mind is challenged to think in new terms, to identify universal themes and topics.

But the connections need not always be between a multitude of books or stories. Single titles of good literature will enrich the curriculum, as well. Individual threads can link two books or a book and an idea. Each reader's schematic background will provide different links from the book to the reader. As children and teachers learn about literature more books will find their way into the classroom. (P) indicates a book most appropriate for primary grade readers. (I) indicates intermediate activities.

BOOKS AND IDEAS FOR EXPRESSIVE ACTIVITIES

Aardema, Verna. *Bringing the Rain to Kapiti Plain*. Illustrated by Beatriz Vidal. Dial, 1981. (P)
A young African boy brings rain to the dry and thirsty pastures of his homeland. The drought threatens the Kapiti Plain until Ki-pat brings rain to the plain.

1. View the Reading Rainbow® program segment from the National Public Broadcasting Network, which features this book.

2. Read another book about rain, such as Mirra Ginsburg's *Mushroom in the Rain*, illustrated by José Aruego and Ariane Dewey (Macmillan, 1974).

Adams, Adrienne. *A Halloween Happening*. Scribner, 1981. (P, I)
   The witches from Adams's *A Woggle of Witches* (Scribner, 1971) are back again in another escapade on a bewitching Halloween.

   1.   Publish a class cookbook featuring some of the witches' gourmet treats: toad tarts, scrambled lizard eggs, wart soup, worm waffles, and candy bats.

   2.   Draw a picture of one of the witches. Name and describe the witch.

Alexander, Sue. *Nadia the Willful*. Illustrated by Lloyd Bloom. Pantheon, 1983. (P, I)
   Nadia has lost her beloved brother. Her father, in his grief, forbids anyone to speak of him. Nadia must speak out and in doing so she helps her father realize that spoken memories will help him too accept his sorrow.

   1.   The setting is in the Bedouin culture in the Sinai. On a world map locate the geographical region that would represent this area. Discuss Bloom's illustrations in relation to actual photographs of the area.

   2.   Extend the theme by reading more books about the death of a loved one.

Booklist—Death of a Loved One

Bartoli, Jennifer. *Nonna*. Illustrated by Joan E. Drescher. Harvey House, 1975.

dePaola, Tomie. *Nana Upstairs, Nana Downstairs*. Putnam, 1973.

Jukes, Mavis. *Blackberries in the Dark*. Pictures by Thomas B. Allen. Knopf, 1985.

Miles, Miska. *Annie and the Old One*. Illustrated by Peter Parnall. Little, Brown, 1971.

Smith, Doris Buchanan. *A Taste of Blackberries*. Illustrated by Charles Robinson. Crowell, 1973.

Zolotow, Charlotte. *My Grandson Lew*. Illustrated by William Pene du Bois. Harper & Row, 1974.

Asch, Frank. *Bear Shadow*. Prentice-Hall, 1985.
   Bear wants to catch a fish but he finds his shadow scares the fish away. Bear tries to get rid of his shadow but he cannot until the position of the sun changes the location of the shadow. (P, I)

   1.   After reading the story once, reread it discussing the illustrations and the effect of the sun on Bear's shadow.

   2.   Follow the discussion in activity 1 with a reading of *Nothing Sticks Like a Shadow* by Ann Tompert (Houghton Mifflin, 1984). In this story Rabbit argues with Woodchuck. Rabbit thinks he can get rid of his shadow. He tries to nail it down, to dig a hole to bury it, and to hide from it in the bushes. When all his efforts fail Rabbit falls asleep. In doing so he finds out that when the sun goes down his shadow disappears.

   3.   Locate and read other "Bear" books by Frank Asch.

4. Read a story about Ground Hog's day where Ground Hog checks for his shadow. Read *A Garden for Groundhog* by Lorna Balian (Abingdon, 1985). This book might also provide a link from the books by Asch to books by Lorna Balian.

5. Read other shadow books. See index.

6. Teach children to play shadow tag. In this game the person who is "it" attempts to catch opponents by stepping on their shadows. The person whose shadow is stepped upon must then become "it" and attempt to step on others' shadows.

Bang, Molly. *Ten, Nine, Eight*. Greenwillow, 1983. (P)
A young black child is being lovingly tucked into bed by her father. As she is readied for bed they count down from ten to one, from ten small toes all washed and warm to one big girl all ready for bed.

1. Use this as a model for your own bedtime countdown rhyme.

2. Read other counting verses. See index.

3. Read Merle Peek's *Roll Over! A Counting Song*. (Clarion, 1981).

Banks, Lynn Reid. *The Indian in the Cupboard*. Doubleday, 1981. (P, I)
A nine-year-old boy accidently brings to life his three-inch plastic toy. At first he is amused by the incident, then he begins to be aware of the responsibility involved. He must feed, protect, and hide the three-inch human being from another time (1870s) and another culture.

1. How would the story have changed if Omri had not found the missing key?

2. Write Little Bear's story for your local newspaper.

3. Read the sequel, *The Return of the Indian in the Cupboard*, by Lynne Reid Banks (Doubleday, 1987).

Blos, Joan W. *Martin's Hats*. Morrow, 1984. (P)
Martin wears many hats as he plays.

1. Describe where Martin goes when he "squeezed into caves dark as under the bed."

2. Collect all kinds of hats worn by various community helpers and career people. Find out something about people who wear the hats that have been collected.

3. Discuss why some of these hats are worn, for example, for protection, identification, or comfort.

4. Read other books about unknown places and things.

Booklist — Unknown Things

Mayer, Mercer. *There's a Nightmare in My Closet*. Dial, 1968.

_____. *There's an Alligator under My Bed*. Dial, 1987.

Sendak, Maurice. *Where the Wild Things Are*. Harper & Row, 1963.

Stevenson, James. *What's under My Bed?* Greenwillow, 1984.

Brenner, Barbara. *The Prince and the Pink Blanket*. Illustrated by Nola Langner. Four Winds, 1980. (P, I)
The king does not like Prince Hal carrying around his pink blanket. That is, until Uncle Maurice comes along with his home movies and photographs to remind the king of his own childhood days.

1.   Discuss the setting of this story. It appears to be medieval but there are movie projectors, telephones, and other modern-day items.

2.   Discuss anachronisms. An anachronism is an item or object out of its time period — for example, when a movie is made about the pioneer days and a commercial jetliner is spotted in the sky in the background. What items would you consider anachronisms in *The Prince and the Pink Blanket*?

3.   Describe items we have not wanted to give up. Read and relate to *Ira Sleeps Over* by Bernard Waber (Houghton Mifflin, 1975).

Brett, Jan. *Annie and the Wild Animals*. Houghton Mifflin, 1985. (P, I)
When Annie's cat disappears Annie is very lonely. She goes hunting for her cat and meets many woodland animals. She tries to make friends but is unsuccessful.

1.   Investigate one of the wild animals in the story. Tell more about that animal in an alliterative paragraph.

2.   The illustrations in this book are vibrant and full of color. Go on a search in your school and library to find other books about animals that have pictures that you like. Share the books with your classmates.

Brittain, Bill. *The Wish Giver: Three Tales of Coven Tree*. Harper & Row, 1983. (I)
In Coven Tree, a small New England town, devilish things begin to happen the day Thaddeus Blinn shows up to sell wishes for 50 cents a wish. Four townspeople purchase the wishes. The first three make wishes which, when granted literally, cause the three of them immense problems.

1.   This book has both a prologue and an epilogue. What is a prologue? What is an epilogue? Discuss why Brittain used them to clarify the story.

2. Pretend Thaddeus Blinn had given you a card with a red spot on it. Would you wish? Why or why not? If you did wish what would your wish be? Be careful with the wording.

3. Make a poster depicting your favorite scene from the book. Include the title and the author's name on the poster.

Brown, Ruth. *The Big Sneeze*. Lothrop, Lee & Shepard, 1985. (P, I)
A farmer is sleeping in his barn when a fly lands on his nose and causes him to sneeze. He sneezes so hard that he sets off a chain of events.

1. Use the pattern to write your own innovation on this text.

2. Think of other things that might make you (or the farmer) sneeze. Make a list.

3. This story illustrates cause and effect. Discuss cause and effect. Then make a list of things that happen in your classroom or home because of some other event. Put the events in the cause or the effect column.

Burch, Robert. *Christmas with Ida Early*. Viking, 1983. (I)
The Sutton family has not been the same since Mrs. Sutton died and the eccentric Ida Early came to be their housekeeper and friend in *Ida Early Comes Over the Mountain* (Viking, 1980). In this sequel, Ida Early continues to lead the family through one escapade after another.

1. Would you like Ida Early to live with your family? Why or why not?

2. Draw a picture of Aunt Earnestine's Christmas gift to Ida. Describe it.

3. Robert Burch has written a book about Ida Early and Valentine's day. He intends to write other books about her. Think of some adventures you would like Ida to have, so you could read about them. Write some of your ideas and then send them to Robert Burch in care of his publisher.

Byars, Betsy. *The Animal, the Vegetable, and John D. Jones*. Delacorte, 1982. (I)
Clara and Deenie are forced to spend a vacation with John D. None of them are happy with the situation but the children's now-divorced parents are interested in seeing how their joined family might get along.

1. Read Chapter 6 of this book and then describe John D.

2. Would you like to have Clara or Deenie as a friend? Why or why not?

3. Make some rules you would have for avoiding doing something foolish.

Calhoun, Mary. *The Night the Monster Came*. Morrow, 1982. (P, I)

Giant footprints, a huge beast seen jumping the fence. Bigfoot lives in the north woods. Andy thinks the monster has come down from the mountains and woods surrounding Andy's home. What will Andy and his family do?

1. Make a life-sized model of the monster—or of how you think the monster really looks.

2. On a world map mark the locations where Bigfoot, the Loch Ness monster, and any other well-known monsters are thought to reside.

Campbell, Rod. *Dear Zoo*. Four Winds, 1982. (P, I)

A variety of flaps and doors reveal hidden animals which arrive from the zoo. The search is an attempt to find just the right animal for a pet.

1. Make a list of the animals in the story and the reasons why they would or would not make good pets.

2. Read Beatrice Schenk deRegniers's *It Does Not Say Meow and Other Animal Riddle Rhymes*, illustrated by Paul Galdone (Clarion, 1972). Use these rhymes as models to write riddles about some of the animals that are sent from the zoo to be a pet. Write the clues and then share with classmates.

Carris, Joan. *When the Boys Ran the House*. Lippincott, 1982. (I)

Mrs. Howard is sick in bed from encephalitis. A visiting nurse helps out, but the bulk of the burden for taking care of his younger brothers and the household falls on Justin's shoulders.

1. In the reference section of your school or public library locate a medical dictionary or encyclopedia and find out about encephalitis.

2. If you were in charge of the house you would need to plan meals and go grocery shopping. Make your meal plans for a week and make the shopping list. Make sure the meals you plan are meals you are able to prepare.

Clifford, Eth. *Harvey's Horrible Snake Disaster*. Houghton Mifflin, 1984. (I)

Harvey's aunt and his cousin Nora have come for a temporary stay with Harvey's family. Nora is strong-willed, obnoxious, creative but crafty, and lies through her teeth. She manages to cause havoc by bringing a snake into the house and letting it loose in the herpetologist's car, causing an accident.

1. If you were Harvey would you have helped keep the snake's escape over the weekend a secret? Explain why or why not.

2. Do you think the story could have really happened? Why or why not?

3. Define the occupation and research to locate more information about herpetology, a branch of zoology. Share the information about the herpetologist's duties and work.

4. On a long snake-shaped piece of butcher paper give information about many different types of snakes, such as their size and the food they eat.

Clifford, Eth. *Just Tell Me When We're Dead*. Houghton Mifflin, 1983. (I)

Jo-Beth's cousin, Jeff, was an orphan living with his grandmother. When his grandmother had to go to the hospital in an emergency situation, Jeff felt abandoned. He ran away to an abandoned Coney Island. Jo-Beth went after him. She finds him but together they encounter criminals. They know they must stay clear and have a difficult time reaching safety.

1. What do you think Jo-Beth wrote in her diary the day that Jeff ran away?

2. Explain the meaning of the title *Just Tell Me When We're Dead*.

3. List at least five attractions or rides that are normally part of an amusement park. Draw an illustration including as many of the listed attractions or rides as you can. Hide Jo-Beth and Jeff somewhere in your picture.

Clifford, Eth. *The Dastardly Murder of Dirty Pete*. Houghton Mifflin, 1981. (I)

Mr. Onetree is tired and ready for a good hot meal but he and his two girls, Jo-Beth and Mary Rose, are lost. In the distance they spot a sign that says "Inn of the Whispering Ghost." The sign is creepy — how creepy they soon find out.

1. Before reading the book discuss what a ghost town is and how it would look.

2. Do you think Mr. Nicely (Sourdough Sam) should have been allowed to wander around the town? Why or why not?

3. Build a small model of the ghost town.

Cone, Molly. *The Amazing Memory of Harvey Bean*. Houghton Mifflin, 1980. (I)

It really did not matter that the other children laughed at Harvey's forgetfulness. More important was that no one seemed to really care about him. A friend, Mr. Katz, saw Harvey as a mere scrap of a boy and he could not bear to let any scrap go to waste. It is Mrs. Katz who helps Harvey improve his memory and who makes his summer one he would remember.

1. Do you think this story could happen in real life? Why or why not?

2. Describe Mr. and Mrs. Katz. What kind of personalities did each of them have? Draw a picture of each of them.

3. Draw a picture of the outside of the Katz home and yard.

4. Draw a picture of the inside of the Katz home.

5. The rhyme Harvey used to remember something is a memory device. Make up your own rhyme to help you remember. Write it down, memorize the rhyme, and try using it the next time you need to remember something.

Coville, Bruce. *The Monster's Ring*. Pantheon, 1982. (I)

Fifth grader Russell Crannaker must get away from the class bully. In desperation he pays a visit to Elives' Magic Supplies where he buys a ring that produces unexpected results.

1. If you were faced with a bully like Eddie, what would you do?

2. Russell told Eddie to "go play in the road, toad." That was Russell's way of saying to go away. Write five more rhyming sentences that tell someone to go away. One example is "Go jump in a boat, goat." Try some others.

3. Imagine that you have a monster's ring and have turned yourself into a monster. Draw a self-portrait of yourself as a monster.

4. You have been invited to advertise this book on national public radio. Write a one-minute advertisement and record it onto a cassette tape to replay to your classmates.

5. Extend the theme of magic by reading either of the following two books. In *The Magic Grandfather* by Jay Williams (Houghton Mifflin, 1979), a boy discovers that he too may be a sorcerer like his grandfather. In *Standing in the Magic* by Gunilla B. Norris (Dutton, 1974), Joel's friend Brady creates some unusual magic with the help of a special ring.

Craig, M. Jean. *The Man Whose Name Was Not Thomas*. Illustrated by Diane Stanley. Doubleday, 1981. (P, I)

A book that will keep readers guessing what really is going on in the life of a non-Thomas's life. As the story is shared the readers will learn many things about the man's life. They will learn about the character's name, home, career, courtship, and marriage through statements about what is not true. Clever illustrations accompany the text.

1. Read the book sharing the information on the right-hand side of the page where the illustrations show exactly what is true about the non-Thomas. Play the guessing game. The real name of the non-Thomas will be revealed at the end.

2. Use the same pattern to create a book about yourself.

Dahl, Roald. *George's Marvelous Medicine*. Knopf, 1981. (I)

George experiments with some magic potions and discovers that his potion has strange powers. At first he tries it out on some of his family's farm animals. When he finds out that the medicine has the power to reduce an animal or a person, he gives the medicine to his pesky grandmother. She is reduced to nothing.

1. Describe the type of child you think George was.

2. Would you like George for your friend?

3. Compare and contrast George's grandmother with your grandmother. Make a chart.

4. Why did the author allow George to reduce Grandma to nothing rather than just making her miniature? Explain.

5. What do you think happened to all the animals that were changed?

Dana, Barbara. *Zucchini*. Illustrated by Eileen Christelow. Harper & Row, 1982. (I)

Zucchini is a ferret born in a rodent house at the Bronx Zoo. He longs for a life outside of the zoo so he makes his way across town and ends up in the 92nd Street ASPCA (American Society for the Prevention of Cruelty to Animals) where he meets Billy.

1. Write a short paragraph describing Miss Pickett and in a second paragraph tell why you would or would not like to be in her class at the ASPCA.

2. Report on the ASPCA. What is the purpose of this association?

3. Draw a picture of the living quarters Billy will make for Zucchini when they arrive at their new home.

4. Investigate information about ferrets. Are they an endangered or a protected species?

Davis, Gibb. *The Other Emily*. Illustrated by Linda Shute. Houghton Mifflin, 1984. (P, I)

Emily finds that another shares her name. She does not like it. She wants to be the one and only Emily.

1. How do you distinguish yourself from others who have your same name?

2. Discuss with your parents the reason you were given the name you were.

3. Make a name booklet for yourself. Research the meaning of your name. Include that information and the information from activity 2 and a picture of yourself in a name booklet.

Degen, Bruce. *Jamberry*. Harper & Row, 1985. (P, I)

A book of word play focusing on berries of all kinds: jamberries, blackberries, blueberries, raspberries and strawberries.

1. Read and reread and enjoy.

2. Hold a berry-tasting party. Include as many types of berries as possible. Discuss the difference between smooth round blueberries and bumpy blackberries. Categorize those that are round and those that have some other shape.

3. Read *Let's Make Jam* by Hannah Lyons (Lothrop, Lee & Shepard, 1975).

4. Make strawberry jam using frozen strawberries and Sure-Jell. Serve on crackers, or serve on pancakes after reading Eric Carle's *Pancakes, Pancakes!* (Knopf, 1970).

5. Make a list of all the ways one might eat berries (pies, shortcake, plain, in muffins). Try to put the information into a rhythmic verse.

6. Draw a picture of many types of berries. Label each type of berry. Then make a chart showing the characteristics of the various types of berries.

dePaola, Tomie. *Marianna May and Nursey*. Holiday House, 1983. (P)

Nursey always dresses Marianna May in white dresses but when Marianna eats orange ice or rolls in the grass she gets her dress orange or green.

1. Share the story with the children but read only to the part where Mr. Talbot proclaims that he has an idea. Make predictions concerning Mr. Talbot's idea.

2. Share the predictions and discuss their merits. Some of the ideas will rival dePaola's ending. Finish reading the book to find out how dePaola thought Mr. Talbot would solve the problem.

deRegniers, Beatrice Schenk. *The Shadow Book*. Photographs by Isabel Gordon. Harcourt, Brace & World, 1960. (P, I)

1. Introduce the subject of shadows with Robert Louis Stevenson's poem "My Shadow" from *A Child's Garden of Verses* (available in a number of editions; please check the card catalog in your school or public library).

2. Read *The Shadow Book*. Discuss: times we will have a shadow, changes in our shadow during the day, differences between shadows.

3. Ask students (small or large group) to make a list of all the things they think they know about shadows. Conduct research, measuring shadows during various times of the day.

4. For additional books to share as class read alouds or to use in a shadows center, see index.

5. Draw an illustration incorporating a "shadow" of an object or objects.

6. Read poems about shadows. Three short shadow poems can be found in Jack Prelutsky's *Read-Aloud Rhymes: for the Very Young*, illustrated by Marc Brown (Knopf, 1986). The titles of the poems (all on page 25) are "Hide-and-Seek Shadow" by Margaret Hillert, "Look" by Charlotte Zolotow, and "Poor Shadow" by Ilo Orleans.

Dillon, Barbara. *What Happened to Harry?* Morrow, 1982. (I)

Harry does not pay any attention to the warnings about the old Blackburn place. It is Halloween, Harvey decides to visit the home anyway, and he becomes a poodle. His human form now belongs to Hepzibah the Hateful. Hepzibah proceeds to become "Harry" in his home and at school, and his family begins to wonder, "What happened to Harry?"

1. If Hepzibah the Hateful were Hepzibah the Nice and she agreed to turn you into something for only twenty-four hours what would you choose and why?

2. Do you think Harry should have gone into the old Blackburn place? Why or why not?

3. Read any one of Scott Corbett's series of "trick" books. The first one, *The Lemonade Trick* (Little, Brown, 1960), introduces a little old lady, Mrs. Graymalkin, who gives Kerby a magic chemistry set. Strange things begin to happen. There are several other books in the series.

Elting, Mary and Michael Folsom. *Q Is for Duck*. Illustrated by Jack Kent. Clarion, 1980. (P, I)

A unique alphabet book that presents more than Q is for Quack. "Q is for Duck. Why? Because a duck quacks." The illustrations are a clever addition to this alphabet riddle book that many ages of children will enjoy.

1. Read the book aloud. Encourage listener participation in the story.

2. Discuss how the listeners knew each answer. Eventually they will conclude that the answer is always an attribute (characteristic) that most people will associate with the animal or thing. For instance, a whale is enormous, and a duck is noted for its quack. The letter, of course, is an important clue.

3. Write a group alphabet book based on this concept. Each child might be assigned a letter of the alphabet.

4. Individuals or small groups might write a complete alphabet book of their own using this pattern. A thematic book might be appropriate, for example, birds, nature, or sports.

5. Publish as a book. Be sure to include author, title, publisher, and date on the title page.

Flieschman, Paul. *The Birthday Tree*. Illustrated by Marcia Sewall. Harper & Row, 1979. (P, I)

Jack's parents plant a tree when he is born. The tree grows and flourishes and finally becomes diseased, mirroring growth and prosperity and finally old age.

1. Discuss family traditions practiced to celebrate the birth of a baby.

2. If your family were to plant a tree in commemoration of you, which kind of tree would you choose and explain why.

Fleming, Alice. *Welcome to Grossville*. Scribner, 1985. (I)

Michael's mother and father are divorcing. Michael, his mother, and sister must move to Humboldt, a town Michael dubs "Grossville." The neighborhood tough guy finds Michael an easy target. In an effort to find his own niche, Michael becomes friends with Ralph, a bird-watching enthusiast who is afflicted with cystic fibrosis.

1. Read *The War with Grandpa* by Robert Kimmel Smith (Delacorte, 1984). Compare Peter's situation with Michael's.

2. Ralph, Michael's friend, had cystic fibrosis. Find out what you can about this disease and make an informational brochure about the disease.

Folsom, Marcia and Michael Folsom. *Easy As Pie: A Guessing Game of Sayings*. Clarion, 1985. (P, I)

From "straight as an arrow" to "tough as nails" to "shy as a violet," this book contains twenty-six common similes. There is a phrase for each letter of the alphabet.

1. Before using this book children should be introduced to some of the similes that are commonplace to adults. A good way to do this is to give some examples, such as "wise as an owl," "light as a feather," "old as the hills." Explain the idea of a simile, and then encourage the children to interview their parents to generate more similes that are used in their family.

2. Share the sayings from the family interviews with the class. Discuss the meanings and why the sayings make sense.

3. Read *Easy As Pie*. After enjoying this book of similes the students might enjoy writing their own book of alphabetical similes. Each child could be assigned a specific letter, or small groups could write a complete alphabet.

4. Introduce the relationship between similes and metaphors. Brainstorm some metaphors. Try to use one metaphor or simile each day in some writing. See if others notice. Make up similes appropriate to things or people in your class, for example, dusty as the chalk erasers.

Fox, Mem. *Hattie and the Fox*. Illustrated by Patricia Mullins. Bradbury, 1987. (P)
A cumulative and repetitive text tells the story of a fox who is lurking behind the bushes and trees ready to attack the goose, the pig, the sheep, the horse, and the cow.

1. Read and encourage the listeners to participate in the refrain.

2. Dramatize the story in readers' theater format.

3. Utilize the script for the readers' theater production to focus on the use of quotation marks.

Freschet, Bernice. *Five Fat Raccoons*. Illustrated by Irene Brady. Scribner, 1980. (I)
Five raccoons search for food from spring to fall. Predators stalk the raccoons throughout the book.

1. Discuss hibernation and the life cycle of raccoons.

2. Make a list of information about raccoons that you think is true. Research to verify your lists.

Fujikawa, Gyo. *The Flyaway Kite*. Grosset & Dunlap, 1981. (I)
When the kite flies away the boys attempt to figure out what to do. In the process they climb a tree.

1. Research the art of kite making in the Orient.

2. Design a paper kite. Make it if you can.

3. Fly a kite.

Gackenbach, Dick. *A Bag Full of Pups*. Clarion, 1981. (P)

Mr. Mullin set out to give away the puppies in his bag. One puppy would herd cows for a farmer, one would do tricks with a magician, one would become a guide dog for a blind man, one would have a home with a lady who would dress him up in clothes, one would ride with the firemen on the fire truck, one would help a hard-of-hearing person know when someone knocked on the door, one would help a dog trainer win prizes, one would be a hunting dog, and finally one would be a pet for a boy.

1. Give away your bag full of kittens. With whom would they find homes? Remember kittens do different things than puppies.

2. Draw a picture of one of the puppies and his or her new master.

3. Tell about one of the puppies' new life.

4. Read a book about caring for a new puppy.

5. Dramatize the story.

6. Count down as the puppies are found new homes.

7. Read other books about dogs and how to care for them, such as the following.

Booklist — Dogs

Gackenbach, Dick. *Pepper and All the Legs*. Seabury, 1978.

Henrie, Fiona. *Dogs*. Watts, 1980.

Hess, Lilo. *A Dog by Your Side*. Scribner, 1977.

Kellogg, Steven. *Pinkerton, Behave!* Dial, 1979. (And other titles about Pinkerton.)

Pinkwater, Jill. *Superpuppy: How to Choose, Raise, Train....* Seabury, 1977.

Thomas, Jane Resh. *The Comeback Dog*. Houghton Mifflin, 1981.

Gackenbach, Dick. *The Perfect Mouse*. Macmillan, 1984. (P, I)

The little mouse's parents did not want her to marry anyone ordinary so they took her to the sun, who was very powerful. They begged the sun to marry her. He declined, saying that the cloud was more powerful. They continued to the cloud, the wind, and the stone wall and finally realized that the ordinary mouse was more powerful than even the stone wall.

1. Read and discuss the story focusing on the evolution of the power.

2. Compare with other versions of this tale. Yashiko Uchida included "The Wedding of the Mouse" on pages 89-94 in her book *The Dancing Kettle, and Other Japanese Folk Tales* (Harcourt, Brace & World, 1949), and I. F. Bulatkin included a version, "The Matchmaking of a Mouse," on pages 82-84 in his collection *Eurasian Folk and Fairy Tales* (Clarion, 1965).

3. Continue the theme of power, in this case the seemingly least significant really having the most power, by sharing Gerald McDermott's *The Stonecutter* (Viking, 1957). A filmstrip/cassette version is available from Weston Woods.

Gaeddert, LouAnn. *The Kid with the Red Suspenders*. Dutton, 1983. (I)
Hamilton Clyde Perkins is plagued with an overprotective mother. He is teased, "Hammie, Hammie, Mommie's little lambie." Ham finally shows his independence by skipping school to go to the Bronx Zoo with his friend Jerry and the bully Rob.

1. Hamilton's mother always packed special lunches for him. Draw a special lunch that you might have packed for Hamilton. Include a list of the special items that you would have packed.

2. Would you have liked to have Jerry for a friend? Why or why not?

3. If you had been Hamilton's classmate and friend how might you have helped him feel better about himself?

Gibbons, Gail. *Boat Book*. Holiday House, 1983. (P, I)
Introduces many types of boats and ships.

1. Use this title as an introduction to the subject of ships and boating. Investigate more detailed information by using the card catalog subject headings: SHIPS and BOATS AND BOATING.

2. Read Donald Crews's *Harbor* (Greenwillow, 1982). This book shows the jobs carried out by ferryboats, fireboats, tankers, tugs, barges, and oceanliners.

3. Make a wall bulletin board of boats. Include student pictures and charts of information.

Gibbons, Gail. *Check It Out! The Book about Libraries*. Harcourt Brace Jovanovich, 1985. (P, I)
This book briefly covers the history of libraries before continuing with a discussion of the various types of libraries (public, school, special collections). A very good overview of the function of a library.

1. Ask each student to choose a subject that interests him or her. Visit the school or public library. The students should use the card catalog, computer listing, or book catalog to locate two or three books on their subject.

2. Follow the same procedure as in activity 1, but this time each child should locate books by a specific author. Information on the flaps of the book jacket will enable students to write a sentence or two about the author or illustrator.

3. Investigate the classification system in the library your students use most frequently. Consult with the professional librarian in your school or public library to learn more about the divisions.

Gibbons, Gail. *Christmas Time*. Holiday House, 1982. (P, I)

Discusses the history and significance of Christmas, explaining why Christmas is celebrated, the meaning of gift giving, and the origins of Santa Claus.

1. Extend the holiday theme by sharing Tomie dePaola's *An Early American Christmas* (Holiday, 1987). Research and begin a discussion of the origins of Christmas customs. Resources that might be helpful with the "gift bearer" tradition include: Jones, E. Willis. *Santa Claus Book* (Walker, 1976); Giblin, James Cross. *The Truth about Santa Claus* (Crowell, 1985); Weil, Lizl. *Santa Claus around the World* (Holiday, 1987).

2. Read other books focusing on this holiday season. See index.

3. To initiate a discussion of beliefs that accompany Christmastime read Chris Van Allsburg's *The Polar Express* (Houghton Mifflin, 1985).

Gibbons, Gail. *Clocks and How They Go*. Crowell, 1979. (P, I)

A simple introduction to the common types of clocks in our households.

1. Bring as many different types of clocks to your classroom or library as are available. Use the information in the book to categorize the clocks. Think of other ways to categorize the clocks.

2. Take a clock apart to show the inner workings. (Make sure you will be able to put the clock back together or that you have someone who can replace the parts.)

3. Invite a watch repair person or a watchmaker to visit with your group. Ask that person to explain how a clock works and how to care for a clock.

4. Read another book about clocks, *The Story of Clocks* by Terry Maloney (Sterling Publishing, 1959).

5. Locate other books about clocks by using the card catalog subject heading CLOCKS AND WATCHES.

Gibbons, Gail. *Deadline! From News to Newspaper*. Crowell, 1987. (P, I)
The activities necessary to produce a newspaper from start to finish are examined. The book describes roles of the various editors, photographers, staff artists, and composing room staff in a small city daily newspaper.

1. Produce a class newspaper.

2. Invite a journalist to visit to describe his or her role in the production of the newspaper. Ask that person to bring the news sheets produced by the big presses and to describe the steps involved in the production of the newspaper.

Gibbons, Gail. *Department Store*. Crowell, 1984. (P, I)
The action behind the scenes in a department store is captured in the illustrations. Before the store opens the store's salespeople are preparing their work stations for the day's customers. Cash registers are opened, then the doors, for the start of the shopping day.

1. Set up a store in your room.

2. List the types of jobs that offer opportunities for careers in the department store industry.

3. Visit with a buyer for a local department store; find out more about the buyer's work.

4. Design a logo and an advertisement for your very own department store. Decide on your store's philosophy and the type and quality of merchandise to be sold. Then sell your store's service through a visual advertisement.

Gibbons, Gail. *Dinosaurs*. Holiday House, 1987. (P, I)
One or two dinosaurs are introduced per page. Each page includes a few facts about the creature pictured. A pronunciation guide is included. *Dinosaurs* includes information about fossils, paleontology, and an explanation of the method used by scientists to deduce facts from dinosaurs' fossilized remains.

1. Use this book as a springboard to research about dinosaurs.

2. Locate other books about dinosaurs by checking the card catalog in your school or public library. Use the subject heading DINOSAURS.

Gibbons, Gail. *Fill It Up! All about Filling Stations*. Crowell, 1985. (P, I)
The services offered by a full-service filling station are highlighted and explained as the illustrations show customers lining up at John and Peggy's service station. New batteries are sold, flat tires fixed, engines repaired, and gas pumped into the autos' gas tank. The last page labels and illustrates the types of tools used in a service station.

1. Team this book with Gail Gibbons's *Tools*. Use the final page of the *Fill It Up* title to present a model for similar panels to be developed by students showing the tools their parents use in their work.

2. Invite community workers into your classroom. Ask them to speak about their daily routine and the tools they use in their work.

3. List the services that a "full-service" station offers. Make a comparable list of the services of a "quick-stop" or "self-serve" station. Compare these lists and discuss which type of station is more valuable in your community. Or are they valuable for different reasons?

Gibbons, Gail. *Fire! Fire!* Crowell, 1984. (P, I)

From the start of a fire in an apartment kitchen, to the phone call to the fire department, to the dispatching of the fire-fighting equipment — the whole fire sequence is covered. Other fire locations are discussed: a fire in a country barn, a forest fire, a waterfront fire. Each of these fires is a little different, in terms of equipment used, methods of putting out the fire, and so forth. An appendix describes fire-fighting equipment, ways to prevent a fire, and what to do if there is a fire.

1. Brainstorm situations or things in your homes that may be a potential cause of fire. Make a class list. Then plan ways to minimize the danger of these things.

2. Visit a fire station.

3. Celebrate National Fire Prevention Week; it is usually designated as a week in the last part of September.

4. Make a diagram of your own house. Plan your escape route in case of a fire. Where would you go to telephone for help?

5. Read the page "What to do if there is a fire...." Make these suggestions into a fire action poster for your school or library.

6. Read "Ways to prevent a fire." Make a house check for dangers. Make a list of any that you find; tell how you would correct the danger.

7. Make a diagram of your neighborhood or city; show the location of the fire stations.

8. Make a diagram of a fire truck. A diagram labels the important parts of an object.

Gibbons, Gail. *Flying.* Holiday House, 1986. (P, I)

The history of flying is covered, from the early attempts in balloons, to dirigibles, to the Wright Brothers' successful attempt. Present-day uses for hot-air balloons, blimps, hang gliders, sailplanes, propeller planes, helicopters, and jet planes are briefly introduced. A double-page spread contains a diagram of the inner sections of a passenger jet. Two of the final pages feature panels depicting the space shuttle flights. The very last page lists the dates and briefly describes eight historic flights.

1. Expand on the theme of flight in planes and balloons by reading more books on the topic of hot-air balloons and flight. See the index.

2. Read about Orville and Wilbur Wright, pioneers in air travel. Make a timeline indicating the important dates in their contribution to the history of air travel.

3. Write a short paper or draw a biographical mural describing the Wright Brothers contribution to the history of flight.

4. Write a poetic biography of the Wright Brothers. Use Maxine Kumin's *The Microscope* (Harper & Row, 1986) as a model.

Gibbons, Gail. *From Path to Highway: The Story of the Boston Post Road.* Crowell, 1986. (P, I)
From 500 years ago to the present day, the development of the Boston Post Road is followed.

1. Make a timeline illustrating the development of the Boston Post Road.

2. Research and find more information about the development of the postal system, from postal rider to the present-day system (see *The Post Office Book: Mail and How It Moves* by Gail Gibbons).

3. Locate the Boston Post Road on a present-day road map. Mark the route with a colored pen. Make it the center of a display about this historical road.

4. At the end of the book Gail Gibbons gives some brief information about five famous travelers of the Boston Post Road. Find out more about these five people.

   • Role-play the famous travelers' appearance in your classroom.

   • Conduct a radio interview of one of the famous travelers; use a cassette tape recorder to record the interview for "broadcast" later.

5. The year is 1673; describe your journey on the Boston Post Road. Put the description in diary form or in the form of a letter to your family which you will send once you reach your destination.

6. Relate the research for the building of this road to the general information about building new roads in Gail Gibbons's *New Roads*.

Gibbons, Gail. *Halloween.* Holiday House, 1984. (P, I)
The legend and customs of Halloween are examined: Jack-o-lanterns, costumes, decorations, scarecrows, the custom of trick-or-treating, bobbing for apples, and other Halloween activities.

1. Use this book as a stimulus for researching, in more detail, the customs of Halloween.

2. Enjoy additional books building on the Halloween or scary theme. See the index.

3. Hold a Jack-o-lantern decorating contest.

4. Divide into groups and audiotape a round-robin scary story.

Gibbons, Gail. *Happy Birthday*. Holiday House, 1986. (P, I)

A pictorial look at the traditions and historical beliefs that have emerged into our birthday celebrations. The intertwining of the traditional or historical belief that resulted in today's custom is most effective.

1. Briefly describe the customs or traditions that surround the celebration of birthdays in your house. Or describe the traditions you would like to have.

2. Read some other books with the birthday theme. See the index.

Gibbons, Gail. *Lights! Camera! Action! How a Movie Is Made*. Crowell, 1985. (P, I)

From beginning script to finished movie, the steps are summarized for the reader. All of those people with special responsibilities are cited. The procedures are divided into three steps: (1) Pre-production, (2) Production, and (3) Post-production.

1. Read *Who Threw That Pie? The Birth of Movie Comedy* by Robert Quackenbush (Albert Whitman, 1979). Use this book as an introduction to movie greats: Georges Melies, John Bunny, Mack Sennett, Mabel Normand, Ford Sterling, Charlie Chaplin, Chester Conklin, Ben Turpin, Buster Keaton, Harold Lloyd, Harry Langdon, Stan Laurel, and Oliver Hardy. Research these performers and their work. Make a "Movie Hall of Fame" bulletin board.

2. Another book that describes the making of motion pictures is *Movies and How They Are Made* by Frank Manchel (Prentice-Hall, 1968). Locate others by using the card catalog subject heading MOTION PICTURES—PRODUCTION AND DIRECTION.

3. Write a script for a short movie about an incident in your life.

Gibbons, Gail. *The Milk Makers*. Macmillan, 1985. (P, I)

From cow to table, the process of milking cows and packaging the milk for selling is covered. One page lists three other types of animals that give milk (goats, sheep, reindeer); another page lists the five most common breeds of dairy cows (Ayrshire, Brown Swiss, Guernsey, Jersey, Holstein-Friesian). A diagram of a cow's stomach is included along with information about the process of actually milking the cow. The final page of the book summarizes the common milk products which can be found in our grocery stores.

1. Have a tasting party featuring all of the dairy products listed on the final page of the Gibbons book. As each of the products is tasted make notes on taste, texture, feel to the tongue, and appearance. Use the words in those notes to create a lyrical verse about the food we eat. To get in the mood to write read some poetry from Shel Silverstein's *Where the Sidewalk Ends* (Harper & Row, 1974) or his *A Light in the Attic* (Harper & Row, 1981), or from Jack Prelutsky's *The New Kid on the Block* (Greenwillow, 1984).

2. For older students gather more information about the production of milk by reading James Cross Giblin's *Milk: The Fight for Purity* (Crowell, 1986). This book looks at the history of milk production in this country and includes a discussion of the importance of milk in the Western world and some of the problems encountered by milk producers. The book also examines more thoroughly the fight in the late 1800s and early 1900s of Nathan Straus and others for laws to mandate the pasteurization of all publicly sold milk. This book will add much for the student who desires to have more facts about the topics introduced in the Gibbons title.

3. Make a chart comparing the five most common breeds of cows for size, color, milk production, and general characteristics.

4. Read Eric Carle's *Pancakes, Pancakes!* (Knopf, 1970). In Carle's story the milk does not go to a commercial packager. Compare and contrast the two methods of obtaining milk.

Gibbons, Gail. *New Roads.* Crowell, 1983. (P, I)

This book briefly introduces every operation necessary to bring a new road into use for motorists, from taking a traffic count before construction to erecting directional signs and landscaping the roadside.

1. The description in the final section of the macadam road includes the notation that the method was invented by John L. McAdam. Find out more about the person and the invention. Interview Mr. McAdam (a student playing the historical part) onto a cassette tape recording for replay as a radio broadcast.

2. Make a cut-away model of a road described in the book.

3. In local history resources locate some reference to the roads and paths that the early settlers in your area traveled or built. Describe their experiences in a dialogue or play.

4. View the film *Career Awareness—Construction*, produced by Xerox Corporation, 1974 (10 minutes). The film depicts the men and women in the big business of earth moving (from sandbox to interstate).

Gibbons, Gail. *Paper, Paper Everywhere.* Harcourt Brace Jovanovich, 1983. (P, I)

The production of paper is traced through the various steps, from logging of the trees to the cutting of the finished product. Games are included that illustrate the diverse uses of paper.

1. This book is an excellent book to use in conjunction with Gibbons's title *Deadline! From News to Newspaper* (Crowell, 1987), since newsprint is a major use of paper manufactured in the United States.

2. For one day keep statistics in your classroom, library, or school about the amount of paper used and for what purpose. Make a graph according to use and amount in various locations.

3. Extend the idea of statistics and what happens in one day by reading Tom Parker's *In One Day* (Houghton Mifflin, 1984). Gather statistics about other aspects of life in your school. How many times is the water fountain used? How many lunches are served in one day? How many pencils are sharpened? How many minutes are spent reading books? Title the book: *In One Day at (name of school).*

Gibbons, Gail. *Playgrounds*. Holiday House, 1985. (P, I)

Various types of playground equipment are introduced, such as swings, slides, and sandboxes.

1. List all of the equipment and play opportunities on your school playground. Categorize the equipment into sets or like groups. Make a chart showing each group.

2. Decide what additional equipment you would like your playground to have. Invite your principal to come into your classroom while you give a persuasive speech extolling the value of the new playground equipment.

3. Design a new playground slide. Draw a picture of the slide and decide how it would be constructed. Make it as elaborate as you wish.

Gibbons, Gail. *The Post Office Book: Mail and How It Moves*. Crowell, 1982. (P, I)

This book, as does many of Gibbons's other books on specific topics, begins with a historical perspective of the topic to be discussed. But the focus is on the present-day operation of the postal service. Through her illustrations Gibbons depicts the variations that are present in our system. For example, on the page where the text reads, "A letter carrier picks up mail from the mailbox," she has used six different panels on the page to show a letter carrier picking up mail from a letter depository box, a rural mailbox, a mailbox on the porch of a residence, a business mailbox, a street corner letter box, and a mailbox on a pier (which the letter carrier reaches by boat). From its initial receipt at the local post office the mail is followed through various sorting and culling operations using zip codes to the final destination city or town where another letter carrier delivers the letter to its addressee.

One might note that Gail Gibbons has illustrated the back of the title page (where the copyright information is listed) with a package and a letter. The letter is addressed to her family, The Ancliffes, using her correct address, Goose Green, Corinth, Vermont 05039. The return address appears to be that of her parents, The Ortmanns, who according to the address live in Florida. Later in the book a letter addressed to "Grace & Harry Ortmann" is used to illustrate the function of the zip code. In an earlier drawing of packages and letters illustrating the placement of zip codes across the United States, a package depicted is addressed to a Barbara Fenton in London, England. One of the people to whom Gibbons dedicated her book *Trucks* is Barbara Fenton.

1. Invite your neighborhood letter carrier to visit with your group. Ask him or her to describe the part the letter carrier plays in moving the mail.

2. Visit a post office.

3. Investigate the operation of the postal service by locating other books on the topic by using the card catalog subject heading POSTAL SERVICE – UNITED STATES.

4. Write and mail a letter to a friend.

5. Design a stamp for the United States Postal Service.

Gibbons, Gail. *The Pottery Place*. Harcourt Brace Jovanovich, 1987. (P, I)

A simplified view of the work of a rural potter. The potter mixes her clay, then throws, bisques, glazes, fires, packs and delivers her pots. Much information is included about the actual pottery-making process. Information about the tools of the potter are included, and parts of the kick wheel are labeled.

1. Visit an art center where potters actually work. If an art center is not accessible perhaps a high school potters' class could offer a resource person to visit your class.

2. Research to find out how long it takes to complete the total process of throwing, glazing, and firing a finished pot. Make a timeline showing the process.

Gibbons, Gail. *The Seasons of Arnold's Apple Tree*. Harcourt Brace Jovanovich, 1984. (P, I)

Gail Gibbons's son Eric Ancliffe developed a special relationship with the apple tree on a hilltop near their home in Corinth, Vermont. This book, dedicated to Eric, is the story of his tree. The book speaks of the tree as Arnold's (Eric's) secret place and follows the boy and the tree through the four seasons of the year. Closeup drawings in small panels in the corner of several illustrations give added information concerning the stage or development of the tree. As Arnold builds a tree house and shades himself from the summer rains, the tree develops blossoms and produces ripened fruit. By fall the tree's green leaves have turned golden. The apples are ready to harvest. With the harvest of apples Arnold's family makes apple pie (the recipe is included) and apple cider (the process is diagramed in a side panel). On Halloween Arnold decorates some of the apples. In the winter the branches of the apple tree are bare but it becomes a home for birds as Arnold uses his tree house as a bird feeder, giving them popcorn and berries to eat. The tree becomes a center for his snow fort and the cycle starts once again when the snow melts away and the tree begins to leaf out.

1. Extend the idea of a secret place by reading Beatrice Schenk deRegniers's *Little House of Your Own*, illustrated by Irene Haas (Harcourt, Brace & World, 1954).

2. Draw an apple tree as it would look in the four seasons of the year.

3. Another book with changing seasons depicted through the use of an apple tree is Virginia Lee Burton's *The Little House* (Houghton Mifflin, 1942). This classic title won the Caldecott Award in 1943 as the most distinguished picture book published during the previous year.

4. Write a description of "your secret hiding place." Where do you go to be alone? Where do you go to think your secret thoughts?

Gibbons, Gail. *Sun Up, Sun Down*. Harcourt Brace Jovanovich, 1983. (P, I)

As a young girl rises in the morning the sun brings shadows through her window. Throughout the day the contribution of the sun is highlighted, from its part in growing wheat to providing the warmth to keep our planet warm. A portion of the book discusses clouds that sometimes cover the sun and bring rain and darkness to the earth below.

1. The following topics are mentioned in the book: clouds, shadows, planets, the sun, solar power plants. Use the brief information to motivate a research activity for more details.

2. Make a diagram of the solar system showing the planets' relationship to the sun.

3. Conduct some shadow research. Begin by reading *The Shadow Book* by Beatrice Schenk deRegniers with photographs by Isabel Gordon (Harcourt, Brace & World, 1960). Refer to the Shadows booklist. See the index.

4. Read Tomie dePaola's *The Cloud Book* (Holiday House, 1975).

Gibbons, Gail. *Thanksgiving Day*. Holiday House, 1983. (P, I)
In the same format as her book entitled *Halloween* Gail Gibbons describes the origins and traditions surrounding the establishment of the Thanksgiving holiday in the United States.

1. Describe the traditional customs your family has for the Thanksgiving celebration.

2. Research the first Thanksgiving to add more details to the information presented here. When was the holiday declared a national holiday? Who was the president responsible for the declaration?

3. Read *The Thanksgiving Story* by Alice Dalgliesh (Scribner, 1954). The story of the first celebration is presented with dignity and avoids stereotypes.

4. Continue the holiday theme by reading poems selected by Lee Bennett Hopkins in his anthology of poetry *Merrily Comes Our Harvest In: Poems for Thanksgiving* (Harcourt Brace Jovanovich, 1978) and in Jack Prelutsky's *It's Thanksgiving* (Greenwillow, 1982).

Gibbons, Gail. *Tool Book*. Holiday House, 1982. (P, I)
A book introducing basic tools used by construction workers and handypersons. The tools are introduced in categories. Tools that measure include: folding and flat rulers; tape measure; level; and square. Tools that cut include: ax; metal shears; hand saw; coping saw; plane; chisel; gouge; and file. Tools that pound include: hammer; sledge hammer; and mallet. Tools that grip include: adjustable wrench; vise; pliers; and open-end wrench. Tools that make holes include: shovel; hand drill (and bits); brace and bit (and brace bits). The final categories include tools that turn screws (screwdriver, Phillips screwdriver), and the various types of objects that hold things together (screws, nails, and nuts and bolts). Things that lift and move things include: claw hammer; jack; and pry bar. The final grouping includes tools that are used to help cover surfaces: putty knife, plaster trowel; and brick trowel. Three options for keeping the tools in order are listed: a toolbox; hardware for hanging the tools on a wall; and a workbench.

1. Invite a construction worker to visit to explain the tools he or she uses. Follow the worker's visit by listing the tools discussed and putting them in categories. Use the book's categories or formulate new categories of your own. Depending on the age of the children you may want to expand on the career aspects of the visiting worker's trade. Be aware that there are various categories of construction worker, some using common tools but others using tools unique to a particular trade. In the construction industry the most common craftspersons

include carpenters, plumbers, sheet metal workers (heating and air conditioning), and electricians. (Option 2: Assign a student or small group of students to interview a worker in each of these areas.)

2. Make cards with each of the tools described, one tool on each card. Create new categories for the tools. Rearrange the tools in the new categories. Write a new text utilizing the new categories you have created.

3. Use Anne Rockwell and Harlow Rockwell's book *The Toolbox* (Macmillan, 1971). This book more closely reflects the toolbox used by people who do their own repairs around the house. Write a toolbox book for each craftsperson who visits or whose work is researched.

Gibbons, Gail. *Trains*. Holiday House, 1987. (P, I)
A simple text explaining the history of locomotives and trains. Types of railroad cars and engines, the function of the rails, and special equipment are discussed.

1. Team this book with Donald Crews's *Freight Train* (Greenwillow, 1978). Set the mood for the study of trains and transportation by oral reading of the Crews title. Accompany the reading with sound effects imitating the clickety clack of the railroad tracks.

2. Make train-shaped paper on which to write train information and stories.

3. If there is an Amtrak station nearby arrange to make a visit.

4. Put a train on a bulletin board. Inside each train car place a book jacket for a book children might be encouraged to read.

5. Use the subject heading TRAINS in the library's card catalog. Locate other books about trains. Make an informational bulletin board about trains.

Gibbons, Gail. *Trucks*. Crowell, 1981. (P, I)
This classic introduction to trucks of all kinds can serve as a springboard to building awareness of the trucks and truck drivers that serve each of our communities.

1. List all the types of trucks that are part of your life during one day's time. This list might include the cafeteria delivery trucks, the mail trucks, grocery delivery trucks, emergency trucks.

2. Ask each student to select a specific truck. The truck should be illustrated on a portion of an 11 x 18-inch sheet of paper. Fold the paper in half so there are two 9 x 11-inch sections. On one section the truck should be drawn and on the other section a text should explain the service performed by this truck and its truck driver. In order to complete the text students may have to interview a person who drives the type of truck illustrated.

3. Invite various types of truck drivers to visit your group to explain about the type of material they move from place to place. Incorporate some career information if appropriate to your age group.

4. Read and discuss other books about trucks.

5. Write a two-page paper about a type of truck you have chosen. Use the text in the titles by Barrett, Ancona, or Bushey in the following booklist to provide a model for the paper you write.

Booklist — Trucks

Ancona, George. *Monster on Wheels*. Dutton, 1974.

Barrett, N. S. *Picture Library: Trucks*. Watts, 1984.

Bushey, Jerry. *Monster Trucks: and Other Giant Machines on Wheels*. Carolrhoda, 1985.

Crews, Donald. *Truck*. Greenwillow, 1980.

Rockwell, Anne. *Trucks*. Dutton, 1984.

Siebert, Diane. *Truck Song*. Crowell, 1984.

Gibbons, Gail. *Tunnels*. Holiday House, 1984. (P, I)
All types of tunnels are examined: tunnels dug by animals for their homes, tunnels built by people, tunnels that go under streets, mountains, and water.

1. Read Cass R. Sandak's *Tunnels* (Watts, 1984). This book focuses more on natural and man-made tunnels—their design, construction, and function—and famous tunnels throughout the world. Using the material in this book and in the Gibbons book make a list of all the types of tunnels in each of the books and categorize them.

2. Gather additional facts about the famous tunnels listed in the books. Who built the tunnels? For what purpose? Where are they located? Include any additional information that may seem appropriate.

Gibbons, Gail. *Up Goes the Skyscraper!* Four Winds/Macmillan, 1986. (P, I)
Much like the book *New Roads* this title examines a construction process from start to finish. First comes careful planning with input from earth samples, surveyors, engineers, and other planners. The roles of architects, the general contractor, and specialty workers are described.

1. List all of the types of construction workers that have a part in building the skyscrapers.

2. Make a career chart for each of the workers. What kind of education is needed for each of the careers? What skills are needed? How does one get into the specific career field?

3. Invite someone from each of the construction workers' specialties to visit with your group. Ask them to describe their work, their background, and the type of construction they have done in your city.

4. Conduct a "construction fair." Basically institute the activity suggested in activity 3 but build booths for the various representatives and ask them to visit at the same time. Children would choose the booth they wish to visit.

5. View the film *A City Grows—the Skyscraper* produced by Coronet Instructional Films, 1977 (approximately 11 minutes). This film takes us from the breaking of the ground to the topping out ceremony. Compare and contrast the information depicted in this film to the information given in the Gibbons book.

6. Read James Cross Giblin's *The Skyscraper Book* (Crowell, 1981).

Gibbons, Gail. *Valentine's Day*. Holiday House, 1986. (P, I)

As with her many other titles, Gail Gibbons begins this book with the historical beginnings of the holiday. Various types of valentines—sentimental, silly, homemade, and store-bought—are discussed briefly. People of various ages are depicted exchanging valentines, and heart-shaped gifts of all types are shown. The final two pages describe how to make your own valentines and how to make your own valentine box.

1. Read the book as an introduction to the coming holiday. Suggest children make valentine boxes that represent themselves.

2. Show the filmstrip cassette of *Valentine's Day* by Gail Gibbons. The filmstrip/cassette is available from Listening Library (HY 246 CFX).

3. Read other books building on the theme of the Valentine's holiday (see booklist following this discussion).

4. Make a valentine for a special person. Use hearts and lace and ribbons.

5. Make a valentine and send it to Gail Gibbons.

Booklist—Valentines

Barth, Edna. *Hearts, Cupids, and Red Roses: The Story of the Valentine Symbols*. Houghton Mifflin, 1982.

Brown, Fern G. *Valentine's Day*. Watts, 1983.

Brown, Marc. *Arthur's Valentine*. Little, Brown, 1981.

Bulla, Clyde Robert. *St. Valentine's Day*. Harper & Row, 1965.

Hopkins, Lee Bennett. *Good Morning to You, Valentine*. Illustrated by Tomie dePaola. Harcourt Brace Jovanovich, 1976.

McCullough, Frances. *Love Is Like the Lion's Tooth: An Anthology of Love Poems*. Harper & Row, 1984.

Prelutsky, Jack. *It's Valentine's Day*. Morrow, 1983; Scholastic pb.

Gibbons, Gail. *Weather Forecasting*. Macmillan/Four Winds Press, 1987. (P, I)

Hailstorms, early frost, drought, hurricanes, snowstorms, rain—all of these weather conditions can be forecast by the professionals who study the weather. Their predictions can look into the next day and to longer periods of time. This book deals with the techniques used to track and gauge the weather and explains why weather forecasting is important to our lives.

1. Ask a meteorologist from a local radio or television studio to visit your class, or take a field trip to a local radio or television studio's weather department.

2. Examine the illustrations and attempt to duplicate some of the less complex instruments to collect your own weather data.

3. Throughout the year keep a day-by-day temperature chart. Temperatures will vary depending on the time of day. So you will want to take the temperature at the same time each day.

4. Record the weather each day.

5. Watch or listen to the evening weather segment on the radio or television. Make a chart of the weather the forecaster predicts each evening. Make a similar chart of the weather that actually occurs the next day.

6. Correlate this book with Tomie dePaola's *The Cloud Book* (Holiday, 1975). Read other books about weather and the clouds. Refer to index in this book to locate booklist of cloud books.

Gibbons, Gail. *Willy and His Wheel Wagon*. Prentice-Hall, 1975. (P, I)

Willy collected wheels. When the collection became too large for him to locate the wheels he wanted when he wanted them, he decided to build a "wheel wagon" and put his wheels into sets (or groups). Once he got them arranged all of his friends started to come around to get replacements for wheels on their bicycles, tricycles, go-carts, and other vehicles. Soon he had many wheels to fix. Then along came a friend who had a toy train with wheels. He tried to flee but his wheel wagon began to roll down the hill; it was out of control. His friends saved the wagon from crashing. The story introduces the concept of "sets" and demonstrates the value of friends.

1. Ask each child to bring to school twenty objects that are alike but not exactly alike, for example, buttons, beads, markers for board games, or simply twenty pieces of paper of varying colors and shapes. When the children have their collections read the story *Willy and His Wheel Wagon*, and discuss sets and the way that Willy classified his wheels. Now ask children to create at least two sets with their collections. Size, shape, color, and use might be part of the criteria. Discuss the sets that were created.

2. Cut out wheels from magazines and newspapers and make a "wheel collage." On the collage place the wheels in sets. Make other collages picturing sets of other objects.

3. Do you think Willy's friends were taking advantage of him? Why or why not? How could he have handled the requests from his friends without losing them as friends.

Gibbons, Gail. *Zoo.* Crowell, 1987. (P, I)

A working day at the zoo is presented, from the beginning when the workers arrive to the time when the night guard locks the gate.

1. List all of the animals named as being part of this zoo. Categorize the animals into their major classes: mammals, reptiles, birds, fish, amphibians. What are the characteristics of each of these animal classes?

2. View the film *Who's Who in the Zoo?* produced by Centron Films in 1974 (approximately 12 minutes). This film explores the work of the various scientists, specialists, and technicians who care for animals in the zoo.

3. Read *What Happens at the Zoo* (Books for Young Explorers Series) by Judith E. Rinard (National Geographic Society, 1984). This book provides additional information on the functions within a zoo and the care and treatment given to the animals that live there.

4. Several zoos have colorful, informative brochures or booklets promoting their zoos. One such zoo is the Milwaukee County Zoo which has superb displays of animals in their natural habitats. Write: Milwaukee County Zoo, 10001 West Bluemound Road, Milwaukee, WI 53226 to request information about the availability and price of their promotional material.

Giff, Patricia Reilly. *Rat Teeth.* Delacorte, 1984. (I)

Radcliffe has several problems, not the least of which are his protruding teeth. His dad and mother are divorced and he has to move with his father to live with Aunt Ida. His new teacher is strict, and he feels lost in the shuffle. In an effort to escape the teasing of his classmates he runs away and spends the day at Macy's only to find out that being away from home is harder than he thought.

1. If you had been Radcliffe's classmate how might you have helped him cope with his new situation?

2. At Macy's Radcliffe met a boy named Jo-Jo Hines. We are not told much more about him. Think about how old he is, what he looks like, and what type of person he might be. Try to decide where he really does live, what kind of family he has, and why he wasn't in school.

3. Radcliffe could not change the way his teeth looked but his classmates teased him anyway. How would you handle people who teased you about something that you could not change?

Gormley, Beatrice. *Fifth Grade Magic.* Dutton, 1982. (I)

Gretchen wanted more than anything a part in the play. When a fairy godmother offered to help, Gretchen was pleased. That is, until things started getting mixed up. That is when Gretchen found out her fairy godmother was an apprentice. Humorous.

1. Describe the spells Errora and Gretchen attempted to cast and explain what went wrong.

2. Create a new book jacket for the book. Be sure to include the title, author's name, and illustrator.

3. Which of Errora's spells did you like best? Explain why you chose that spell.

Gould, Marilyn. *Golden Daffodils*. Addison-Wesley, 1982; Harper & Row, 1982. (I)

Daffodils were a symbol of hope and beauty to Janis. This fall Janis needed hope more than ever. She had cerebral palsy and she was starting a new school and she wanted to be "just another student" at that school. She does meet good friends, including Barney Fuchs, and her cousin Rhoda is close at hand. But Cheryl and Garth set out to be deliberately nasty and unkind to Janis. Janis and her friends triumph but not before some moving episodes.

1. Why do you think Cheryl and Garth were so nasty to Janis?

2. Barney wanted Janis to visit his brother David. Why do you think he wanted that?

3. At the beginning of the book, the author quotes a poem by Wordsworth. Copy that poem onto a large piece of paper, then illustrate the poem. Attempt to show the feelings that Janis may have had for daffodils.

4. Daffodils were a personal symbol for Janis. Design your own personal symbol and use it on stationery and elsewhere. Explain why this is your symbol.

5. Marilyn Gould used the title "A Host of Daffodils" as her working title for this story while she was writing the book. What does that phrase mean?

6. Read the sequel to this book, *The Twelfth of June* (Lippincott, 1986).

Graham, John. *I Love You, Mouse*. Illustrated by Tomie dePaola. Harcourt Brace Jovanovich, 1976. (P, I)

A patterned story that uses many animals, such as a mouse and a piglet to tell a story.

1. Read the story aloud. It is a story you will want to read several times letting the children participate in the reading as soon as they recognize the pattern.

2. Use in conjunction with Mary Ann Hoberman's *A House Is a House for Me*, illustrated by Betty Fraser (Viking, 1978). This book will give several additional animals and their homes.

3. With older children follow the same procedure to model the writing procedure, but follow the group activity by giving children the names of unusual animals with which they may not be familiar. Ask them to research the animals to find out the necessary information: what the baby animals are called, where they live, and what they do. Once they have located the necessary information they will need to use that information to write a verse. Collect these verses, with illustrations, into a class book.

4. Before binding the verses into a class booklet, you may wish to display the verses on a bulletin board. Be sure to include a title page giving the title of the innovation text as well as the title of the book upon which the verses are based.

Greer, Gery and Bob Ruddick. *Max and Me and the Time Machine*. Harcourt Brace Jovanovich, 1983. (I)

Steve buys a time machine for $2.50. Max is very dubious about the real worth of the machine but nevertheless assists Steve in hooking it up. Before either of them can blink they find themselves in the thirteenth century. Steve has entered the Middle Ages in the body of Sir Robert Marshall, the swashbuckling Green Falcon. Max is Sir Marshall's horse. Their adventure lasts three days and includes jousting with an evil knight, rescuing a beautiful damsel, and confronting death. Just in time they are catapulted back into the twentieth century.

1. This story is known as a "time shift" story because the setting of the story shifts from one time period to another. Tell about both time settings used in the story, using information you can glean from the story.

2. How was Sir Robert Marshall's personality different from or similar to the personality of Steve?

3. Explain why you would or would not go to Dr. Gathergoods if you were sick. Use the information in the book to help you explain the reasons for your decision.

4. Another novel that shifts back into other periods of history is *Time Cat* by Lloyd Alexander (Holt, Rinehart & Winston, 1963). Locate that title and read one of the nine episodes. Compare that story with the novel about Max and Steve.

Griffith, Helen V. *Foxy*. Greenwillow, 1984. (P, I)

Jeff is on a trip to Florida with his parents who had visited the state before Jeff was born. Jeff gains the confidence of an abused dog which cowers when approached. Jeff's relationship with the dog and his conflicts with Amber provide for several suspenseful episodes.

1. The story takes place in the Florida Keys. How does the author establish the geographical setting through her text?

2. List ten animals mentioned in the story. Choose one to tell more about. Make a chart giving at least five facts about this type of animal.

Grimm Brothers. *The Devil with the Three Golden Hairs*. Retold and illustrated by Nonny Hogrogian. Knopf, 1983. (P, I)

Common themes are present in tales from various countries. Details, names, and exact incidents may be different but the basic story lines are often very similar. A boy was born to a poor couple who knew that luck would follow their child throughout his life. It was foretold that during his fourteenth year the young boy would marry the king's daughter. The king did not like this prophecy. He attempted to destroy the child to keep the prophecy from coming true. In the end he sets a seemingly impossible task for the boy; the boy must pluck three golden hairs from the head of the devil.

Hogrogian's paintings are set against white backgrounds. The paintings seem to spill out of their frames, beckoning the reader to come into the fantasy. Each set of two pages is illuminated with one full-page framed illustration. The opposite page is often illustrated with an unframed illustration further enhancing the text. Each of the paintings is brilliant, particularly the vibrant red of the devil's cape and the red wine flowing from the fountain.

1. Nonny Hogrogian has retold a German folktale first collected by the Grimm Brothers. Several other retellings of this tale are available in various editions of folktales collected by the Grimm Brothers. One such collection is *The Brothers Grimm, Popular Folk Tales*, translated by Brian Alderson (Doubleday, 1978). "The Three Golden Hairs of the Devil" is found on pages 170-77 of this book. I. F. Bulatkin has included a similar tale of Russian origin in a collection of tales, *Eurasian Folk and Fairy Tales* (Criterion, 1965). The tale, found on pages 9-21, is called "The Three Golden Hairs of Granddad Sol." Compare and contrast two versions of this story.

2. Write a paper comparing at least two versions of the "golden hairs" story.

Grimm, Jacob and Wilhelm Grimm. *Favorite Tales from Grimm*. Illustrated by Mercer Mayer. Macmillan, 1982. (I)
This collection of tales from the German stories of the Grimm Brothers contains several traditional stories. Mayer's elaborate illustrations give each tale an interpretation that cannot be fully appreciated through the text alone.

1. Compare and contrast the tales in this collection with retellings from other sources. There are many collections of Grimm tales available and many books retelling a single tale in the Grimm tradition. Locate these stories in your library by searching for entries in the card catalog under GRIMM, JACOB or GRIMM BROTHERS. Use the table of contents in each collective volume to locate specific tales.

2. Use this book as a motivator for a "Grimm Brothers Read-In." Using the card catalog locate as many Grimm tales as are available in your school or public library. Set up a Grimm Brothers Read-In display. Set aside twenty minutes each day for a week or two to read the stories of the Grimm Brothers. The tales may be read silently or aloud. At the end of the read-in discuss the fairy tales. Charts of favorite tales, with saddest tale, most romantic tale, and so on, could be developed. Compare and contrast the story grammar and illustrations in a tale retold and illustrated by different authors and artists. Other activities could include making posters for favorite tales and developing puppet plays.

Gwynne, Fred. *A Chocolate Moose for Dinner*. Windmill, 1976.
A little girl hears phrases spoken by her parents and pictures them in her mind. Her parents' mention of chocolate mousse for dinner brings the literal picture of a chocolate moose coming for dinner. Other words bring up equally confusing images of gorilla war and shoetrees.

1. Before reading this book plan ahead and manage to discuss one of the phrases and its figurative meaning each day. For example, on day one serve a small portion of chocolate mousse to your students as a special treat. Discuss the name of the treat. Be sure to share the spelling as well. On the second day share a special afternoon drink of juice in the afternoon and propose a toast to someone's good efforts that day. Acquaint the students with

the term "toast." On the third day discuss guerilla warfare. On following days focus on the other phrases in the book, such as, "have a shoe tree," "prey on other animals," "be in an arms race," "sleep on an idea," and "build a wing on a house."

2. Once the phrases have all been introduced read the story. You will be able to confirm the children's understanding of the figurative phrase by the expressions of humor that are exhibited when they see the illustrations for the literal interpretation of the phrase.

3. Interview parents to find out some other phrases our parents or family members use that might be illustrated. Draw the illustrations.

4. Extend the fun with the literal and figurative meanings of more phrases by reading one of the other titles by Fred Gwynne: *The King Who Rained* (Windmill, 1970); *Sixteen Hand Horse* (Simon & Schuster, 1987); or *A Little Pigeon Toad* (Simon & Schuster, 1988).

5. Anthony Browne has written *Gorilla* (Knopf, 1983). In the background of one of the illustrations is a poster of a gorilla outfitted as a guerilla fighter. One might read the text and see if any of the children spot the poster as illustrative humor on Browne's part. Cite other examples of illustrative humor in this book.

Hahn, Mary Downing. *Daphne's Book*. Clarion, 1983. (I)

How could Jessica handle this? No one liked Daphne and now Jessica was stuck with her for this school project. Nothing could get her out of the situation. Would people begin to think Jessica was strange and odd too? As Jessica and Daphne get to know one another Jessica begins to understand the problem. It is their friendship that brings a solution to Daphne's situation.

1. Make a list of ten words that describe Daphne, Jessica, and yourself. Who are you more like? Explain.

2. Would you want to have Daphne for your friend? Jessica? Michelle? Tracy? or Sherry? Explain why or why not.

3. Create a book jacket for *The Mysterious Disappearance of Sir Benjamin Mouse*, the book the girls were writing.

4. Read *Bear's House* by Marilyn Sachs (Doubleday, 1971). Discuss how a fellow classmate might help the young girl in this story.

Hale, Irina. *Brown Bear in a Brown Chair*. Atheneum, 1985. (P)

A brown bear sits undistinguishable in a brown chair. He attempts to make himself visible by finding a chair where he will not blend into the upholstery.

1. Choose a pattern (wallpaper, material, painted, colored) and make a chair and a bear.

2. Write a story about your bear and why he is the pattern he is. Perhaps the pattern is from one of your favorite shirts, from your family's kitchen curtains, or from the wrapping paper that wrapped your favorite package last December. Or perhaps the pattern is that of your bedroom wallpaper.

Hall, Donald. *Ox-Cart Man*. Illustrated by Barbara Cooney. Viking, 1979. (P, I)

A year in the life of a family in nineteenth-century New England. The focus is on the annual cycle of planting, growth, and harvest interwoven by strong strands of handcraft, trade, and conservation.

1. On a map locate the six states that compose the area known as New England. This story takes place near Portsmouth, New Hampshire. Mark that location also.

2. Discuss what life might have been like in the 1800s.

3. Read the book or view the videotape available from Live Oak Media, or view the National Public Broadcasting's Reading Rainbow® segment featuring *Ox-Cart Man*.

4. Research to confirm the ideas presented during the discussion generated during activity 2.

5. Compare life in the nineteenth century with life in your community today.

6. Schedule an Ox-Cart Man Day. Invite local artisans to your school to demonstrate the art of making corn husk dolls, birch brooms, woven items, and other handcrafts.

Hall, Lynn. *Danza*. Scribner, 1982. (I)

Paulo, a sensitive Puerto Rican boy, finds his beautiful Paso Fino horse near death. This is the story of Paulo's relationship with his powerful grandfather and the American, Major Kessler, who join with Paulo in helping Danza recover from the near-fatal condition.

1. Write a possible ending to the story, if Major Kessler had not been willing to help Paulo. What if

   • another person took Major Kessler's role in the story?

   • Paulo and his grandfather aided Danza on their own?

   • Paulo gave up the horse?

   • the outcome for Danza was not positive?

2. Research breeds of horses. What are the characteristics of a Paso Fino horse? Where did this breed of horse originate? Compare Paso Fino horses to three other major breeds of horses.

3. Investigate the different ways a horse can be a champion, including show horse, race horse, and rodeo horse. Describe the characteristics of a champion.

4. Plot Danza's travels on a political map of Central and North America.

5. Read Barbara Berry's *The Thoroughbreds* (Bobbs-Merrill, 1974). This book traces the history of thoroughbreds.

Hall, Lynn. *Half the Battle*. Scribner, 1982. (I)

A hundred-mile horse race of endurance. Loren Liskey puts himself, his brother, and their horses through a grueling schedule of conditioning and practice for the ride. Loren's jealousy mounts as his brother, Blair, gets all the attention just because he is blind. Loren's jealousy brings him to take drastic action to ensure that he will get the recognition that he feels he deserves.

1. If Loren suddenly lost his sight and Blair regained his, how do you think Blair would treat Loren?

2. Research endurance rides. Where are the major races held? What are the obstacles? Are there any outstanding champions today?

3. Read one other book about a blind person (fiction or nonfiction). Compare how that person dealt with blindness with the way Blair coped with his sightlessness. See index.

Hall, Lynn. *The Horse Trader*. Scribner, 1981. (I)

Karen is fifteen. Her trusted friend Harley Williams promised to find her a nice little mare. He does, but when Karen realizes that Lady Bay is a foundered horse her faith in Harley Williams and their friendship is called up for re-examination.

1. Read about the auctions on Assateague and Chincoteague Islands, located off the coasts of Maryland and Virginia. Marguerite Henry writes of the auctions in *Misty of Chincoteague*. See the Bookshelf entry for that book for additional sources and activities.

2. What is a foundered horse? How does a horse become foundered? What are the symptoms and the effects?

Hall, Lynn. *The Something Special Horse*. Scribner, 1985. (I)

Mr. Eklund buys and sells horses for the animal food market. When Chris discovers that his father has bought an especially attractive and healthy horse at one of the weekly sales, Chris suspects that the horse is more than what she appears. Chris decides that he must defy his father and take the horse to a professional stable over forty miles away. After reaching Greencrest Farms Chris does ask for help and they are able to trace the owner. A sequel is suggested by the loose ends that exist even as the story ends.

1. Lynn Hall raises horses and often writes about Paso Fino horses. In this story, however, the gray mare was an Andalusian. Research information about this breed of horse and other breeds of horses. Make a chart of your information. Include in a display the chart and some books about horses that you think your classmates may wish to read.

2. Make a bibliography of books by Lynn Hall that your library has in its collection. Bibliographies should include the author, title, publisher, and copyright date. Alphabetize first by author, then by title.

3. At the end of the book, Chris felt that he could "handle whatever was to come." When his dad arrives at Greencrest Farms what do you think will happen?

4. Write the ending to this story. What happens to Chris and to the horse, Lacy.

Hall, Lynn. *Tin Can Tucker*. Scribner, 1982. (I)

After she runs away from a group home, Ann Tucker finds a permanent family with the rodeo circuit. This is an unpretentious novel filled with the precise details of the rodeo circuit, as well as some memorable characters and rodeo scenes. An entertaining upbeat winner.

1. Read another book about runaways or foster care. Compare the two stories and the chief protagonists in each story. Read Betsy Byars's *The Pinballs* (Harper & Row, 1977) or Katherine Paterson's *The Great Gilly Hopkins* (Crowell, 1978). See the index for additional titles.

Hanson, June Andrea. *Winter of the Owl*. Macmillan, 1980; Scholastic pb, 1982. (I)

Janey is wild about her horse. As a colt her horse was wild and unbroken, and Janey had worked hard to tame him; the colt was her special friend. But now the ranch her father and grandfather operated is losing money and her father has ordered the horse sold. The money is needed to buy food for the other stock on the ranch. What can Janey do? Can she find a way to keep the horse? Janey's relationship with her grandfather was the focus of Hanson's first novel *The Summer of the Stallions* (Macmillan, 1979). At the end of that book Janey found the colt which she took home to train. That colt is the focus of this book.

1. Explain the significance of the title *Winter of the Owl*.

2. Read another horse story. In the card catalog in your school or public library use the subject heading HORSES-FICTION. Marguerite Henry and Lynn Hall have each written several excellent horse stories.

Heller, Ruth. *Chickens Aren't the Only Ones*. Putnam, 1981. (P, I)

Many different animals lay eggs and this book discusses several of them. Reptiles, birds, snakes, and of course hens are mentioned.

1. Make a list of animals that do lay eggs.

2. Use the list from activity 1, to begin a chart of egg characteristics. Use the chart to compare and contrast the size, shape, and color of each of the animals' eggs.

3. Illustrate the various shapes of eggs: bubble-like eggs, capsule-like eggs, eggs hanging on strings, eggs in sacs, big eggs, and little eggs.

4. Read *Seven Eggs* by Meredith Hooper, illustrated by Terry McKenna (Harper & Row, 1985). The book describes the animal that hatches from each of six eggs. The seventh and the last one is hatched "On Sunday ... and out came seven chocolate eggs." Each of the baby animals was given a chocolate egg, including "one for you." Use a plastic egg filled with chocolate eggs to duplicate the end of the story.

5. An animal that is hatched from an egg after the egg is expelled from the body is called "oviparous." Create your own oviparous animal. Use magic markers to show the colors of the animal. Be sure to tell about the size of the animal's egg, incubation period, where the animal lives, and what it eats.

6. How does an egg grow into a chicken? Why can't you hatch a chick from your breakfast egg? From tiny egg cell to wet, wobbly baby bird, it takes twenty-one days for a chick to hatch. *Egg to Chick* by Millicent E. Selsam and illustrated by Barbara Wolff (Harper & Row, 1970; Harper Trophy, 1987) explains the answers to these questions. The book is well written and uses many simple but accurate drawings to expand on the information given in the text. While this book is designated by the publisher as an I Can Read book, the book is equally informative for the older child who needs a well thought-out explanation.

7. View the National Public Broadcasting Reading Rainbow® segment featuring Millicent E. Selsam's *Egg to Chick* (Harper & Row, 1970; Harper Trophy, 1987).

8. Read other books about poultry and eggs. See index.

Henry, Marguerite. *Misty of Chincoteague*. Illustrated by Wesley Dennis. Rand McNally, 1947. (I)
Misty was the colt of Phantom, a descendant of the Spanish horses that struggled to Assateague Island when a ship was wrecked in a storm. Once each year the wild horses are herded across the channel to Chincoteague Island where the horses are sold on Pony Penning Days. Paul and Maureen have their hearts set on buying Phantom and are thrilled when they find out that they can also purchase her colt, Misty. Through the colt, the two children are able to gentle Phantom and win an exciting race. But Phantom escapes to the island leaving Misty behind with her human friends.

1. This story is based on true events. Assateague Island and Chincoteague Island are located off the coasts of Maryland and Virginia. Pony Penning Days are still held, during the last week of July, each year. Research to find out more about the islands and Pony Penning Days. In addition to general reference sources Jack Denton Scott's *Island of the Wild Horses* (Putnam, 1978) and K. M. Kostyal's article "All the Pretty Little Ponies: Chincoteague's Roundup" in *National Geographic Traveler* (Summer 1985, II: 2, pp. 118-127) will be useful sources. Accompanying the Kostyal article are several interesting photographs by Medford Taylor.

2. Write a letter to the Chincoteague Chamber of Commerce requesting information. The address is: Chincoteague Chamber of Commerce, P.O. Box 258, Chincoteague, VA 23336. Other sources of information include: District Naturalist, Assateague Island National Seashore, P.O. Box 38, Chincoteague, VA 23336, and Refuge Manager, Chincoteague National Wildlife Refuge, P.O. Box 62, Chincoteague, VA 23336.

3. Make Chincoteague Pot Pie. The ladies' auxiliary serves this dish during Pony Penning Days on Chincoteague Island. Search cookbooks to find a suitable pot pie recipe, rename the recipe Chincoteague Pot Pie, and arrange to make the recipe in class or send the recipe home with a note encouraging a family meal.

4. Read the sequel, *Stormy: Misty's Foal*. Illustrated by Wesley Dennis (Rand McNally, 1963).

5. Collect pictures of horses from magazines and newspapers to make a collage of horses. Title the collage "Marguerite Henry's World of Horses." Display the collage on a bulletin board with information about the many other horse stories written by Marguerite Henry.

6. For teacher background about Marguerite Henry and her writing read Marguerite Henry's article "A Weft of Truth and a Warp of Fiction" in *Elementary English* (October 1974, Volume 51, pp. 920-955). In this article Henry discusses the origin of the idea for her book *San Domingo: The Medicine Hat Stallion* (Rand McNally, 1972).

7. Even though books of fiction are generally said to be stories that are not true, there is much research that must be done before the book is written. The events must be believable. Marguerite Henry is one of those authors who spends a great deal of time doing research. In a film produced by Pied Piper, *Story of a Book, 2nd Edition*, Marguerite Henry tells the story of how her book *San Domingo: The Medicine Hat Stallion* came to be. The film will introduce children to Marguerite Henry and her books while giving them an insight into the writer's craft.

8. Introduce the theme of animals in books by utilizing "Animals" a filmstrip/cassette in Pied Pipers' *Literature for Children* series. "Animals" is one of four titles in the series 2. In the filmstrip/cassette Marguerite Henry's *King of the Wind* (Rand McNally, 1948) is featured. Several other titles by Henry are mentioned in the narrative.

Hoban, Lillian. *Arthur's Halloween Costume*. Harper & Row, 1984. (P)
   Arthur, the lovable monkey, gets ready for his favorite holiday, Halloween. He has trouble choosing a costume. Will he be scary or will he win a prize?

1. Make a list of costumes for Halloween.

2. Categorize the list of costumes into scary, fairytale, imaginative, or any other category that is appropriate.

3. Draw a picture of you in your favorite Halloween costume.

4. Tell about your scariest moment on Halloween.

Hoberman, Mary Ann. *A House Is a House for Me*. Illustrated by Betty Fraser. Viking, 1978. (P, I)
   A patterned rhyming story featuring various types of animals and things and their homes, both real and fanciful.

1. Read the story aloud and encourage the children to join in on the refrain, "but a house is a house for me." A big book version is available from Scholastic Books.

2. Use in conjunction with *I Love You, Mouse* by John Graham. See Bookshelf entry for that book. Both deal with animals and homes.

3. Make a list of words that rhyme.

4. Make a list of real and fancile homes.

5. Paint a mural of different houses.

6. Describe your own house.

7. Make a model of your house. If your classmates make models of their houses perhaps you could make a model of your school community.

8. Investigate types of houses in other cultures.

9. Read Harvey Weiss's *Shelters: From Tepee to Igloo* (Crowell, 1988).

10. Write some additional verses for *A House Is a House for Me*.

Hogrogian, Nonny. *Apples*. Collier Macmillan, 1972. (P, I)

A wordless fable. Colored pencils appear to have been used to execute these vibrant but softly colored illustrations which detail a story of the town's inhabitants who eat apples and abandon the apple cores on the ground. As each apple core is left behind a small tree sprouts. Each of the trees grows larger as the next tree begins to sprout. Finally an entire apple grove yields a harvest of red apples for the apple vendor who picks the apples and carts them off to presumably start the whole scenario once again.

1. Make a list of the people and animals that contributed to the apple orchard (boy, rabbit, crow, girl, hen, pig, goat, dog, sheep).

2. Wordless books are excellent vehicles to promote speaking and writing activities. For activity suggestions and a wordless booklist refer to the index.

Hogrogian, Nonny. *The Contest: An Armenian Folktale*. Adapted and illustrated by Nonny Hogrogian. Greenwillow, 1976. (P, I)

Two robbers, Hrahad and Hmayag, find that they are betrothed to the same woman. Ehleezah is described as "the sweetest girl in our mountains." The men meet on their way to a neighboring province and decide that they should have a contest to decide which of them will actually get to marry Ehleezah. The contest was to determine which of them was the cleverest thief in the mountains. The winner would marry Ehleezah. During the course of the contest jewels were stolen from the same man three times and Ishkhan's palace walls were scaled, one of his chickens eaten, and the Ishkhan's own bedroom entered. The Ishkhan was asked to determine which of the two was the cleverest but his answer did not settle the matter. The following morning the two robbers decided that Ehleezah was not deserving of either of them and that the province could provide a profitable future for them both. They remained in the new province while "back in Erzingah Ehleezah, too, had discovered a new future." This last phrase is illustrated with a picture of Ehleezah being serenaded by a bearded man.

The illustrations of the woman, Ehleezah, bring to mind the maiden who gets the blue bead in *One Fine Day* (Macmillan, 1971). The final illustration of Ehleezah and her new suitor definitely look like Nonny Hogrogian herself and her husband, David Kheridan. Since both Hogrogian and Kheridan are of Armenian descent it is not surprising that their own bone structure, hair coloring, and other physical features should provide an authentic image for an Armenian folktale.

1. Examine the tapestry-like endpapers and the tapestry borders on Hogrogian's full-color illustrations. Note the colors used and the patterns which repeat in each design. Try using oil pastel chalk to create some tapestry-like designs. Use the designs to frame favorite paintings.

2. Suppose that Hmayag and Hrahad were not robbers. What might they have done to prove their cleverness?

3. Describe what you would do to prove your cleverness if you were involved in a contest.

4. Look at the last picture in the book, the one showing Ehleezah and her bearded friend. Describe the "new future" that these two people will have together. Do you think that this friend is a robber? Why or why not?

Hogrogian, Nonny. *Handmade Secret Hiding Places*. Overlook Press/Bookstore Press, 1975. (P, I)
An instruction book giving simple directions for the building of such hiding places as a "Behind the Stairs Hideout," "The Leafy Lean-To," and "The Four Poster Arabian Tent." These directions, along with the directions for seven other hideouts, are written in cursive print. The directions are simple and should allow for anyone who is able to decipher cursive print to build a hideout.

1. Read the directions and make the hideout that is described. Have someone take a picture of you in the hideout. Bring the picture to share with others.

2. Write directions for the building of a hideout that you have designed.

3. Illustrate your handmade secret hiding place.

4. Write a short description of your secret hiding place.

5. Describe the things you do (or would do) in your handmade secret hiding place.

Hogrogian, Nonny. *One Fine Day*. Macmillan, 1971. (P)
Hogrogian was awarded the 1972 Caldecott Award for the illustrations in this cumulative tale. The fox is so thirsty that he laps up the old woman's milk, so the woman cuts off the fox's tail. He begs for the return of his tail and the woman agrees if the fox gives her back her milk. So the fox goes first to the cow asking for milk, she asks for grass, and so he goes to the grass, and so the story goes until he gets a blue bead from the peddler to give to the maiden.

1. Write another cumulative story telling another story about the fox and his tail. Create another sequence of action.

2. During your next school party play pin the tail on the fox.

3. Choral read the story.

Hogrogian, Nonny. *Rooster Brother*. Macmillan, 1974. (P, I)

Nonny Hogrogian first heard this story from her husband, David Kheridan, who heard the tale as a child from his father. On his name day Melkon, a small but clever boy, was sent to the bakery to have a rooster put in the oven for their supper. On the way from the bakery, the cooked rooster was stolen by three bandits. Melkon vowed to make them pay. When Melkon was finished the bandits had had enough of Rooster Brother so they left the town of Adana and never returned. The endpapers foreshadow the illustrations with giant red poppies that grace the green fields. Within, Melkon is shown waiting for his rooster to be roasted while he picks poppies on the hillside. The illustrations are vibrant and in full color. Traditional homes are shown in the background of several pictures. The bandit who leaves his suit at the tailor shop has the same general characteristics as Nonny Hogrogian's husband, David Kheridan. The heathery garments in vibrant blues, magentas, oranges, and browns are colors familiar to the Armenian culture.

1. Locate Armenia on a world map. Discuss its location and some of the history behind the culture of the people. Use an encyclopedia entry for Armenia.

2. Discuss how this story reflects the culture of the Armenian people. Discuss the characteristics of their culture that we might deduce from this story. Research if these deductions are accurate in the location today.

3. Discuss the unstated moral of this story. What do you think the moral is? What makes you think that that is the message in this story? Explain.

Holl, Kristi D. *Just Like a Real Family*. Atheneum, 1984. (I)

Twelve-year-old June Finch's class is scheduled to visit the local nursing home where each student is to become a friend to one of the residents. June was looking forward to a relationship with a warm grandmotherly woman. Instead, she was paired with grouchy old Franklin Cooper who makes it plain that he does not want any part of June and her visits.

1. Explain the new definition of a potato and of an egg which readers of this novel will have. Would you choose to be a potato or an egg? Explain.

2. Describe how Mr. Cooper changed during the course of the story.

3. Tell what you think will be the relationship between Mr. Cooper, June, and her mother in one year.

4. Make a chart illustrating some of the wildflowers Mr. Cooper and June might have found if they had gone for a walk in a nature park near your home.

5. Read the sequel to this book, *No Strings Attached* (Atheneum, 1988).

Hurwitz, Johanna. *Baseball Fever*. Morrow, 1981.

Ezra Feldman loved baseball. His favorite team was the New York Mets but his specialty was baseball history. Ezra's European father thought Ezra ought to learn how to play chess. Neither one could see the virtue in the other's interest.

1. Define "baseball fever."

2. How do you think this story would have ended if Mr. Feldman had not met Mr. Strauss?

3. Ezra used the names on t-shirts to create silly sentences. He used the words on the shirt to make an acronym for his own statements. For example, YALE became "You are large enough" and COLUMBIA became "Can only ladies' umbrellas maim big intelligent alligators?" Draw a paper t-shirt representing a popular t-shirt or t-shirts worn in your locale. After several are posted on a bulletin board try to make your own silly sentences for each of the posted t-shirts.

Hutchins, Pat. *Good-Night, Owl!* Macmillan, 1972. (P, I)
Owl cannot sleep because of all the animals and the noise they are making: bees buzz, the robin peeps, and more animals keep owl from his sleep. But at night it was the owl who screeched and kept the other animals awake.

1. Make a picture book of animals and the noises they make.

2. Choose one of the animals in the book and give some more information about that animal.

3. Read *Why Mosquitoes Buzz in People's Ears* by Verna Aardema (Dial, 1975). The book is filled with the sounds of animals from the jungle.

Kheridan, David and Nonny Hogrogian. *Right Now.* Knopf, 1983. (P, I)
The feeling of happiness is conveyed through simple verses. Plans for the days ahead, happenings in the past are recounted but each verse ends in a statement about "right now" and the joy in the simple events of today. The thoughts of the past and the future are pictured in black and white illustrations while the statements about "right now" are colorful paintings comfortably displaying a sense of wonder and joy.

1. Read the verses. Discuss past or future and the ending sentence which always conveys a thought about "right now." How does Nonny Hogrogian make a distinction between the present and the future or past? Discuss the story grammar.

2. Write some verses about an event that occurred last night. Complete the verse with a statement of the present. Keep the verse you write in the same pattern as Kheridan's verses.

3. Make a class book. Each member of the class could complete and illustrate a parody of the last sentence in the book. "Sometimes I wish I could _____ like a _____ , but right now I like just being me." On that page print the completed sentence and place a picture of the student below the sentence. The student should autograph the page. On another page, the student should tell a little about himself or herself. These two pages could be posted on a special "Just Me" bulletin board and later combined in book form for the children to read.

Krauss, Ruth. *This Thumbprint*. Harper & Row, 1967. (P)
    A small-sized book that contains a story illustrated completely with thumbprint characters, best to be shared in a small group so that the illustrations can be seen adequately.

1. Read the story and then allow students to draw their own characters using their thumbprints. Use *Ed Emberley's Great Thumbprint Drawing Book* (Little, Brown, 1977) as an additional source of ideas.

2. Create a family or class picture using thumbprint illustrations. If appropriate write stories to go along with the thumbprint illustrations.

3. Use in October. October 9, 1915 is the date The International Association for Criminal Identification (fingerprinting) was established. On October 24, 1904 the St. Louis Police department was the first to adopt a fingerprinting system.

Lobel, Arnold. *The Rose in My Garden*. Illustrated by Anita Lobel. Greenwillow, 1984. (P, I)
    "This is the rose in my garden./This is the bee/That sleeps on the rose in my garden." A lyrical cumulative verse that unfolds an ever-blooming garden bursting with hollyhocks, marigolds, zinnias, daisies, and other flowers.

1. Just right for continued exploration of the cumulative verse form. Read other titles (see booklist following) that use a variation of the "This is the house that Jack built" verse.

2. Give each child a package of flower seeds to begin growing his or her own garden. Paste a title and author square on the flower seed package recognizing the involvement of *The Rose in My Garden* in the activity.

Booklist—Cumulative Verses and Tales

Emberley, Barbara. *Drummer Hoff*. Illustrated by Ed Emberley. Prentice-Hall, 1967.

Heilbroner, Joan. *This Is the House Where Jack Lives*. Illustrated by Aliki. Harper & Row, 1962.

"The House That Jack Built." In *The Three Bears and 15 Other Stories* by Anne Rockwell. Crowell, 1975; Harper Trophy, 1984.

"The Old Woman and Her Pig." In *The Old Woman and Her Pig and 10 Other Stories* by Anne Rockwell. Crowell, 1979. The paperback edition of the same book is published under the title of *The Three Sillies and 10 Other Stories to Read Aloud* by Anne Rockwell. Harper Trophy, 1986.

Wood, Audrey. *The Napping House*. Illustrated by Don Wood. Harcourt Brace Jovanovich, 1984. (P, I)

Major, Beverly. *Porcupine Stew*. Illustrated by Erick Ingraham. Morrow, 1982. (P, I)

One evening Thomas spots a porcupine in his grandfather's hayfield. That night he dreamed that he and his cat, True Blue, were in attendance at the Porcupine Parade and Picnic. During the porcupine festivities he sees a quill-throwing contest, talks to the young porcupine, and samples porcupine stew.

1. Thomas's grandfather has some sayings which during the course of the story are shown to have multiple meanings. Give at least two meanings for each of the following phrases:

   • make a fine, mouth-watering porcupine stew

   • throw his quills

   • dog decorated with a porcupine's quills.

2. Research to find out true facts about porcupines.

3. Make a list of true information about porcupines that was also in *Porcupine Stew*.

Mauser, Patricia Rhoads. *A Bundle of Sticks*. Atheneum, 1982. (I)

Day after day, Ben Tyler came home from school black and blue. Ben did not know how to retaliate or fight Boyd and he knew it. After attending kajukenbo school Ben did feel much more confident and was able to face Boyd. In a dramatic conclusion to Ben's kajukenbo lessons, Ben earns his purple belt.

1. Sifu explained to Ben the real reason or purpose of kajukenbo. Tell how Ben demonstrated an understanding of that purpose.

2. Kajukenbo is a combination of *ka*rate, *ju*do, *ken*po, and *bo*xing. Research the martial arts and explain the basic elements in each of these sport forms.

3. The name kajukenbo is an acronym. That is a word that is made up of the first letters or syllables of other words. Other acronyms include: NATO (North Atlantic Treaty Organization), WACS (Women's Army Corps), SEALS (sea, air, and land divers) and scuba (self-contained underwater breathing apparatus).

4. Boyd is described as a "bully." How would you define a bully? Explain how Boyd's behavior fits your definition of a bully.

Mayer, Mercer, reteller. *The Pied Piper of Hamelin*. Macmillan, 1987. (P, I)

This tale is basically the same tale told in Robert Browning's lengthy poem about the stranger who rids a rat-infested German town of its vermin. When he is cheated and not given his rightful pay he leads the children of the town away. Mayer does add a few twists of his own. In this version the Pied Piper enters with a "strange wind" instead of the traditional gentle tap. In traditional versions a lame child is left behind because he cannot keep up with the rest. In Mayer's version the Pied Piper heals the boy and sends him back as a messenger to tell the townspeople of the children's fate. The boy becomes a bard singing about the events of Hamelin and their moral, "a promise is a promise." The retelling echoes some of Browning's language in the text, and only the ending strays significantly from the traditional tale. However, with the reworked ending the tale has been turned into a powerful parable.

1. Compare the parable aspects of this retelling with the many stories of Leo Lionni, including *Frederick, The Alphabet Tale*, and *Swimmy.*

2. Compare the art in the Mayer retelling with the art in the Schwarz versions of the "Pied Piper of Hamelin." (Browning, Robert. *The Pied Piper of Hamelin.* Illustrated by Lieselotte Schwarz. Scroll Press, 1970. [Schwarz is a German artist whose paintings are suggestive of Silesian peasant art. She uses bright primary hues and massive figures in her bold child-like interpretive illustrations. Traditional verse.])

3. Compare the story grammar and illustrations from the Mayer and the Schwarz versions with the versions in the following booklist.

4. With older students use the novels that embellish the narrative poem. Compare and contrast the story with any of the picture book versions listed in activity 2 or 3. The novels are Delia Huddy's *Time Piper* (Greenwillow, 1979) and Gloria Skurzynski's *What Happened in Hamelin* (Four Winds, 1979).

Booklist — Pied Piper of Hamelin

Bartos-Hoppner, Barbara. *The Pied Piper of Hamelin.* Illustrated by Annegert Furschshuber. Lippincott, 1987.

Baumann, Kurt, reteller. *The Pied Piper of Hamelin.* Illustrated by Jean Claverie. Methuen, 1978.

Browning, Robert. *Pied Piper of Hamelin.* Illustrated by Kate Greenaway. Warne, 1889.

Browning, Robert. *Pied Piper of Hamelin.* Illustrated by C. Walter Hodges. Coward, McCann & Geoghegan, 1971.

Mayer, Mercer. *A Silly Story.* Parents, 1972. (P, I)
A young boy is sitting on a rock under a tree with his dog, when he gets his first silly thought, "perhaps I am a rock, a dog, or a tree, thinking I am me." Later he thinks maybe he is where he is not, and at night he thinks that "perhaps I am my pillow and my pillow is really me." In the end he has a silly thought but he does not remember it because he falls asleep.

1. This story is full of imaginative thoughts. Add some more of your own. What if I'm really not at my typewriter but am my typewriter and the typewriter is typing on me? What if I just think I'm eating an egg but the egg is really me?

2. Compare and contrast the story grammar in the story with this traditional childhood verse:

    I wonder how it feels to fly high in the sky ... like a bird.

    I wonder how it feels to sit on a nest ... like a bird.

    I wonder how it feels to catch a worm in the morning ... like a bird.

    I feel funny ... maybe it is wondering how it feels to be like a child.

Mayer, Mercer. *A Special Trick*. Dial, 1970.

Many of us who have read stories about encounters with witches, sorcerers, wizards, or magicians would think twice about messing around with one of these people with magical power. In a story of the sorcerer's apprentice, the apprentice got into trouble when he used magic words that he knew too little about. If you were told how to cast a spell would you use the information? Would you create a magic potion and not know how to find an antidote? In this book, *A Special Trick*, Elroy visits a magician's tent.

1. Write a paragraph telling what you would do if you found an old book of magic spells.

2. Read one of the following books to see how other people handled magic spells and words they did not know enough about. After reading one of the following books make a poster advertising the book to other members of your class.

Booklist – Magic Spells

Corbett, Scott. *The Lemonade Trick*. Little, Brown, 1960.

Coville, Bruce. *The Monster's Ring*. Pantheon, 1982.

Dahl, Roald. *George's Marvelous Medicine*. Knopf, 1981/1982.

dePaola, Tomie. *Strega Nona*. Harcourt Brace Jovanovich, 1986.

Galdone, Paul. *The Magic Porridge Pot*. Seabury, 1976.

Towle, Faith. *The Magic Cooking Pot*. Houghton Mifflin, 1975.

Mayer, Mercer. *Appelard and Liverwurst*. Illustrated by Steven Kellogg. Four Winds, 1978. (P, I)

Appelard is a poor farmer in Cyclone County, a county that has more hurricanes, cyclones, tornadoes, and thunderstorms than any other county in the United States of America. The Z. P. Zanzibus circus, Appelard's barn, and many other places and buildings have been destroyed by the tornadoes. Appelard's mule blew away in the cyclone of '65. He has been too poor to replace the animal and therefore he has no way to plow his fields, raise crops, earn money. Since he has no money he cannot rebuilt the barn that also blew away years ago. But when the baby rhinosterwurst shows up, Appelard knows that he is on the way to riches. The rhinosterwurst is named Liverwurst and becomes a part of the family. When there are problems in town, Liverwurst's mother arrives in town to rescue her baby from jail. Now Appelard has two rhinosterwursts on his hands.

1. Read the story aloud to the point where Appelard, Liverwurst, and the other animals come across Z. P. Zanzibus on the road. Predict what will happen next. How will Appelard solve his problem?

2. Tell about the heritage of the rhinosterwurst. Who do you think its ancestors were? Explain your answer.

3. In a paragraph describe the scene pictured on pages 32 and 33.

4. Write a story of the next adventure which involves Liverwurst and Appelard.

5. In what period of time do you think this story takes place? Explain what in the story made you determine the time period of this story.

Mayer, Mercer. *I Am a Hunter*. Dial, 1969. (P, I)

A little boy hunts snakes in his backyard. His father does not like his hacking the hose in two. The boy fights the giant in the alley. His mother does not like it when he knocks over all of the garbage cans. He plays fireman and saves a burning house next door from burning down. The drenched woman next door does not like having her house sprayed with water. When he plays doctor his sister would rather not be sick. When he eats like a caveman his father makes him eat with a fork and knife. In the bathtub he is a sea captain until his parents tell him to finish his bath and get to bed. He is a sea captain and sails away.

1. Add other examples of imaginary play opportunities that could get the little boy into trouble. Add other episodes to this story (before the sea captain sails away).

2. Write a sequel to this story. What happens to the boy when he sails away on the sea. Will he ever come back?

3. Compare and contrast with John Burningham's *Time to Get Out of the Bath, Shirley* (Crowell, 1978).

Mayer, Mercer. *Liza Lou and the Yeller Belly Swamp*. Four Winds, 1980. (P, I)

The Swamp Monster and three other unfriendly characters threaten Liza Lou. She must find a way to escape from the Swamp Monster, the Swamp Haunt, the Gobblygook, and the Swamp Devil.

1. Before you read the book, draw a picture of what you think a "Swamp Monster," "Swamp Haunt," "Gobblygook," and "Swamp Devil" look like.

2. Write a scene where you are in a boat rowing down the waterway and the Swamp Haunt rises out of the swamp and blocks your rowboat from continuing on. What are you going to do? What do you have in your boat that might be helpful? Write a paragraph to tell how you escape from the Swamp Haunt.

3. After reading the book, make a list of the tricks Liza Lou uses to escape from the four swamp creatures.

4. After reading the book, draw a second picture of each of the swamp creatures. Compare and contrast these drawings with the drawings you made before reading the story. Explain how reading the book helped you formulate the mental image of these creatures.

Mayer, Mercer. *One Monster after Another*. Golden Press, 1974. (P, I)

Calm enough in the beginning, Sally Ann mails a letter to Nancy Jane but before it can be picked up by the mailman a Stamp-Collecting Trollusk steals the letter and gabbles away. As we follow the letter from monster to monster we meet a Letter-Eating Bombanat, a Bombanat-Munching Grumley, a Wild-'n-Windy Typhoonigator, a Paper-Munching Yalapappus, a Bombanat-Collecting Grithix, and the official mailman who finally delivers the letter to Nancy Jane.

1. Make a list of the monsters that are in the story.

2. Draw a Purse-Collecting Grihgtihee.

3. On the next to the last page we see Nancy Jane with her suitcase walking toward other houses, presumably to visit Sally Ann at 219 Faddle Street. Tell what happens when the Purse-Collecting Grihgtihee snatches Nancy Jane's purse. Be creative and imaginative.

Mayer, Mercer. *There's a Nightmare in My Closet*. Dial, 1968. (P, I)

A little boy is so afraid of the nightmare lurking in his bedroom closet that he faithfully closes the closet door every night before going to sleep. One night the boy decides to confront his nightmare. Wearing his army helmet, he waits, barricaded behind his pillow with his toy cannon, his pop gun, and his toy soldiers. The only way to quiet the nightmare is to take him by the hand and tuck him into bed, which the little boy does. Then the little boy (at the monster's request) closes the closet door and crawls into bed beside the nightmare.

1. Give each student a sheet of paper, 8½" x 11" or larger. Direct the children to:

    *   Fold the paper in half so that the sheet is 8½" x 5½" doubled.

    *   Keep the fold at the top and draw a closet door so that the bottom of the door will be at the bottom edge of the paper (not the folded edge).

    *   Draw their own bedroom on the paper, incorporating the closet door into the picture. The picture should keep the folded edge at the top of the room, as if the fold was the ceiling edge.

    *   Cut the closet door open on the right side and across the top of the door. This should allow the closet door to be folded back, to open and close the closet.

    *   Draw a nightmare on the inside paper so that it is visible through the closet door when it is opened.

    *   Glue the insides of the folded page together. Take care not to glue shut the door so it can open and close.

    *   Write: "There's a Nightmare in My Closet by Mercer Mayer" on the back of the nightmare picture.

    This activity will help develop creative expression as well as give students further practice in developing their listening skills and auditory processing skills. Those students who have difficulty processing auditory instructions may have to be given the instructions step by step. In those cases group instructions might be taped so that students needing the instructions repeated might go to a listening center and go through the instructions at their own pace. After the group experience, individual students may wish to use the tape recorder to follow the directions once again.

2. Introduce the story with this traditional folk rhyme:

> In a dark dark wood, there was a dark dark house.
> In the dark dark house, there was a dark, dark room.
> In the dark dark room, there was a dark, dark closet.
> In the dark, dark closet, there was a dark, dark shelf.
> On the dark, dark shelf, there was a dark, dark box.
> In the dark, dark box, there was a (pause) MONSTER!

(During the pause, pick up a black box and extract a monster as you say the word.)

3. Memorize the folk rhyme in activity 2 and recite as a choral reading.

4. Make paper or sock monsters. Stuff them for a three-dimensional effect. If the monsters are small enough they might be put into a black box to accompany the choral reading.

5. Continue the poetry theme with some of the following.

Booklist—Monster Poems and Riddles

Moore, Lilian. "The Monster's Birthday." In *Spooky Rhymes and Riddles*. Scholastic, 1972.

Prelutsky, Jack. *The Headless Horseman Rides Tonight: More Poems to Trouble Your Sleep*. Illustrated by Arnold Lobel. Greenwillow, 1980.

_____. "The Lurpp Is on the Loose." In *The Snopp on the Sidewalk and Other Poems*. Greenwillow, 1976/1977.

_____. *Nightmares: Poems to Trouble Your Sleep*. Illustrated by Arnold Lobel. Greenwillow, 1976.

Sarnoff, Jane and Reynold Ruffins. *The Monster Riddle Book*. rev. ed. Scribner, 1978.

Mayer, Mercer. *There's an Alligator under My Bed*. Dial, 1987. (P, I)
   A little boy is sure that there is an alligator under his bed. His parents give him no sympathy since they "never saw it," so the boy forms a plan of attack. He leaves a trail of food from his bed through the house to the garage door. As the alligator gobbles up the goodies, fresh vegetables, fruit, and the "last piece of pie" the boy follows him to the garage. When they arrive in the garage the boy locks the door. The boy then leaves a note for his father, telling him that there's an alligator in the garage and that he should wake him up "if you need help."

1. Compare and contrast the main character in this story with the main character in *There's a Nightmare in My Closet* and *There's Something in My Attic* (Dial, 1988), both by Mayer.

2. Extend the theme of monsters and strange things by reading one or more of the following books about monsters and unexplained noises. Use these books to stimulate additional exercises comparing and contrasting such elements as story grammar, main character, and setting in any two of the stories.

3.   Use the illustrations in *There's an Alligator under My Bed* to help set the time period of the story — 1950s, 1960s, 1970s, 1980s. (Note: The illustrations showing the little boy's toys include a hot wheels tricycle and robot transformer-type toys.)

Booklist — Monsters and Strange Noises

Crowe, Robert L. *Clyde Monster*. Dutton, 1976.

Flora, James. *The Great Green Turkey Creek Monster*. Atheneum, 1976.

Mosel, Arlene. *The Funny Little Woman*. Dutton, 1972.

Sendak, Maurice. *Where the Wild Things Are*. Harper & Row, 1963.

Stevens, Kathleen. *The Beast in the Bathtub*. Illustrated by Ray Bowler. Gareth Stevens Children's Books, 1985.

Stevenson, James. *What's under My Bed?* Greenwillow, 1983.

Stone, Jon. *The Monster at the End of This Book*. Illustrated by Mike Smollin. Western Publishers, 1977.

Ungerer, Tomi. *The Beast of Monsieur Racine*. Farrar, Straus & Giroux, 1971.

Viorst, Judith. *My Mama Says There Aren't Any Zombies, Ghosts, Vampires, Creatures, Demons, Monsters, Fiends, Goblins, or Things*. Illustrated by Kay Chorao. Atheneum, 1973.

Willis, Jeanne. *The Monster Bed*. Lothrop, Lee & Shepard, 1986.

Winthrop, Elizabeth. *Maggie and the Monster*. Illustrated by Tomie dePaola. Holiday House, 1987.

Zemach, Harve. *The Judge: An Untrue Tale*. Illustrated by Margot Zemach. Farrar, Straus & Giroux, 1969.

Mayer, Mercer. *You're the Scaredy-Cat*. Parents, 1974. (P, I)
  A rather typical story of two boys who are going camping in the backyard. When they have managed to scare one another with their spooky stories they each declare the other a scaredy-cat.

1.   Write your own stories to make a scaredy-cat out of one of your friends.

2.   Who do you think was the real scaredy-cat in this story?

3.   How old do you think the boys are? Why do you think so? Explain your answer.

Mayer, Mercer. *What Do You Do with a Kangaroo?* Four Winds, 1973. (P, I)

What do you do with a kangaroo, or an opossum, a llama, a raccoon, a baby moose, a grown Bengal tiger, a camel—you throw them out. Then if you can't throw them out, you let them stay—in your bed.

1. Think up other preposterous situations with other animals and add episodes to the book following the same pattern as the book.

2. Share the story with children using Scholastic's Big Book of this title. The book is available as a Big Book, standard-sized paperback and paperback with cassette tape and teaching guide.

3. Read the story to the very end where the little girl says that she cannot throw the animals out—discuss what could be done to solve her problem. There will be no right or wrong answer. Be sure to say that situations can be handled in many different ways. The author has one idea and "we" have some other ideas. Discuss how we would illustrate our ending.

McGinnis, Lila Sprague. *The Ghost Upstairs*. Hastings, 1982. (I)

For over seventy years, Otis White has lived in (and haunted) the house next door to Albert Snook's family home. Now the old house is being torn down to make way for a new library. Otis moves into Albert's house. This is the story of Albert's relationship with Otis.

1. Otis was intrigued by the many new things in Albert's room. These things had not been invented seventy-five years ago when he had died. Look around your classroom and make a list of five things that you think might not have been invented seventy-five years ago. Then research to verify your ideas. You might use the encyclopedia to help in your research. Be sure to use the index. Check your library's reference section too.

2. Why did Otis decide to live in the library? What things will he take to the library with him?

3. Read the sequel, *The Ghost Alarm*, by Lila McGinnis (Hastings, 1989).

4. Would you consider Otis a "poltergeist?" Why or why not?

5. Read another book with a ghost as the chief protagonist. See the index of this book for reference to the booklist of ghostly tales.

McInerney, Judith Whitlock. *Judge Benjamin, Superdog*. Holiday House, 1982. (I)

A large St. Bernard is the caretaker, custodian, and all-around pet of the O'Riley family. The family includes children ages 3, 8, and 10 and before the story ends a new baby. The dog protects the family from thieves, traffic accidents, and most importantly from a tornado.

1. The author says that this story is really the story of her own family and their beloved St. Bernard. Are there any parts in this story that you think could not have really happened?

2. Draw a picture of the episode that you think was the most exciting or humorous.

McPhail, David. *Snow Lion*. Parents, 1982. (P, I)

Lion finds his jungle home too hot for comfort. He packs his bags and searches for a cooler place to visit. He discovers snow in the mountains and longs to share it with his jungle friends.

1. When Lion packs his bag to look for a cooler place where might he go? Make a list of places which will be cool.

2. Make a snow cone. Crushed ice and strawberry syrup makes a delicious treat.

3. Make a magic snow picture. You will need white construction paper, a white crayon, blue tempera paint (diluted with water), and a paint brush. Use the white crayon to draw a snow picture on the construction paper. Everything which is to be white must be colored in solid. Using the brush lightly apply the blue tempera wash over the picture and the white crayon will appear revealing the snow picture against the blue background.

4. Compare what happens in this story to the fate of the snow in Ezra Jack Keats's *The Snowy Day* (Viking, 1963).

Miller, Moira. *Oscar Mouse Finds a Home*. Dial, 1985. (P)

Oscar decides that he must find a home of his own when his family's attic home gets too crowded with his little brothers and sisters.

1. Describe the home you think Oscar might find, a nice quiet home.

2. Describe a quiet place where you can go to be alone.

3. Read *I Love You, Mouse* by John Graham, illustrated by Tomie dePaola (Harcourt Brace Jovanovich, 1976). In this book various animals find their young a home where they can be safe.

Most, Bernard. *If the Dinosaurs Came Back*. Harcourt Brace Jovanovich, 1978. (P, I)

How would dinosaurs fit into our lives if they were to exist today? What if the dinosaurs came back?

1. Discuss knowledge children already have about dinosaurs. Where did they live? How big were they? Are they living today?

2. Would it be possible for dinosaurs to come back? What might enable dinosaurs to be part of our life now? Would it have been possible for some dinosaur eggs to have been frozen beneath the polar ice cap — and just now discovered and hatched?

3. After the discussion, read the book. Be sure to share the illustrations.

4. Brainstorm a list of other suggestions for the dinosaurs.

5. Write and illustrate some of the ideas for other things the dinosaurs could do "if the dinosaurs came back."

Nic Leodhas, Sorche. *Always Room for One More*. Illustrated by Nonny Hogrogian. Holt, Rinehart & Winston, 1965. (P, I)

The now-classic tale of Lachie MacLachlan and his good wife and his bairns to the number of ten. Lachie and his family lived in the Scottish heather. Every traveler that passed their door was invited into their home, as there was "always room for one more." As the small cottage filled with family and travelers another room and then another was added so there would always be "...room for one more."

1. Before reading the story discuss Sorche Nic Leodhas's "About the Story" note appearing at the end of the story. Define and discuss the Scottish words that she felt necessary to use in the story and song.

2. A folk song that tells the story of Lachie and his family is included at the end of the book. Ask your music teacher to help you sing this folk song. Scottish folk songs are partly told and partly sung.

3. This book won the Caldecott Award in 1966. That same year three books were designated as Caldecott honor books. These books were *Hide and Seek Fog* by Alvin Tresselt, illustrated by Roger Duvoisin (Lothrop, 1965); *Just Me* by Marie Hall Ets (Viking, 1965); and *Tom Tit Tot* by Joseph Jacobs, ed., illustrated by Evaline Ness (Scribner, 1965). Look at the illustrations in the four books. If the children are not aware of which of the four did win the Caldecott Award, discuss which one they think should have won and why. If the children know that *Always Room for One More* brought this award to Nonny Hogrogian discuss why the children think the Caldecott committee chose her book (and the illustrations) over the illustrations of the other three books.

Nic Leodhas, Sorche. *Ghosts Go Haunting*. Illustrated by Nonny Hogrogian. Holt, Rinehart & Winston, 1965. (P, I)

A collection of "true" ghost stories told to the author at clan gatherings. These tales are Scottish in origin and told to the author as true fact. The stories vary from one about a ghost who is displeased with being a ghost to a man who learns to believe in the existence of supernatural beings. Nonny Hogrogian uses woodcuts to illustrate this novel-length collection of tales.

1. Read one of the tales. Do you think the story is true? Explain your reasons for thinking as you do.

2. After reading several ghost stories either collect a true story from a friend and write it down in story form or tell a ghost story that might have happened to you.

3. Read other modern ghost stories. Refer to the index for the Ghosts booklist.

Nixon, Joan Lowery. *Maggie, Too*. Harcourt Brace Jovanovich, 1985. (I)

Margaret (Maggie) has lived with her father ever since her mother died when Maggie was two. Now her dad, a movie director, is marrying a young actress and has sent Maggie off to live with her maternal grandmother. As soon as Maggie arrives the action begins. Grandma Landry's two daughters show up, a burglar is captured, and Maggie comes to realize that it is not only herself that has had to make some adjustments to the new situation. Maggie ends up planning to stay with her grandmother for the next school year. That story is told in *Maggie Makes Three* (Harcourt Brace Jovanovich, 1986).

1. Do you think Margaret had a "right" to be angry with her father for sending her off to live with her grandmother for the summer? Explain why or why not?

2. Explain why Margaret wanted to win the trip to Cancún, Mexico for herself, and why she later changed her mind and placed her grandmother's name on the entry.

3. At the end of the book, Margaret decides that she would like to be called "Maggie." Explain why Margaret/Maggie made that decision.

4. Locate information about the city of Cancún, Mexico. Write at least ten facts about the city.

5. Draw a map of Mexico. Locate Cancún on that map. Label the Mexican states around Cancún and put in other major cities, landmarks, mountains, and rivers.

6. Draw a picture of Flowerpot.

Noah's Ark. Illustrated by Nonny Hogrogian. Knopf, 1986. (P, I)

Nonny Hogrogian's ancestors came from Armenia near Mount Ararat, where Noah's Ark is said to have come to rest. The Bible provides the text, Hogrogian provides the visual interpretation of this event. The beautiful illustrations washed with sunny colors provide a warm interpretation of the events of the time.

1. Compare and contrast Hogrogian's depiction of the Noah's Ark episode with other artists' illustrative depictions.

Booklist—Noah's Ark

Fussenegger, Gertrud. *Noah's Ark*. Lippincott, 1987.

Duvoisin, Roger. *A for the Ark*. Lothrop, 1952.

Singer, Isaac Bashevis. *Why Noah Chose the Dove*. Farrar, Straus & Giroux, 1974.

Spier, Peter. *Noah's Ark*. Doubleday, 1977.

Notes for comparison — The Duvoisin book and the Singer book (illustrated by Eric Carle) use a different perspective to depict Noah's story. The Spier book and the Hogrogian book both use the Bible text as the direct basis for their book. Peter Spier's *Noah's Ark* won the 1978 Caldecott Award for "the most distinguished American picture book for children." In his Caldecott acceptance speech at the American Library Association's annual convention in Chicago, Illinois on June 27, 1978, Spier spoke of having wanted to illustrate Noah's story for years. When he went to the library and checked *Books in Print* he found out that there were over twenty Noahs in print. After obtaining as many of the versions as he could he looked at what other artists had done with Noah. He concluded that invariably Noah's water voyage was depicted as a "joyous, sun-filled Caribbean cruise." The story of the flood did not show any of God's wrath. None of them hinted at the unpleasant side of the story. Peter Spier's book attempts to give that perspective. Look at Hogrogian's book and discuss it in light of what Peter Spier has to say about the other Noah books. Keep in mind that Hogrogian's book was not yet published when Peter Spier made his comments.

Hogrogian, Nonny. *The Glass Mountain*. Retold and illustrated from a Grimm Brothers' Fairy Tale. Knopf, 1985. (P, I)

In this tale, originally entitled "The Raven," a princess is turned into a raven and is imprisoned atop a glass mountain until a young man overcomes obstacles to set her free. Hogrogian has used hand-marbled papers as endpapers and as frames for her luscious paintings that illustrate this tale of enchantment. The Queen, exasperated with her young child's constant activity, laments that if only the child were a raven, she could fly away and the Queen would have some peace. The Queen had no sooner uttered that statement than the baby was transformed into a raven and flew away to a dark woods. Years later a young man chances upon the raven and is asked to free her of the enchantment. As in other folktales the number three is important. When the young man fails in his mission, the raven leaves him with three gifts: food, a golden ring, and a letter. With the help of the food that replenished itself the young man enlisted the help of a giant. The giant took the young man to the mountain but from there the man had to climb the mountain on his own; he tried but kept falling back. The Princess waited in the castle at the top of the mountain. He was filled with grief when he was unable to reach her. He built a small hut at the foot of the mountain. One day outside of the castle three scoundrels argued. One had a stick that would open any door. The second had a cloak that made anything it covered invisible. The third scoundrel had a horse that could go anywhere, even up the side of the mountain. With the promise of something more valuable than money, the man convinced the three to let him "try out" their possessions. With the aid of the magic possessions he climbed the mountain and released the Princess from her enchantment. The two were married.

1. Make marble paper as Hogrogian used for the backdrop of the illustrative paintings. Ezra Jack Keats also used marbleized paper for the background in many of his illustrations. A procedure for making marbleized paper is included in the information about Keats. See index.

2. Compare tales of enchantment from other cultures. Transformation of an animal or a person is part of the "Beauty and the Beast" story found in Andrew Lange's *The Blue Fairy Book*, illustrated by Reisie Lonette (Random House, 1959). "The Frog Prince" is another popular Grimm tale using this motif. One version of "The Frog Prince" can be located in the Grimm Brothers' *Tales from Grimm*, translated and illustrated by Wanda Gag (Coward McCann, 1936). Henry Rowe Schoolcraft's *The Ring in the Prairie: A Shawnee Legend*, edited by John Bierhorst, illustrated by Leo Dillon and Diane Dillon (Dial, 1970), uses the motif as does a Norwegian story of the "Widow's Son," which can be found in

Ingri d'Aulaire and Edgar d'Aulaire's *East of the Sun and West of the Moon* (Viking, 1938, 1969). A Japanese tale with this motif, "Gombei and the Wild Ducks," found in Yoshiko Uchida's *The Sea of Gold and Other Tales from Japan*, illustrated by Marianne Yamaguchi (Scribner, 1965), will provide an interesting enchantment tale to compare with the modern-day fantasy by Roald Dahl, *The Magic Finger* (Harper & Row, 1966).

Park, Barbara. *Skinnybones*. Knopf, 1982. (I)
Alex Frankovitch is the skinniest kid on his team, in his class, and everywhere he is. His sense of humor is superb but it does not help him much when T. J. Stoner arrives at Alex's school. T. J. Stoner is a great little league baseball player. He takes after his older brother who plays professional ball with the Chicago Cubs. Alex is the least talented member of his baseball team. T. J. is the hit of the day when he is about to pitch his 125th straight win. Everyone congratulates T. J. and laughs at the fool Alex has made of himself. But the laughter turns to admiration when the principal uses the intercom to congratulate T. J. and Alex. Alex has won the Kitty Fritter TV contest and will get a chance to appear in a national TV commercial. Both T. J. and Alex end up being celebrities.

1. Steve Garvey (once the first baseman for the San Diego Padres) was Alex's idol. An idol is someone a person admires and respects. Choose someone you idolize and write a short paper telling about that person's life and why you admire and respect him or her.

2. Why do you think Alex resented the attention being given to T. J.?

3. Would you like to have T. J. or Alex, or both, as a friend? Explain why or why not.

4. Read the sequel, *Almost Starring Skinnybones*, by Barbara Park (Knopf, 1988).

Parrish, Peggy. *Amelia Bedelia*. Harper & Row, 1963.
Amelia is a zany housekeeper who interprets all of her directions in literal terms. She actually dresses a chicken and wraps the steak in bows.

1. Introduce the idea of mixed-up meanings for words by reading Jack Prelutsky's poem "My Brother's Head Should Be Replaced" in Prelutsky's *The New Kid on the Block* (Greenwillow, 1984). In this poem a boy tries to put the halves of a tomato together with tomato paste.

2. Make a list of words that could bring interesting images to mind. For example, make butter fly and draw a house wing.

3. Correlate with the Gwynne titles: *A Chocolate Moose for Dinner* (Windmill, 1976), *The King Who Rained* (Windmill, 1970), *Sixteen Hand Horse* (Simon & Schuster, 1987), and *A Little Pigeon Toad* (Simon & Schuster, 1988). See Bookshelf entry for Gwynne's *A Chocolate Moose for Dinner*.

Patrick, Gloria. *A Bug in a Jug and Other Funny Rhymes*. Illustrated by Joan Hanson. Scholastic, 1970. (P)

The verse featured in the title reads, "This is jug. This is a rug. This is the jug on the rug. This is a bug. This is the bug in the jug on the rug." Using the same building pattern other verses feature: a louse in a house, a cat on a mat, a bee up a tree, a ewe at the zoo, and a friend at the end (of the book).

1. Use the pattern of individual verses to create some of your own.

2. Read other books about bugs, cats, ewes, and friends.

3. Extend the focus on bugs by reading the insect poems on pages 72 to 75 in Jack Prelutsky's *The Random House Book of Poetry*, illustrated by Arnold Lobel (Random House, 1983). Also read Eric Carle's *The Grouchy Ladybug* (Crowell, 1977) and Roach VanAllen's *I Love Ladybugs* (DLM Teaching Resources, 1985).

Paulsen, Gary. *Dogsong*. Bradbury, 1985. (I)

This 1986 Newbery Honor book tells the adventure of an Inuit (Eskimo) teenager who takes a 1,400-mile trek by dog sled in order to avoid the encroachment of modern ways. The trip takes him across ice, tundra, and mountains in search of his own song.

1. Research a Native American group in the United States—the American Indians, the Inuits (Eskimos), or the Hawaiians. Write an abc book for the group that is researched. See the index to locate alphabet books to use for models.

2. When Columbus arrived in America there were over 700,000 people living in present-day Alaska and the continental United States. He called them all "Indians." In fact, each tribe had its own name, language, and culture. Later, historians grouped the tribes by common characteristics. The following partial list will give some idea of these groupings.

   • Plains Indians: Crow, Sioux, Cheyenne, and Comanche tribes.

   • Southwest Indians: Hopi, Navajo, and Pima tribes.

   • Woodlands Indians: Chickasaw, Seminole, Iroquois, and Delaware tribes.

   • Northwest Coast Indians: Chinook and Yurok tribes.

   • Great Basin Indians: Shoshoni and Paiute tribes.

   • California Indians: Wintun and Pomo tribes.

   Research to locate the common characteristics that bind the various groups of tribes together. Locate the geographical home of these tribes, their style of houses, their crafts, and means of earning a living.

3. The name Eskimo comes from the American Indian word meaning "eaters of raw meat." But the native Eskimo people prefer to call themselves Inuit, which means "people," and their land Inuit Nunangat, meaning "people's land." The Inuits hunt for their food and have invented several types of vehicles for transportation across the icy land and across the waters. Research the kayak, plank sled, umiak, and frame sled.

Peet, Bill. *Cyrus the Unsinkable Sea Serpent*. Houghton Mifflin, 1975.

Cyrus, a giant sea serpent, was gentle and considerate. Others thought he looked frightening and fearsome, as fearsome as some of his adventures on the high seas.

1. Compare and contrast the type of "person" you feel Cyrus is with the type of person you are.

2. Create another adventure for Cyrus.

3. Draw a giant sea serpent on a long piece of butcher paper. Name and describe him or her. Tell about this sea serpent Cyrus.

4. Research the Abominable Snowman, Big Foot, or the Loch Ness Monster. Make a chart showing the information about these monsters—where they are generally sighted, their size, and what they are thought to do.

5. Add Cyrus, the sea serpent, to the monster chart you made in activity 4.

Pevsner, Stella. *Me, My Goat, and My Sister's Wedding*. Clarion, 1985. (I)

Doug and his friends Frank and Woody are conned into paying Oliver to let them take care of his goat while Oliver is on a two-week backpacking trip. The boys arrange for the goat to stay in their clubhouse at the back of Doug's yard. They plot to use the goat to make money by renting the goat's services to "mow" people's lawns. The goat brings about the expected turmoil when Doug's sister plans her garden wedding. Later, Oliver and his villainous father arrive to pick up the goat. Doug's father follows Oliver and his father and convinces them to let Doug have the goat. The conclusion has the goat returning to the clubhouse at the back of Doug's family's yard, Doug's sister's wedding concluding without any more calamities, and Doug's niece becoming friends with him and promising to return soon.

1. Draw a picture of Rudy, at Doug's sister's wedding. Add the title of the book and the author's name and display the picture with the book in your classroom or library.

2. Tell what you think Doug's father said to Oliver's father to convince him that Doug should have the goat.

3. Pretend that you are going to help Missy decide what kind of dog she should get. Locate a book about different breeds of dogs. Decide which one you would recommend to Missy. Make a brochure about that breed telling how to care for that kind of dog, what to feed it, and so on. Illustrate the front of the brochure.

Pfeffer, Susan Beth. *Courage, Dana*. Delacorte, 1983. (I)

Seventh grader Dana Parker finds herself thrust into the limelight when she dashs out in front of a car to save a young boy. She is immediately hailed as courageous and that causes her some problems. In an attempt to show her best friend, Sharon, that she is really brave, Dana spends a night in the cemetery. On her way home she chances onto a situation which will really test her courage.

1. What do you think you would have done about the paint-spraying incident if you had seen the incident? Explain why you would have acted as you did.

2. Several other books deal with a bully causing problems for someone else (see the following list). Locate one of them and compare the bully in each of the stories with Charlie from this story.

3. Make a list of five ways that you could test your courage.

Booklist—Bullies

Carrick, Carol. *What a Wimp!* Clarion, 1983.

Fleming, Alice. *Welcome to Grossville*. Scribner, 1985.

Gaeddert, LouAnn. *The Kid with the Red Suspenders*. Dutton, 1983.

Mauser, Patricia Rhodes. *A Bundle of Sticks*. Atheneum, 1982.

Prelutsky, Jack. *My Parents Think I Am Sleeping*. Greenwillow, 1985. (P, I)
Poems for the child who doesn't always go to sleep when he or she is sent to bed.

1. Make a picture of yourself in bed with strange things going on outside of your door.

2. Choose your favorite poem and memorize it. Share it with your class.

3. Read other books by Jack Prelutsky.

Rayner, Mary. *Mrs. Pig's Bulk Buy*. Atheneum, 1981. (P)
The piglets love ketchup. They put ketchup on everything Mrs. Pig fixes for them, and so they are delighted when Mrs. Pig stocks up on ketchup. That is, until they realize that it is the only thing they will be eating.

1. Make a list of foods the piglets put ketchup on. Make a list of foods you put ketchup on.

2. Draw a picture of all the food the piglets ate after Mrs. Pig bought up all the ketchup. (Picture will include: tomato ketchup, bread with ketchup, ketchup soup, cereal with ketchup, ketchup sandwich.)

3. Compare and contrast the lesson in this book with the lesson in Russell Hoban's *Bread and Jam for Frances* (Harper & Row, 1964).

4. How do you think this story would have been different if the piglets had liked chocolate syrup on everything and Mrs. Pig had bought a large stock of chocolate syrup. Tell or write the story.

Roberts, Willo Davis. *The Pet-Sitting Peril*. Atheneum, 1983. (I)

Nick Reed is eleven years old and wants to earn money. He begins with just one customer, Mr. Haggard, but soon he has many more customers. His pet-sitting takes him to an apartment building. Strange happenings occur while he is sitting. When he calls the police he becomes a suspect. He continues his pet-sitting, and one night finds that he is alone in the apartment building except for the animals. That's the night the arsonists return to finish the job.

1. Mystery writers often throw out "red herrings" during their story. A red herring is a false clue meant to lead the reader off-track. Explain in your own words the red herring that the author put in the book regarding the manager, Mr. Griener, Clyde and Ron, Mr. Haggard, Al and Greg, and the owner, Mr. Hale.

2. Write a newspaper article about Nick's heroic deeds in saving the Victorian mansion and helping to capture the arsonists.

3. Would you have stayed overnight in the Hillsdale apartment building? Why or why not?

Rockwell, Anne and Harlow Rockwell. *The Emergency Room*. Macmillan, 1985. (P)

Shows what goes on in the emergency room of the hospital and describe much of the hospital equipment.

1. This book makes an excellent book to read after a visit to a hospital since it will help review much of what occurred or what the children might have seen during their hospital trip.

2. For children who may be scheduled for surgery or for hospital tests this book might be used to introduce a discussion on the topic.

3. Make and discuss a home first-aid kit. A standard-sized school box or a shoe box makes a good container. Make a list of items that should be in a first-aid kit, then either place the real items into the box or make paper cutouts of the items. Send the box home asking that parents replace the paper cutouts with the real items. The box should be kept in the home or in the car for emergencies.

Rockwell, Thomas. *How to Eat Fried Worms*. Illustrated by Emily Arnold McCully. Dell, 1973. (I)

Billy sets out to win a bet by eating fifteen worms, one each day. At first he has difficulty swallowing the worm. He does but then his problem becomes more complex as the days go on.

1. Introduce the book by reading "Willy Ate a Worm Today" by Jack Prelutsky in *The New Kid on the Block* (Greenwillow, 1984).

2. Make chocolate-covered worms with Chinese noodles and melted chocolate. Serve as Billy eats his fourteenth worm. Purchased gummy worms might be a suitable substitute.

Roos, Stephen. *My Horrible Secret*. Delacorte, 1983. (P, I)

Eleven-year-old Warren Fingler cannot throw or catch a ball and soon he is going to be expected to go to summer baseball camp. Warren's brother is a very popular athlete in town and everyone expects Warren to be much like his brother. A series of incidents and a broken arm keep him from having to attend the camp but his secret is out. His brother, Warren, and his friend Laurel promise to help Warren learn to throw and catch a ball so he can get rid of his "horrible secret."

1. Do you think anyone could have really kept the secret of his inability to throw and catch a ball until he was in fifth grade? Why do you think that one could or could not keep something like that a secret?

2. Explain why Warren thought that falling off Spitfire was the "best break he ever had."

Roy, Ron. *Where's Buddy?* Clarion, 1982. (I)

Mike is supposed to be watching his younger brother Buddy but he isn't paying too much attention and Buddy slips off. When it is noticed that Buddy is not around a search is undertaken. Buddy is diabetic and if he isn't found there is a real chance that he could go into an insulin shock. Mike and his friends manage to find Buddy in a cave in a coma. They do bring him around with a drink of coke but then are threatened with the rising tide.

1. The author included a lot of information about juvenile diabetes in this story. List some of the information about diabetes that you found in this book. Research and learn more. Share this information with the rest of the class.

2. Do you think Mike should be reprimanded for his inattention to his parents' request to watch Buddy?

3. Are you ever left to care for younger sisters or brothers? Describe how you feel when you really want to play with your friends instead.

Sendak, Maurice. *Alligators All Around*. The Nutshell Library. Harper & Row, 1962. (P, I)

An abc book that describes the activities of an alligator family using alliterative two-word phrases for each letter of the alphabet. Weston Woods has available a filmstrip cassette of the book.

1. Make a dictionary card for each letter of the alphabet. On each card write words that begin with that letter.

2. Write each of the alphabetical phrases on large sheets of newsprint. Ask individuals or pairs of students to illustrate each phrase with their own idea of the phrase's meaning.

3. Use the text pattern as a model to create another abc book.

4. Ask each child to draw himself or herself as an alligator doing the thing that he or she likes to do best. Use the alligators to create a class mural. Phrases could be added to describe the alligators' antics.

Sendak, Maurice. *Chicken Soup with Rice*. Harper & Row, 1962. (P, I)
Poems for each month of the year. Each month's poem contains the refrain "cooking once, cooking twice, cooking chicken soup with rice."

1. Read the book. Encourage the children to choral read the refrain. Scholastic has a big book version of this title.

2. As the poem is being read children should stand during their birthday month. When the verse is finished for their month they should sit down.

3. Write additional chicken soup with rice verses. Illustrate the verses.

4. Sendak dedicated this book to a very good friend and neighbor, Ida Perles. Sendak thought of her as a second mother. Ida Perles's belief in the curative powers of tender loving care and in good home cooking was the inspiration for the book. After explaining the meaning behind Sendak's dedication discuss a dedication each child might make in a book he or she has authored.

Sendak, Maurice. *Hector Protector and As I Went Over the Water*. Harper & Row, 1965. (P, I)
Two Mother Goose rhymes with Sendak's interpretation through his illustrations. He has expanded two little-known rhymes into stories of their own. Hector is a small rebellious boy who hates green and the queen. The story is told in twenty-four pictures. In the second rhyme a boy conquers a boat-swallowing dragon with the greatest of aplomb.

1. Set up a Mother Goose corner. Use the card catalog in your public or school library to locate other editions of the Mother Goose verses.

2. Hold a Mother Goose Read-In to search for other variations of the "Hector Protector" verse. Compile a list of favorite rhymes found and a list of those Mother Goose books that contain a Hector Protector verse. But if you can't find another version don't be concerned—enjoy the other verses for their rhymes.

3. Make your own illustrations for "Hector Protector."

4. Many authors are writing parodies of Mother Goose verses (see following list). Try these for fun and to motivate students to write more innovations on the rhymes. Older readers will enjoy them more than younger children.

Booklist—Mother Goose

Briggs, Raymond. *The Mother Goose Treasury*. Coward McCann, 1966.

Caldecott, Raymond. *Hey Diddle Diddle Picture Book*. Warne, n.d.

dePaola, Tomie. *Tomie dePaola's Mother Goose*. Putnam, 1985.

Greenaway, Kate. *Mother Goose: or the Old Nursery Rhymes*. Warne, 1882.

Lobel, Arnold. *The Random House Book of Mother Goose*. Random House, 1986.

Opie, Iona and Peter Opie. *A Family Book of Nursery Rhymes*. Watts, 1969.

Rackham, Arthur. *Mother Goose: The Old Nursery Rhymes*. Watts, 1969.

Tudor, Tasha. *Mother Goose*. Walck, 1944.

Wildsmith, Brian. *Brian Wildsmith's Mother Goose*. Watts, 1964.

Booklist — Fun with Mother Goose

Arneson, D. J. *Mother Goose Is Dead*. Illustrated by Tony Tallaarco. Dell, 1967.

Kelly, Walt. *The Pogo Stepmother Goose*. Illustrated by the author. Simon & Schuster, 1954.

Larche, Doug. *Father Gander: Nursery Rhymes, The Equal Rhymes Amendment*. Illustrated by Carolyn Marie Blattel. Advocacy Press, 1986.

Merriam, Eve. *The Inner City Mother Goose*. Illustrated by Lawrence Ratzkin. Simon & Schuster, 1969.

Sendak, Maurice. *Higglety Pigglety Pop! or There Must Be More to Life*. Harper & Row, 1967. (P, I)
 A literary fairy tale with multiple themes. Written to immortalize Sendak's Sealyham terrier, Jennie.

1. Throughout many of Sendak's books the familiar theme of eating reoccurs. Examine this book and look for the references to food. Extend this idea to other books by Sendak.

2. Sendak used a baby picture of himself as a model for the illustration of the baby in this book. Draw a baby character using one of your own baby pictures as the model. Display the drawings along with the photographs.

3. The pig uses sandwich boards to advertise the leading lady. Create a sandwich board to advertise the leading character in a favorite book.

Sendak, Maurice. *In the Night Kitchen*. Harper & Row, 1970. (P, I)
 New York City is transformed into a surreal kitchen furnished skyline. Mickey falls from his bed into the night kitchen and transforms bread dough into an airplane which he uses to fly off into the night. During his adventure he collects milk for the cake and saves the day (night).

1. Discuss in terms of the trilogy and theme envisioned by Sendak (see entry for Sendak's *Outside Over There*).

2. In many of Sendak's illustrations in his various titles he put in objects, names, and animals that had a personal significance. In this book he included several references to names of people in his life. Make a list of all the names on buildings, streets, and objects in this book. Then research Sendak's life to see what connections you are able to make. Refer to the Critical Reading section in the preceding chapter where personal references in Sendak's books are discussed.

Sendak, Maurice. *One Was Johnny*. The Nutshell Library. Harper & Row, 1962. (P, I)

A reverse counting book which includes the concept of deletion or subtraction. Johnny lives by himself until he is disturbed by one obnoxious animal after another. Not knowing what to do, he begins to count backward with the threat, "And when/I am through/If this house isn't empty/I'll eat/all of you!!!!" The house emptied and Johnny is alone to enjoy his solitude.

1. Make large number cards. Give each card to a child who stands in numerical order. As the book is read the child with the appropriate numbered card sits down until all are seated (the house is empty).

2. Read another countdown book. Try Molly Bang's *Ten, Nine, Eight* (Greenwillow, 1983).

3. Locate and read other counting books to extend the theme.

4. Write another counting book of your own.

Booklist—Counting Books

Carle, Eric. *My Very First Book of Numbers*. Crowell, 1974.

Feelings, Muriel. *Moja Means One: Swahili Counting Book*. Dial, 1971.

Keats, Ezra Jack. *Over in the Meadow*. Four Winds, 1972.

Langstaff, John. *Over in the Meadow*. Harcourt, Brace & World, 1957.

Mendoza, George. *The Marcel Marceau Counting Book*. Doubleday, 1971.

Wildsmith, Brian. *Brian Wildsmith's 1, 2, 3*. Watts, 1965.

Sendak, Maurice. *Outside Over There*. Harper & Row, 1981. (P, I)

A story of a young girl who is to watch her baby sister while her mother is painting. The goblins take the baby and Ida must follow them in order to rescue her sister. Her sister is found among identical-looking ice babies. Ida does rescue her sister and returns to her home just before her mother is finished.

1. Sendak felt this was the third in his trilogy of books focusing on children and their ability to deal with their fears. Discuss how this book fits that theme. Utilize the other two books, *Where the Wild Things Are* and *In the Night Kitchen*, as part of the discussion.

2. Discuss the theme of this story.

3. Discuss Sendak's admiration of the composer Mozart, which he tried to show in the book. (He says that he set the book in the period of Mozart; in one place Mozart is a black silhouette playing his flute while Ida is in the foreground.)

Sendak, Maurice. *Pierre*. The Nutshell Library. Harper & Row, 1962. (P, I)

A moral tale that has Pierre repeating "I don't care." His attitude gets him into dire trouble— and out of it in the end. It is a rhythmic poem and a fantasy in one.

1. Retell the story using hand puppets. Five puppets (Pierre, mother, father, lion, doctor) will be needed, plus the narrator.

2. View the filmstrip/cassette available from Weston Woods.

3. *Pierre* is an example of a story with a swallow motif. Many folk stories play on this theme. Swallow stories are basically of three types:

   - The hero is swallowed by the monster (or enemy) and is disgorged or emerges in safety when the enemy is killed. (Some versions of "Little Red Riding Hood" would belong to this category.)

   - Swallows own children, neighbors, or others, is killed, and those swallowed emerge alive. ("Unanana and the Elephant" would fit into this category.)

   - The act of swallowing accounts for various natural phenomena. (The Paiute Indian story of how the sun swallows the stars, which explains why the stars disappear at dawn, is an example of this type.)

   Read several of the following stories with the swallow motif. Without stating the theme, ask the children to discuss with you the common elements of each of the stories as they relate to one another.

Booklist—Stories with the Swallow Motif

Aardema, Verna. "The House in the Middle of the Road." In *Behind the Back of the Mountain: Black Folktales from Southern Africa*. Illustrated by Leo Dillon and Diane Dillon. Dial Press, 1973. (A Zulu tale)

Arbuthnot, May Hill, et al. "The Cock, the Mouse, and The Little Red Hen." In *The Arbuthnot Anthology of Children's Literature*, 230. 3rd ed. Scott, Foresman, 1971.

deRegniers, Beatrice Schenk. *Laura's Story*. Illustrated by Jack Kent. Atheneum, 1979.

Hogrogian, Nonny. *The Renowned History of Little Red Riding Hood*. Crowell, 1967.

Hyman, Trina Schart. *Little Red Riding Hood*. Holiday House, 1983.

Kent, Jack. *The Fat Cat*. Parents, 1971. (A Danish folktale)

Minard, Rosemary. "Unanana and the Elephant." In *Woman Folk and Fairy Tales*. Houghton Mifflin, 1975.

Schmidt, Karen. *The Gingerbread Man*. Scholastic, 1985.

Sendak, Maurice. *Where the Wild Things Are*. Harper & Row, 1963. (P, I)

When Max acts like a wild thing he is sent to bed without supper. He takes off across the ocean and in and out of days on an adventure that takes him to where the wild things are. He commands the wild things during their wild rumpus. When he smells the aroma of food he goes back over the ocean and returns to his room where his supper is still hot.

1. Read the story in readers' theater form. Write the script for three parts, a chorus of wild things. Two or three people may choral read the part for each of the three voices. The chorus would include the rest of the group.

2. Write a tale of "Where the Tame Things Are." How would the story have been different?

3. Write "Max Returns to Where the Wild Things Are."

4. Make large wild things using butcher paper. Trace the outline onto another piece of paper. Color that drawing as if it were the back of the wild thing. Staple the two parts together and stuff with crumpled newspapers. Display.

5. Listen and react to the story as it is read without viewing the illustrations. After listening to the story ask children to draw their idea of a wild thing. Reread the story and share the children's pictures of the wild things along with the illustrations from the book.

6. Extend the theme by reading other titles from the booklist for monsters and strange noises in the Bookshelf entry for Mayer's *There's an Alligator under My Bed*.

Shreve, Susan. *The Flunking of Joshua T. Bates*. Knopf, 1984. (I)

Joshua must repeat third grade. He is just as smart as his classmates but he cannot read, at least not well enough to go on to fourth grade. When he returns to school in the fall he is taunted and his parents and friends pity him. His only salvation is the new teacher, Mrs. Goodwin. From her Joshua learns that even "losers" can be winners.

1. Read *Frankie Is Staying Back* by Ron Roy (Clarion, 1981). Compare Frankie and Joshua. Compare and contrast the two boys' situations. Discuss the point of view from which each of the stories is being told. Compare how each of the boys deals with his problems.

2. Describe how you would help a classmate who is repeating a grade. How would you make him or her feel comfortable in your classroom?

Shub, Elizabeth, translator. *About Wise Men and Simpletons: Twelve Tales from Grimm*. Etchings by Nonny Hogrogian. Macmillan, 1971. (P, I)

Etchings created by Nonny Hogrogian are reproduced in halftones. Each story in this collection is illustrated by an etching. The stories include: "About a Fisherman and His Wife," "The Wolf and the Seven Kids," "Briar Rose," "About Elves," "Rapunzel," "About Simpletons," "The Water of Life," "Rumpelstiltskin," "The Six Swans," "King Thrushbeard," "Hansel and Gretel," and "The Bremen Town Musicians." These retellings are sparse and without embellishment. The language is direct and presents the structure of the tale in simple terms. These tales present an opportunity to compare and contrast with other versions retold from the Grimm source. Two collections that will be useful for this purpose include: *The Brothers Grimm: Popular Folk Tales*, translated by Brian Alderson and illustrated by Michael Foreman (Doubleday, 1978), and *The Random House Book of Fairy Tales*, adapted by Amy Ehrlich and illustrated by Diane Goode (Random House, 1985). Both of these volumes are illustrated with full-color plates which will provide material for comparison to the etchings of Hogrogian. The Random House collection contains tales from a variety of sources including several from the Grimm tradition.

1. Compare the story grammar in "Briar Rose" from the collection translated by Shub with the tale titled "Briar-Rose; or, The Sleeping Beauty" contained in the Alderson collection cited above. Both tales are part of the Grimm tradition from Germany.

2. Compare the "Briar Rose" tales originating from the Grimm tales with Charles Perrault's French tale "The Sleeping Beauty in the Wood" found in *The Random House Book of Fairy Tales*. Among the noticeable differences is the mention of a total of thirteen fairies in the Grimm version. One of them is not invited to the baby's christening because the king and queen had only a dozen golden plates. The thirteenth, angry that she is not invited, puts a curse on the baby princess. The curse is modified by the twelfth fairy who had not yet bestowed her gift on the baby. In Perrault's retelling seven fairies are invited to the christening. An eighth fairy thought to have died years ago arrives at the dinner. The king orders a place set for the eighth fairy, but since only seven place settings of gold had been made the eighth place was set with less rich tableware. A young fairy fearing the worst hid behind the curtain in the hope of undoing any evil curse that the old fairy was planning.

3. Compare "The Bremen Town Musicians" with "Jack and the Robbers," a tale from the Appalachian mountain region. "Jack and the Robbers" has been recorded as part of *The Jack Tales* by Richard Chase (Houghton Mifflin, 1943). A filmstrip cassette version of "Jack and the Robbers" is contained in a series available from Pied Piper Productions, *First Choice: Authors and Books—#4-Jack and the Robbers*. This kit contains a filmstrip and two cassettes, one of them an interview with Richard Chase who collected the Appalachian tales.

4. Compare and contrast versions of "Hansel and Gretel" with the version collected by Elizabeth Shub and illustrated by Nonny Hogrogian. See index.

5. Use the filmstrip cassette "Fairy Tales" available from Pied Piper Productions. "Fairy Tales" is one part of the *Literature for Children Series: 2*. The "Fairy Tales" title presents a Japanese tale and a puppet version of "Hansel and Gretel." The discussion included in the presentation discusses the origins of fairy tales, fairy tale collectors and authors, and the geographic diversity of fairy tales. Using the card catalog to locate fairy tales is explained.

6. For comparison suggestions for "Rumpelstiltskin" see the index entry.

Silverstein, Shel. *Who Wants a Cheap Rhinoceros?* Macmillan, 1983. (P, I)
    A story of all the marvelous things a rhinoceros can do around the house. And the animal is cheap so "who wants a cheap rhinoceros?"

1. Read the story. Then list all of the wonderful things the rhinoceros could do.

2. Add some more uses for a cheap rhinoceros.

3. Read Bernard Most's *What If the Dinosaurs Came Back* (Harcourt Brace Jovanovich, 1978). Then tell what you would have a dinosaur do around your house.

4. Choose another animal and tell of all the wonderful things that animal could do around the house. For example, a porcupine might keep away intruders, provide skewers for shish kebabs, and be a "bush" in your front yard. A lion could be a tawny-colored pillow in your family room, a monument in your front yard, and a "watch lion" for your home.

Singer, Isaac Bashevis. *The Fearsome Inn*. Translated by the author and Elizabeth Shub. Illustrated by Nonny Hogrogian. Scribner, 1967. (P, I)

Hogrogian's rich full-color watercolors illustrate this tale of enchantment. The fearsome inn belongs to Doboshova, the witch. During the winter when it stormed and snowed, travelers stumbled into the inn where Doboshova and her half-devil husband, Lapitut, practiced their witchcraft on their unsuspecting guests. Leibel, the cabala student, with the aid of a piece of magic chalk, manages to outwit the evil innkeepers, rescue his fellow victims, and break the spell cast over the inn.

1. This tale refers to the Jewish Passover. Research the origin of that religious event. How does it relate to this story?

2. Illustrate the celebration gathering that lasted for seven days and seven nights when the silvery moon cast a light over the entire landscape.

3. Draw a picture of the barren countryside as it looked while it was under the curse of Doboshova and Lapitut. Draw a companion picture of the countryside once it was no longer spellbound.

Skurzynski, Gloria. *Lost in the Devil's Desert*. Lothrop, Lee & Shepard, 1982. (I)

Left alone on the Mojave Desert with only the clothes on his back, Kevin must draw on all of his past conversations with his father about desert survival. Three days are filled with struggles to survive. When Kevin does manage to reach civilization he is badly burned and swollen but at the end of the story we know he will live.

1. How do you think the story would have ended if Santiago, the shepherd, had not crossed paths in the desert with Kevin? Explain your rationale for thinking as you do.

2. In one episode, Kevin sits very still to keep from being bit by a rattlesnake. If he had been bit, explain what he should have done. A first-aid manual may help you research what should be done in such a situation. Remember, Kevin had limited resources.

3. This is just one of Skurzynski's adventure books. Locate others by using the card catalog in your school or public library.

Skurzynski, Gloria. *Trapped in Slickrock Canyon*. Lothrop, Lee & Shepard, 1984. (I)

Gina and Justin are cousins. Their fathers are identical twin brothers who have gotten together on Justin's father's ranch. Gina's parents have recently separated. She and her father have come to the ranch so that the brothers can mountain climb together. Gina is a city girl and seems to be a novice at rock climbing and exploring the mountains in the region. Justin must entertain his cousin while she is there so he takes her on a hike to see an Anasazi petroglyph. When they arrive they surprise vandals working to remove the ancient artwork. The vandals discover that they have been seen and set out in pursuit of the two youngsters. A storm and a mishap which injures Justin's leg force the two of them to spend the night on a rock shelf. In the morning Gina leaves Justin while she goes for help, and the vandals are captured and punished. The petroglyph was removed from the mountain but was undamaged so it will be displayed in an area museum. The cousins have developed a lasting friendship.

1. Find out what you can about petroglyphs. What are they and where have any been found?

2. What kind of family life do you think Gina will have with her parents?

3. Tell the story of what happens when Gina comes to the ranch with her father, next summer.

4. What do you think was the most exciting part of this story? Explain why you think that was the most exciting part.

5. Make a poster illustrating Gina's favorite term "maximal." Use cutouts from magazines, newspapers, and your own drawings to show what you think are maximal-type objects and events. Write MAXIMAL in big letters at the top of your poster.

Smith, Robert Kimmel. *The War with Grandpa*. Delacorte, 1984. (I)

Peter did not want to give up his room to his grandpa. He loved him but he liked his own room. Grandpa moves into Peter's room and Peter finds himself moved to the third floor, which has none of the interest of his old room. Peter begins to play pranks on Grandpa, a childish way to retaliate. Grandpa is quick to show Peter that two can play the game. In the end the family discovers another solution to their problem and all is well once again.

1. Peter loved to read the *Encyclopedia Brown* series by Donald Sobol and *The Great Brain* series by John D. Fitzgerald. Read one of the books in either of these series and then tell how Peter is different from or similar to Leroy or Tom.

2. Make a list of pranks that Peter and Grandpa played on each other. Categorize each entry on the list as a nuisance or as a mean trick. Explain how you decided which belonged in the mean category.

Sobol, Donald. *Encyclopedia Brown and the Case of the Mysterious Handprints*. Morrow, 1985. (P, I)

Who hid the blond wig in the trash can near the yacht club? Why does Tyrone have a black eye? What about the mysterious handprints outside Mr. Heiden's cottage? Ten-year-old LeRoy (Encyclopedia) Brown, a super sleuth and his partner, Sally Kimball, track down clues and make some startling discoveries—puzzling problems of missing property, sabotaged races, a frame-up involving the boy-wonder himself, and even a case of unrequited love. Between the two of them they manage to keep Idaville in order. The book contains several short stories full of subtle clues which allow readers to pit their skills against those of Encyclopedia and Sally Kimball.

1. Use this title to introduce the character, Encyclopedia Brown. Read aloud one of the stories. Discuss the clues and attempt to solve the case. After discussion turn to the end of the book and read the solution to the mystery.

2. Gather other Encyclopedia Brown books together and encourage children to read the stories in pairs. Discuss and attempt to reason through the clues to solve the mystery.

3. Locate other mysteries by using the card catalog in your school or public library. Use the subject heading MYSTERY AND DETECTIVE STORIES.

Speare, Elizabeth George. *The Sign of the Beaver*. Houghton Mifflin, 1983. (I)

Matthew and his father travel to the wilderness in Maine to land that they have purchased. This is the 1700s and the land is wild country. Matthew and his father clear a homestead and build a cabin for their family. Matthew's father leaves Matthew to care for the homestead while he returns to their former home to get Matt's mother, sister Sarah, and the new baby. Unknown to Matthew, Matthew's father finds his family seriously ill and cannot return to the homestead immediately. Matthew is left for many months in the wilderness. He is badly stung by bees and needs to be cared for. Indians befriend him. The Indians and Matthew become friends and helpmates. Matthew is faced with an important decision. The Indians are moving north, to get away from the advancing settlers, and they want Matthew to go with them. He hasn't heard from his family for months.

1. What decision do you think you would have made if you had been faced with the same situation as Matthew? Explain the reasons why you would have made that decision.

2. Draw a picture of how you think the inside of the cabin looked when Matthew's family finally arrived at the homestead. Reread Chapter 25 if you need help recalling the items that were in the cabin.

3. Elizabeth George Speare has won the Newbery Award twice and this book was named a Newbery Honor book for 1983. Research and write a brief explanation about the importance of the Newbery Award. A good place to start your research is in the *World Book Encyclopedia*. Use the index to help you locate the article on children's literature and on the Newbery Award.

4. Read other books dealing with survival in the wilderness.

Booklist—Wilderness Survival

Dalgleish, Alice. *The Courage of Sarah Nobel*. Scribner, 1954.

Fritz, Jean. *The Cabin Faced West*. Coward McCann, 1958.

George, Jean Craighead. *Julie of the Wolves*. Harper & Row, 1972.

_____. *My Side of the Mountains*. Dutton, 1959.

O'Dell, Scott. *Island of the Dolphins*. Houghton Mifflin, 1960.

Tate, Joan. *Wild Boy*. Harper & Row, 1973.

Steig, William. *Amos and Boris*. Farrar, Straus & Giroux, 1971.
   A small mouse, Amos, meets a whale, Boris, on the ocean. Boris saves Amos's life. Years later the two meet again but this time Amos is able to help Boris.

   1. Compare and contrast with Aesop's fable "The Lion and the Mouse."

   2. Discuss the story grammar focusing on sequence of events within the plot.

Steig, William. *The Amazing Bone*. Farrar, Straus & Giroux, 1976. (P, I)
   The adventure of a magical bone that rescues the heroine from the clutches of robbers and a villainous wolf.

   1. The book has many interesting words. Choose some of the words to make a crossword puzzle. A computer program from Broderbund called Crossword Magic is a user-friendly program that facilitates the creation of crossword puzzles.

   2. In most cases the meanings of the words can be ascertained from the context. Discuss. Some of the words that might be interesting to discuss include: converse, gawking, pumpernickel, dawdled, doggers, sprig, odoriferous, ravenous, frazzled, wretch, gaffers, crullers, flabbergast, surrendered, avail, flourish, minuscule, and mantlepiece. You will be able to find others.

Stevens, Carla. *Anna, Grandpa, and the Big Storm*. Clarion, 1982. (P, I)
   The story of the Great Blizzard of 1888 is told through the story of Anna and her grandfather. Anna's family had invited Grandpa to stay with them. Grandpa was lonely and wanted something to do so he decided to walk with Anna to her school. The wind began to blow and the two of them decided that they should follow Anna's mother's advice and take the El (elevated train). They did and they were caught with several other passengers who had to be rescued by firemen and teams of horses. Anna, her grandfather, and two new friends finally made it home.

   1. What do you think might have happened if Anna had not helped the other passengers, herself, and Grandpa?

   2. Explain why Grandpa decided that he might stay in the city with Anna and her father.

   3. Research information about the real Blizzard of 1888. Did the blizzard really occur? Give some additional facts about the blizzard and confirm the facts that Stevens included in her book.

4. Draw a picture of Grandpa and Anna walking to school.

5. In several of the *Little House* books by Laura Ingalls Wilder, the Ingalls family must deal with snowstorms and blizzards. Locate the books by Wilder and find the chapters in each book that deal with blizzards. Read those chapters and compare the Ingalls family's experiences with the experiences of Anna and her grandpa.

Tashjian, Virginia A. *Three Apples Fell from Heaven: Armenian Tales Retold*. Illustrated by Nonny Hogrogian. Little, Brown, 1971. (P, I)

Nine traditional tales told to the author by her mother. In the author's note Tashjian explains that Armenian folktales always have a traditional, formal beginning and ending. The beginning, "Once there was and was not," is the title for another collection of stories by Tashjian and illustrated by Nonny Hogrogian. This collection takes its title from the traditional ending, "Three apples fell from heaven: one for the teller, one for the listener, and one for all the peoples of the world." Some storytellers use a variation of that ending, "Three apples fell from heaven: one for the one who asked for a story, one for the one who told it, and one for the one who gave ear to it."

These folktales tell of the goodness of common people. The stories make fun of the faults common to all people. Since these tales are so universal in nature they provide excellent material to discuss and write about.

1. Use the following information to locate stories that may be compared and contrasted with stories from the Tashjian collection.

   • "The King and the Shepherd." Compare and contrast with "Clever Manka," which may be found in *The Shepherd's Nosegay* by Parker Fillmore (Harcourt, Brace & World, 1920, 1948) and *The Arbuthnot Anthology of Children's Literature* by May Hill Arbuthnot, et al. (Scott, Foresman, 1961, 1971.)

   • "The Lazy Man." This story describes the laziness of some common folk. One tale that may be used to compare and contrast is *A Treeful of Pigs* by Arnold Lobel, illustrated by Anita Lobel (Greenwillow, 1979).

   • "The Hare's Kidney" and "The Gift of Gold." Each of these stories proves the saying that "money does not bring happiness." Discuss how these two stories do that. Compare and contrast the message in each of these stories with the Greek tale of King Midas. Two versions are located in *The Arbuthnot Anthology of Children's Literature* by May Hill Arbuthnot, et al. (Scott, Foresman, 1961, 1971). The first, entitled "Midas," has as its original source *The Age of Fable; or Beauties of Mythology*, by Thomas Bullfinch (J. E. Tilton, 1863). The other story is entitled "The Golden Touch" and is originally from *A Wonder Book for Girls and Boys* by Nathaniel Hawthorne (Dodd, 1934). This story was also published as a book entitled *The Golden Touch* by Nathaniel Hawthorne. This single tale is illustrated by Paul Galdone (McGraw-Hill, 1959).

   • "The Enormous Genie." Compare and contrast to the Norwegian tale "The Lad Who Went to the North Wind." One source for this tale is *The Arbuthnot Anthology of Children's Literature* by May Hill Arbuthnot, et al. (Scott, Foresman, 1961, 1971). The original source for this tale is *Popular Tales from the Norse* by Peter Christian Asbjørnsen and Jørgen Moe, translated by Sir George Webbe Dasent (David Douglas, 1888).

Taylor, Theodore. *The Trouble with Tuck*. Doubleday, 1981. (I)

Friar Tuck was a beautiful golden retriever but he was blind. When he began to go blind Helen knew she had to do something. She attempted to help him and the only thing she could think of was to obtain a guide dog for him. The guide dog school could not give her a dog at first but eventually did find a dog that was to be retired. Helen set out to train the black and brown German shepherd to work with Tuck. The task was more difficult than she might have thought. Many frustrating days culminated with success. Helen unleashed Tuck and he paraded home with his new guide dog, Lady Daisy. As Tuck had twice previously saved Helen's life, Helen now saved Tuck's life.

1. Investigate Seeing Eye dogs and Guide dogs. Discover how the dogs are trained. Is there a difference between Seeing Eye dogs and Guide dogs? Be ready to share your information with the rest of the class.

2. Tuck had saved Helen from a man who was about to attack her. Put yourself in Helen's place, *without* Tuck. What would you do to save yourself?

3. If Helen had not been able to obtain a guide dog for Tuck, what do you think would have happened to the dog? How would the story have changed?

The Thirteen Days of Yule. Illustrated by Nonny Hogrogian. Crowell, n.d. (P, I)

The introduction by Anthony Murray explains the background of this Scottish version of an old carol that may be compared to "The Twelve Days of Christmas." In this verse the items being given are unusual. On the first Yule day a papingo—ay is given. On the following days the items given include: three partniks, three plovers, a gray goose, three starlings, three goldspinks, a bull that was broon, three ducks a merry laying, three swans a merry swimming, an Arabian baboon, three hinds a merry hunting, three maids a merry dancing, and three stalks o'merry corn. Watercolors accented with pen and ink lines illustrate each gift as it is added to the collection sent by the king to his lady.

1. List the items sent by the king. Ask that each item be researched and illustrated on a large piece of tag board. As the carol is read aloud display the illustrated object. When the carol is completed each of the items should be displayed and the cumulative rhyme repeated.

2. Read the traditional English carol "The Twelve Days of Christmas." Compare with the Scottish version of the carol. One source for the English carol is *The Doubleday Christmas Treasury: A Collection of Stories, Poems, Carols and Traditions*, compiled by Jane Olliver (Doubleday, 1986).

Thomas, Patricia. *"Stand Back," said the Elephant, "I'm Going to Sneeze!"* Illustrated by Wallace Tripp. Lothrop, Lee & Shepard, 1971.

When the elephant sneezes things happen. Monkeys fall off trees. Feathers are blown off birds. Leopards lose their spots.

1. Read the title, predict what will happen when the elephant sneezes. It will help children predict if they know where elephants normally live, as well as something about the geographical region.

2. What will happen if another elephant is standing on the other side of all of the animals and sneezes in the other direction? Tell the story. (This would cause all the actions to be reversed, that is, the leopards would be spattered with all their spots, the birds would be speared with their feathers and the monkeys would jump back into the trees.)

Tusa, Tricia. *Libby's New Glasses*. Holiday House, 1984. (P, I)

Libby does not want to wear glasses. She knows that everyone at school will tease her so she decides to run away. She goes to the beach and finds an ostrich with its head in the sand. Libby tries to get him to raise his head by telling him how slender his legs and neck are, as well as how beautiful his feathers are. The ostrich finds that he has the confidence to raise his head and face Libby. It is then that Libby sees that the ostrich wears glasses, too. Together they set out to see what they can see with their new glasses.

1. Extend the theme of new glasses by reading Marc Brown's *Arthur's Eyes* (Little, Brown, 1980).

2. Make frames for Hollywood-style glasses from cardboard. Add sequins, paper butterflies, and other decorations. Attach one corner of the frames to a pencil or dowel stick (as a holder). The pencil or stick will allow the frames to be held up to the eyes.

3. Plan and hold an Eyes Have It Day. Make a list of famous people who wear eyeglasses. Display the Hollywood frames on a bulletin board. Feature and display as many books as can be found that include people who wear glasses. One example is *Harriet the Spy* by Louise Fitzhugh (Harper & Row, 1964). In this book Harriet is an interesting young girl who finds herself in a number of difficult situations because of her insistence on being totally honest in her observation journal. Harriet is shown on the cover wearing glasses. Encourage the children to hunt down their own book heroes that wear glasses.

Vasilisa the Beautiful. Translated by Thomas P. Whitney. Illustrated by Nonny Hogrogian. Macmillan, 1970. (P, I)

A Russian counterpart of the "Cinderella" tale collected by the Brothers Grimm. The spinning motif popular in the "Rumpelstiltskin" tales is also part of this story. This tale includes the traditional characters from Russian folklore, Baba Yaga, and the symbolic black, red, and white horsemen. When Vasilisa's mother dies she leaves her daughter a doll which provides for Vasilisa when her stepmother and stepsisters treat her with jealousy. The skull light that Baba Yaga gives Vasilisa burns her stepmother and stepsisters to ashes. Vasilisa wins the heart of the prince when she weaves fine cloth from thread she has spun and makes the cloth into shirts fit only for the prince. Her foster mother and her father are then invited to live the rest of their days in the castle with Vasilisa and her prince. The book is handsomely illustrated in full-color illustrations highlighting the richness of the tale.

1. Use this title to focus on the "Cinderella" theme, particularly the tales from the German (Grimm) and French (Perrault) traditions. Refer to the index entry for the Cinderella booklist.

2. Learn more about the character Baba Yaga. In *Funk & Wagnalls Standard Dictionary of Folklore: Mythology and Legend*, edited by Maria Leach (Funk & Wagnalls, 1949), Baba Yaga is described as "a female supernatural of Russian folklore." She is a witch that steals and cooks her victims. She prefers young children and often lives in a little hut in a clearing in a distant forest, surrounded by a picket fence topped with skulls. She is the guardian of the fountains of the water of life.

3. Read Ernest Small's *Baba Yaga* (Houghton Mifflin, 1966). This single tale is illustrated in corrugated cardboard block ink prints by Blair Lent. He has used watercolor overlays. In this story Baba Yaga is portrayed in the text as a fascinating and harmless witch who likes only bad children, while Lent's illustrations show her to be an old hag and very frightening in appearance. In *Vasilisa the Beautiful* the text speaks of her eating those who dare trespass on her property (which is more menacing than the harmless image portrayed in Small's tale). The Hogrogian illustrations, which do not dwell on her evil ways, portray her as a haggard but kindly-looking witch. However she does drive Vasilisa from her cottage when she thinks that Vasilisa is blessed.

4. Read more Russian folktales. An excellent source is Virginia Haviland's *Favorite Fairy Tales Told in Russia* (Little, Brown, 1961). The collection is illustrated by Herbert Danska. Compare the traditional characters found in the tales.

Viorst, Judith. *If I Were in Charge of the World and Other Poems*. Atheneum, 1981. (P, I)
A collection of poems detailing the things "I" would do if I were in charge of the world. "If I were in charge of the world, I would cancel oatmeal, Monday mornings, and allergy shots."

1. Continue the pattern to describe the things that you might cancel.

2. Make a list of things that you would not want to cancel. Make a list of at least ten "no cancel" items.

Wallace, Bill. *Shadow on the Snow*. Holiday House, 1985. (I)
The men in the area knew they must find the panther that was killing the livestock. As the men form a search party to find the dangerous animal, Tom is left behind to care for his grandfather. When his grandfather hurts himself Tom decides he must ride his precious (and pregnant) horse to his friend Justin's farm to get help for his grandfather. The ride to Justin's brings the danger all of the ranchers have been dreading. Note: This book was published in paperback by Archway/Bantam with the title *Danger on Panther Peak*.

1. Describe the friendship between Tom and Justin.

2. Tell why the panther posed a threat to the ranchers.

3. Write a newspaper article telling about the search for the dangerous panther and all the destruction the panther had caused.

4. Write a second newspaper article telling about the killing of the dangerous panther. Be sure to mention the damage the panther had been responsible for in previous days.

5. Discuss the two titles for this book. Which is the better title. Explain why.

Walter, Mildred Pitts. *Brother to the Wind*. Illustrated by Leo Dillon and Diane Dillon. Lothrop, Lee & Shepard, 1985. (P, I)

Emeke, an African boy, wishes to fly. He must learn to trust the advice of the Good Snake and only then will his wish come true.

1. Read other folktales from Africa. Use the card catalog in your school or public library to search the subject index for FOLKLORE-AFRICA.

2. Use this and other African tales to bridge to the culture of the black South. A collection of American black folktales that will provide stories to compare and contrast with the stories of Africa is Virginia Hamilton's *The People Could Fly: American Black Folktales* (Knopf, 1985). This volume is illustrated by Leo Dillon and Diane Dillon. An audiocassette tape of selected readings from this collection is available from Knopf.

Whitney, Thomas P., translator. *The Story of Prince Ivan, the Firebird, and the Gray Wolf*. Illustrated by Nonny Hogrogian. Scribner, 1968. (P, I)

Rich tapestry-like paintings give this tale life. The story is of a king and his three sons. He sends each on a mission to capture the prized firebird. Prince Dimitry and Prince Vasily are jealous older brothers; they set off together to conquer the challenge. Prince Ivan is the youngest son. He travels through the country and encounters a gray wolf who aids him in reaching the firebird. When Prince Ivan attempts to steal the firebird he impetuously takes the golden cage. That causes him to be captured. In return for his freedom he must travel through thirty-nine countries and in the fortieth obtain the horse with the golden mane. Prince Ivan arrives in the fortieth country only to be captured when he attempts to take a golden bridle. In order to obtain his freedom this time he must travel another thirty-nine countries and in the fortieth get Princess Elena the Beautiful. With the help of the gray wolf, Prince Ivan is able to accomplish these tasks. And on the return trip, the gray wolf transforms himself into a fake Princess Elena and later transforms himself into a fake horse with a golden mane. Each time the king of the fortieth kingdom to which he has traveled is fooled into believing that he has received the true person or animal and turns over the prize to Prince Ivan.

However, when Prince Ivan reaches his home kingdom with the Princess Elena, the horse with the golden mane, and the firebird he finds that he is very tired and stops to sleep. While he and Princess Elena are sleeping Prince Dimitry and Prince Vasily happen upon them and in a plot to claim the princess and the treasures for themselves, they murder Prince Ivan. They threaten Princess Elena, telling her that she must tell the king that they had obtained the treasures. Thirty days later the gray wolf returns to the spot where he had left Prince Ivan and finds him dead. With the help of some crows who fly to get some water living and water dead he heals Prince Ivan. Prince Ivan arrives at the castle just in time to prevent Princess Elena's marriage to one of his brothers. Upon learning of his two eldest sons' evil deeds the king has them imprisoned in a dungeon. Prince Ivan and Princess Elena marry and live happily ever after.

1. Read other Russian folktales and formulate some ideas about the commonality of the tales. This tale is similar to the quest tales that are told in many cultures. Russian folktales often involve tasks and trials, transformations, and tricksters. Russian tales are often longer and more involved than those from other countries and often set forth a series of tasks that must be accomplished. This story involves two traditional characters, the firebird and the youngest son, Ivan. As in the folklore of other countries, the number three is often significant. In this case Ivan must accomplish three tasks before he can return to his father's kingdom.

In the tale "The Fire-Bird and the Princess Vasilisa," found in *Vasilisa the Beautiful*, translated by Thomas P. Whitney and illustrated by Nonny Hogrogian (Scribner, 1968), it is a horse, rather than a wolf, who advises his young master and so saves his life. The firebird theme runs throughout Russian folklore and was the inspiration for Stravinsky's "Firebird" music. Baba Yaga is often depicted as a wicked witch. Koshchei, the Deathless One, is another evil character in Russian folklore.

2. Make a list of common elements that can be identified as being part of several Russian tales. (See index of this book for booklist "Russian Folklore".)

3. Make a chart showing the location of Russia and giving some facts about the country, especially information about the climate and types of land in each area. Where are the plains and the forests? What kind of weather is prevalent in each region of the country? What are the major crops and largest cities?

4. Using the information located and presented in activity 3 attempt to determine the setting of the Russian tales read.

Williams, Jay. *Everyone Knows What a Dragon Looks Like*. Illustrated by Mercer Mayer. Four Winds, 1976. (P, I)
A Chinese folktale set in the City of Wu. This city is saved from the wild horsemen of the north because of the faith of a young boy.

1. Before reading the story, ask children if they do know what a dragon looks like. Ask them to draw their idea of a dragon. After reading the story compare their depiction of a dragon with Mayer's illustrations.

2. Read other books with a dragon theme.

3. Compare this Chinese folktale with traditional tales from other lands. What elements in this tale mark it as being set in China? What elements in the comparison tales give information as to the setting from which the tale originated.

Booklist—Dragons

Grahame, Kenneth. *The Reluctant Dragon*. Illustrated by Ernest H. Shepard. Holiday House, 1953.

Hodges, Margaret. *Saint George and the Dragon*. Illustrated by Trina Schart Hyman. Little, Brown, 1984. (Caldecott Award Book, 1985).

Troughton, Joanna. *Sir Gawain and the Loathly Damsel*. Dutton, 1972.

Williams, Vera B. *A Chair for My Mother*. Greenwillow, 1982. (P)
A very special chair is found for a little girl's mother. It is a wonderful, beautiful, fat, soft armchair. It is covered in velvet with a pattern of red roses.

1. Think about the kind of chair your father or mother would like. Take out crayons, pencils, or paint and make a picture of the chair you might choose for your parent.

2. How will you earn the money to buy this special chair for your mother or father?

3. Tell about another special gift that you might wish to give to one of your parents or grandparents. Write about this special gift. Tell what it will look like, where you will buy the gift, or how you will make it. Draw a picture of the gift.

4. Read Franz Brandenberg's *A Secret for Grandmother's Birthday* (Greenwillow, 1975).

Winthrop, Elizabeth. *The Castle in the Attic.* Holiday House, 1985. (I)

William does not want his housekeeper and nanny, Mrs. Phillips, to leave to go back to England. In an attempt to keep her there he miniaturizes her using a special medallion. William then finds that he must enter the castle where he has put Mrs. Phillips and fight the wicked magician, Alastor, in order to release her.

1. The following words were used in the story. Explain what you think they mean. You may make drawings to explain some of the terms if you wish. The words are: drawbridge; shield; scullery; allure; portcullis; lance; buttery; minstrels gallery; armory; sword; and wardrobe.

2. Sir Simon thought that William went to school for "too long of a time." Why do you suppose he thought that?

3. What do you think will happen if someone steals the medallion from Mrs. Phillips while she is on the ship?

4. Draw a picture of an imaginary castle. Include a moat, drawbridge, and a mean dragon to guard the gate. You may wish to find the book *Castles* by David Macauley (Houghton Mifflin, 1977).

Wood, Audrey. *The Napping House.* Illustrated by Don Wood. Harcourt Brace Jovanovich, 1984. (P, I)

A cumulative rhythmic tale that features a dreaming child, a dozing dog, a snoozing cat, a slumbering mouse, and a wakeful flea. "This is a house, a napping house, where everyone is sleeping." The house is a wonderful country home on a rainy afternoon just made for a nap and a granny.

1. Compare and contrast this tale to "The House That Jack Built" or the "Old Woman and Her Pig." "The House That Jack Built" can be found in Anne Rockwell's *The Three Bears and 15 Other Stories* (Crowell, 1975; Harper Trophy, 1984). "The Old Woman and Her Pig" can be found in Rockwell's *The Old Woman and Her Pig and 10 Other Stories* (Crowell, 1979) or the paperback edition of the same book published under the title of *The Three Sillies and 10 Other Stories to Read Aloud* (Harper Trophy, 1986).

2. Other tales to compare and contrast with *The Napping House* include: *This Is the House Where Jack Lives* by Joan Heilbroner, illustrated by Aliki (Harper & Row, 1962), and *Drummer Hoff* by Barbara Emberley, illustrated by Ed Emberley (Prentice-Hall, 1967).

3. The book begins as the "napping house" and with the Grandmother on the bottom. Examine and discuss the story line to ascertain the pattern in the characters' size and in the action line.

4. What would be a good name for the house at the end of the story?

5. When the Woods's young son Bruce outgrew his desire for naps, they found that he rested quite nicely at his granny's cozy, relaxing house. Audrey Wood began calling her mother's house "the napping house." Those three words inspired *The Napping House*. Discuss special places we might choose to sleep, rest, or play. What cozy spot do you have for relaxing moments?

6. Use the pattern of the story and of those in activity 1 to write another verse about something at your school or library.

Wright, Betty Ren. *The Dollhouse Murders*. Holiday House, 1983. (I)
   Amy resents always having to take care of LouAnn, her mentally handicapped sister, everywhere she goes. When they visit Aunt Claire and discover the dollhouse in the attic, strange things begin to happen that provide the clues to solve a murder from years before.

1. How do you think Aunt Claire's life will change now that the murder has been solved?

2. Make a poster advertising this book. Try making the poster three-dimensional with dollhouse doors that open and furniture that looks real. Be sure to put the book's title and the name of the author on the poster.

3. How did Aunt Claire help Amy reconcile her feelings and responsibilities about LouAnn?

4. Extend the theme of children and their relationships with a mentally handicapped sibling by reading another title.

Booklist — Handicapped Siblings

Byars, Betsy. *Summer of the Swans*. Illustrated by Ted Coconis. Viking, 1970.

Friis-Baastad, Babbis. *Don't Take Teddy*. Translated by Lise McKinnon. Scribner, 1967.

Little, Jean. *Take Wing*. Little, Brown, 1968.

Wrightson, Patricia. *A Racecourse for Andy*. Illustrated by Margaret Horder. Harcourt Brace Jovanovich, 1968.

Appendix

ADDRESSES

Alaska ABC Book/Paws IV Publishing
P.O. Box 2364
Homer, AK 99603

Abingdon Press
201 Eighth Avenue South
P.O. Box 801
Nashville, TN 37202

Advocacy Press
P.O. Box 236
Santa Barbara, CA 93102

Aladdin Books (Imprint of Macmillan's Children's Books)
866 Third Avenue
New York, NY 10022

Albert Whitman & Company
5747 West Howard Street
Niles, IL 60648.

Alfred A. Knopf
201 East 50th Street
New York, NY 10022

Algonquin Books of Chapel Hill
P.O. Box 2225
Chapel Hill, NC 27515

American Library Association
50 East Huron Street
Chicago, IL 60611

Archway Paperbacks/Pocket Books
1230 Avenue of the Americas
New York, NY 10020

Atheneum Books (Imprint of Macmillan's Children's Books)
866 Third Avenue
New York, NY 10022

Bantam Books
666 Fifth Avenue
New York, NY 10103

BFA Educational Media
468 Park Avenue South
New York, NY 10016

Bradbury Press
(Imprint of Macmillan's Children's Books)
866 Third Avenue
New York, NY 10022

Broderbund Software
17 Paul Drive
San Rafael, CA 94903

Caedmon
1995 Broadway
New York, NY 10023

Children's Book Council
67 Irving Place
New York, NY 10003

Children's Literature Association
210 Education Building
Purdue University
West Lafayette, IN 47907

Children's Press
5440 North Cumberland Avenue
Chicago, IL 60656

Churchill Films
662 North Robertson Boulevard
Los Angeles, CA 90069

Clarion Books
(A Ticknor & Fields: Houghton Mifflin Company)
52 Vanderbilt Avenue
New York, NY 10017

Coronet/BFA. See Coronet/MTI.

Coronet/MTI Film & Video
108 Wilmot Road
Deerfield, IL 60015

Crowell Publishers (Harper Junior Books Group)
10 East 53rd Street
New York, NY 10022

Crown Publishers, Inc.
225 Park Avenue South
New York, NY 10003

David R. Godine Publishers
306 Dartmouth Street
Boston, MA 02116

Delacorte Press
1 Dag Hammarskjold Plaza
New York, NY 10017

Dial Books for Young Readers
2 Park Avenue
New York, NY 10016

DLM Teaching Associates
One DLM Park
Allen, TX 75002

Dodd Mead Publishers
71 Fifth Avenue
New York, NY 10003

Dutton Children's Books
2 Park Avenue
New York, NY 10016

E. P. Dutton. See Dutton Children's Books.

Farrar, Straus & Giroux
19 Union Square West
New York, NY 10003

Four Winds Press
(Imprint of Macmillan's Children's Books)
866 Third Avenue
New York, NY 10022

Frederick Warne/Viking Kestrel
Children's Book Marketing Department
40 West 23rd Street
New York, NY 10010

G. K. Hall Publishers
70 Lincoln Street
Boston, MA 02111

Gareth Stevens Children's Books
7317 West Green Tree Road
Milwaukee, WI 53223

Garrett Press
South Barre
Vermont 05670

Godine. See David R. Godine.

Golden Press
850 Third Avenue
New York, NY 10022

Green Tiger Press
1061 India Street
San Diego, CA 92101

Greenwillow Books
(A division of William Morrow & Company)
105 Madison Avenue
New York, NY 10016

Grosset & Dunlap (Putnam & Grosset Group)
51 Madison Avenue
New York, NY 10010

Hall. See G. K. Hall.

Harcourt Brace Jovanovich, Inc.
1250 Sixth Avenue
San Diego, CA 92101

Harper Junior Books
10 East 53rd Street
New York, NY 10022

Henry Holt & Co.
115 West 18th Street
New York, NY 10011

Holiday House
18 East 53rd Street
New York, NY 10022

Houghton Mifflin Company
2 Park Street
Boston, MA 02108

Instructor
545 Fifth Avenue
New York, NY 10017

International Reading Association
800 Barksdale Road
P.O. Box 8139
Newark, DE 19714-8139

Jewish Publication Society
1930 Chestnut Street
Philadelphia, PA 19103

KidStamps, Inc.
P.O. Box 18699
Cleveland Heights, OH 44118

Knopf. See Alfred A. Knopf.

Laurel-Leaf/Dell Publishers
1 Dag Hammarskjold Plaza
New York, NY 10017

Libraries Unlimited, Inc.
P.O. Box 3988
Englewood, CO 80155-3988

Library Journal
249 West 17th Street
New York, NY 10011

Lippincott Publishers
10 East 53rd Street
New York, NY 10022

Listening Library, Inc.
P.O. Box L
Old Greenwich, CT 06870

Little, Brown & Company
34 Beacon Street
Boston, MA 02108

Live Oak Media
P.O. Box 34
Ancramdale, NY 12503

Lodestar Books (Imprint of E. P. Dutton)
2 Park Avenue
New York, NY 10016

Lothrop, Lee & Shepard Books
(A division of William Morrow & Company)
105 Madison Avenue
New York, NY 10016

Macmillan Children's Books
866 Third Avenue
New York, NY 10022

Margaret K. McElderry Books
(Imprint of Macmillan's Children's Books)
866 Third Avenue
New York, NY 10022

Morrow Junior Books
(A division of William Morrow & Company)
105 Madison Avenue
New York, NY 10016

National Council of Teachers of English
1111 Kenyon Road
Urbana, IL 61801

National Geographic
17th & M Streets N.W.
Washington, DC 20036

Orchard Books
(A division of Franklin Watts, Inc.)
387 Park Avenue South
New York, NY 10016

Oxford University Press
200 Madison Avenue
New York, NY 10016

Philomel Books (Putnam & Grosset Group)
51 Madison Avenue
New York, NY 10010

Picture Book Studio
60 North Main Street
Natick, MA 01760

Pied Piper Productions
719 West Broadway
Glendale, CA 91204

Price Stern Sloan Publishers
360 North La Cienega Boulevard
Los Angeles, CA 90048

Puffin Books/Viking Kestrel
Children's Book Marketing Department
40 West 23rd Street
New York, NY 10010

Putnam & Grosset Publishing Group
G. P. Putnam's Sons
51 Madison Avenue
New York, NY 10010

Raintree Publishers
310 West Wisconsin Avenue
Milwaukee, WI 53203

Random House
201 East 50th Street
New York, NY 10022

Random House/Miller-Brody School Division
Department 9277
400 Hahn Road
Westminister, MD 21157

Scholastic Hardcover/Paperback Publishers
730 Broadway
New York, NY 10003

School Library Journal
249 West 17th Street
New York, NY 10011

Scott, Foresman & Company
1900 East Lake Avenue
Glenview, IL 60025

Scribner's Books for Children and Young Adults
(Imprint of Macmillan Publishing Company)
866 Third Avenue
New York, NY 10022

Seabury Press. See Clarion Books.

Simon & Schuster Books for Young Readers/Little Simon
1230 Avenue of the Americas
New York, NY 10020

Society for Visual Education, Inc. (SVE)
1345 Diversey Parkway
Chicago, IL 60614-1299

Spoken Arts
310 North Avenue
New Rochelle, NY 10801, or

Spoken Arts
P.O. Box 289
New Rochelle, NY 10802

Stemmer House
2627 Caves Road
Owings Mills, MD 21117

Sterling Publishing Company
2 Park Avenue
New York, NY 10016

Sunburst Communications
39 Washington Avenue
Pleasantville, NY 10570

Teaching (formerly *Early Years*)
325 Post Road West
Westport, CT 06880

Troll Associates
100 Corporate Drive
Mahwah, NJ 07430

U.S. Government Printing Office
Public Documents Office
Washington, DC 20402-9325

Viking Kestrel. See Viking Penguin.

Viking Penguin Children's Books/Viking Kestrel
Children's Book Marketing Department
40 West 23rd Street
New York, NY 10010

Walker and Company/Books for Young Readers
720 Fifth Avenue
New York, NY 10019

Warne. See Frederick Warne.

Watts
387 Park Avenue South
New York, NY 10016

Westminster Press
925 Chestnut Street
Philadelphia, PA 19107

Weston Woods
Weston, CT 06883

Whitman. See Albert Whitman.

Willowisp Press
401 East Wilson Bridge Road
Worthington, OH 43085

Yearling/Dell Publishers
1 Dag Hammarskjold Plaza
New York, NY 10017

Index